Eunuchs

for the

Kingdom

of

Heaven

Eunuchs

FOR THE

Kingdom

OF

Heaven

Women, Sexuality and
the Catholic Church

UTA RANKE-HEINEMANN
Translated by Peter Heinegg

D O U B L E D A Y
New York   London   Toronto   Sydney   Auckland

PUBLISHED BY DOUBLEDAY
a division of Bantam Doubleday Dell Publishing Group, Inc.
666 Fifth Avenue, New York, New York 10103

DOUBLEDAY and the portrayal of an anchor with a dolphin
are trademarks of Doubleday, a division of
Bantam Doubleday Dell Publishing Group, Inc.

Book design by Chris Welch

Library of Congress Cataloging-in-Publication Data
Ranke-Heinemann, Uta, 1927–
[Eunuchen für das Himmelreich. English]
Eunuchs for the kingdom of heaven: women, sexuality and the Catholic Church by
Uta Ranke-Heinemann; translated by Peter Heinegg.—1st ed.
p.   cm.
Translation of: Eunuchen für das Himmelreich.
Includes bibliographical references.
1. Sex—Religious aspects—Catholic Church—Controversial literature.
2. Catholic Church—Doctrines—Controversial literature. I. Title.
BX1795.S48R3613   1990
241'.66'08822—dc20   89-48951
CIP

ISBN 0-385-26527-1

to my husband

CONTENTS

Contents

There are eunuchs born so from their mother's womb, there are eunuchs made so by human agency and there are eunuchs who have made themselves so for the sake of the kingdom of Heaven.

Matthew 19:12

Introduction

THE DISTRICT COURT'S JESUS

I*n the session* held on July 14, 1981, the District Court of Hamburg, Section 144, convicted Henning V., the editor-in-chief of a satirical magazine, of insulting religious creeds and affronting church institutions. The defendant was ordered to pay a fine of some 3,200 deutschemarks (about $1,700). In justifying its sentence the district court argued: "The Christian faith, which is based on the person of Jesus Christ as the essential core of what the Christian Church believes, consists in God's revelation of himself to humanity in the person of Jesus Christ. He is characterized as the Redeemer, whose life was free from any kind of sin and sensual pleasure." Even though not everything about the formulation of the decision may be clear, theologically and grammatically, still the court evidently determined "in the name of the people" that Jesus was a thoroughly "lust-free," i.e., joyless Redeemer.

Presumably the court did not quite mean what it said. Free from any kind of sin—fine, but free from any kind of sensual pleasure, that can't be. Otherwise Jesus would be turned into a real wretch, and with that sort of assertion the court itself might offend people's religious feelings. The court does disallow Jesus any and all pleasures, but it probably has only one of these in mind; and that wouldn't be the intellectual sort, also called joy, but a physical-carnal pleasure. There are several levels of this, from listening to music through enjoyment of food and drink (Jesus was called a "glutton and tippler" by his enemies, Mt. 11:19; Lk. 7:34) down to the last and lowest, sexual pleasure. The court is obviously thinking of the worst form, namely sexual

|

3

|

pleasure. And with regard to this, it would seem that the judgment was: Jesus had nothing of the sort. At the same time the court connects sexual pleasure so closely with the concept of "sin" that one more legal point should be clear: Sexual pleasure is not a good thing. Here the court seems to be following the old Catholic view that there can be no sexual pleasure without sin. Sexual joylessness with such a negative approach to pleasure, however, must ipso facto mean hostility to pleasure; and actually Jesus *was* that kind of sexually "listless" and lust-hating Redeemer—as celibate theologians have always seen him.

This hostility to pleasure had consequences, and not only for the defendant in Hamburg, who got off with a fine. It had a vast number of consequences for many people in history, and for the most part those consequences were far more serious; sometimes they were lifelong or even lethal. In Emperor Charles V's "Penal Rules" of 1532 Article 133 imposed the death penalty for the use of contraceptives—which implied the seeking of sensual pleasure outlawed by the Church. And even in this century, e.g., in the Nazi period, pious hostility to pleasure played an important role in deciding the fate of human beings. Take the question, among others, of how to handle patients with hereditary diseases, and how "to protect the national community, in justifiable self-defense, from these vermin" (Cardinal Faulhaber). In a conversation with Hitler the cardinal objected to the Führer's plans to have the "vermin" sterilized. It was the old hostility to pleasure, supposedly stemming from Jesus, that led Cardinal Faulhaber to oppose Hitler's plans for sterilization and to make a case instead for transferring the noxious individuals to an internment camp—that is a concentration camp. But more on this later.

Back to the beginning, to the joyless Jesus. Jesus' hostility to pleasure had implications, first of all, for the married life of his mother: Before his birth he laid down conditions for Mary's being allowed to become his mother. According to the teaching of the Church, Jesus would have taken no pleasure at all in the whole process of redemption, he would not have become man to begin with, or he would have looked for another mother, if Mary had taken pleasure in bearing more children besides himself. This was explained by Pope Siricius in the fourth century, who claimed that in such an event Jesus would not have accepted Mary as his mother: "Jesus would not have chosen birth from a virgin, had he been forced to look upon her as so unrestrained as to let that womb, from which the body of the Lord was fashioned, that hall of the eternal king, be stained by the presence of male seed. Whoever maintains that, maintains the unbelief of the Jews" (letter to Bishop Anysius from the year 392). Bearing children is thus a lack of continence, a plunge into pleasure. Conceiving a child, except from the Holy Spirit, is a defilement and uncleanness. And this was not just the personal opinion of an individual pope, as proved by the Catholic dogmatic theologian Michael Schmaus, who says that with his assertions Siricius was bearing witness to "the unanimous teaching of the Church" (*Catholic Dogmatics,* Vol. 5, p. 109).

Jesus' hostility to pleasure also had consequences for the theologians' image of other women. Women present an image of inferiority, since, unless they busy themselves with self-sanctification—as virgins do—they are only good for having children. But you can't have children without having sex and "being stained by the presence of male seed." Thus Jesus' hostility to pleasure meant that sexual enjoyment was excluded from Christian marriage as much as possible and often subject to threats of eternal damnation.

The same disapproval of pleasure affected the priestly way of life, which had to be remote from the moral slums of everyday existence. Hostility to marriage logically leads to the celibate life of the priesthood. And so it is no wonder that the great Mariologist and despiser of marriage, Pope Siricius, stood in the forefront of the battle against the marriage of priests. He had a decisive influence on the development of celibacy when in his letter to the Spanish bishop Himerius of Tarragona (385) he labeled it a *crimen* for priests to continue having relationships with their wives after their ordination. He called that an *obscoena cupiditas.* (At the beginning of the evolution of celibacy most priests were still married; only after 1139 were priests no longer allowed to marry.)

5

Another letter by this sexual neurotic, from the year 390, is aimed at Jovian, who thought that married life was just as good as a virginal life. In about the year 388 Jovian developed some almost Lutheran ideas about marriage and virginity. He came to Rome during the papacy of Siricius and persuaded a number of "consecrated" virgins and male ascetics to get married. He posed the question to them: "Are you better than Sarah, Susanna, Anna, and many of the holy women and men in the Bible?" On the Virgin Mary, Jovian was of the opinion that Mary had indeed conceived Jesus as a virgin, but not borne him as one, because in giving birth Mary's bodily virginity had come to an end. Thus he contested the doctrine of the so-called "virginity in birth," that is, he denied that Mary's hymen remained intact during childbirth. But early on such a foregone biological conclusion was an outrage to pious ears, as it is now. Some respected ascetical laymen turned to Pope Siricius and called for the condemnation of the heretic. Thereupon Siricius excommunicated him and eight of his followers (391).

And so in the case of Siricius we already find many typically Catholic features joined together: Hostility to pleasure, leading to hostility to marriage, leading to celibacy, and, in keeping with all this, the doctrine of the Virgin Birth and Mary's perpetual biological virginity. Pope Siricius left behind only seven letters, which almost without exception display his sexual pessimism. This nonsensical hatred of marriage and the body, as expressed by Pope Siricius and many others, became so dominant in the Catholic Church that it is widely taken to be the sum total of Catholic teaching, and could even find an echo in the judgment of a German district court.

Siricius is one of the many milestones in a long history that turned Christianity from something which if it wasn't, it should have been—namely, the site of the individual experience of the love of God open to all, a love in which the body has its natural and divinely ordained place—into the reign of an unmarried ruling caste over a largely married mass of people treated as minors. This was a perversion of the work of the man from whom Christians get their name. Face to face with a Lord of the Church who no longer reveals God's nearness to men and women and his compassion for them, because he has been made into the listless and lust-hating Christ of the bedroom inspectors and conjugal police, a person can no longer recognize himself as someone whom God loves, but only as someone who is impure and worthy of damnation.

I

NON-CHRISTIAN ROOTS OF CHRISTIAN SEXUAL PESSIMISM

I*t is not true* that Christianity brought self-control and asceticism to a pagan world that delighted in pleasure and the body. Rather, hostility to pleasure and the body are a legacy of Antiquity that has been singularly preserved to this day in Christianity. Christians did not teach licentious, dissolute pagans to hate pleasure and control themselves; instead, the pagans had to acknowledge that the Christians were almost as advanced as they were. The pagan Greek personal physician of Emperor Marcus Aurelius, Galen (second century), found it praiseworthy that the Christians, despite their deficient philosophy, translated into reality authentic virtues that he held in high esteem, such as lifelong sexual continence. He writes: "Most people cannot follow a coherent argument. That is why they need parables, which they make good use of. Similarly nowadays we see people called Christians who draw their faith from parables and miracles. And yet sometimes they behave just like those who live according to a philosophy. For their scorn of death and its aftermath becomes evident to us every day, as does their sexual continence. For they have not only men but women too who live their entire lives sexually continent. Their numbers include individuals who have reached a stage in their self-discipline and their self-control which is not inferior to that of genuine philosophers" (Richard Walzer, *Galen on Jews and Christians,* London, 1949, pp. 19–20).

Sexual pessimism in Antiquity is derived, not, as it would be later in Christianity, from the curse of sin and punishment for it, but predominantly from medical considerations. Pythagoras (sixth century B.C.) is reported as saying that one should indulge in sex in the winter, but not in the summer, make moderate use of it in the spring and fall, but that it was harmful to health in every season. To the question of what was the best time for love, he answered: When you want to weaken yourself (Diogenes Laertius, *Life of the Philosophers,* VIII). The ancients, by the way, believed that women are not harmed by sexual intercourse, since unlike men they are not affected by the loss of energy through the loss of semen. The sexual act is presented as dangerous, hard to control, harmful to health, and draining. Xenophon, Plato, Aristotle, and the physician Hippocrates (fourth century B.C.) all look on it in this way. Plato (d. 348/47 B.C.) writes in the *Laws* about the Olympic victor Issos of Tarentum: He was ambitious and "possessed in his soul the technique and the power of restraint." Once he began devoting himself to his training, "it was said that he never touched a woman or a boy." Hippocrates describes the fate of a young man who died insane after a twenty-four-day illness that began with a simple upset stomach. Previously he had overindulged in sexual pleasure (*Epidemics* III, 18). Hippocrates thought that man (the male) gave the body the greatest amount of energy by withholding his semen, because excessive loss of semen led to tabes dorsalis and death. Sexual activity was a dangerous drain on one's energy. Soranus of Ephesus (second century A.D.), personal physician of Emperor Hadrian, considered continual virginity salubrious. The only justification for sexual activity was the begetting of posterity. Soranus describes the harmful effects of going beyond the bounds of procreation.

In his *History of Sexuality,* Michel Foucault (d. 1984) pursues these voices from Antiquity. According to Foucault, in the first two centuries of the Christian era sexual activity was judged with increasing severity. Physicians recommended abstinence, counseling virginity instead of pleasure-seeking. The philosophers of the Stoa condemned all extramarital sex and demanded conjugal fidelity from both spouses. Pederasty was rated less favorably than before. During these two centuries the bond of marriage was strengthened; sexual relations were allowed only in marriage. Sexuality and marriage became one. The Greek moralist and historian Plutarch (d. ca. 120), one of the most prominent and popular authors in world literature, praises Laelius, who in his long life had intercourse with one and only one woman, his wife (*Parallel Lives, Cato the Younger, 7*).

This increasingly stern and reductive assessment of sex was shaped by the Stoa, the greatest school of ancient philosophy, which lasted from about 300 B.C. to 250 A.D. To this day the word "Stoic" stands for stolid, passionless behavior. While Greek philosophers in general accorded pleasure-seeking considerable importance for the humane ideal of life, the Stoics, especially during the first two centuries of the Christian era, changed all that. They rejected the quest for pleasure. The positive effect of this rejection was the concentration of sexual activity on marriage. But to the extent that carnal pleasure became suspect, marriage was also called into question and celibacy was valued more highly. Marriage was treated as a concession for those who could not contain themselves, a permit to indulge in lust for those who found lust indispensable. The rigoristic preference of celibacy and abstinence to marriage was already outlined in Stoicism and came to fulfillment in the Christian ideal of virginity. The Stoic suspicion of pleasure thus led on the one hand to marriage's being rated higher than a whole spectrum of sexual activities, but on the other hand it also led to a discrimination against marriage in favor of total renunciation of physical pleasure and passion.

The Stoic Seneca, who in the year 50 was appointed tutor to the eleven-year-old Nero and was forced by Nero to commit suicide in the year 65 (for allegedly conspiring against the Emperor), argues in an essay "On Marriage": "All love for someone else's wife is shameful. But it is also shameful to love one's own wife immoderately. In loving his wife the wise man takes reason for his guide, not emotion. He resists the assault of passions, and does not allow himself to be impetuously swept away into the marital act. Nothing is more depraved than to love one's spouse as if she were an adulteress. Those men, however, who say they couple with a woman only to beget children for the sake of the state or the human race, should at least take the animals for their models, and when their wives' wombs swell, they should not destroy their posterity. They should show themselves to be not suitors, but husbands." This passage pleased the lust-hating Father of the Church Jerome so much that he quoted it against Jovinian, the lover of pleasure (*Against Jovinian* I, 49). John Paul II is still talking about adultery with one's own wife. "Do nothing for the sake of pleasure," is Seneca's basic principle (Letter 88, 29). His younger contemporary Musonius, who was active as a teacher of Stoic philosophy to many members of Rome's ruling class, declared that any act of intercourse not serving procreation was immoral. According to Musonius, only marital sex, and only when it was aimed at procreation, was in keeping with good order. Anyone who was intent simply on pleasure, even if he kept within the bounds of marriage, was reprehensible. The first-century Stoics were thus the fathers of the twentieth-century birth control encyclicals. Musonius explicitly rejects contraception; for the same reason he also comes out against homosexuality: the sexual act has to be an act of procreation.

The Stoics did, however, value marriage, above and beyond its procreative function, as a union for mutual assistance (Musonius, *Reliquiae* XIII). Aristotle stated that no bond is closer than that existing between parents and their children, whereas Musonius (ibid., XIV) regarded love between husband and wife as the strongest tie of all. While Aristotle stresses the subordination of woman to man, and describes women as inferior in virtue to men, for Musonius men and women are equally virtuous. Musonius advocates equal rights and education for women, an idea all too seldom copied by the Catholic hierarchy, with its barefoot-in-the-kitchen attitude. Christianity too speaks of marriage as "mutual assistance," but at bottom women are looked upon here simply as assistants to the men: Eve was made to help Adam and not the other way around.

And from the time of Thomas Aquinas on, Aristotle was elevated to the status of a quasi-Father of the Church on women's issues. Common to both the Stoics and the Christians was a certain disembodiment of marriage, insofar as the sexual realm is detached from it and viewed only under the aspect of pleasure or procreation. The marital act remains in the sphere of carnal pleasure; attempts to integrate it fail, and it continues to be stamped by the mistrust toward all pleasure-seeking. The notion that sex has to be a procreative act, but otherwise has to be looked up under the negative heading of pleasure, not under the heading of love, has left an enduring imprint on Christianity.

In Seneca we find an idea that would later disastrously prompt Christian morality to concentrate on sex. Seneca is writing to his mother Helvia: "If you reflect that sexual pleasure has been given to man not for enjoyment, but for the propagation of his race, then if lust has not touched you with its poisoned breath, that other desire will also pass you by without touching you. Reason strikes down not only the individual vices, but all of them together. The victory takes place only once and in all respects." That means that morality is essentially sexual morality. To be vigilant here is to be vigilant, period.

The ideal of virginity did not begin with Christianity. The wonder-worker Apollonius of Tyana (first century), his biographer Philostratus reports, took a vow of virginity that he kept his whole life long. And the naturalist Pliny the Elder, who died in the eruption of Vesuvius in 79, praises the elephant as exemplary because it mates only every two years (*Natural History* 8, 5.). Pliny is referring here to the ideal concept of purity that prevailed in his day. And Pliny's chaste elephant was destined to have a great future and a long career among Christian theologians and in Christian devotional literature. Thus we find him in Richard of St. Victor (d. ca. 1173), Alain de Lille (d. 1202), and in an anonymous summa from the thirteenth century (*Codex latinus Monacensis* 22233), as well as in the Dominican William Peraldus (d. before 1270). In the case of Francis de Sales, the bishop of Geneva (d. 1622), the elephant appears in the *Introduction to the Devout Life* from the year 1609. (cf. Michael Müller, *Die Lehre des hl. Augustinus von der Paradiesesehe*, pp. 74 and 207; John T. Noonan, *Contraception*, 1986[2], p. 248.) And as always he is the model for married people.

Francis de Sales writes: "He is only a clumsy animal and yet the most dignified one alive on earth and the one with the most understanding . . . He never changes his mate and tenderly loves the one he has chosen, with whom, however, he mates only every three years, and that only for five days and in so hidden a manner that he is never seen at this act. But he does show himself on the sixth day, on which he immediately goes straight to the river, where he washes his whole body, not returning to the herd before cleansing himself. Is that not a good and honest nature?" (3, 39). In keeping with the Christian rage for continence, Francis has given Pliny's elephant an extra year of chastity. Pliny's text reads: "Out of modesty elephants never mate except in secret . . . They do it only every two years and then, it is said, never for more than five days. On the sixth they bathe in the river. Until then they do not return to the herd. They are unacquainted with adultery" (*Natural History* 8, 5).

In a book that is still popular among pious Catholics in German-speaking countries, *Stories about the Life of Jesus by Anna Catharina Emmerich, as Recorded by Klemens von Bretano*, we meet the elephant once again. Indeed he has now become part and parcel of Jesus' message, appearing at numerous points of the visions, e.g.: "Jesus spoke too of the great depravity of procreation in mankind, and said that people must abstain after conception, citing the chastity and continence of the elephant as proof of how far humans stood behind the nobler animals on this matter" (dictated on November 5, 1820). The young couple at the marriage of Cana are deeply impressed by this. "At the end of the meal the bridegroom once again came all by himself up to Jesus and spoke very humbly to him, explaining how he felt himself to be mortified to all fleshly desire, and would gladly live with his bride in continence, if she granted this to him. And the bride too came all by herself to Jesus and said the same thing; and Jesus called them both together and spoke with them about marriage and purity, which is so pleasing to God" (dictated on January 2, 1822). The Catholic journal *Offertenzeitung* wrote in September 1978 about Emmerich, the stigmatized visionary nun, who died in 1824: "One could scarcely find a greater antitype to the enjoyment of this world by our nonpraying contemporaries than the love, suffering, and penance of this follower of Christ who lived entirely in God." The *Offer-*

tenzeitung is hoping that "this great servant of God will soon be beatified."

The negative assessment of sexual pleasure that prevailed in Stoicism and was characteristic of the first two centuries after Christ was further strengthened by the invasion of pessimism, which shortly before the birth of Jesus came out of the East, probably from Persia, made its way into the West, and would prove to be the most dangerous competition for Christianity. This movement, which called itself *gnosis* (knowledge), believed that it had recognized the worthlessness and baseness of all existing things. It preached abstinence from marriage, meat, and wine. As early as the New Testament we find the lines being drawn against Gnosticism and its contempt for existence. The First Letter to Timothy ends with the sentence: "O Timothy . . . avoid the godless chatter and contradictions of what is falsely called knowledge." The body is for the Gnostics the "corpse with senses, the grave that you carry around with you." The world does not come from the hands of a good God, but from demons. Only the soul of man, that is, his actual self, his ego, comes like a spark of light from another world, a world of light. It is captured by demonic powers and banished into this world of darkness. The soul of man thus finds itself in a foreign land, in a hostile environment, chained to the dark prison of the body. Seduced by the clamor and the joys of the world, it is in danger of not finding its way back to the god of light from whom it originates. For the demons try to intoxicate it, because without the sparks of light the world, this creation of the demons, falls back into chaos, into darkness.

Gnosticism is a passionate protest against the idea that existence is good. It is governed by a deep pessimism, which stood in opposition to the world view of late Antiquity. It is true that the Greeks were familiar with the depreciation of matter—talk about the body as the prison of the soul goes back to Plato (*Gorgias* 493 A)—but the cosmos (= beauty and order, cf. "cosmetics") was a unified, graduated structure from bottom to top without a break between matter and spirit. The demonization of all corporality and all matter was unknown before the invasion of Gnosticism.

This invasion of negation was so powerful that it proved capable of transforming Antiquity's feelings for life. The cheerful image of Antiquity sketched by German classicism has been invalidated by research into Gnosticism. The philosophy of Neoplatonism (extremely important for Augustine), which developed in the first half of the third century and characterized the end of Antiquity, was influenced by Gnosticism's understanding of life and general mood. Admittedly, Plotinus (d. 270), the leading mind in Neoplatonism, wrote a work against the Gnostics, but to a large extent he was infected by Gnostic pessimism and flight from the world. "He seemed to be ashamed of having a body," writes his biographer Porphyry (d. ca. 305; *The Life of Plotinus*, § 1). Neoplatonism demanded from its followers an abstinent, indeed an ascetical life. Neoplatonism had a fate similar to that of Christianity: Much as it struggled against Gnosticism from the very beginning, it was contaminated by Gnostic hostility toward the body.

Judaism in particular was unreceptive to asceticism until the invasion of Gnosticism, as manifested, for example, in the Qumran sect. The world and the matter were not thought of as evil. Jews did not consider overcoming the world and the denial of life an act of piety. And Judaism's clinging to the *one,* good God as the creator of everything in existence weakened the pessimism and the world-denying Gnostic influences on the Qumran sect. There is no sexual pessimism in the Judaism of the Old Testament. Nevertheless many Catholics find such pessimism already rooted in the Old Testament, specifically in the Book of Tobit, which was composed in about 200 B.C. Actually the credit for laying this biblical foundation for sexual asceticism has to go to the Church Father Jerome (d. 419/20). In his translation of the Bible into Latin (the Vulgate), which to this day is considered authoritative for the Catholic Church, he altered the text, skewing it toward the ideal of virginity. According to the Catholic Wetzer/Welte *Kirchenlexikon* (1899) Tobias survived his wedding night "because of the continence of the newlyweds." For his wife Sarah had already had seven husbands die on her, each during the wedding night; and a grave had already been dug for Tobias as

well. But he did not die. While it says in the original version that
on the first night the pair slept together, Jerome makes Tobias
wait three nights before consummating his union with Sarah.
And when Tobias approaches her, after three nights of prayer, he
utters words that come not from Judaism, but from Jerome: "And
now, Lord, you know that I am not taking this sister of mine out
of lust, but only out of love of offspring" (Tob. 8:9). This forged
statement has been cited by all rigoristic theologians to this day as
an argument for the exclusively procreative purpose of marriage.
Tobias originally said, quoting from Gen. 2:18, "It is not good for
man to be alone"; but Jerome simply drops that sentence in order
not to confuse the issue. In the more recent Catholic translations
of the Bible Jerome's interpolations and omissions have been canceled. And the time has long passed when the bishop of Amiens
and the pastors of Abbeville could charge brides and grooms a fee
for a dispensation if they were unwilling to observe the three "Tobias nights," but intended to have intercourse on the first night.
Voltaire (d. 1778), by the way, saw a connection between the fees
paid the bishop of Amiens and the so-called *jus primae noctis,* the
privilege of the feudal lord to be the first to cohabit with his
female subjects on their wedding night. In fact there does seem
to be a connection between the continence of the young husband
for God's sake, as described in Tobias' case (from the pen of
Jerome), and the continence of the young husband for the sake of
the ruler's privilege, as expressed in the *jus primae noctis,* and,
finally, the bishop's charging money to dispense couples from that
privilege. The idea is the same: The right to the wedding night
belongs in the first instance to the feudal lord or the Lord God.
For Protestants, one might add, the whole Book of Tobit, with or
without the "Tobias nights," does not belong in the Old Testament, but in the so-called Apocrypha (noncanonical writings).

Thanks to the discoveries at Qumran on the Dead Sea in 1947,
we can get a better picture of the desert-dwelling sect from the
time of Jesus that has been known since Antiquity under the
name of the Essenes. The influence of Gnosticism and its sexual
asceticism, which was in itself alien to Judaism, can be clearly
seen in this sect. It was not, admittedly, a purely monastic com-

munity, since married people could also be part of it, but the great cemetery to the east of Qumran shows that the full-fledged members, the ones that set the tone, were monks. Even the layout of the graves testifies to the privileged position of the unmarried and the inferior status of women and children. The settlement was totally destroyed by the Romans in 68.

The Jewish idea of a good Creation by a good Creator God was severely impaired by the influence of Gnosticism. The world, according to Qumran, is darkness under Satan's dominion. We find a similar Gnostic expression in the Gospel of John, since for all the polemics against Gnosticism it had a significant influence on the New Testament. Neither in the New Testament nor in the Jewish sect at Qumran, however, was the Jewish idea of the *one,* good God ever abandoned.

On the subject of the Essenes the Jewish historian Josephus (d. ca. 100) writes: "Jews from birth . . . turn away from the joys of life as if from an evil thing and embrace continence as a virtue. They judge marriage unfavorably, but they accept the children of others, so long as they are still at an age when they can be trained. They are on their guard against the inconstancy of women, convinced that no woman is true to her husband . . . Neither shouts nor any other kind of noise disturbs the consecrated silence of the building . . . But to people outside it sounds like a grimly horrible mystery. This silence is the consequence of their constant observance of sobriety and their custom of taking just enough food and drink for satisfaction . . . They are emphatically convinced that the body passes away and that matter does not last, but that souls are immortal eternally and forever . . . About souls they believe that they came forth from the most rarefied aether . . . If they were freed from the shackles of the flesh, then they would feel as if they had been released from long imprisonment and would soar back on high in blessed joy . . . There is, however, yet another group of Essenes . . . They believe that whoever renounces marriage is neglecting an essential task in life, namely the begetting of offspring, that is, they think that if everyone had the same opinion as the others, the human race would soon come to an end. But they test their future wives for three years, and if these . . . prove their capacity for bearing children, then the marriage is entered into. They do not have intercourse during pregnancy, which goes to show that they do not marry for reasons of lust, but for the blessing of children" (*The Jewish War* II, 8, 2–13).

While the Jewish sect at Qumran, in keeping with the un-Jewish Gnostic influence, proposed an extreme form of the rejection of marriage, in Philo of Alexandria, the Jewish-Greek philosopher and contemporary of Jesus, we meet a synthesis of Jewish and Greek thought. At the beginning of the Christian era this cultivated Jew constituted a bridge from Judaism to the Greek world, from Jewish faith to Greek philosophy; and, strongly influenced by that philosophy, he tried to familiarize his non-Jewish contemporaries with the Hebrew Bible. This mixture of Judaism and Greek thought (primarily Stoicism) reads as if Philo were already the first Christian Father of the Church, at least with regard to his notions of marriage. But Philo remained a Jew in that he did not support the ideal of virginity, which was developing in early Christianity.

When Joseph was in Egypt, says Philo, he told his would-be seductress, Potiphar's wife: "We descendants of the Hebrews have quite peculiar customs and practices. When contracting marriage, we come pure to pure virgins; and we set as our goal not lust but the begetting of legitimate children" (*On Joseph* 9, 43). In his explanation of the Mosaic law on adultery Philo speaks of "lecherous men, who in their frantic passion practice all too lustful intercourse, not with another's wife, but with their own" (*On the Individual Laws* 3, 2, 9). Philo means that coitus in marriage should take place only in the hope of having children, not for sexual enjoyment. For this reason he praises Abraham's polygamy, because in his opinion it was occasioned not by the longing for pleasure, but by Abraham's wish to increase his posterity. Indeed Philo takes his idea of procreation as the sole meaning and purpose of marriage further than had Greeks and Jews before him: If someone knows about the barrenness of a woman from a former marriage and marries her despite that, then he is "tilling a poor and stony land," he is acting only from motives of sensual pleasure, and that must be condemned. But if the infertility of the wife is determined only after the marriage has been contracted, then it is pardonable for the husband not to dismiss his wife. The last ramifications of this notion that marriage has to be a procreative fellowship were not removed from Canon Law until 1977: Now the husband need only be capable of having intercourse, not of having children, in order to contract a valid marriage.

Philo sharply criticizes contraception: "Those who during intercourse bring about the destruction of the seed are undoubtedly enemies of nature" (*On the Individual Laws* 3, 36). And because of the sterility of their sexual acts he also sharply condemns homosexuals: "Like a bad farmer, the homosexual lets the fertile land lie fallow and toils night and day with the sort of land from which no fruit at all can be expected." Philo, who thought like a Greek about many things, was altogether Jewish in his aversion to homosexuality: "One must proceed ruthlessly against these men, in accordance with the prescription of the Law, that the effeminate man, who falsifies the stamp of nature, should be killed without hesitation, and should not be allowed to live a day, indeed not for an hour, since he shames himself, his house, his fatherland, and the whole human race . . . because he pursues unnatural pleasure and for his part works toward the desolation and depopulation of the cities . . . when he destroys his seed" (*On the Individual Laws* 3, 37–42).

II

THE ANCIENT TABOO AGAINST MENSTRUAL BLOOD AND ITS CHRISTIAN CONSEQUENCES

One *particular taboo* of Antiquity that Christianity went along with prohibited intercourse with a menstruating woman. Philo, like the physician Soranus of Ephesus (second century A.D.), argues that conception cannot take place during menstruation, and so he forbids intercourse with menstruating women. Fresh menstrual blood, he says, keeps the womb moist, and "Moisture not only weakens the vitality of the seed, but totally cancels it" (*On the Individual Laws*, 3, 6, 32). This is Philo's justification for the ban in Leviticus 20:18: "If a man lies with a woman having her sickness, and uncovers her nakedness, he has made naked her fountain, and she has uncovered the fountain of her blood; both of them shall be cut off from among their people."

The Old Testament itself does not explain this atrocious penalty. We do learn, however, in Leviticus 15:19–24 that God defines a menstruating woman as unclean for seven days, and anyone who touches her or anything she has touched or anything touched by someone she has touched is also unclean. In Antiquity both Jews and pagans were convinced that menstrual blood was, in effect, poisonous. But whereas for Philo the menses damaged semen so that conception could not occur, the Roman naturalist Pliny the Elder (d. 79 A.D.) maintained that sex with a woman having her period was forbidden because children conceived during menstruation were sick, or had purulent blood serum, or were born dead (*Natural History* 7, 15, 87).

Around the year 200 the Church Fathers Clement of Alexandria (d. 215?) and Origen (d. 254) [echoed two centuries later by Jerome (d. 420)] claimed that children conceived during menstruation were born impaired. As Jerome wrote: "When a man has intercourse with his wife at this time, the children born from

2 1

this union are leprous and hydrocephalic; and the corrupted blood causes the plague-ridden bodies of both sexes to be either too small or too large" (*Commentary on Ezekiel* 18, 6).

"Whoever has relations with his wife during her period," warns Archbishop Caesarius of Arles (d. 542), "will have children that are either leprous or epileptic or possessed by the Devil (Peter Browe, *Beiträge zur Sexualethik des Mittelalters,* p. 48). In his encyclopedic work *Etymologies,* which was widely read for hundreds of years, Isidore of Seville (d. 636) states that, "After touching [menstrual blood] fruits do not sprout, blossoms fade, grasses wither . . . iron rusts, brass turns black, dogs that taste it get rabies" (Browe, p. 2). Like Philo, Isidore thought that the damage done to semen during menstruation made conception impossible. According to Abbot Regino of Prüm in Eifel (d. 915) and Burchard of Worms (d. 1025), the priest in the confessional had to ask about intercourse during menstruation.

The major theologians of the thirteenth century, men such as Albert the Great, Thomas Aquinas, and Duns Scotus, forbid intercourse with a menstruating woman as a mortal sin on account of the harm to the children. Berthold of Regensburg (d. 1272), the most celebrated preacher in the same century, makes it clear to his listeners: "You will have no joy from any children conceived during the menses. For they will either be afflicted by the devil, or lepers, or epileptics, or humpbacked, or blind, or crook-legged, or dumb, or idiots, or they will have heads like a mallet . . . and should you have been away from your wife for four weeks, indeed, should you have been away for two years, you should take good care not to desire her . . . You are, after all, upright people, and you see that a stinking Jew avoids this time with great diligence" (F. Göbel, *Die Missionspredigten des Franziskaners Berthold von Regensburg,* 1857, pp. 354–55). Berthold mentions the Jews ("stinking" Jews, as Christian anti-Semitism would have it) because in the Middle Ages the fact that so few Jews contracted leprosy was often explained by their careful avoidance of intercourse with menstruating women. The peasants, on the other hand, were especially prone to leprosy; and Berthold attributes this to their having intercourse with their wives during menstruation (Browe, p. 4).

Even Jan Hus, who was burned at the stake at the Council of Constance in 1415—but not for his opinions on this point, which more or less all the Council Fathers shared—believed that hunchbacked, squinting, one-eyed, epileptic, lame, and diabolically possessed children were the consequence of sex with a menstruating woman (Browe, p. 5).

In the following centuries, thanks to medical progress, the notion that the handicapped were conceived during menstruation was slowly abandoned. By the sixteenth century Luther's adversary, Cardinal Cajetan (d. 1534), spoke of intercourse during menstruation as only a "venial sin" (*Summula Peccatorum* 1526, under the heading "matrimonium"). Thomas Sanchez (d. 1610), a moral theologian who set the standard on questions of marriage for his own century and the following centuries, writes that many theologians no longer view intercourse during menstruation as sinful, but that most consider it a venial sin, because there is something "improper" about it, and it shows a lack of self-control. He himself, Thomas Sanchez, agreed with the latter assessment. He no longer believed that the practice damaged the fetus, since this could very seldom be proved. Under certain circumstances intercourse with a menstruating woman could even be sinless, if there was a sufficient reason to justify it, such as the wish to overcome a strong carnal temptation or to ease marital strife (*The Holy Sacrament of Marriage* Book 9, Disp. 21, n. 7).

Some theologians committed to Jansenism (the revival of strict Augustianism in the seventeenth century) saw the situation differently. The Belgian Laurentius Neesen (d. 1679), for example, considered intercourse with a menstruating woman a mortal sin for the partner who demanded it (Heinrich Klomps, *Ehemoral und Jansenismus*, p. 190). Most of the Jansenists, however, speak of venial sin in this case. Alphonsus Liguori (d. 1787), the most important moral theologian of the eighteenth century, and the one who set the tone for Catholics in the nineteenth and early twentieth centuries, follows Thomas Sanchez, so that up until the beginning of this century intercourse with a menstruating woman was generally looked upon as a venial sin (Dominikus Linder, *Der Usus matrimonii*, p. 218).

The idea of a menstruating woman's receiving Holy Communion was consistently frowned upon all the way into the Middle Ages, although more severely in the Eastern Church than in the West. Patriarch Dionysus of Alexandria (d. 264/65), a disciple of Origen, said it was pointless to ask whether a woman might thus take Communion, "because pious, devout women would never even think of touching the sacred table or the Body and Blood of the Lord" (*Ep. can.*[2], PG 10, 1281 A). The papal legate Cardinal Humbert, who in 1054 brought about the great Schism between the Eastern and Western Church that took place in Constantinople, criticized the Greek Church for this discriminatory practice. The famous twelfth-century canonist of the Orthodox Church, jurist Theodore of Balsamon (d. after 1195), patriarch of Antioch, defended the custom, as did the Coptic patriarch of Alexandria Cyril III (d. 1243). The Maronites did not abolish it until 1596 (cf. Browe, pp. 9 and 10).

The West took a more moderate position. Pope Gregory the Great (d. 604) did not forbid menstruating women from coming to church or receiving Communion, but he praised women who abstained from the Eucharist at this time. For Gregory menstruation is the result of sin: Women should not "be forbidden to go to church. Nor should they be forbidden to receive Communion in these days. But when a women does not dare, because of her great reverence, to go there, she is to be praised. The menstrual period is no sin, it is a purely natural event. But the fact that nature is so perverse, that it appears stained even without man's will, *that* comes from a sin" (*Response to the English Bishop Augustine,* 10th Answer).

This imbalance led to conflicting legislation in the West. In some cases Communion was forbidden to women having their period, in others it was permitted. The Prague canon Matthias of Janow (d. 1394), for example, attacked priests who would not admit such women to the Eucharist. He argued that priests should not inquire about such matters in the confessional, "since that is neither necessary nor useful nor decent" (Browe, p. 14). But as late as 1684 in the Black Forest village of Deckenpfronn menstruating women stood outside the church door "and actually do not go in, they stand as if they were in the pillory," as the church record reports (cf. Browe, p. 14).

Menstruation proved to be especially fatal to women's chances for holding church offices. Theodore of Balsamon writes that, "At one time deaconesses used to be ordained in keeping with the laws of the Church. They were allowed to approach the altar, but because of their monthly impurity they were ousted from their place in the liturgy and from the holy altar. In the honorable church of Constantinople deaconesses are still selected, but they no longer have access to the altar" (*Responsa ad interrogationes Marci* [resp. 35]; cf. Ida Raming, *Der Ausschluss der Frau vom priestlichen Amt,* 1973, p. 39).

Blood from childbirth (lochia) was considered still more harmful than menstrual blood, which prompted bans on intercourse similar to those that applied to menstruating women. Women who had just given birth caused additional problems for the antisexual Christian Church, for example when they had to be buried. To begin with, according to the Synod of Trier, which was held in 1227, new mothers had to be "reconciled with the Church." Only then would they be allowed to go to church. This "churching" ceremony, as it is now called, was an amalgam of Jewish laws of ritual purity (even Mary was not allowed to reenter the Temple until forty days had passed and a sacrifice of purification had been offered) with a characteristically Christian pillorying of sexual pleasure and defamation of women.

Women who died in childbirth before being "reconciled" with the Church were often denied burial in the cemetery. Several synods—Rouen in 1074 and Cologne in 1279—opposed this policy and argued for the same kind of burial that other Christians got (Browe, p. 20). Writing to Elector Johann of Saxony in 1530 on behalf of the Imperial Diet of Augsburg, Martin Luther notes that in the papal Church, "Women who die in childbirth are buried in a special ceremony." They were not laid out, as others would be, in the middle of the Church, but at the door (*Briefwechsel* 7, Calw/Stuttgart 1897, p. 258). In the diocese of Ghent, as a deanery conference of 1632 prescribed, women who died before they could be churched were buried in secret (Browe, p. 21).

Though they had a long struggle for the right to a normal burial, women who had just given birth had to struggle even longer for the right to return to church without undergoing a special purification. On January 13, 1199, Pope Innocent III imposed an interdict on France because the French King was living in an invalid marriage with his mistress Agnes of Meran. The interdict ordered all the churches in France to be closed, and to be opened only for infant baptisms. The Pope "strictly" forbade women to come to church for purification, and since they had not been "churched," they were also not permitted to take part in the baptism of their children. Only after the interdict was lifted could they be readmitted by the priest. The interdict lasted over a year, until the King dismissed Agnes of Meran.

This was in contradiction to what the same Pope, Innocent III, had written in 1198 to the Archbishop of Armagh, in reply to the question of whether the Mosaic law on women who had just given birth was still applicable in the Church. No, said Innocent, "but if women prefer to stay away from church for a while out of reverence, we believe we cannot reprimand them" (*Ep.* I, 63; cf. Browe, p. 26). When it comes to discriminating against women, the Both-And approach, on the one hand yes, on the other hand no, has always been useful.

The custom of purifying women after childbirth has lasted almost up to the present. The *Kirchenlexikon* of Wetzer/Welte (1886) describes "churching" in this way: "Like the catechumens and penitents, the woman who has just had a child must first stand, or kneel, outside the church door; and only when she has been solemnly purified by sprinkling with holy water and the prayer of the priest is she led into the church. This is similar to what still happens today with catechumens and to what used to happen before with public penitents on Holy Thursday" (Wetzer/Welte I, 1711). As late as the 1960s the practice of "churching" was still strictly adhered to. In 1987 a woman wrote me as follows: "I can recall how terribly ashamed my mother once was. In 1960 my younger sister was born. My mother was not allowed to be present at the baptism because she had not yet been 'churched.' Some time later in the afternoon she sneaked off all by herself to church, where the pastor 'churched' her. Only then could she attend services again."

III

THE NEW TESTAMENT, AND HOW IT WAS MISUNDERSTOOD: THE VIRGIN BIRTH, CELIBACY, AND THE REMARRIAGE OF DIVORCED PERSONS

In the development of Christian sexual morality the immediate determining influences were Judaism and Gnosticism: Judaism as we found it in a contemporary of the first Christians, namely Philo of Alexandria (d. ca. 45–50 A.D.); and Gnosticism, insofar as it promoted the ideal of celibacy and subordinated marriage to the single life. It is true that Christians resisted the invasion of Gnostic pessimism, and that during the first Christian centuries the Gnostics were the peculiar opponents of the Christians. But the idealization of virginity as closer to God was adopted by the Christians from their opponents; and it even infiltrated the New Testament, although only to a small extent.

Thus in Revelation John speaks of the 144,000 who sing a new song before the throne of God: "It is these who have not defiled themselves with women, for they are virgins; it is these who follow the Lamb wherever he goes; these have been redeemed from mankind as first fruits for God and the Lamb" (Rev. 14:4). Here, right in the New Testament, Gnosticism has triumphed over the Jewish legacy of the Old Testament, which never talks like that. In the next verse Revelation does quote Isaiah 53:9, "And in their mouth no lie was found, for they are spotless," but Isaiah has nothing in that passage about the "virginally pure."

Elsewhere in the New Testament, however, Gnosticism and its hostility to sex and marriage are rejected. 1 Timothy 4:3 warns against "liars whose consciences are seared, who forbid marriage . . ." In his address "To the Christian Nobility of the German Nation" (1520) Luther cites this verse against the papacy: "And now the see of Rome, out of its own wickedness, has come up with the idea of forbidding priests to marry. This it has done on orders from the devil, as Paul proclaims in 1 Tim. 4: 'Teachers will come with teachings from the devil and forbid people to marry.' This had led to a great deal of misery, and was the reason why the Greek Church broke away. I advise that everyone be left free to get married or not to get married." And in "On the Babylonian Captivity of the Church" (1520) he writes: "I know that Paul commands: 'A bishop should be the husband of one wife.' And so we drop all these cursed human regulations, which have crept into the Church, causing only the multiplication of great dangers, sin and evil . . . Why should my freedom be taken away from me by someone else's superstition and ignorance?"

And finally, in the Schmalkaldic Articles of 1537 Luther argues: "They were completely unjustified in forbidding marriage and in burdening the divine state of the priesthood with the demand of continual celibacy. In doing so they have acted like anti-Christian, tyrannical, unholy scoundrels, occasioning all sorts of terrible, ghastly, countless sins against chastity, in which they are caught to this day. Neither we nor they have been given any power to make a female creature out of a male, or a male out of a female, nor did they have the power to separate these, God's creatures, or to forbid people to live together honorably in marriage. That is why we refuse to accept their confounded celibacy, but rather wish that people be free to choose marriage, as God has ordained and established it. For St. Paul says in 1 Tim. 4, it is a teaching of the Devil."

The New Testament's presentation of the Virgin Birth should not be understood as expressing hostility to sex and marriage, although it has been misunderstood in this sense. The Old Testament did not promise a biological Virgin Birth, nor did the New Testament wish to describe such a birth as a historical event.

Matthew 1 and Luke 1 use the Virgin Birth as a metaphor, like other metaphors in the New Testament. As for the prophet Isaiah (eighth century B.C.) he never speaks of a Virgin Birth at all. The supposed promise of the Virgin Birth by the prophet does not correspond to the Hebrew text. In Isaiah 7:14 it says: "Behold, a young woman (alma) shall conceive and bear a son, and shall call his name Immanuel." The appearance of the word "virgin" in Matthew 1:23 comes from the Septuagint, the Greek translation of the Bible (third century B.C.), which translates the word *alma* as *parthenos* (virgin). The Hebrew word *can* mean virgin, but need not do so any more than every young woman *must* have preserved her virginity. But even if Isaiah had spoken of a virgin, that would not have meant a virginal conception. In that case the passage means only that the woman of the child being awaited was a virgin before he was engendered. It does not mean that the procreation of the child would take place in a supernatural fashion and would do no harm to her virginity.

We don't know what young woman or virgin Isaiah had in mind when he spoke with King Ahaz in Jerusalem during the Syro-Ephraimite war in 734 B.C. But when he gave the king the "sign" of the young woman who would become pregnant, he was in any case talking about an event in the near future, not about something that would take place after more than seven hundred years. Isaiah says of the child Immanuel: "He shall eat curds and honey when he knows how to refuse the evil and choose the good. For before the child knows how to refuse the evil and choose the good, the land before whose two kings you are in dread will be deserted" (Is. 7:15–16). In the years 733 and 732 B.C. the Assyrians conquered both the kingdoms of Damascus and Israel. The danger threatening King Ahaz from both those sources thus passed him by. And the child Immanuel, born to the young woman, would still have been small, not yet at the age of discretion, still eating, as the prophet had put it, curds and honey.

Thus there is nothing about the Virgin Birth in the Old Testament. Even in the New Testament this notion cannot be found in the work of the earliest author, namely Paul. And the earliest Gospel, Mark, also says nothing about it. In the Gospel According to John, Jesus is expressly referred to as the son of Joseph (1:45 and 6:42). John, by the way, invokes the Old Testament in identifying Jesus: "Philip [one of the twelve apostles] found Nathanael, and said to him, 'We have found him of whom Moses in the law and also the prophets wrote, Jesus of Nazareth, the son of Joseph' " (1:45).

The legend of the Virgin Birth is found only in Matthew and Luke. But even in the case of these two Gospels the metaphor of the Virgin Birth occurs only in the more recent strata of the text, not in the oldest. The genealogies of Jesus in Matthew 1 and Luke 3 come from a time when Joseph's being the father of Jesus was taken completely for granted. These parts of the Gospels aim to prove that Jesus is a descendent of David through Joseph, which presupposes that Joseph is Jesus' actual father. And Mary quite matter-of-factly refers to Joseph as Jesus' father in Luke 2:48.

Only in the more recent strata of these two Gospels do we find the Virgin Birth used as a metaphor to express God's special initiative in salvation history. Here the New Testament does not intend to be read as a documentary report, nor to be taken literally, any more than the description of Adam's creation from a clod of earth in Genesis. Both are expressive images for the concept that the creation of the first man and the creation of the "second man" (as Paul calls Jesus in 1 Corinthians 15:47) are the work of God.

The image of the Virgin Birth corresponds to the legends and metaphorical language of Antiquity which trace the descent of famous individuals back to the gods. According to Suetonius, Augustus was considered a son of Apollo, Plutarch tells us that Alexander was conceived by a thunderbolt that struck his mother's womb (or so she dreamed). It was reserved to Christians to take this sort of image literally, in the biological sense, with respect not to the pagan gods, but to their own Christian God, as late as the twentieth century. This is not to deny that many ancient pagans took the images glorifying great men for reality, but educated and enlightened pagans did not. The situation was probably the case described by Plutarch: "There was a woman living in Pontus who claimed that she was pregnant by Apollo.

Naturally enough many people doubted her story, but there were also many who believed her" (*Parallel Lives, Lysander,* 26).

David Friedrich Strauss, one of the most famous Protestant theologians of the nineteenth century, showed how the process of ongoing historicization could transform a metaphor from Antiquity into a concrete account of personal chastity with a life of its own. Thus in his *Life of Jesus* (1835) he tells of Plato's nephew Speusippus, who mentions a widespread Athenian legend that Plato was a son of Apollo: Until Plato was born, it was claimed, his father, Ariston, refrained from intercourse with his wife, Periktione (Diogenes Laertius 3, 1, 2). In the same way, Strauss said, the legend of Jesus' birth from a virgin limited Mary's virginity until Jesus' birth: "But he knew her not until she had borne a son; and he called his name Jesus" (Mt. 1:25). Plato acquired brothers and sisters, and Jesus acquired brothers and sisters. They are mentioned both in Mark (6:3) and Matthew (13:55). The fact that the New Testament reports the existence of Jesus' brothers and sisters shows, by the way, that the metaphor of the Virgin Birth was not understood in a sexual pessimistic sense, as it increasingly was during its historicization over the centuries.

After New Testament times, from the second century on, Jesus' brothers and sisters were first turned into stepbrothers and stepsisters from the first marriage of Joseph, now a widower (Proto-Gospel of James 9, ca. 150); and finally in about 400 Jerome made the stepbrothers and stepsisters over into male and female cousins; and maintained that it was "godless, apocryphal daydreaming" to believe that Joseph had children from a first marriage. According to Jerome, only a virginal Joseph would be appropriate for a virginal Mary (*Ad Matth.* 12). Thus Mary was a virgin after as well as before the birth of Jesus. The last vulnerable window in her virginity was closed as early as the second century, when in the Proto-Gospel of James (19–20) a midwife declared that Mary's hymen remained undamaged during the birth of Jesus. The New Testament metaphors of Virgin Birth thus took on an independent status as the story of Mary's private chastity and biological intactness.

To recapitulate: The prophet Isaiah referred in the eighth

century B.C. to a young woman who would conceive. The New Testament began by molding this statement into the metaphor for a Virgin Birth as an expression of God's special initiative in the creation and existence of Jesus. In the ensuing centuries this metaphor was elaborated into a detailed account of Mary's abiding virginity before, during, and after Jesus' birth. Coincidentally, this development of the Virgin Birth metaphor also established—and this is the gravest consequence of the historicization process—that God is a kind of man, for he deals with Mary in a quasi-masculine fashion. As the well-known Catholic dogmatic theologian Michael Schmaus writes, "What is otherwise achieved through the action of a male, was done to Mary by God's omnipotence" (*Mariology*, p. 107).

The growing tendency to place an antisexual construction on passages from the New Testament with no antiphysical, antisexual connotations was not confined to the metaphor of the Virgin Birth. This sexually pessimistic process of reinterpretation can be seen quite clearly in the case of another passage, which to this day is thought of as a comment by Jesus on celibacy and one of the mainstays of the practice. In his "Letter to All the Priests of the Church" on Holy Thursday, 1979, John Paul II refers to "celibacy for the sake of the Kingdom of Heaven," about which Jesus is supposed to have said, "He who is able to receive this, let him receive it" (Mt. 19:12). Jesus, in fact, is not speaking here about celibacy at all, but the passage has been cut and trimmed to make it do so; and as such it has become the favorite motto of all defenders of celibacy up to and including John Paul II.

But we need consider only the subject put before Jesus to know what he is talking about in his answer. He is not asked about celibacy, and hence is not discussing that. He is questioned by the Pharisees about divorce, whereupon he proposes a thesis that was unheard of at this time, when a man could divorce his wife simply for burning his dinner (thus Rabbi Hillel, in contrast to the stricter Rabbi Shammai). Jesus says: "Whoever divorces his wife and marries another woman commits adultery" (Mt. 19:9). Even his disciples object to this teaching; and Jesus says, "Not all men can receive this saying" (Mt. 19:11), and he adds that there is a self-castration for the sake of the Kingdom of Heaven (Mt. 19:12). This statement, which is naturally to be understood metaphorically, has an immediate grammatical connection (through the word "for") with the preceding debate over divorce. The issue here is voluntary renunciation of remarriage, which Jesus treats as adultery. "Unmarried" or "incapable of marriage" (thus the New English Bible) are common but erroneous translations of the Greek word *eunuchoi*.

It must be admitted that this saying about psychic self-castration is one that has bewildered many people, and not just the disciples. Jesus himself says, "He who is able to receive this, let him receive it." But whatever one's response to it, it deals not with the incapacity for marriage or the principled rejection of it (as many readings of this text imply), but with renouncing adultery; and hence it has nothing to do with celibacy. Need we say that the whole institution of celibacy was based—and still is today, practically speaking—on a foolish objection by the disciples? Their protest boils down to the idea that it would be better not to marry at all *because* that way one loses one's sexual freedom, and the possibility of getting rid of one's wife.

Thus Jesus is repudiating adultery and divorce. And the disciples object that it would be better not to get married (if you can't get divorced). They are the sort of people who do not receive Jesus' saying. They think it's better to live with a woman without a strong, indissoluble bond, if that means what Jesus says it does, namely, that one may never have another woman. When Jesus thereupon says to them, "He who is able to receive it, let him receive it," he is not making their objection into part of the Gospel—because that objection is simply a male chauvinist protest, and how pathetic that celibates are always invoking this objection—but Jesus stands by his message. He means what *he* said, and not the protest by his polygamously minded disciples, whom Jesus' demand rubs the wrong way.

What stuns the disciples is not Jesus' teaching about the single life or celibacy, about which he says nothing whatsoever, but his teaching about marriage and divorce; and this *was* something new. The disciples appeal to Moses, who allowed "one to give a certificate of divorce, and to put her away." But Jesus answers: "For your hardness of heart Moses allowed you to divorce your wives, but from the beginning it was not so." In making his case Jesus cites the story of creation: "Have you not read that he who made them from the beginning made them male and female, and said, 'For this reason a man shall leave his father and mother and be joined to his wife, and the two shall become one flesh'? What therefore God has joined together, let not man put asunder" (Mt. 19:3–12).

Becoming one flesh is for Jesus a total, irrevocable act of union, more than a mere temporary connection. On it is based the indissolubility of marriage. Thomas Aquinas (d. 1274) later grounded the permanence of marriage on concern for the children, whom the wife could not raise all by herself. But Jesus says nothing about children. Nor does he speak of becoming one flesh for the purpose of having children. His new teaching, which is the old truth "from the beginning," argues the indissoluble oneness of the spouses.

Jesus' teaching, by which he goes back to before Moses, to the origins, struck his listeners as outrageous. The alternative to Rabbi Hillel's interpretation was Rabbi Shammai's view, which set stricter conditions, but did not contest the possibility of divorce. Jesus' words turned his disciples' understanding of divorce upside down. The Jews understood "Thou shalt not commit adultery" as having different implications for men and women: For the man, only intercourse with someone else's wife was adultery; for the wife, intercourse with anyone but her husband was adultery. The man could only violate someone else's marriage; one's own marriage is violated only by the wife. The reason for this is that the wife was considered not a man's partner, but his possession. By committing adultery the wife was depreciating her husband's possession, while the husband was depreciating another man's possession. Adultery was a kind of crime against property. Thus intercourse with an unmarried woman did not constitute adultery for the man.

Jesus' teaching revokes this privileged masculine concept of adultery. He also revokes polygyny, which Jews thought had been granted by God. Judaism in Jesus' day—apart from the Qumran sect—affirmed polygamy. That meant that a man could never violate his own marriage. The wife belonged to her husband, but the husband did not belong to his wife. Jesus' way of reading the creation story destroys the whole patriarchal position. No wonder the disciples thought that under those circumstances it would be better not to marry at all. That sort of marriage was not what they had in mind.

We can find a parallel to the passage on divorce in Matthew's account of the Sermon on the Mount (Mt. 5:27–28): "You have heard that it was said, 'You shall not commit adultery.' But I say to you that every one who looks at a woman lustfully has already committed adultery with her in his heart." As we all know, Jesus also has something to say about other subjects in the Sermon on the Mount. But, with the increasing stress of sexual offenses in comparison with all other areas of human deficiency, divorced and remarried people were given special treatment in the Catholic Church, although sowers of discord were not. Now as in days gone by the chief sins of humanity are located in the bedroom and not, for example, on the battlefields.

The Sermon on the Mount, the noblest Christian utopia, is divided into two parts. The larger (by far) section is considered unattainable and impractical. Only the remarriage of divorced people is, by exception, enforced and subject to a special penalty, even though when addressing this subject Jesus said—in fact said twice—that not everyone could receive it. Granted, denying the idea of the indissolubility of marriage, canceling the possibility and the ideal of radical solidarity, constitutes a breakdown of common life. But the belief that failure on this point weighs more heavily than all kinds of human failure is a product of the Church's sexual pessimism. It is altogether wrong to appeal to Jesus to justify this celibate rigorism. With Jesus, positive warmth toward marriage and women, indeed toward all of humanity, was the guiding principle. In contrast, this rigorism is hostile toward women, and often enough plainly inhuman, no longer affirming a principle for the sake of people, but sacrificing people *to* a principle.

As far back as the time when the New Testament was composed exceptions were made to the prohibition against the remarriage of divorcees. This can be seen in the two so-called Matthew clauses (Mt. 5:32 and 19:9). The tenor of the longer text (Mt. 19) makes it quite clear that Jesus is stressing the indissolubility of marriage, while emphasizing that not everyone can "receive" this. From the very beginning exceptions were made in practice, namely, in the case of adultery (or "unchastity"). And so an exemption was later introduced into the text that interrupts the train of Jesus' thought. The Protestant Church and the Eastern Church—which has been separated from the Roman Catholic Church since 1054—translate this clause correctly in the sense of weakening Jesus' strict position that divorce and remarriage run counter to the will of God. Hence they translate the crucial phrase as "except for adultery." In contrast, the Catholic Church translates it as "not even for adultery," disregarding the early Church, which inserted this formula to begin with. Thus in the Eastern Church and in the Protestant Church the remarriage of divorced people is allowed, while it is decisively rejected in the Roman Catholic Church.

But Rome was not always as strict as it is today. The Spanish Synod of Elvira (beginning of the fourth century) and the Synod of Arles (314) treated men and women differently: A woman who remarried was excommunicated for life; the man was not excommunicated, only advised not to remarry, and he was admitted to Communion. Some Fathers of the Church—Origen (d. 25/54), Epiphanius (d. 403), Basilius (d. 403)—allowed exceptions to the prohibition against the remarriage of divorcees. Epiphanius and Basilius permitted only men to remarry and only under certain circumstances. In a similar vein Augustine (d. 430) writes: "The man who dismisses his wife after catching her in adultery and then marries another obviously should not be equated with those who dismiss their wives for reasons other than adultery and get married again. In the Sacred Scripture it is by no means clear [*obscurum est*] whether someone who is doubtlessly allowed to dismiss his wife for committing adultery is himself to be viewed as an adulterer when he afterward marries another woman. I for one believe that he commits a venial sin in this case" (*De fide et operibus* 19). Theodore, archbishop of Canterbury (d. 690), the

Frankish Synods of Verberie (756) and Compiègne (757), and the Collection of Canon Law by Burchard of Worms (d. 1025) all issue special regulations for the remarriage of divorced people. The reform pope Gregory VII (d. 1085), who enjoined celibacy on the clergy and fought against married clerics, at the same time opposed remarriage—for the same reasons of hostility to sex.

Nevertheless, even after Gregory's reforms many theologians still argued for exceptions to the indissolubility of marriage. Among them were Luther's adversary, Cardinal Cajetan (d. 1534), as well as Luther himself and Erasmus of Rotterdam (d. 1536). It was not until 1563 that the Council of Trent unequivocally proclaimed that the remarriage of divorced persons for any reason whatever was forbidden. Canon 7, which makes this stipulation, was, however, toned down somewhat at the request of Venice. The Venetians, who were then a colonial power, were afraid of difficulties with their Greek Orthodox subjects on the islands of Crete, Cyprus, and Corfu; and in their petition to the council they called attention to the fact that, "Everyone knows that the Greeks have kept the custom of dismissing an adulterous wife and marrying a new one. In this, as they say, they are following a very old custom of their fathers. They were never condemned on that account by any council for this, although this usage was well known to the Roman Church." The original wording by the Council of Trent had been to the effect that if anyone said that one could remarry in the case of adultery, then he would be excommunicated. As a result of the Venetian intervention Canon 7 now reads that "If anyone says that the Church errs in teaching" that one may not remarry, then he is excommunicated." Even Pius XI in his encyclical *Casti connubii* (1930) took a similar line, with his eye on the Greek Church. That is, the Greek practice of remarriage was not condemned, but only the person who says that the Catholic Church is in error. To the popes their infallibility is still more important than their rigorism toward the remarried.

Jesus, as we have seen, did not say anything at all about celibacy. He simply corrected, to his disciples' horror, the biases of a polygamous society contemptuous of women, and sketched an ideal image of marital unity. But his teaching was later reinterpreted by celibate theologians into a call to renounce marriage, while his words on becoming one flesh were transformed into praise of celibates as the eunuchs for the Kingdom of Heaven.

On another issue too the New Testament has been misunderstood in an antisexual sense. John Paul II falsely sees the obligatory celibacy of the Catholic Church as not only recommended by Jesus himself, but in addition as an "apostolic doctrine" (Letter to All the Priests of the Church on Holy Thursday, 1979, ch. 8). In reality all apostles were married. It is interesting to trace the course of translations and interpretations of the New Testament, and to see how over the course of the centuries the wives of the apostles were turned into a sort of housekeepers. This was because of the increasing effort to make the apostles appear to be celibates, until the current pope raised them to the level of preachers and teachers of obligatory celibacy.

But "apostolic doctrine" teaches that all officeholders in the Church have the right to get married. Paul declares in 1 Corinthians 9:5 that all the apostles and Peter, who is despite that still considered the first pope, were married and took their wives along on missionary trips. He points out that he has this right too. The question of the marriage of priests was a large contributing factor to the breaking away of the Eastern Church (1054), in which simple priests, but not bishops, are allowed to get married, and later of the Protestant Church (sixteenth century), in which both pastors and bishops may marry. For this reason it is worthwhile to take a closer look at 1 Corinthians 9:5, since a false translation of this passage has, since the year 400, prevented aspirants to the Roman Catholic priesthood from stumbling onto their apostolically guaranteed right to marry—especially when they know too little Greek. The passage says literally: "Don't we have the right to be accompanied by a sister (meaning a Christian woman) as a wife, as the other apostles and the brothers of the Lord and Cephas?"

This right of the apostles slowly turned into the right to take along a woman as a helping sister, first, by translating "wife" as "woman," and second, from 1592 on, by reversing the terms "a sister as a woman" to putting "a woman as a sister," thereby eliminating every trace of wives. Jerome (d. 420), who was the father of the Vulgate and an outstanding philologist, correctly translated the Greek *gunē* as *uxor*, which unambiguously means "wife," as late as 383. But after 385 he preferred the word *mulier*, which means both "wife" and "woman" and made his translation read: The apostles had the right to be accompanied by a "sister as a woman" (*mulier*). Jerome had come to the conclusion that the passage dealt with female servants and not wives. This change of mind took place as a result of the letter that Pope Siricius wrote in 385 to the Spanish bishop of Tarragona, saying that he found it "indecent," indeed "criminal," when priests continued having intercourse with their wives and begetting children after their ordination.

In 1592, then, contrary to the original Greek text, contrary to the correct word order in Jerome (a sister as a wife), and contrary to the twenty-eight Vulgate manuscripts with the correct word order, the Vulgata Clementina, now the official edition of the Latin Bible, made the crucial change. It did so on the basis of two less valuable Vulgate manuscripts in which the Greek text was translated in the wrong order (a woman as a sister). In this way the passage on the right of the apostles to be accompanied by their wives was completely garbled and rendered harmless (on all this cf. Heinz-Jürgen Vogels, *Pflichtzölibat*, 1978).

There are still more passages proving that compulsory celibacy is not an apostolic doctrine (e.g., 1 Tim. 3:2 and Tit. 1:6). There it says that a bishop should be the "husband of one wife," meaning he should not have remarried after divorce, in accordance with Jesus' teaching on adultery and polygamy. But these passages are not especially popular with the defenders of celibacy, no more than Peter's mother-in-law (Mk. 1:30).

Paul, it is true, speaks about the greater availability of the unmarried person for the Lord (1 Cor. 7), but this cannot be enlisted in support of compulsory celibacy, since the same epistle (1 Cor. 9:5) expressly mentions his right to take his wife on missionary journeys as the other apostles do—the very passage that has been neutralized by transposing the words "women" and "sister." Just how far the Pope, as an unmarried successor of the married Peter, has distanced himself from Peter and John Paul can be seen from the fact that we can't imagine him speaking of his right to have a wife and to take her with him on his pilgrimages all over the world. Yet this would be altogether in the spirit of the New Testament. Clement of Alexandria, a Church Father, wrote in around the year 200 that, "Even Paul has no misgivings about addressing his wife in one of his letters (Phil. 4:3), whom he did not take along with him only so as not to be hindered in the exercise of his office. Hence he says in a letter: 'Don't we have the right to take a sister with us as a wife, like the rest of the apostles?' " (*Miscellanies* III, 53). It is not without interest to note, then, that in around 200 people still knew that Paul had been married. Later on, as virginity became increasingly idealized, the attempt was made to stylize him—wrongly—as a lifelong celibate.

Paul was a Pharisee (Phil. 3:5). He mentions that, it might be added, with pride, since the word had not made it into the synonym for self-righteous hypocrite that it unfortunately became thanks to the anti-Semitic self-righteousness and hypocrisy of Christians. According to the German Protestant theologian Joachim Jeremias, Paul was at the time of his conversion an ordained pharisaic scholar, hence a middle-aged man; and so, since in Jesus' day the age for marriage was in general around eighteen to twenty, he was married. For the attitude of the Scribes to marriage and celibacy was perfectly clear: It was a man's unconditional duty to marry. Tradition attributed to Rabbi Eliezer Ben-Asau (ca. 90) the saying that, "Whoever does not engage in procreation is like someone who spills blood" (Yebamoth 63b; Strack and Billerbeck, *Kommentar zum Neuen Testament aus Talmud und Midrasch,* II, p. 373). Jeremias thinks that when Paul wrote First Corinthians he was a widower (*Zeitschrift für die neutestamentliche Wissenschaft* 28 [1929], 321–23).

Still another passage of the New Testament was misunderstood as advocating celibacy. Some Christians influenced by Gnostic hatred of the body had asked Paul whether it might not be good for a man not to touch a woman (1 Cor. 7:1). Most celibate commentators to this day read this verse ("It is well for a man not to touch a woman") as Paul's answer, although in it Paul is simply repeating the question that was posed to him. In this way the heresy of the Gnostics was turned into apostolic support for celibacy and the ideal of virginity. Against its own intentions the New Testament was taken over by the rising tide of sexual pessimism.

In the face of the Corinthians' question, whether a man should not touch a woman, Paul works out his view of marriage. He finds that every man should have his wife, and every woman her husband. He stresses that married couples should not heed the person who is urging them to abstinence in the Gnostic fashion, but that on the contrary everyone has the duty of acceding to the wishes of his or her partner for sexual union. Thus he does not side with the man who is arguing for marital continence. He expressly states: "Do not refuse one another except perhaps by agreement for a season, that you may devote yourselves to prayer." And he goes on to say: "But then come together again, lest Satan tempt you through lack of self-control."

This is followed by verse 6, which Augustine misunderstood, and on which he built his disastrous theory of the excuse for marital intercourse. In Augustine's opinion intercourse is a culpable act and needs a justification: the child. Verse 6 in Paul reads: "I say this by way of concession, not of command." The word "this" could refer either to "Do not refuse one another, except . . . for prayer" or to "But then come together again," since both are present in verse 5. Is Paul conceding (Augustine translates "concede" as "forgive") the Corinthians intercourse, or is he conceding their abstention from marital sex for the sake of prayer? More likely it is the latter. He leaves it up to them—he does not command them—to abstain from intercourse for prayer. But if he means the former, then Paul is saying that he doesn't want his concession to be understood as a command to engage in sex, but as their right; in other words he leaves it to their discretion. In any case the whole passage has to be read in the light of verses 2 and 5: "Because of the temptation to immorality, each man should have his own wife, and each woman her own husband," and "Do not refuse one another."

The tenor of the whole discussion is in any case not in favor of the Gnostic supporters of sexual abstinence. Instead, Paul rebukes people who have withdrawn from their partners out of misunderstood piety. He cites avoiding immorality as a motive for marriage and marital intercourse. Granted, this does not sound very sensitive, but given the Gnostic question, "Is it good for a man not to touch a woman?" it is an extremely clear answer. We note that there is no talk here of having children, Augustine's most important excuse for marital sex. Thus Paul's position contrasts with the Church's emphasis, predominant even today, on procreation as the purpose of the conjugal act.

The section in the seventh chapter of First Corinthians where Paul comes to speak about the greater single-mindedness of unmarried people begins with the words: Now concerning the unmarried, I have no command of the Lord, but I give my opinion . . ." (1 Cor. 7:25) Almost all Catholic theologians, including John Paul II, see Jesus' words on divorce in Matthew 19 as the supreme moment of celibacy and monasticism (concentrating on the disciples' objection, "If such is the case of a man with his wife, it is expedient not to marry," and on Jesus' answer, "Not all men can receive this saying"—though he meant *his* saying, not the disciples' objection). In contrast with this, Paul says that he is unaware of any saying by Jesus about remaining unmarried. Celibate fantasy has in the meantime filled such crucial gaps in Jesus' message.

As for Paul himself, there is some evidence that, unlike Jesus, he was not completely free from Gnostic tendencies. Admittedly, he writes, Jesus did not speak out about the unmarried state, but he wished to pass on his personal opinion. There follow axioms such as, "Are you free from a wife? Do not seek marriage" (1 Cor. 7:27). But behind such statements probably lies the intense, proximate expectation of the second coming of Christ and the end of the world. Paul himself says, "in view of the impending distress" (7:26). From this perspective his remark, "Are you free from a wife? Do not seek marriage," should be assessed no differently from other statements by Paul made in this expectation, such as: "Everyone should remain in the state in which he was called. Were you a slave when called? Never mind. But if you can gain your freedom, make use of your present condition instead" (7:20–21). If we keep in mind Paul's conviction that the Parousia would occur in his own lifetime (1 Thes. 4:17), we can no more view him as an advocate of celibacy than as an advocate of slavery.

The third passage of the New Testament that deals at some length with marriage (apart from Matthew 19 and I Corinthians 7) is the Letter to the Ephesians (5:22–32). It is still disputed whether this letter was written by Paul. In any case we cannot help noticing that while in 1 Corinthians 7 the word "love" is not mentioned in connection with marriage, Ephesians impressively says: "Husbands, love your wives, as Christ loved the church and gave himself up for her . . . Even so husbands should love their wives as their own bodies. He who loves his wife loves himself . . . 'For this reason a man shall leave his father and mother and be joined to his wife, and the two shall become one flesh.' This mystery is a profound one . . ."

It is worth mentioning that in all three New Testament passages on marriage we find no reference to the generation of children, which later became increasingly important in Catholic sexual morality and pushed into the background all other purposes and motives for marital intercourse. That doesn't mean that Jesus, Paul, and the author of Ephesians want to exclude procreation; it does show, however, that we can speak meaningfully about marriage without immediately talking about children.

The Jewish sect of Qumran, which was influenced by Gnosticism, is of great importance to New Testament scholarship because Jesus, John the Baptist, and the apostles lived for decades, so to speak, alongside it. The baptismal site above where the Jordan empties into the Dead Sea was only nine to twelve miles from the Qumran settlement. While Jesus was not an ascetic, there is a lot of evidence that John the Baptist was influenced by Qumran, and "may even have been a member [of the sect]" (*Religion in Geschichte und Gegenwart,* vol. 5, 1961, 751). The difference between them was apparent even to their contemporaries. Jesus says: "John came neither eating nor drinking, and they say, 'He has a demon'; the Son of man came eating and drinking, and they say, 'Behold, a glutton and a drunkard, a friend of tax collectors and sinners'" (Mt. 11:18–19). Thus, even as Jesus did not follow the ascetical style of Qumran, however physically close to Qumran he may have been, so we also see in him no tendency toward a high esteem for virginity as a means to come closer to God. Jesus belongs to the Old Testament tradition, which is alien to such thinking. He is trying to get Judaism back to its roots: to the idea of the creation of a man and a woman who become one flesh and are therefore inseparable.

Jesus' relation to Old Testament tradition and to Judaism is also important for a question recently brought up once again by the Jewish scholar of religion, Ben-Chorin, who argues that Jesus was married. It is quite thinkable that the Gnostic-ascetic slant on Christianity, which appeared very early on, has shaped not only the teaching of Jesus as interpreted by those who preached it, but also the image of the person of Jesus himself; so that today we take it for granted that Jesus never married, whereas there is not the slightest hint about this in the New Testament. In contrast to this, Ben-Chorin presents a "chain of indirect proofs" for Jesus' being married: "When Luke observes (2:51–52) that the boy Jesus was obedient to his parents, this obviously means that he adapted to the rhythm of civic life . . . the next life situation is decisively important: an eighteen year old beneath the wedding canopy (*la-chupa*). If, as is expressly reported, the young Jesus deferred all his particular interests until his emergence into public life and subordinated himself to the will of his parents, then with all probability we may assume that they sought out for him a suitable bride; and that he, like every young man, especially like those who studied the Torah, entered the married state. The Talmud observes: 'A twenty year old youth who lives without a wife is plagued by sinful thoughts' (bKiddushin 29 b), for 'a man is always in the thrall of desire, from which only marriage frees him' (bYabmuth 63a). A Tosephta (supplement-cum-commentary) on Yabmuth 88 passes down a harsh remark by Rabbi Eliezer Ben-Asai: 'Whoever renounces marriage violates the commandment to increase and multiply; he is to be looked upon as a murderer who lessens the number of the beings created in the image of God.'

"Of the many hundred rabbis from the Talmudic period known to us by name only one, Ben-Asai (2nd century A.D.), was not married. According to one reading, even this bachelor was briefly married to a daughter of his teacher, Rabbi Akiba, but later remained single so as to devote himself exclusively to the Torah. He was sharply criticized for this by his colleagues: 'Some preach well and act well, some act well and don't preach well, but you preach well and don't act well.' Ben-Asai answered them: 'What can I do? My soul clings to the Torah. The world can be maintained by other people' (bYabmuth 63b). The fine preaching and not-so-fine behavior of Ben-Asai consisted in the fact that he taught all the commandments, but evaded the fundamental commandment: 'Be fruitful and multiply,' by being celibate . . .

"This needs to be kept in mind when we look at Jesus' career . . . If he had scorned marriage, then his opponents among the Pharisees would have reproached him with that, and his disciples would have asked him about this sin of omission . . . It should not surprise us that we hear nothing about this, for we also hear nothing about his education as a child, about his vocational training and practice. We hear only that he returned to Nazareth to live the thoroughly normal life of a Jew. Since we also learn nothing about the wives of the later disciples, as we do, with very few exceptions, about the wives of most of the teachers of the Law from Jesus' time, this chapter remains within the framework of matters of course. Later on in the narratives the only women mentioned are those who make an appearance in the public life of Jesus" (Shalom Ben-Chorin, *Mutter Mirjam,* 1982, pp. 92 ff.)

Another argument for Ben-Chorin's thesis is that when Paul says that he knows of no saying by Jesus on celibacy, but can present only his personal opinion (1 Cor. 7:25), that can hardly be made to square with the notion that Jesus was unmarried. Though Paul may have had no saying by Jesus before him, if he could have cited the example of Jesus the celibate, he would hardly have been satisfied with pointing to the lack of a specific saying. There is no way he would have failed to mention the unusual example set by Jesus' own life—if Jesus had set it.

IV

THE CHURCH FATHERS TILL AUGUSTINE

A*lthough Jesus was* no ascetic and no eulogist of virginity, the ideal of virginity gradually spread through the Christian world. While being taken to Rome, Bishop Ignatius of Antioch, who was thrown to the wild animals around the year 110—one of the privileges of the Romans consisted in the fact that prisoners condemned to death in the provinces were transported to the capital to provide entertainment in one of the circuses—wrote seven letters that are considered important evidence for the period immediately after the New Testament. In the letter to Bishop Polycarp of Smyrna he mentions the people who "live in chastity to honor the flesh of our Lord." He does not praise such individuals, however. Instead he warns them of "arrogance," and continues: "If he boasts, he is lost; and if he takes himself to be more than a bishop, he has fallen prey to destruction." Evidently the higher value of virgins, at least in their own eyes, was an issue that even then could not be overlooked and was causing problems for the bishops, who at that time were still married.

Around 150 Justin Martyr writes: "From the first we have either entered marriage, with the sole purpose of raising children, or we have renounced getting married and remain wholly continent" (1 *Apology* 29). In connection with this Justin tells a story, which meets with his complete approval, about a young Christian man who had applied to the Roman governor for permission to be castrated. Back in the first century the Emperor Domitian (d. 96) had made castration subject to criminal punishment. And Emperor Hadrian (d. 138) had explicitly extended this prohibition even to those who voluntarily agreed to be castrated. That was his way of taking action against the rigoristic antisexual and antimarital tendencies (predominantly Gnostic) of his time. Hadrian instituted the death penalty for anyone who was castrated without official permission, as well as for the doctor who performed the operation. Justin writes: "So that you can be sure that unbridled dissipation is not a secret element in our religion, I add this story: Once one of our people in Alexandria directed a petition to the governor, Felix, to allow his physician to remove his testicles; for the doctors there declared they were not allowed to do this without the governor's permission. And when Felix refused to give the order under any condition, the young man remained unmarried and contented himself with the conviction he shared with his supporters" (1 *Apology* 29).

The young man Justin describes wanted to use his castration to send a message about the high moral and ascetical standards of the Christians, and to counter the aspersions of moral inferiority cast upon Christianity. In his "apologies" (defenses of Christianity) Justin strove to characterize Christians—still a defamed minority at the time—as politically reliable and morally elevated individuals. The fact that he chose to mention the young man in this context shows that virginity was capable of impressing his contemporaries. The account of the young man and his attempt to become a eunuch is supposed to recommend Christianity to the audience. Justin is trying to get them not to shake their heads but to applaud.

Christians did not yet view themselves as the teachers of the world, which would be living in darkness without them. They were not thought of as having to furnish the pagans and atheists with models of good behavior. It was the other way around: The pagans labeled the Christians "atheists," and the Christians wanted to show that they could match the high ideals of the pagans. That was what Justin had in mind. Public opinion at that time was swayed by the idea—stressed by first- and second-century Stoics—that marriage had to serve exclusively for procreation, as well as by the pessimistic, Gnostic, body-hating idealization of virginity. Christianity did not invent reverence for virginity, which in no way comes from Jesus. Rather Christians adapted themselves to their environment, and then they dragged the ideal of virginity all the way into the twentieth century—and its end is not yet in sight—as a hallmark of true and original Christianity. This was after practically everyone else, including many from their own ranks, namely the Protestants, had long since given up this old, obsolete pagan custom.

Granted, in the post-apostolic period there was a centuries-long, embittered struggle between the Church and the Gnostics; but this led to reciprocal influence: Justin's young man from Alexandria with his longing for castration and the approval of such piety by Justin show what deep inroads Gnostic contempt for the body had already made into Christianity. On the other side, many Gnostics for their part had integrated Jesus into their system as a redeemer from matter, who disguised himself in a phantom-body (bodies are material, and hence evil) and preached to the soul of men, informing them how they could escape from the prison of the body and enter after death into the pure Kingdom of Light.

The Gnostics rejected the resurrection of the body. Some of them considered themselves Christians—higher level Christians than the simple believers. But the lines of division are blurred, and while Justin (d. 165) (a Church Father) cherished marriage—though only for procreation—his disciple Tatian (d. 180) drifted completely away into the Gnostic camp and became the head of the "Abstainers," for whom marriage was "lewdness" (Clement of Alexandria, *Miscellanies* III, 12, 89). Many Christians, especially in Rome and Alexandria, were in danger of being swamped or absorbed by Gnosticism.

One man who was fully dedicated to the struggle against Gnosticism was the "most learned of the Fathers," as Jerome later called him, Clement of Alexandria. Around the year 200 Alexandria was the center of both Christian and Gnostic learning. Clement attacked the Basilidians. Basilides was a Gnostic who taught in Alexandria from about 120 to 140. According to Clement, the now commonplace twisting of Jesus words on remarriage (Mt. 19) into an argument for celibacy stems from the arch-heretics, the Gnostics. Clement writes: "The Basilidians say that the Lord, in reply to the apostles' question if it would not be better not to marry, answered: 'Not all men can receive this saying,' . . . which they interpret to mean, approximately, the following . . . 'Those who have made themselves unfit for marriage make this decision because of the consequences that grow out of marriage for them, because they fear the trouble that one has in acquiring the wherewithal for living' " (*Miscellanies* III, 1, 1). Later on Clement interprets the passage correctly. And it is high time for the Pope and all the Church's celibates to realize that after eighteen hundred years of error they can now bury their favorite passage on celibacy and the single life, and recognize their reading for what it is: a biased misinterpretation by the Gnostics. Celibacy is based on a misunderstanding. Clement rightly says that the passage in Matthew 19 refers to divorce: "As for Jesus' statement that, 'Not all men can receive this saying,' . . . they [the Basilidians] do not know that after his [Jesus'] saying about divorce, some asked, 'If such is the case of a man with his wife, it is not expedient to marry,' and that thereupon the Lord said: 'Not all men can receive this saying, but only those to whom it is given.' For the questioners wanted to know just this, whether he would allow someone to marry another woman when his wife had been condemned and repudiated for immorality" (*Miscellanies* III, 50, 1–3).

Clement here defends Jesus' original words against appropriation by the antimarital Gnostics. Thus while Clement defends marriage against the Gnostics as God-given and good, on the other hand he remains totally caught up in the Stoic ideal of *apathia* (no-feeling) and the Stoic idea that marriage is exclusively at the service of procreation. In this he is a true precursor of papal encyclicals on birth control. He takes this so far that he even foists a Stoic misinterpretation on Paul (1 Cor. 7), who doesn't so much as mention having children, but speaks only of avoiding immorality: " 'Do not refuse one another,' says the Apostle, 'except perhaps by agreement for a season.' Here with the words, 'Do not refuse one another,' he is referring to the marital duty of begetting children, which he also made clear before with

the words: 'The husband should give to his wife her conjugal
rights, and likewise the wife to her husband' " (*Miscellanies* III,
107, 5). Clement also alludes to the fact that Paul (1 Cor. 7:2)
sees marriage as a means for satisfying one's sex drive, but this is
hardly of any importance to his concept of marriage (*Miscellanies*
III, 15).

Clement employs the comparison from agricultural life that
was popular with the Stoics. "Thus it is not right to become
enslaved to the pleasures of love and to be lustfully intent on the
fulfillment of one's desires; just as it is wrong to give oneself up
to excitement by irrational passions and to long to become impure. Like the farmer, the married man is permitted to sow his
seed only when the season allows" (*Paedagogus* II, 10, 102, 1).
Adultery with one's own wife also puts in an appearance, one of
the theme songs of the rigorists, from Philo to John Paul II.
Clement writes: "One commits adultery with one's own wife if
one has commerce with her in marriage as if she were a harlot"
(*Paedagogus* II, 10, 99, 3). In keeping with his Stoic ideal of
hostility to sexual pleasure, Clement rejects intercourse with
pregnant spouses (*Paedagogus* II, 92, 2) or between older partners
(*Paedagogus* II, 95, 3) as counter to the Christian ideal.

On September 16, 1968, Cardinal Frings gathered together in
Cologne all the deans and university professors from his diocese
and, while referring to, among others, Clement of Alexandria, he
sought to hymn the praises of *Humanae vitae*. He pointed out that
Clement had forbidden intercourse with an older wife, which
clearly showed that from the beginning the Church had striven
and spoken out for the encyclical on birth control. From the
beginning, perhaps, but not from the very beginning, i.e., Jesus
or Paul. Hostility to sexual pleasure is a Gnostic-Stoic legacy,
which as far back as Clement was superimposed on the Christian
Gospel ("Good News"), and which spoke of pleasure as if it were
a source of pollution. Clement then comes to speak about the
famous Stoic "finger," which would later assume great importance again, thanks to Augustine: "For if the reason taught by the
Stoics does not even allow the wise man to move his finger any

which way, how much more must the seekers of wisdom affirm their dominion over the organ of generation?" (*Paedagogus* II, 10, 90, 1).

Clement of Alexandria at least had a proper grasp of Jesus' saying about self-castration for the sake of the Kingdom of Heaven (Mt. 19). But the same saying was doubly misunderstood by Origen, his famous successor at the Alexandrian school of catechesis and the most important theologian of the Greek Church. Origen (d. 254) read Jesus' words not only as an exhortation to celibacy, but as a literal command. At the age of eighteen, in his quest for Christian perfection, Origen castrated himself, invoking the Christians who had done so before him (*Commentary on Mt. 15:3*). Later he recognized his error in taking the passage about eunuchs literally, but he still saw celibacy as higher in the eyes of God. Even in his own lifetime Origen was considered the most important theologian. His rich disciple and thankful patron, Ambrosius, whom he had converted from Gnosticism to Christianity, paid for his seven stenographers, seven copyists, and a whole series of female calligraphists. He was a strict ascetic who never touched meat, wine, or women. No theologian in Christian Antiquity was more controversial than Origen, the most significant but also the most unclassifiable Church Father before Augustine. Although three hundred years after his death (553) he was condemned by the Church for false teachings, e.g., on the human soul, his influence on the leading theologians of both the East and the West has been great.

Origen links together Jewish-Christian faith in the one, good God as the creator of the body and of matter, of marriage and generation, *and* Gnostic contempt for the body. Body and matter, he says, do derive from the one, good God (and not from a wicked creator, as in the original, pre-Christian Gnosticism), but the body is not the good God's first thought. According to Origen, it is rather a kind of punishment, a "chain," a "prison" that owes its existence to a prior Fall of pure souls. These notions of Origen were condemned by the Church.

Still other arguments had consequences for the theology of marriage; for example, Origen warns against judging Lot's daughters too harshly just because, since they could not find husbands, they got children for themselves by having intercourse with their father. Such incest, he says, was far more chaste than the chastity of many people. Wives should examine their conscience and see whether they really approach their husbands only for the sake of children and whether, once they have conceived, they cease to have relations with them, as the daughters of Lot did. Quite a few women, he says, indulge unceasingly in lust; they are worse than animals, which will have nothing to do with sexual intercourse once they have conceived. As the apostle says, even the works of marriage should be performed for the glory of God. This is the case when they are carried out purely for the sake of having offspring (*In genesim homiliae*, 5, n. 4). The idea that it is better to have children with one's own father than to avoid conceiving children with one's own husband would have a long post-Augustinian career.

Origen influenced Gregory of Nyssa (d. 395), the younger brother of Basil the Great (familiar to modern tourists from the many cathedrals of St. Basil). Gregory distanced himself from the concept of a Fall of souls before they were incorporated into human bodies, which contradicted the Old Testament. But Origen's hatred of the body remained intact. Gregory, who was, by the way, a married bishop, dealt with an issue that would later concern the two great pillars of Catholic sexual morality, Augustine and Thomas Aquinas, namely, did Adam and Eve have sexual intercourse back in Paradise? (For a discussion of what follows cf. Michael Müller, *Die Lehre des hl. Augustinus von der Paradiesesehe und ihre Auswirkung in der Sexualethik des 12. und 13. Jahrhunderts bis Thomas von Aquin*, 1954) Gregory answers: No. Prelapsarian life was like that of the angels, who multiply without marriage and sexual reproduction. We cannot imagine what such propagation looked like, "but it is a fact" (*De hominis opificio* 17).

God had, however, foreseen the Fall, and he knew that man would give up his equal status with the angels and would seek out fellowship with lower forms of life. And so, when he created man, he provided him with animal sexuality, "which in no way corresponds to the loftiness of our creation." Gregory sees this double decision expressed in the creation story: "God created man in his own image," it says first; then follows the sentence, "Male and female he created them" (Gen. 1:27). This implies, Gregory says, that sexual differentiation, being a man or woman, is only a belated addition to the true nature of human beings. The only thing made in God's image is human nature, not sexual differences, which are merely a later accouterment of the completed "image and likeness," an animal component intended only for the animals (*De hominis opificio,* 16–17, 22).

Later Augustine and medieval theologians would see man's likeness to God only *"ubi sexus nullus est,"* where there is no sexual difference. The core of human nature, said Augustine, is not touched by sexuality (*De trinitate* XII, VII, 12). These celibate theologians wondered why right after, "God created man in his own image," the text says, "male and female he created them," since in their opinion there was no connection between the first and second statement. They never understood that the full sexuality of the one, whole, spiritual-personal human being is more than his or her sexuality, more than his or her merely biological capacity for reproduction. Sexuality is not a simply regional, functional determination, but a peculiar feature of the essence of man that goes back to his absolutely earliest, psychophysical origins, a peculiar feature that helps to shape, each time in a special way, all the definable dimensions of the human being, and is also shaped by each of them. Sexuality is not something that a person simply *has* along with many other things, but a fundamental way of *being* in all things, and hence something without which his or her other existential acts and relations cannot actually be thought and realized. Because sexuality is trans-regional it is extremely difficult to give a definitive description of human masculinity and femininity. It would have to be supplied with fresh nuances for the individual differences of the person. And hence such attempts at definition always lay themselves open to the accusation of confusing historically conditioned gender roles and models, or reproductive capacity, with the essence of sexuality, or else of absolutizing one sex and thus one-sidedly defining the other in terms of it.

In any case, despite his hostility to the body and sex, Gregory was prevented by Christianity's Jewish legacy from lapsing completely into Gnosticism and the Gnostic hatred of the flesh. Sex, he maintains, was created by God (even if he did so only because he foresaw the Fall), and hence it is good. The sexual organs are precious, because with them man (through procreation) fights against death (*Oratio catechetica magna* 28). In Paradise, however, humanity's animal nature, i.e., our maleness and femaleness, did not yet have any consequences. When Adam was still naked, "not yet covered with mortal pelts, he looked on God's face, he did not yet know any pleasure in looking and tasting, but simply rejoiced in the Lord, and his helpmeet assisted him in this" (*De virginitate* 12).

Only after the Fall, Gregory says, did our present form of life begin, did man's animal constitution come into operation: Humans reproduced like animals. And with animal procreation animal passions came into effect. Man was originally made in the image of God, that is, without passion. The passions do not belong to man's true nature, they were at first peculiar to the animals: The carnivorous animals subsist through rage, the weak ones through fear, and the species are maintained through the longing for pleasure (ibid., 18). As God's image man would have remained free from passions. He would have devoted himself to whatever he freely chose in accordance with the judgment of his understanding (ibid., 12). "We look forward with longing to the time of completion, in which human life will again be redeemed and placed back in its blessed original condition" (*De hominis opificio*, 22). The resurrection will be the "return" to the first angelic mode of life, the "restoration" of our erstwhile state. For Christ says: At the resurrection they will neither marry nor give in marriage (*De hominis opificio*, 17).

John Chrysostom (d. 407), the greatest preacher of the Eastern Church (called *chrysostomos*, or golden mouth, since the sixth century) was more strongly oriented toward the Bible, although on many points he shared Gregory of Nyssa's antisexual thinking, e.g., the idea that Adam and Eve had no sexual intercourse in Paradise. "In keeping with God's will man and woman dwelt in

Paradise like angels, enflamed by no sensual lustfulness. . . . There was no desire for intercourse, there was neither conception nor birth nor any sort of corruption." They lived in pure virginity "as in heaven, and they were blessed in commerce with God." Woman was created by God as a help for Adam, as a creature who possessed the same nature, was gifted with reason and speech, and could "offer him much consolation" (*In genesim homiliae* 15, 3, 4). As opposed to this, Augustine, who was especially convinced of woman's inferiority, asserted that in solitude a man means more to a man than woman does. On the other hand Chrysostom himself experienced consolation in solitude from a woman: He wrote seventeen letters from exile to his most faithful supporter, the widow Olympias in Constantinople.

The Fall ended Adam and Eve's Edenic idyll of virginity. "Along with that happy life our first parents simultaneously lost too the ornament of virginity . . . After they had laid aside this royal garment and forfeited the heavenly jewel, receiving in exchange the destruction of death, the curse, the pains, and a laborious life, in the wake of all this came marriage, that mortal and slavish garment" (*De virginitate* 14; *In genesim homiliae* 18, 1). Marriage, therefore, comes from disobedience, from the curse, from death. Virginity and immortality, marriage and death belong together (*De virginitate* 14; *In genesim homiliae* 18, 4).

Like Gregory of Nyssa Chrysostom was convinced that in Paradise there was asexual reproduction. How this took place, he did not know: "What marriage, then, begot Adam? What birth pangs brought forth Eve? Many myriads of angels pay homage to God, and yet none of them came into existence through propagation, through birth, through pangs and conception." God could have likewise multiplied men and women without marriage, "whether in the same way as Adam and Eve, or in a different way, I cannot say" (*De virginitate* 14–15, 17). Chrysostom shifts God's command, "Increase and multiply," which was spoken in Paradise immediately after the creation of man and woman (Gen. 1:28), to after the expulsion from Eden. He writes: "Grow and multiply, said the divine Physician, when nature exploded, when it could no longer master the uproar of the passions and when amid this storm it had no other harbor to flee to" (*De virginitate* 17, 19).

It's surprising that Chrysostom clings to the idea of Adam and Eve's permanent virginity in Paradise though he has to fly in the face of the Old Testament to do so. The superimposition of Gnostic depreciation of marriage and exaltation of virginity upon the Jewish Bible is apparent in Chrysostom's work, even though he pays close attention to the biblical text. Marriage is only the "child's garment," which grown-ups, those who have reached the full maturity of Christ, lay aside in order to put on the garment of virginity (*De virginitate* 16).

As for the purpose of marriage, Chrysostom follows the Pauline Letters more closely than any of the other Church Fathers. He thinks that marriage *was* instituted for "the begetting of children," but, far more importantly, to extinguish the fire of nature. Chrysostom reminds us that Paul says, "Because of the temptation to immorality each man should have his own wife"—not in order to have children. And he bids spouses come together not so that they may become the parents of many children, but so that Satan may not tempt them. Now that the earth has been populated with humans, "there remains only one goal: prevention of debauchery and lust" (*De virginitate* 19, 19). "One must take a wife for the sole purpose of fleeing sin and freeing oneself from every sort of lewdness" (*quales ducendae sint uxores* 5; likewise *hom. in illiud: propter fornicationes* [1 Cor. 7:2]). Marriage for Chrysostom is a concession to human weakness.

Thus while Augustine and the tradition that follows him take procreation to be the single legitimate purpose of marriage, Chrysostom sees things differently. Granted, his terminology (like Paul's in 1 Corinthians) is not personal enough, but, like Paul, he argues that marriage exists for the interests of the spouses and must not be seen as a means to the end of procreation. He has no prohibition against intercourse with pregnant or post-menopausal wives. Chrysostom knows Scripture too well to say, as Canon Law did until 1983, "The first purpose of marriage is the begetting of children." More than any Church Father before him Chrysostom saw marriage primarily as a "remedy for concupiscience" (to use a later term). For his contemporaries, however, the great Church Fathers such as Ambrose, Jerome, and Augustine, the Stoic notion of the child as the first and only legitimate end of marriage is once again triumphant.

Chrysostom sharply—and inconsistently—condemns contraception. This is a legacy of Stoicism, which Chrysostom could no more avoid than he could the Gnostic ideal of virginity. Toward the end of his sermon on Ephesians 5:22–33, where he finds a splendid tribute to married love, he says: "Whoever gets married in this way and with these intentions will not be much inferior to the monks and unmarried people." But he *will* be inferior. That was something that none of the Church Fathers doubted and none of the higher-ups in the Church doubts, even today.

According to Ambrose (d. 397), bishop of Milan, freely chosen virginity is a virtue that first came into the world thanks to Christianity. We can hardly imagine nowadays how important the ideal of virginity was in the fourth and fifth centuries, how profoundly it influenced the religious imagination. Virginity was *the* Christian virtue. Ambrose considered it the uniquely new feature that Christianity brought into the world, the fulfillment of the Old Testament's promises. "This virtue is in fact our exclusive property. The pagans do not have it, it is not practised by the wild primitive peoples. It is found nowhere else among living creatures. Though we share the same air with all others, and participate in all the aspects of an earthly body, though we are no different from others in our birth, yet we escape the miseries of nature, which is otherwise the same, only by virginity, while virginal chastity seems to be held in reverence by the pagans, but is nonetheless violated (even though it is placed under the protection of religion), and is persecuted by the wild tribes, and totally unknown to all other creatures" (*De virginibus* I, 3–4).

Ambrose wanted priests to cease having intercourse with their wives (*De officiis* I, 50, 248). In a number of his writings he glorifies virginity, especially the order of consecrated virgins, who at that time—at least in the West—did not yet live in convents, but made up a class by themselves in the community. Such virgins were supposed to lead a retired life in their families, devoted to prayer, fasting, and sanctification.

Ambrose led the way in the condemnation of Jovinian, who had maintained that virginity was not more pleasing to God than marriage. Besides that he doubted that Mary had remained a virgin during Jesus' birth. After Pope Siricius had excommunicated Jovinian and his eight followers in Rome, he sent word to Ambrose about his decision. Ambrose, who was a great enemy of Jovinian to begin with, convoked his own synod in Milan and excommunicated Jovinian and his supporters on his own account. Emperor Theodosius, a friend of Ambrose, had Jovinian scourged with a lead-tipped whip and exiled on the island of Boa. The only report we have on the death of Jovinian comes from Jerome in the year 406: Jovinian, he said, did not breathe forth his soul, he "belched it forth between pheasants and pork" (*Against Vigilantius* I).

Ambrose doesn't say that marriage should be fled like a sin, but avoided like a burden (*On Widows* 13, 81). In connection with 1 Corinthians Ambrose does mention the therapeutic nature of marriage: "In saying that it was better to marry than to burn, the Apostle was evidently recommending marriage as a remedy for protecting all those who would otherwise be endangered" (*On Widows* 2, 12). But the actual purpose of marriage, according to Ambrose, is procreation. Hence he vehemently condemns intercourse with pregnant women. Like the Stoics before him he cites the example of animals as his model: "Even the animals show us, with the dumb language of their behavior, that they are inspired by the instinct to maintain the species and not by a greedy desire for sexual union. For as soon they note that their wombs are pregnant, they no longer indulge in sexual intercourse and the lustfulness of lovers, but instead they take parental cares upon themselves. Humans, by contrast, pay no attention either to the child in the womb or to God. They besmirch the former and anger the latter. Control your carnal appetite and look upon the hands of your creator, who is forming a human being in the mother's womb. He is at work, and you would desecrate the sanctuary of the womb with your lust? Either take the animals for your model or fear God" (*Commentary on the Gospel of Luke* I, 44). Ambrose likewise forbids intercourse among older couples: "Every thing has its time . . . Thus certain times have been assigned to marriage too, at which the generation of children is fitting. So long as the vigor of youth continues, so long as there is hope for the blessing of children . . . the desire for commerce between the sexes is permissible. But for older spouses age itself draws the boundaries for performing the works of marriage, and the suspicion of incontinence, which is and deserves to be a source of shame, bids them cease from the act. Even young spouses usually cite the desire for children as their justification, thinking that in this way they can make excuses for the fire of their youth with the wish for offspring. How much more ignominious would it be for older people to engage in an act that even young ones are embarrassed about admitting. Still more, even young married persons who mortify their heart in abnegation from the fear of God, often renounce those works of youth as soon as they have conceived" (*Commentary on the Gospel of Luke* I, 43).

As theology increasingly became the business of bachelors, sin was more and more placed in the realm of sex. With the growth of its sexual neurosis, with its commitment to making lay people into monks, Christianity distanced itself from its Jewish roots in the Old Testament and from Jewish life in general. Virginal Christianity condemned carnal Judaism: The eight sermons Chrysostom delivered against the Jews in 387 in Antioch were one long calumny. He described the Jews as "carnal," "lascivious," and "accursed." "Here we find assembled the arsenal of all the weapons that have been directed against the Jews to this day" (Friedrich Heer, *Gottes erste Liebe: Die Juden im Spannungsfeld der Geschichte,* p. 67). In 388 when the Christians of Kallinikon, a town on the Euphrates, burned down a synagogue at the instigation of their bishop, the Emperor Theodosius ordered the synagogue to be rebuilt at the bishop's expense. Ambrose protested: "I declare that I set fire to the synagogue, indeed, that I gave them the command to do this, so that there would be no place left where Christ is denied . . . What is more important, the notion of order or the interests of religion?" *Epistle* 40, 11). When the Emperor hesitated, Ambrose interrupted the mass and addressed him in the presence of the gathered community, saying he would not go on until the Emperor revoked his order. In this way Ambrose got the Christian arsonists off scot free; and he has gone down in church history as the upright Christian who stands his ground, even in the face of the Emperor.

It is an error, by the way, to think that anti-Semitism came from below. It came from above, for example, from a bishop like Ambrose of Milan, Father of the Church. "Here too we must continually bear in mind one fact—even though famous theologians, even now, falsely claim that the opposite is true: In Christian Europe anti-Semitism comes from above, not from below, from the people or the underclass. It derives from theology, from theological concepts of the world and history. The cliché-ridden image of the Jew, was created on high, only to be put into practice, with horrible results, by the lower classes" (Heer, p. 80).

No Church Father wrote more offensively about marriage or more contemptuously about sex than Jerome (d. 420). And at the same time no Church Father was so beloved by women, or lived as much with them (in physical proximity), or loved women, in his desexualized way, as much as Jerome. In 382, when he was in his mid-thirties, he came to Rome and became the spiritual adviser and center of an ascetical group of rich Roman aristocratic women. One member of this female circle gathered around Jerome was Paula; she came from an old family, was in her early thirties, a widow with five children. Paula's daughter, the intelligent Eustochium, learned Greek and Hebrew from Jerome so she could study the Bible. Under his direction she became the first woman from the Roman nobility to live as a consecrated virgin. In 383 Blesilla, another daughter of Paula, died at the age of twenty. Jerome was accused of letting her starve to death with his recommendations on fasting; and on the occasion of her burial a strong wave of opposition to the "detestable mob of monks" (*Epistle* 39, 6) swept over Rome. In 386 Jerome moved with his spiritual lady-friends to Bethlehem, where he (with inherited money) and Paula (contributing the lion's share) financed a monastic settlement with hostels for pilgrims and a school. Paula was in charge of the women's monastery, Jerome of the men's (they were not far apart). When Paula died in 404, Jerome was so downcast that for a time he was unable to work; and he did not long survive the death of his "daughter," Eustochium, in 419. His final letters resound with grief for Eustochium.

While he was still in Rome, Jerome had an argument with a layman named Helvidius, who talked about Jesus' brothers and sisters in the context of the New Testament (Mk. 6, Mt. 13). In 383 Jerome wrote a piece "Against Helvidius on the Perpetual Virginity of Mary." The reasons and exegetical considerations that Jerome cites against Helvidius are essentially the same as those the Catholic Church advances to this day. According to Jerome, Mary laid the foundations of virginity for both sexes, and the moral superiority of virginity becomes clear in her person. The reality was the other way around: Virginity was not prized because Mary was always a virgin, rather Mary was made a perpetual virgin because virginity was so highly prized.

In connection with the Marian controversies of the day mention should also be made of Bishop Bonosus of Sardica, a supporter of Helvidius. Like Helvidius, Bonosus argued that after the birth of Jesus Mary led a normal married life with Joseph and had more children. Bonosus also denied the doctrine of Mary's virginity *after the birth of Jesus.* But this sort of normal married life for Mary was and still is an immoral, intolerable idea in the eyes of most clerical celibates. And so Bishop Bonosus was excommunicated by Pope Siricius.

In Bethlehem (393) Jerome wrote his two books against the heretic Jovinian for doubting Mary's intact condition *in giving birth* and maintaining that virginity did not rate more highly with God than marriage. In making his case Jerome slandered marriage so vigorously that Paula's son-in-law, the senator Pammachius, tried to remove all copies of this work from circulation. Jerome, for example, incorrectly attributes the sentence, "It is well for a man not to touch a woman," (1 Cor. 7:1) to Paul, instead of to the Corinthians who made inquiries of Paul. He then writes: "Thus it must be bad to touch a woman. If indulgence is nonetheless granted to the marital act, this is only in order to avoid something much worse. But what value can be recognized in a good that is allowed only with a view to preventing something worse?" (*Against Jovinian* I, 7). In this polemic Jerome quotes a maxim by a certain Sextus, whom he at first took for the martyr Pope Sixtus II (d. 258), but which originally came from a pagan collection.

Sextus' maxim, as edited by Jerome, says that, "Anyone who is too passionate (*ardentior* = more burning) a lover of his wife is an adulterer," (*Against Jovinian* I, 49) and was attributed during the Middle Ages to Jerome himself. It was destined to become part of the standard repertoire of the Catholic pleasure-hating tradition up to and including John Paul II. Thomas Aquinas, who was the second pillar, along with Augustine, of Catholic sexual morality, repeats the idea. Marriage, he argues, is aimed at procreation, and therefore the man who loves his wife too passionately contravenes the good of marriage and can be labeled an adulterer (*Summa Theologiae* II/II q. 54 a. 8). Pope John Paul II took up the notion of adultery with one's own wife in the general audience of October 8, 1980, and corroborated it (*Der Spiegel*, n. 47, 1980, p. 9).

Jerome mentions the only good thing that he could extract from marriage in a letter to Eustochium: The fact that "it produces virgins. I gather the rose from the thorns, the gold from the earth, the pearl from the mussel" (*Epistle* 22, 20). Thus he says that "the begetting of children is allowed in marriage, but feelings of sensual pleasure such as those had in the embraces of a harlot are damnable in a wife" (*Commentary on Ephesians* 5:25). Jerome stresses that after conception spouses should devote themselves to prayer rather than to physical intimacy. What is prescribed in the animal world by the law of nature itself, namely no more mating after fertilization, is something that human beings should freely affirm. If they do, they will receive a heavenly reward for abstaining from pleasure (*Commentary on Ephesians* 5:25).

Jerome did have one consolation for wives: "I do not deny that holy women are to be found among the wives, but only when they have stopped being mates, when they imitate virginal chastity even in the constraining position that the married state brings with it" (*Against Helvidius* 21). Blesilla lived up to this ideal of virginity. After seven months of marriage she became a widow, and under Jerome's direction dedicated herself entirely to God, that is, to celibacy. In his letter of condolence to Paula, written a month after Blesilla's death, Jerome emphatically praises the deceased because "the loss of her virginity caused her more pain than the death of her husband" (*Epistle* 39, 1).

V

FAMILY PLANNING IN ANTIQUITY: INFANTICIDE, ABORTION, CONTRACEPTION

T*he issue of* contraception has played a continuous role in the Church's celibate, antipleasure regulation of marital sex, particularly since the time of Augustine. Since Christian doctrine on this point took shape against the background of pre-Christian and non-Christian family planning, we need to survey the practice of birth control in the ancient world. The methods used were killing the newborn, abortion, and contraception (see John T. Noonan, *Contraception*, 1986[2]).

It was not until the year 374 that, under the influence of Christianity, infanticide was legally defined as murder. Seneca (d. 65), for example, had looked upon it as an everyday event in Rome, as a reasonable way of acting, to drown misshapen or sickly infants (*De ira* I, 15). Suetonius (d. second century) mentions the exposure of newborns as a matter left to the discretion of the parents (*Gaius Caligula* 5). Plutarch (d. ca. 120) writes in his life of Lycurgus (ninth century B.C.), the founder of the

Spartan constitution, that among the Spartans infants were first examined by the elders, and weak or deformed babies were flung over the precipice of Taygetos so they would not be a burden to the state. He further reports that the mothers of newborns bathed them in wine, not water, because the sickly and epileptic ones could not tolerate this and died (*Parallel Lives, Lycurgus* 16).

In this connection there is an informative passage in Tacitus (d. 120 A.D.), the most important opponent of Judaism in pagan Antiquity. His polemic against the Jews is among the bitterest things he wrote. As part of the long series of reproaches he levels against the Jews, this "race hateful to the gods," he also blames them for not killing their overly numerous newborns. This passage is indicative of how natural it seemed in Tacitus' day to dispose of unwanted or physically handicapped babies, and also of the fact that the Jews were, in this respect as in so many others, exceptions to the general rule. He writes: "To establish his influence over this people for all time, Moses introduced new religious practices, quite opposed to those of all other religions. The Jews regard as profane all that we hold sacred; on the other hand, they permit all that we abhor . . . They likewise offer the ox, because the Egyptians worship Apis. They abstain from pork, in recollection of a plague, for the scab to which this animal is subject once afflicted them." Tacitus alludes here to the supposed skin disease that, according to the Egyptian priest Manetho (third century B.C.), was the reason why the Egyptians ousted the Jews from their country. This was a piece of counterpropaganda by the Egyptians against the Jewish account of the exodus from Egypt with God's help.

Tacitus continues: "The Jews are extremely loyal toward one another, and are always ready to show compassion, but toward every other people they feel only hatred and enmity . . . Although as a race they are prone to lust, they abstain from intercourse with foreign women; yet among themselves nothing is unlawful. [Note: It is interesting that Tacitus criticizes the Jews for their boundless sexual appetite, just as the Church Fathers, in promoting the ideal of virginity, would later attack the "carnal" Jews for rejecting celibacy. Christians got that ideal from first- and

second-century pagans, not from the Jews.] They adopted cir-
cumcision to distinguish themselves from other people by this
difference. Those who are converted to their ways follow the
same practice, and the earliest lesson they receive is to despise
the gods, to disown their country, and to regard their parents,
children, and brothers as of little account. However, they take
thought to increase their numbers; for they regard it as a crime to
kill any late-born [i.e., posthumous or unwanted] child, and they
believe that the souls of those who are killed in battle or by
the executioner are immortal; hence comes their passion for begetting children and their scorn of death . . . The Egyptians
worship many animals and monstrous images; the Jews conceive
of one god only, and that with the mind alone: they regard as
impious those who make from perishable materials representa-
tions of gods in man's image . . . Therefore they set up no statues
in their cities, still less in their temples; this flattery is not paid
their kings, nor this honour given to the Caesars . . . King An-
tiochus [2nd century B.C.] endeavoured to abolish Jewish superstition and to introduce Greek civilization; the war with the
Parthians, however, prevented his improving this basest of peoples." And Tacitus calls the Jews a "people which, though prone
to superstition, is opposed to all propitiatory rites" (*Histories* V,
3–13, translated by John Jackson, Loeb Library of Classics). By
the way, the same practice that Tacitus finds contemptible in the
Jews he praises in the Germans. He writes: "Setting a limit to the
number of children or killing a late-born child is considered a sin,
and good customs accomplish more here than good laws elsewhere" (*Germania,* ch. 19). Tacitus sees the Jews as people who
like to wage war, strengthened by their faith in the resurrection
of fallen warriors, even while they speak out for the protection of
newborns.

In a questionnaire distributed by the *Frankfurter Allgemeine
Zeitung* in 1984, the Polish Catholic priest Henryk Jankowski,
Lech Walesa's confessor and his companion on his trip to meet
the Pope, was asked what qualities he most prized in a man. The
answer was: manliness and courage. The qualities he most prized
in a woman were piety and the willingness to have children.

Masculine courage—meaning primarily courage in battle—and female fertility add up to the old Jewish ideal, which Tacitus rejected, in Christian guise. Terrifying as it is that Tacitus takes the murder of unwanted babies for granted, and thankful as we must be to Judaism and Christianity for turning the West's moral consciousness in their direction, we can't help being brought up short by Tacitus' assessment of the Jews as having nothing against death on the battlefield but strenuously opposed to limiting the number of their children. Christian bishops today, with their commitment to the campaign against the pill and abortion on the one hand and to the arms race on the other, with their much greater readiness to defend the unborn than the already born, scarcely strike us as schizophrenic any more, after two thousand years of schizophrenia. But the pagan Tacitus would presumably find Christians notable for the same thing that irritated him about the Jews: inconsistency.

Thus before Christians took up the cause, the Jews were concerned about the life of all newborn infants and likewise took a stand against abortion. The Jew Philo of Alexandria (d. ca. 45–50), a contemporary of Jesus, who on these issues sounds like a Church Father, expressly connects abortion and infanticide. Having declared his objections to abortion, he writes: "At the same time this prohibition forbids another great injustice as well, namely the exposure of children, a crime that has become customary among many other peoples as a result of their innate inhumanity" (*On the Individual Laws* 3, 20, 110). Philo complains that there are parents who strangle their babies or hang weights on them and drown them or expose them in deserted places to be eaten by wild animals and birds of prey. These parents, he says, are guilty of murder. Their offense, he says, is connected with their lust, "for they are lustful when they have intercourse with their wives not for the begetting of children and the perpetuation of the human race, but simply sate their lust through intercourse like boars or rams" (ibid., 3, 20, 113).

We cannot help noticing that Philo the Jew reproaches pagan baby-killers with lust, while Tacitus the pagan levels the same charge at Jews who protect their babies ("among themselves nothing is unlawful," "they are prone to lust"). In the fist two centuries of the Christian era the notion that morality was essentially sexual morality could be found among pagans, Jews, and Christians alike. It was a widespread legacy of Stoicism or Gnosticism that has been preserved to this day among Christians and remains a preferred subject for disqualifying people of different faiths. The unanimity of Tacitus and Philo in charging their opponents with lust can be explained by the fact that in the first two centuries of the Christian era contempt for the body, rooted in various philosophies, had prepared the way for a sexual caste system: On the one hand those who were beyond "lust" (both Tacitus and Philo claimed to be part of this group), and on the other the "lustful," who continued having children, whether they let them live or not.

Neither Tacitus nor Philo, neither Jews nor pagans, took the step leading from despising the "lustful" to the total asceticism of the reverend celibates. It was reserved to the Christians alone consistently to look upon the whole lot of married folk and producers of children as a lower, more sinful species of person while regarding virgins and unmarried people as a higher and holier state. It was Christian bias, in other words, that thrust married men and women down into second-class status.

Early Christianity adopted from the Jews its rejection of the exposure or outright killing of infants. Justin Martyr (d. ca. 165) writes: "We have learned that the exposure of newborn children is also an evil thing, if only because we see that almost all of them, not just the girls but the boys too are led into vice" (I. *Apology* 27). Evidently many children were found and saved. "And furthermore it is to be feared that one of the exposed children, if he or she is not picked up, will die, and so we shall become murderers" (ibid., 29). Lactantius, a Church Father whom Constantine appointed tutor to the prince in 317, writes in his *Divine Instructions* (304–13) about the pagans: "They strangle their own children or, if they are too pious to do that, they expose them" 5, 19, 15).

Infanticide and abortion were often mentioned together and

equated. In the Letter of Barnabas from the first half of the second century we read: "You shall not kill either the fetus by abortion or the newborn" (19, 5). In his petition to the Emperor Marcus Aurelius (177), the Christian philosopher Athenagoras writes that Christians "call women who take medications to induce an abortion murderers" and "forbid the exposure of a child, because it is the same as killing a child" (35). The Church Father Tertullian writes in 198 that pagans are accustomed to kill newborns, "either by drowning, or by exposing them to cold or death from hunger or the dogs . . . But we are not permitted, since murder has been prohibited to us once and for all, even to destroy . . . the fetus in the womb. It makes no difference whether one destroys a life that has already been born or one that is in the process of birth" (*Apology* 9:7–8). At the end of the second century the Roman lawyer Minucius Felix, who was a Christian, addressed the pagans as follows: "I see you now exposing newborn children to the wild beasts and birds, now ending their lives in a deplorable manner by strangling them. Some women take medicines to destroy the germ of future life in their own bodies. They commit infanticide before they have given birth to the infant" (*Octavius* 30, 2). Ambrose (d. 397) too speaks of both cases as murder. He writes: "The poor expose their children, the rich kill the fruit of their own bodies in the womb, lest their property be divided up, and they destroy their own children in the womb with murderous potions. And before life has been passed on, it is annihilated" (*Hexaemeron* 5, 18, 58).

On January 16, 318, Emperor Constantine issued an order forbidding fathers to kill their grown children for crimes, as the right of *patria potestas* had allowed them to do. But it was not until February 7, 374, more than a half-century after Christianity had become a recognized and privileged religion in the state, that infanticide too was legally branded as murder.

In Rome there were laws governing abortion (as we shall see, they did not take the rights of the fetus into consideration, but merely protected the rights of the husband and the life of the mother). But in the early Christian era they underwent no changes, even though from the very beginning Christians were committed to defending the unborn and attacking abortion. The Cornelian law, which Sulla had enacted in 81 B.C. against the purchasing and administering of poisoned drinks, was applied both to potency and fertility potions and to the contraceptive and abortifacient kind. If a man or woman who had been given the potion died, the person supplying it was executed. Thus the concern, once again, was for adults, not for the fetus.

The abortion law promulgated by Emperor Septimius Severus (d. 211) and Caracalla (d. 217) stipulated that a woman who tried to abort her pregnancy was to be sent into exile, "for it is dishonorable for a wife to deny her husband children with impunity." All this, obviously, was designed to protect the interests of the husband. Unmarried women seeking abortions were not punished. And this law too did not deal with the protection of the fetus as such.

Protection of the unborn first began to be enforced on the grounds of the sharp criticism that Christians voiced on abortion. We know that abortion was common in the Roman Empire, from the fact, for example, that Seneca (d. 65) praised his mother because, unlike many others, "she did not destroy the hope of children conceived in her womb" (*Ad Helviam* 16, 1).

From the start Christians borrowed from Jewish tradition in sharply condemning abortion. The Didache, also called "The Teaching of the Twelve Apostles," from the first half of the second century, speaks of "child-murderers, who go the way of death, who slay God's image in the womb" (5, 2). The Spanish Synod of Elvira at the beginning of the fourth century, condemned abortion under pain of lifelong excommunication. In 314 the Synod of Ancyra laid down ten years of church penance for women who engaged in fornication and then destroyed its consequences. The decisions of this synod were frequently cited by later councils in both the East and the West. The Apostolic Constitutions, a compilation from the fourth century, condemned the killing of a fetus that had already taken shape (7, 3, 2). The canons of St. Basil (d. 379), which set a standard for legislation in the Eastern Church, condemned without exception all women who underwent abortions, without respect to the degree of development of the fetus. The punishment was the same as that determined by the Synod of Ancyra: ten years of penance.

The oldest documents on contraceptive practices come from Egypt. These are papyrus finds from the nineteenth to the eleventh century B.C. They mention prescriptions for vaginal tampons that were supposed to block or kill the sperm. The tampons were saturated with such substances as acacia gum, honey, and crocodile feces. Greco-Roman science looked primarily to three works, Aristotle's (d. 332 B.C.) *On the History of Animals*, Pliny's (d. 79) *Natural History*, the best and most comprehensive scientific encyclopedia in Antiquity, and the *Gynecology* of the physician Soranus of Ephesus, who was active around the time of the Emperors Trajan and Hadrian (early second century) in Rome. The *Gynecology* was the most important source of knowledge about contraception for the Roman Empire, as it was in turn for the Arabs and through them for medieval Europe.

The first contraceptive these authors mention is potions. Pliny gives only one recipe: a concoction of rue (also an abortifacient), attar of roses, and aloe (*Natural History* 20, 51, 142–43). Soranus deals with contraceptive potions under the heading, "Should one use abortifacient and contraceptive drugs, and how?" He claims three potions are good for birth control: a mixture of panax juice, rue seed, and Cyrenaican juice blended with wax and served in wine; secondly a mixture of wallflower seed, myrtle, myrrh, and white pepper dissolved in wine, to be drunk for three successive days. Finally, he prescribes a mixture of sour honey with gillyflower seeds and cow parsnip. Soranus advises care, since "these medications not only prevent conception, but also destroy what has already been conceived." Although these drugs could also cause an abortion, they were primarily designed for contraception. Soranus warns that they can lead to severe irritations in the head and digestive tract as well as to vomiting (*Gynecology* I, 19, 60–63).

The second method used in Antiquity was not to let the sperm into the uterus. Aristotle thought that conception would be rendered more difficult by making the cervical labia slippery. "That is why some people anoint the part of the womb that the seed enters with cedar oil, lead salve, or a salve made of incense and olive oil" (*On the History of Animals* 7, 3, 583a). Soranus recommends a mixture of old olive oil, honey, juice from the balsam tree or cedar resin, to be placed in the womb. He also thinks soft wool in the orifice of the uterus will be effective, or wool soaked in wine, and into which stone-pine bark and the tanning agent from Venice sumac have been dissolved (*Gynecology* I, 19, 61–62).

For the third kind of contraception an anointment was applied to the penis. This was supposed either to kill the sperm or, like a pessary, to close the uterus upon entering the vagina. Pliny recommends cedar gum (*Natural History* 24, 11, 18).

In addition to these methods one was also advised to observe the sterile times in a woman's cycle. The school of Hippocrates (fifth century B.C.) had come to the conclusion that the fruitful period came immediately after menstruation (*Diseases of Women* I, 38). Soranus held the same belief. He writes: "The uterus, in which a lot of blood has collected during menstruation can, it is true, very easily discharge the pent-up blood, but it is not capable of admitting and holding the semen." He thinks that one woman or another might conceive during menstruation, but "scientific considerations lead to the conclusion" that the menstrual period is not the right time for conception. Soranus also argues that the time before menstruation is unfavorable for conception, because the womb is already incorporating material into it and so has difficulties in accepting the seed. The best time for conception, he says, is immediately after menstruation (*Gynecology* I, 10, 36).

One subject of broad interest in Antiquity was *euteknia*, the blessing of good, healthy children. The first important element in *euteknia* was the age of the parents. According to Plato, a man has the finest offspring between his thirtieth and thirty-ninth year, a woman between her sixteenth and twentieth. Aristotle recommends "setting the marriage age for girls at eighteen, for men at thirty-seven or somewhat less." Xenophon praises the laws of Lycurgus (founder of the Spartan Constitution) and the measures he took so that parents in good health would produce healthy issue. Girls who wished to be mothers were not allowed to drink wine or only when it was diluted with water. They were also supposed to play sports. Lycurgus "instituted races and contests of strength between women like those between men."

The best moment to aim for *euteknia,* Soranus says, is immediately after menstruation; the worst offspring are born from intercourse immediately before. For just as the stomach, when it is full of food, is inclined to vomit, in order to eject its contents, so with the womb when it is full of blood. After menstruation, on the other hand, the womb regains its appetite. This is shown by the fact that after menstruation women are especially inclined to the sexual act. It's interesting, by the way, to note how women have been talked, or have talked themselves, into believing their libido is at its maximum during the most fruitful phase of their cycle, though that phase has varied, depending on the state of medical science at the time. On September 16, 1968 when Cardinal Frings gathered the deans and professors in Cologne, hoping to make *Humanae vitae* (the encyclical on the birth control pill) more palatable to them, he argued that the marital act was by its very nature an act of procreation, since a woman's libido was at its highest during her fertile days. To that extent the cardinal's views and those of Soranus of Ephesus agree. But since in the meanwhile science shifted the fertile phase from its placement by Soranus, the supposed naturally directed maximum libido was also shifted. Female libido evidently takes its cue from scientists. Or rather maximum libido is a construct of moralists, or else women locate their libido wherever it is especially advisable, for the sake of greater fertility, or wherever it is downright forbidden, should the woman not desire to get pregnant: Prohibitions too can encourage libido.

Finally the ancient world was familiar with the use of amulets. Soranus rejects them with a blast of contempt (*Gynecology* I, 19, 96). But his judgment could not eradicate the widespread faith in such devices. Pliny recommends that women "who have children swarming all around them and whose fruitfulness therefore is in need of a remedy" wear an amulet made from a certain kind of spider. It was supposed to be bound into a piece of deerskin and put on before sunrise (*Natural History* 29, 27, 85).

Coitus interruptus is not mentioned in the scientific works of Greco-Roman authors, either because it was taken for granted or because even then people preferred recommending methods that were predominantly to be used by the woman.

Since contraceptive potions also had abortifacient effects, they caused problems for ancient medicine. Soranus, the most important author in this field, wrote that he faced this problem with every potion that he prescribed. Soranus was strongly influenced by Stoicism, and so his standards for permitting abortion were strict: He allowed it only when the birth meant danger for the mother. He thought that contraception was better than abortion (*Gynecology* I, 19, 60–61).

Even during the Christian era of the Roman Empire Soranus enjoyed great prestige. Tertullian made use of one of his writings. Even Augustine, the great opponent of contraception, calls him a "very noble medical author" (*Against Julian* 5, 14, 51). And the Christian court physician of the Christian Emperor and lawgiver Justinian (sixth century), the high dignitary Aëtios, even lists contraceptives advised by Soranus—and recommends them himself. This suggests that Christians in the first centuries were freer on the matter of birth control than the Catholics of today. The married physician Aëtios clearly judged the issue less rigorously than the celibate Church Fathers, such as Chrysostom and Jerome, who took a position on contraception.

Chrysostom speaks of married couples who don't want any children and therefore "kill the newborn" or "thwart the beginning of life" (*Hom.* 28 on Mt. 5) It isn't clear whether this "thwarting" refers to abortion or contraception. Chrysostom speaks unequivocally about contraception in another passage. Addressing Christian husbands who "scorn their wives and seek out whores," he admonishes them: "Why do you scatter your seed where the field is intent on destroying the fruit, where all means to frustrate pregnancy are used, where murder is perpetrated before birth can occur? You not only let a harlot be a harlot, you make her into a murderess . . . There is in fact something worse than murder—I don't know what to call it—for such women do not kill something that has taken shape, but prevent it from taking shape. Do you despise the gift of God and contend against his laws? Do you make the antechamber of birth the antechamber of carnage? Woman, made for reproduction, becomes, because of you, a tool of murder. For she is expert in this sort of deed and with it prepares your destruction, so that she may always be used and desired by her lovers, so that she may drain ever more money from them. And even if that destruction comes from her, you are the guilty one. Idol worship too arises here. In order to look pretty, many of these women use magic, drink-offerings, philters, poisoned potions, and countless other things. Even after such shamefulness, after death and sorcery, this business still seems harmless to many men, even to many men who have wives. And among the latter a whole fountainhead of mischief arises, since poisons are prepared not to harm the harlot's womb, but the offended wife . . . wars without end, continual struggles, and quarreling is the order of the day" (*Homily 24 on the Letter to the Romans*). Chrysostom raised the stakes even higher in this rhetorical assault by characterizing contraception as "murder, worse than murder," thereby outdoing all the writers of the Greco-Roman world, none of whom had equated semen with a human being.

The prevailing view in Antiquity was Aristotle's notion that the animation of the masculine fetus did not take place until forty days after conception, while the female fetus acquired a human soul only ninety days after conception. Before then the fetus had first a vegetable, then an animal soul (*On the History of Animals* 7, 3, 583b). This temporal difference in the genesis of the soul in men and women would not have been simply a matter of time, but of human quality, since the soul belongs to man sooner than it does to woman. The soul, i.e., the essence of humanity, is something masculine rather than something feminine.

A similar idea about the inferiority of women probably underlies the Old Testament: According to Leviticus 12:1–5 a woman is unclean forty days after the birth of a son, eighty days after the birth of a daughter. The ninety days before the emergence of the female soul in Aristotle and the eighty days of uncleanness in the Old Testament are fused together in Christian tradition, so that a soul was attributed to the female fetus eighty days after conception.

In keeping with this idea about successive animation, the term "murder" was incorrect not only for contraception but also for early abortion. Augustine follows Aristotelian biology in writing that no soul can live in an unformed body, and so there can be no talk of murder here (*On Exodus* 21, 80). Jerome too writes in a letter to Aglasia: "The seed gradually takes shape in the uterus, and it does not count as killing until the individual elements have acquired their external appearance and their limbs" (*Epistle* 121, 4).

Nevertheless, Jerome too is inconsistent and speaks exaggeratedly of "murder" with reference to contraception. In a letter to Eustochium he writes to warn about some consecrated virgins: "Some even ensure barrenness by the help of potions, murdering human beings before they are fully conceived. Others, when they find that they are with child as a result of their sin, practice abortion with drugs, and so frequently bring about their own death, taking with them to the lower world the guilt of three crimes: suicide, adultery against Christ, and child murder" (*Epistle* 22, 13, translated by F. A. Wright Loeb Library of Classics).

VI

AUGUSTINE

T*he man who fused* Christianity together with hatred of sex and pleasure into a systematic unity was the greatest of the Church Fathers, St. Augustine (d. 430). His importance for Christian sexual morality is unquestioned, and it set the standard for condemnation of "artificial" contraception by Paul VI (1968) and

John Paul II (1981). Augustine is the theological thinker who paved the way not just for the centuries, but for the millennia, that followed. The positions taken by Augustine had a decisive influence on the great medieval theologians, for example Thomas Aquinas (d. 1274), and on Jansenism, that reawakening of severe prudishness in seventeenth- and eighteenth-century France. Augustine's authority in the realm of sexual morality was so overwhelming that we shall have to take a closer look at his ideas. Like many neurotics he radically separates love and sexuality. As the Viennese historian Friedrich Heer wrote, "The catastrophic process of the desexualization of love was given an emphatic push forward in the West by Augustine" (*Gottes erste Liebe: Die Juden im Spannungsfeld der Geschichte,* pp. 69, 71).

Augustine was the great creator of the Christian image of God, the world, and humanity that is still widely accepted today. He took the contempt for sex that saturates the work of the Church Fathers, both before him and in his own day, and to it he added a new factor: A personal and theological sexual anxiety. Augustine connected the transmission of original sin, which plays so great a role in his system of redemption, with the pleasure of sexual intercourse. For him original sin means eternal death, damnation for everyone who has not been redeemed by God's grace from the *massa damnata,* to which all people belong. Augustine insists that not all persons will be redeemed, e.g., unbaptized children are lost.

Augustine was so fixated on the damnation of unbaptized children that one of his opponents, Bishop Julian of Eclanum, a Pelagian, sharply attacked him: "Augustine, you are far removed from religious feelings, from civilized thinking, indeed from healthy common sense, if you think that your God is capable of committing crimes against justice that are scarcely imaginable even for the barbarians." Julian called Augustine's God "a persecutor of infants, who throws tiny babies into the eternal fire" (Augustine, *Against Julian* I, 48).

Augustine once told the following story to his community during a sermon: A child died when he was still taking instructions for baptism, in other words a catechuman. In despair over his eternal damnation his mother brought the corpse to the shrine of St. Stephen. The child was raised from the dead, only to be baptized and die again, in the certainty of having now avoided the "second death," that is, Hell (*Serm.* 323 and 324).

The respected Parisian professor of theology Johannes Beleth (d. ca. 1165) forbade dead pregnant women to be laid out in church since their unborn children had not been baptized. Before such women could be buried in a consecrated cemetery, the child had to be cut out of their body and buried outside the cemetery. Fortunately this pious custom was not practiced everywhere. Church laws in Norway, for instance, expressly forbade the operation (Peter Browe, *Beiträge zur Sexualethik des Mittelalters*, p. 23). But the very existence of the prohibition points to the ghastly consistency of Augustine's teaching on original sin.

Pelagius and Julian of Eclanum entered the pages of Church history as great heretics. But Augustine, with his inhuman doctrine, has remained the determining spiritual force till this day, though the Church is slowly beginning, despite him, to let unbaptized children into heaven after all. Not too long ago Karl Rahner asked: "Was it all false, the case made by Pelagius and Julian of Eclanum against the apparently universally triumphant Augustine? Were they not in many respects vindicated afterward in a slow development that has lasted to our day?" (*Theologie der Gegenwart*, 1977, 2, 76).

There is another teaching of Augustine's that has likewise had devastating consequences, namely, the doctrine of the way original sin is passed on to little children, that is, to everyone. Augustine thought that when Adam and Eve disobeyed God and ate the forbidden fruit of Paradise, "they were ashamed and covered their sexual parts with fig leaves." He concludes from this that "this is where it comes from" ("ecce unde"). He means that what they were both trying to hide was the place whence the first sin is transmitted (*Sermons* 151, 8). Thus, according to Augustine, sexual intercourse or, more precisely, sexual pleasure is what carries original sin on and on, from generation to generation. "Christ was begotten and conceived without any fleshly pleasure and so he also remained free from every kind of defilement by original sin" (*Enchiridion* 13, 41).

At a time of AIDS-anxiety we can imagine what it meant to think and feel that sexual pleasure infected the child with original sin. This linking of pleasure and sin was not definitively abandoned until the last century. That was why the "Immaculate Conception" was not declared a dogma until 1854. This doctrine is known to modern men and women primarily because they constantly confuse it with the Virgin Birth. Many people believe that the dogma of the Immaculate Conception refers to the point in time when Mary conceived Jesus from the Holy Spirit. But it actually refers to the moment when Mary herself was conceived by her mother without original sin. So long as the Church clung, with Augustine, to the idea that original sin was transmitted through the act of generation, it was impossible to speak of Mary's immaculate conception. For Augustine only Jesus was free from original sin, because he came into the world without any sexual act. And conversely in order to be free of original sin he had to come into this world in a virginal birth.

In 1140 Bernard of Clairvaux, an ardent venerater of Mary, decisively opposed the institution of a feast in Lyon to honor Mary's Immaculate Conception. He argued that to claim Mary was preserved from original sin meant that one must also assume that Mary too was the product of a virgin birth.

Augustine was the father of a fifteen-hundred-year-long anxiety about sex and an enduring hostility to it. He dramatizes the fear of sexual pleasure, equating pleasure with perdition in such a way that anyone who tries to follow his train of thought will have the sense of being trapped in a nightmare. He laid such a heavy moral burden on marriage that we cannot be surprised if people unnaturally oppressed by it were stung into rejecting Christian sexual morality lock, stock, and barrel.

However significant Augustine's conversion (387) may have been for theology, it was a disaster for married people. He prepared for conversion by dismissing, at age twenty-nine, the woman with whom he had been living for twelve years, and who had borne him a son, Adeodatus (= God-given), when he was just seventeen. He kept the boy, while this woman ("she was one who had come my way because of my wandering desires and my lack of considered judgment; nevertheless, I had only this one woman"), whose name he never mentions, swore to be faithful to him even as he sent her away. He called his relationship to her a "mere pact made between two people whose love is lustful and who do not want to have children—even though, if children are born, they compel us to love them" (*Confessions* IV, 2, translated by Rex Warner, 1963, NAL).

Augustine strictly practiced contraception, observing his partner's infertile days, although his vigilance was frustrated by a miscalculation that blessed him with Adeodatus. But after his conversion he turned into a fanatical opponent of all contraception. Part of the reason why he wanted to avoid pregnancy during his love affair was that he was unwilling to marry the woman, who did not belong to his social class. His mother, St. Monica, plotted against the liaison, and saw to it that his mistress went back to Africa, because she was preparing her son for a suitable marriage. But the rich bride chosen by Monica was not yet of marriageable age, and Augustine would have had to wait another two years for her, so he took another lover. "The woman with whom I was in the habit of sleeping was torn from my side on the grounds of being an impediment to my marriage, and my heart, which clung to her, was wounded and broken and dripping blood. She had returned to Africa after having made a vow to you [God] that she would never go to bed with another man, and she had left with me the natural son I had had by her. But I, in my misery, could not follow the example of a woman. I had two years to wait until I could have the girl to whom I was engaged, and I could not bear the delay. So, since I was not so much a lover of marriage as a slave to lust, I found another woman for myself . . . Nor was the wound healed which had been made by the cutting off of my previous mistress. It burned, it hurt intensely, and then it festered, and if the pain became duller, it became more desperate" (*Confessions* VI, 15).

After his conversion his bad conscience over his own betrayal of his first lover was transformed into a contempt for sexual love in general. As guilty as he may have felt, he thought the fault lay less in himself than in the evil pleasure of the sexual act. Augustine's pessimistic sexual morality is simply a repression of his bad sexual conscience, his aversion to women a continual ferreting out of the culpable cause of his failure.

Augustine's aversion to conception was not due merely to the fact that he did not wish to marry his lover. (It is not true, by the way, that he *could* not marry her "for legal reasons." That is one of the many justifications that some theologians tried belatedly to bestow upon the great Church Father.) Rather the primary reason was that during the time of his love affair he belonged to the Gnostic sect of the Manichees, which had a wide following among the cultivated classes, but was forbidden by the Roman state because they practiced contraception and abortion. Founded by the Persian Mani (b. 216?), Manichaeism was the last great religious movement in the East after Christianity and before Islam. Mani styled himself as the Holy Spirit promised by Jesus. According to him, the earth was "the kingdom of boundless darkness," fashioned by the devil. Procreation was a diabolical act, because man was a particle of light trapped in a body generated by demons. The Manichaeans, like all strict Gnostics before them, rejected the Old Testament, because it tied the good God in with the creation of the world, whereas the world and the body derived from the evil Demon.

The Manichaeans demanded a completely ascetical life from their full members, "the elect." But only a few people were capable of this. Most belonged to an inferior second class of Manichaeans, who were, like Augustine, simply "hearers," i.e., they lived with their spouses or lovers, but pledged to avoid the incarceration of the spiritual man, meaning procreation. After he converted, the affirmation of pleasure and denial of procreation that marked his Manichaean period turned into an affirmation of procreation and a denial of pleasure: The Manichaean became a Christian.

In a sense he also turned from a second-class Manichaean into a first-class one, because Christians and Manichaeans agreed in rating celibacy higher than the simple married state (where

Christians had children and Manichaeans practiced birth control). One of the reasons, after all, that Manichaeism had such a wide following at the time of Augustine was that with its ideal of virginity it fit in well with Christianity and was viewed by many people as a loftier form of the Christian faith.

During the painful period spent with his second mistress Augustine busied himself with Neoplatonic philosophy, especially Plotinus. Plotinus combined Gnostic flight from the world and recognition of its futility with knowledge of the one true and good God. Unlike the original Gnostics and the Manichaeans, he did not trace evil back to an autonomous evil principle but thought of it as a deviation from the one True and Good. Augustine's ascetical Neoplatonic bent, his urge to break away from everything earthly and beloved on this earth, his turn toward the one true God was finally shifted to an escapist version of Christianity by an accidental visit. One day a compatriot of his from Africa, Ponticianus, dropped by and called his attention to the first monk, the Egyptian Anthony (ca. 300), whose life, written by the Church Father Athanasius (d. 373) was being more and more widely disseminated in the West and had already found many imitators. Augustine was profoundly impressed. And when Ponticianus left, Augustine said to his friend Alypius: "What is wrong with us? What is this which you have heard? The unlearned rise up and take heaven by force, while we (look at us!) with all our learning are wallowing in flesh and blood" (*Confessions* VIII, 8). There follows the famous scene in the garden, which took place in Milan in 386, Augustine's immediate conversion to Christianity. This fits into the process of repressing the betrayal of his mistress in favor of a conversion to asceticism or, concretely, a depreciation of marriage vis-à-vis celibacy.

While in the garden Augustine heard a child's voice singing, "Take up and read, take up and read." He took the Bible, which was lying open in the garden and read: "Let us conduct ourselves becomingly as in the day, not in reveling and drunkenness, not in debauchery and licentiousness, not in quarreling and jealousy. But put on the Lord Jesus Christ, and make no provision for the flesh, to gratify its desires" (Rom. 13:13–14). The image of the enemy is clear: lust, evil pleasure, sexual desire, carnal craving. Augustine writes: "It was as though my heart was filled with a light of confidence and all the shadows of my doubt were swept away . . . For you converted me in such a way that I no longer sought a wife nor any other worldly hope" (*Confessions* VIII, 12).

Augustine's conversion to Christianity, from love of pleasure to hatred of it, took place by classifying women as stimulants and ignoring them as partners. And to this day male celibate clergy are still putting women in their place. On Holy Saturday, 387, Augustine had himself baptized, along with his son Adeodatus, by Ambrose, the eulogist of virginity, whom he greatly revered. Three years later the motherless eighteen-year-old boy, Adeodatus, died, "the son of my flesh, begotten by me in my sin" (*Confessions* IX, 6, translated by Rex Warner). Augustine dearly loved him.

In almost all Catholic manuals of theology we read that as a Christian Augustine defended "the holiness of marriage" against the Manichaeans. But this has to be corrected: he merely defended marital *procreation* against the Manichaeans. None of the Church Fathers had any idea what marriage was all about, least of all Augustine, neither during his Manichaean period, when he lived with his lover, and certainly not in his monastic-episcopal period, after he became a Christian.

The method of contraception that was used by the Manichaeans and that Augustine subjected to a barrage of scorn is the only one that has the Church's blessing today. At the synod of bishops held in Rome in 1980, at which contraception was sharply rejected, only this method received approval from the highest authorities. Around this time there were appearances on the TV news by a Catholic couple (a sort of Knaus-Ogino-cervical-mucus model couple), who had been called in to advise Pope John Paul II in person.

The following is not meant to criticize that form of "rhythm," but curiously enough Augustine would have greeted this couple not as a papal model, but as "adulterers" and "whoremongers." That is the vein in which he addresses the Manichaeans: "Didn't you warn us before to watch as carefully as possible for the time after the monthly period, when a woman may be expected to conceive, and to abstain from intercourse at this time, lest a soul be enclosed in the flesh? It follows from this that, in your opinion, marriage was not intended to beget children but to satisfy desires" (*The Morality of the Manichaeans* 18, 65).

In Augustine's day the medical profession was convinced that the most fruitful phase in a woman's cycle came immediately after menstruation. In another passage Augustine tackles the same issue even more forcefully: "The birth of children is what you most abhor in marriage, and thus you turn your 'hearers' into adulterers of their own wives, when they are on the alert to see that their wives do not conceive . . . They wish to have no children, for whose sake alone marriages are contracted. Why then aren't you the sort of people who forbid marriage . . . if you are trying to take away what constitutes marriage in the first place? For if that is taken away, husbands are shameful lovers, wives are harlots, marriage beds are bordellos, and fathers-in-law are pimps" (*Against Faustus* 15, 7).

It was altogether in keeping with Augustine, Thomas, Jerome, the Stoics, Philo, in short with the whole antipleasure tradition that on October 8, 1980, at a general audience in Rome the Pope spoke about adultery with one's own wife. But the Pope didn't mean, as Augustine did, those who used the rhythm method; he referred only to those who used the so-called "unnatural" methods. Augustine called rhythm "the pimp's method," whereas Pope John Paul II in *Familiaris Consortio* does not cite it under the heading of contraception, but separates it out from the other, evil methods, and puffs it in hymn-like language: "The decision for the natural rhythms implies an acceptance of the times of the person, the woman, and thereby too an acceptance of dialogue, of mutual respect, of common responsibility." It means "living personal love in its claim to fidelity."

Only when he comes to the other methods of birth control does the Pope link up again with Augustine, as he speaks of "a falsification of the inner truth of married love," because they "surrender God's plan to arbitrariness and manipulate and debase human sexuality." In *Familiaris Consortio* the Pope calls upon theologians "to elaborate the anthropological and at the same time the moral difference between contraception and recourse to rhythm."

The theologians must feel overtaxed by the Pope's demand—he'll have to elaborate that difference all by himself. Because, to quote Germany's best-known moral theologian, Franz Böckle, "We should not be surprised when troubled pastors and most of all pressured lay people can't understand the metaphysical difference between the 'natural' and the 'unnatural' methods." While for Augustine contraception is contra-ception, the Pope asks theologians to discover differences where there are none, theologically speaking, the only distinction being medical. We may be glad that at least the rhythm method has been permitted—in the Eastern Church the hierarchy is still quite fixated on Augustine, and hasn't even made as much progress as the Western Church—but progress vis-à-vis Augustine shouldn't consist in the Pope's picking, with wiredrawn logic, and blessing one method. Rather he should finally leave the whole question in the hands of married people, whom it concerns in the first place.

Since 1981 the Pope has once more taken a little turn on the issue of rhythm. On September 6, 1984, again during one of his weekly general audiences, within the framework of the eighth in a series of twelve addresses on birth control, John Paul II warned the faithful not to "misuse" the church-approved method of birth control. This would happen if married couples were to try "for dishonest reasons" to keep [the number of children] below the birthrate that is morally right for their family." Actually, the Pope should neither interfere in the question of methods nor talk about a "morally right" birthrate, nor suspect married people's reasons as being "dishonest."

Unlike the Pope, therefore, Augustine did not divide contra-ception into two categories, allowed and disallowed: It was all forbidden. He lashes out especially at the method now approved by John Paul II, because his opponents, the Manichaeans, and he himself in his youth had used it in preference to others. But there are also passages in which he refers to the so-called artificial methods: "Sometimes (*aliquando*) this lustful atrocity or atrocious lust goes so far as to acquire poisons for infertility (*sterilitatis venena*) . . . so that the wife becomes her husband's harlot, or he an adulterer with his own wife" (*Marriage and Lasciviousness* I, 15, 17). This principle was destined to go on to play a large role in the Church's battle against contraception. It was cited in 1962 during Vatican II, for example, by Ernesto Cardinal Ruffini, archbishop of Palermo, in the basilica of St. Peter, to condemn the birth control pill.

Yet another passage by Augustine concerning contraception was destined to play at least as disastrous a role as the ones we have already discussed. He wrote: "It is impermissible and shameful to practice intercourse with one's wife while preventing the conception of children. This is what Onan did, the son of Judah, and that is why God killed him" (*The Adulterous Relations* 2, 12). The fact that Onan died after engaging in coitus interruptus, which displeased God, has gone a long way toward neuroticizing many married couples, who have been continually reproached with this passage in this century, particularly by Pius XI. In 1930 he wrote: "Hence it is no wonder that Holy Scripture attests that the divine majesty prosecutes such reprehensible conduct with the highest degree of hatred, indeed God has already punished it with death. Augustine calls our attention to this when he writes: 'Marital intercourse, even with one's legitimate spouse, is forbidden and immoral, if the awakening of new life is prevented. This is what Onan, the son of Judah did, and on account of that God killed him' " (*Casti connubii,* 1930). God pursues "with the highest degree of hatred" those who practice contraception. This the Pope added from his own rich invention, to intensify an already shocking story.

The Pope deliberately overlooks the fact that Onan's offense was not against marriage, but the law of succession. Onan, whose death has served many purposes, is turned into a man who wanted "to avoid the burden, but taste the pleasure anyhow." In *Casti connubii,* the first anti-birth control encyclical of this century, Onan is used to strike fear into the hearts of married couples.

Who was the man after whom onanism was so incorrectly named? Incorrectly, because he was not engaged in masturbation but in coitus interruptus: The custom of levirate marriage dictated that if a man died childless, his next male relative, normally his brother, had to beget a child upon his brother's widow, and so provide him with an heir for his name, his line, and his property. The story of Onan is reported in Genesis 38:7–10: "Judah's firstborn was wicked in the sight of the Lord, and the Lord slew him. Then Judah said to Onan, 'Go into your brother's wife, and perform the duty of a brother-in-law, and raise up offspring for your brother.' But Onan knew that the offspring would not be his; so when he went in to his brother's wife he spilled the semen on the ground, lest he should give offspring to his brother. And what he did was displeasing in the sight of the Lord, and he slew him also." Augustine cited this passage as a warning against birth control because it fit in with his anticontraceptive campaign. Others, such as Jerome and Thomas Aquinas, were more careful, and made no such use of the text.

The Manichaeans wanted to stop procreation lest any more sparks of light be captured in diabolical matter. Still they allowed their second-class adherents, the so-called "hearers," to marry, if they bore no children. But for Augustine, the convert, procreation became the only goal and purpose of marriage, while he saw pleasure as an evil. "I am convinced," he wrote, "that nothing turns the spirit of man away from the heights more than the caresses of woman and those movements of the body, without which a man cannot possess his wife" (*Soliloquies* 1, 10).

The goodness of procreation and the evil of pleasure were the twin premises that led to his strict demands on married couples. And since the second premise is false, the result was a calamity. For right as Augustine was to oppose the Manichaeans, he was largely wrong in his struggle against the Pelagian bishop Julian of Eclanum. The Pelagians had a positive attitude toward sexual pleasure. They looked upon it as natural, in no way as sinful, rather as a special advantage of marriage. From Augustine's point of view that proved the Pelagians denied original sin.

Julian was the son of a Catholic bishop, came from the Apulian upper class. He was a married priest, an educated man (meaning that he had learned Greek). His wife Titia was the daughter of the Catholic bishop Aemilius of Benevento. Julian was made bishop of Eclanum in 416, but then in the Pelagian controversy (Augustine's greatest battle) he was excommunicated and driven from office by Pope Zosimus in 418. For Julian, Augustine always remained "the African." After a checkered wandering life Julian died some time after 450 in Sicily. At the end he was a private tutor in a Pelagian family. Some friends wrote on his grave: "Here lies Julian, a Catholic bishop." But Augustine, the celibate, conquered Julian, the married man, and with him all married men.

Like the Church Fathers before him and in his own day, Augustine asks whether Adam and Eve had sexual intercourse back in Paradise: "The question is asked, quite properly, how we should imagine the union of man and woman before they sinned, and whether the blessing, 'Increase and multiply and fill the earth' is to be understood in the carnal or spiritual sense," he writes in 389. "For we can also think of this blessing in a spiritual sense, and assume that only after the Fall was it transformed into fleshly fertility" (*De gen. contra Manichaeos* I. 19). Augustine could also imagine what this sort of spiritual fertility looked like: "What should the woman help the man do? To bring forth spiritual fruits, namely good works to the praise of God, in a spiritual relationship" (ibid., 2, 11). He concludes that in Eden the connection between man and woman was asexual (ibid., I, 19).

But then Augustine began to waver. In 401 he said there were three possibilities: Either the blessing at Creation, "Increase and multiply," should be understood mystically and metaphorically; or else Adam and Eve might have "had children without intercourse, in some other way—by the gift of the almighty Creator, who could have made them himself without parents." Or, finally, the children of Adam and Eve could have been begotten through sex. In this particular work (*De bono con.* 2) Augustine did not wish to commit himself on this difficult question.

In a work begun shortly afterward, *De genesi ad litteram,* whose composition went on until 415, he once again mentioned the possibility that in Paradise children were begotten without intercourse. Perhaps they were bred through purely spiritual love, "uncorrupted by desire" (3, 21). But in the course of the same piece he decided that even in Eden reproduction took place through the sexual act. Augustine came to this realization thanks to his disdain for women. He corrected the old error of Gregory of Nyssa and John Chrysostom—who denied the existence of sex in Paradise—with a new error, a bit of misogynistic nonsense that Thomas Aquinas would later approvingly quote: "I don't see what sort of help woman was created to provide man with, if one excludes the purpose of procreation. If woman is not given to man for help in bearing children, for what help could she be? To till the earth together? If help were needed for that, man would have been a better help for man. The same goes for comfort in solitude. How much more pleasure is it for life and conversation when two friends live together than when a man and a woman cohabitate" (*De genesi ad litteram* 9, 5–9). In Paradise, Augustine says, there *was* sexual intercourse, because in intellectual matters woman would have been no help to man, but God, as we know, created woman as a help for man, according to the biblical, male-conceived account of Creation.

Women may well have been astonished to know that they were good only for reproduction, and unqualified for anything having to do with mind and intelligence. This idea was formulated by Thomas Aquinas (d. 1274) in connection with Augustine as follows: Woman is simply a help in procreation (*adiutorium generationis*) and useful in housekeeping. For a man's intellectual life she has no significance. Thus Augustine was the brilliant inventor of what Germans call the three K's (*Kinder, Küche, Kirche*—children, kitchen, church), an idea that still has life in it, in fact it continues to be the Catholic hierarchy's primary theological position on woman.

In his opus magnum, *The City of God,* written between 413 and 426, Augustine explains: "There is no denying the obvious evidence of bodies of different sex, which shows that it would be a manifest absurdity to deny the fact that male and female were created for the purpose of begetting children, so as to increase and multiply and fill the earth" (XIV, 22, translated by Henry Bettenson, Penguin 1972). He now characterized his earlier opinion as absurd and recanted it in his *Retractations,* begun three years before his death.

Thus there was sex in Eden, and the Manichaean idea that procreation came from the devil was rejected. But what about pleasure? Was there sexual pleasure in Paradise? Augustine's answer is, of course, no. Before the Fall sex took place free from all the excitement that accompanies it today. In Eden the will ruled the sexual organs, as it nowadays does the hands and feet. "Why shouldn't we believe that before the Fall men could control the sex organs just as they could the other limbs?" (*De genesi ad litteram* 9, 10). "We move our hands and feet to perform their special functions, when we so will; this involves no reluctance on their part, and the movements are performed with all the ease we observe in our own case, and in that of others . . . Then why should we not believe that the sexual organs could have been the obedient servants of mankind, at the bidding of the will, in the same way as the other, if there had been no lust, which came in as the retribution for the sin of disobedience?" (*The City of God* XIV, 23). "Then [had there been no sin] the man would have sown the seed and the woman would have conceived the child when their sexual organs had been aroused by the will, at the appropriate time and in the necessary degree, and had not been excited by lust" (ibid., XIV, 24). "Then without feeling the allurement of passion goading him on, the husband would have relaxed on his wife's bosom in tranquillity of mind and with no impairment of his body's integrity" (ibid., XIV, 26).

Augustine thought that when sexual pleasure reaches its climax, it not only escapes the control of the will, but "there is an almost total extinction of mental alertness; the intellectual sentries, as it were, are overwhelmed. Now surely any friend of wisdom and holy joys who lives a married life . . . would prefer, if possible, to beget children without lust of this kind. For then the parts created for this task would be the servants of his mind, even in their function of procreation, just as the other members are its servants in the various tasks to which they are assigned. They would begin their activity at the bidding of the will, instead of being stirred up by the ferment of lust" (ibid., XIV, 16).

Augustine devotes an entire chapter of *The City of God* (XIV, 24) to proving his abstruse idea that man in Paradise (in other words, the ideal person) fully controlled his sexual organs with the will. He notes that, "Some people can even move their ears, either one at a time or both together. Others without moving the head can bring the whole scalp—all the part covered with hair—down toward the forehead and bring it back again at will. Some can swallow an incredible number of various articles and then with a slight contraction of the diaphragm, can produce, as if out of a bag, any article they please, in perfect condition . . . We observe then that the body, even under present conditions, is an obedient servant to some people in a remarkable fashion beyond the normal limitations of nature . . . If this is so, is there any reason why we should not believe that before the sin and its punishment of corruptibility, the members of a man's body could have been the servants of man's will, without any lust, for the procreation of children? . . . because he did not obey God, [man] could not obey himself."

But whence comes this unique situation of the sexual organs, that they are not "moved by the will," but "excited by lust"? Augustine answers: ". . . the retribution for disobedience is simply disobedience itself" (ibid., 15). The body bids the mind obey, so that man may become aware of his disobedience to God (ibid., 24). Punishment for the Fall was first exacted on the realm of sexuality (ibid., 20). The attitude of the Church's celibate hierarchy is that the locus par excellence of sin is sex, a view based on Augustine's pleasure-hating fantasies.

The fact, noted by Augustine, that some people can wiggle their ears was thus destined to have consequences, as late as this century, as proof that procreation was originally lustless. Some readers have tried to excuse Augustine's nonsense on voluntary control of orgasm by citing his deficient knowledge of the human nervous system, as if the root of his argument was a medical error. But this defense is a mistake. One way or another Augustine would have managed to make sexual pleasure the result of the Fall. He didn't care about medicine; he wanted to ban pleasure, and any means of underpinning that ban was fine for him. The Stoic ideal of *apathia,* of self-control, together with its specific (and characteristically Augustinian) horror of lust, and not the state of ancient medical science, were the reasons why he discriminated, in a way that has lasted for centuries, against an essential part of human existence. "We must never allow ourselves to believe that God's blessing, 'Increase and multiply and fill the earth,' would have been fulfilled through this lust by the pair who were set in Paradise. It was, in fact, after the sin that this lust [*libido*] arose. It was after the sin that man's nature felt, noticed, blushed at, and concealed this lust; for man's nature retained a sense of decency, although it had lost the authority to which the body had been subordinate in every part" (ibid., 21).

In the last decade of his life Augustine drew marginally closer to the Pelagians on the subject of lust. He conceded the possibility of lust in Eden, of a totally curbed and harnessed sort. In his polemic against the Pelagians from the year 420 (*Contra duas epistolas Pelagianorum*) he maintains that in Paradise either intercourse took place wholly without pleasure, or that pleasure was aroused at the bidding of the will, when reason found it necessary to engage in sex for procreation. "If you prefer to accept the latter form as the one that prevailed in Paradise, if it seems good to you that in this happy condition children were bred through such a fleshly desire (*concupiscentia carnalis*), which neither hastened ahead of nor trailed behind the command of the will, which it had to follow and did not transgress, then we have no objection" (I, 17).

Thus toward the end of his life he granted lust—checked by will and reason—a place in Paradise. In the last thing he wrote, his "Incomplete Work Against Julian" (429/30), composed immediately before his death, he took up the problem of lust one more time: it seems to have bothered him to the very end. Julian had argued that sexual desire was the body's sixth sense, and a neutral energy, which could be used well or ill. The present form of the sexual drive, he said, was the same as in Paradise. Augustine insisted, however, that in any case sexual intercourse must have taken place differently in Eden: Either there was no lust then, and in that case lust is a vice, or it was present then, but at the will's bidding, and in that case it has gotten worse through sin, for in Paradise sexual pleasure would have been so constituted that "it occurred only with the will of the soul" (6, 22) and did not "suppress the thought of the mind as overwhelming pleasure" (4, 39). In any case Augustine calls sexual pleasure, in its present-day form, an "evil" (4, 23). Indeed it can be labeled a "sin, because it arose because of sin and strives for sin" (1, 71). As we see he took his sexual phobia with him to the grave.

In Augustine's view, sexual pleasure, which darkens the mind and disobeys the will, lowers human reproduction to the level of the animals: "This reproductive power, then, was not removed by man's sin. 'Man, placed in a position of honor is brought to the level of the beasts,' and he breeds like the beasts. And yet there is still the spark, as it were, of that reason in virtue of which he was made in the image of God; that spark has not been utterly put out" (*The City of God* XXII, 24).

Married couples make good use of this evil of lust only when they wish for the sole purpose of marriage, namely reproduction, before and during every sexual act. Against Julian, Augustine stressed in 422: "What cannot occur without lust should not, however, occur because of lust" (5, 9). And further: "If there was any other way to have children, then every act of sexual intercourse would quite obviously be a surrender to lust and hence a bad use of this evil." But because nobody can be begotten in any other way, married couples who have sex for the purpose of procreation are making "a good use of this evil" (*Against Julian* 5, 46).

Hence Louise Brown, the first test-tube baby, half succeeded in being Augustine's ideal child, because she was conceived by her mother without physical pleasure. The only disturbing feature is that the semen was obtained by masturbation from the lustful father. But if the semen had been surgically removed, then we would have attained a more or less paradisiacal state, meeting all of Augustine's demands and conditions. If we ignore the anesthetic, there is also no darkening of the mind here, which Augustine found so upsetting about sex and which Thomas Aquinas would sharply criticize later.

Just how much honor was bestowed on a pleasure-free conception can be seen in the Virgin Mary. Her image was elevated to what was then and in our century largely remains the state-of-the-art in celibacy: She conceived Jesus virginally, without having to be ashamed about lust, and for that reason she also gave birth painlessly (*Enchiridion* 41). Other women, unfortunately, were left with the curse for the Fall: "In pain you shall bring forth children" (Gen. 3:16).

Neither virgin birth nor *in vitro* fertilization are ordinary circumstances, and in the usual, unprivileged method of breeding lust cannot be excluded—Augustine writes that he had never met a husband who could claim that he "had sexual relations only in the hope of conception" (*De bono con.* 13). And so he has a prescription: With lust one has to distinguish between "feeling" and "seeking." "Distinguish these two clearly," he admonishes. Physical sensation is good, physical desire is a bad impulse. Thus intercourse is good when it takes place with the right intention (meaning, a child). But it is a sin when the spouses surrender to lust (*Against Julian* 4, 29).

After advising this sort of marital schizophrenia in his last book, interrupted by death, Augustine cut short his life work. But for pious married couples a problem now began that could never be solved and that revived in every Augustinian renaissance, for example in Jansenism. The forty-eight-year-old Louis XIV once complained to the confessor of his second wife, Madame de Maintenon, about her lack of enthusiasm during the marital act. Whereupon the confessor, Monsieur Godet des Marais, bishop of Chartres, pointed out to her: "What a grace it is to do out of pure virtue what so many women do without merit, because they perform it with passion." The person who feels nothing at all is the most deserving in the eyes of God.

Augustine found in Paul, as he thought, proof that seeking pleasure in sex is a sin. Paul seems to be paying his respects to all celibates in the principle supposedly derived from him, "It is good for a man not to touch a woman: (1 Cor. 7:1). This thesis, actually advanced by the Corinthians and cited at the beginning of Paul's response, has with few exceptions been misread to this day. Paul then says, "I say this by way of concession [= I leave it up to you], not of command." But Augustine (1 Cor. 7:6) translates this, "I say this by way of pardon" (*venia*), and makes it refer to the resumption of sexual relations.

Again and again he argues in his writings that intercourse in marriage obtains forgiveness from the apostle. "By granting pardon, the apostle is evidently denouncing it as a fault" (*De peccato originali* 42). Or, "Where pardon has to be granted, there are no reasons for denying the presence of guilt" (*De nuptius et concupiscentia* 1, 14). And in his very last work, "Against Julian," he says, "The apostle would not grant pardon, if he did not acknowledge that there was a sin here" (*Against Julian* 4, 29).

But intercourse for procreation is guiltless even for Augustine, and so the pardon for guilt from intercourse can refer only to sex that is engaged in not out of "lust for generation" but "lust for lust" (*De nuptiis et concupiscentia* 1, 14). Naturally, Augustine reminds us, we should not overstrain the apostle's readiness to forgive. Even in married sex one can incur mortal sin by an excess of sensual pleasure. Such a lack of self-control is not covered by the apostle's willingness to concede and forgive, because in that way one becomes "an adulterer" with one's own wife (*Against Julian* 2, 7, 20). This theme of lust-inspired marital sex as a mortal sin would continue to fascinate and preoccupy the popes and theologians all the way into our century, as we see, for example, in the condemnation of the book by Van de Velde.

Despite the effect of sensual pleasure, which because of original sin has acquired such an uncanny power over humans, under certain circumstances married sex *is* pardonable, hence only a venial sin, and indeed is sinless if the couple wants children. This is due, says Augustine, to the "three goods of marriage," which from the time of early Scholasticism on have been called the "goods that excuse marriage." These three "goods" make intercourse tolerable, justify it morally, compensate for the evil of lust, and offset it, provided that the lust is not excessive.

The three goods are children, fidelity, and the indissolubility of marriage. "The good of marriage is threefold. Fidelity, offspring, and the sacrament. Fidelity does not permit sexual relations to take place outside the marriage. The good of offspring causes the children to be accepted with love, to be well nourished and brought up conscientiously. The sacrament prevents the marriage from being dissolved and a dismissed wife from remarrying" (*De genesi ad litteram* 9, 7). With the help of these compensating factors, Augustine says, marital sex is either excused (entirely free from guilt) or pardonable (a venial sin). Intercourse is guilt-free only when it takes place for procreation. Intercourse out of lust, since it occurs within marriage, is pardoned by the Apostle because of the good of fidelity and is thus not free from guilt, but only pardonable.

There is still one question left, because it takes two people to have intercourse. Perhaps one person is having sex out of lust, the other is not. Augustine has thought of this too, and drawn a distinction: Whoever *demands* sex from the other (except for the sake of procreation) commits a pardonable, that is venial, sin. But whoever *performs* intercourse at the request of the other, but personally does not feel lust or seek it, is excused. He or she does not need the apostolic pardon. Somewhat inconsistently with his thesis of procreation as the only legitimate goal of marriage, Augustine also rates the act of *debitum reddere* (marital sex on demand) as guilt-free: "Duty entails no guilt, but demanding duty above and beyond the need for procreation is a venial sin" (*Sermons* 51, 13). Spouses have a strict obligation not to deny their partner, lest he or she fall into a still more serious sin. Thus Augustine does not deny the Pauline character of marriage as a "remedy for concupiscence."

Quite in line with Augustine, the bishop of Chartres advised Madame de Maintenon, after Louis XIV complained about her lack of lust in bed: "One is obliged to serve as a refuge for the weakness of the man, who would otherwise go astray." The fact that, thanks to her frigidity, she felt nothing only heightened her merit.

It is hardly necessary to add that Augustine rejected intercourse with a woman who was menstruating or pregnant or postmenopausal: "True marital chastity avoids intercourse with a menstruating or pregnant woman; indeed it refrains from any marital encounter where there is no longer any prospect of conception, as with older people" (*Against Julian* 3, 21).

The one-sided view of marriage as an institution for breeding, the total elimination of the personal component in sex, and the effort to repress sexuality lead Augustine to such statements as these: The Christian's eye must always be trained on eternal life. The more he loves what is immortal, the more vehemently he will hate what is transitory. That is why the Christian husband detests the mortal connection and turns to what "can enter with us into that kingdom." To this end he aims to form his wife. "He loves the fact that she is human, and hates the fact that she is a woman" (*On the Sermon on the Mount* 1, 15 and 1, 41).

Given the stress he places on procreation, it comes as no surprise that Augustine finds polygamy better than loving and desiring just one woman for her own sake. "I rather approve using the fertility of many women for an unselfish purpose than the flesh of a single woman for her own sake. For in the first case one is striving for a benefit that was appropriate for those Old Testament times, while in the second case we are dealing merely with the satisfaction of a lust aimed at earthly pleasure. That is why those to whom the apostle in 1 Cor. 7:6 forgivingly concedes carnal intercourse with a woman stand on a lower level of the way to God than those who despite their many wives have no other goal in their marital cohabitation than the begetting of children" (*De doctrina christiana* 3, 18).

Of course, Augustine does not intend to introduce polygamy, which he restricts to Old Testament times. In his view polygamy does not contradict the order of creation, but polyandry does. For, he believes, wives are their husband's servants. "Now a slave never has several masters, but a master does have several slaves. Thus we have never heard that the holy women served several living husbands, but we do read that many holy women served one husband . . . That is not contrary to the nature of marriage" (*De bono conjugali* 17, 20). In the contract for civil marriage in the Roman law of Augustine's day there was no passage about the subordination of the wife to the husband (cf. Kari Elisabeth Børresen, *Subordination et équivalence*, 1968, pp. 82–83). By contrast Augustine points to the Christian marriage contract, undersigned by the bishop, which stresses the subordination of the wife to the husband. *Sermons*. 37, 6, 7, and 332, 4). Augustine also has a shining example handy for Christian slave/wives, namely his mother, Monica. He writes: "When she reached marriageable age she was given to a husband whom she served as her master . . . She endured his infidelities and never had a single quarrel with him on this subject. . . . There were many wives with husbands much milder than hers who went about with their faces disfigured by the marks of blows, and when they got together to talk they would often complain of the way their husbands behaved. But my mother, speaking lightly but giving serious advice, used to say that the fault was in their tongues. They had all heard, she said, the marriage contract read out to them and from that day they ought to regard it as a legal instrument by which they were made servants; so they should remember their station and not set themselves up against their masters." Augustine goes on to say that the fact that Monica was never beaten by her irascible husband Patricius (Augustine's father) persuaded a number of wives to follow her example. "Those who followed it found that they had every reason to thank her for it; those who did not were still bullied and kept under" (*Confessions* IX, 9, translated by Rex Warner). The claim that Christianity meant liberation for women is as false as it is long-lived.

For Augustine hatred of pleasure was still more important than his emphasis on the procreative purpose of every conjugal act. This can be seen in the fact that he pleads for so-called Josephite marriage, that is, total continence in marriage, as reflected in many lives of the saints. He writes to a woman who lived with her husband in total abstinence, "Your husband does not cease to be your spouse because of the joint abstinence from carnal relations. You will rather remain all the more devout as spouses, the more devoutly you keep this resolution" (*Epistles* 262, 4).

In Augustine's eyes virginity is morally higher than marriage with sex, and again marriage without sex is higher than marriage with it. The husband and wife reach greater heights of moral development by jointly renouncing intercourse. "Anyone in our day who has arrived at perfect love of God surely has no more than spiritual desire for children" (*De bono conjugali* 3, 3; 8, 9; 17, 9).

Owing to the spirit-killing power of sexual pleasure Augustine calls for continence on Sundays and feast days, in Lent and the catechumenate (preparation period for baptism), and in general at prayer time. Prayer pleases God better, he says, when it is spiritual, that is when a person is free from carnal desires (*De fide et operibus* 6, 8). Augustine was not alone in making such demands. His contemporary Jerome writes: "The apostle says, one cannot pray during the time that one has relations with one's wife. Thus if prayer is made impossible by coitus, then this is certainly still more true for what is more than prayer, the reception of the body of Christ . . . I speak to the consciences of those who communicate on the same day that they have marital relations" (*Epistles* 48, 15). Origen (d. 253) too forbade sex before communion: "He comes thoughtlessly into the sanctuary of the church who comes there after the conjugal act and its impurity, so as presumptuously to receive the Eucharistic bread. He dishonors and desecrates what is holy" (*Select. in Ezech.* ch. 7).

The Apostle Paul's directive is turned upside down, since it begins with the principle, "Do not refuse one another." He goes on to speak of mutual agreement by the husband and wife. Voluntary suspension of intercourse in order to pray slowly turned into a strictly regulated prohibition against sex during the time before and after prayer, all of Sundays and feast days, the whole of Lent, and otherwise too as far as possible. We have yet to come to the central Christian problem of what happens when one wishes to beget a child on Sunday.

VII

THE EVOLUTION OF CELIBACY

Catholic celibacy has pagan roots. The prescriptions of celibate purity derive from the Stone Age of religious consciousness. They grew out of the awe at the unapproachably numinous or the fearsome divine. In the Gospel of God's love they make no sense.

Many pagan priests castrated themselves so that they would not be stained by sex, but be pure and holy mediators between the people and the god or goddess. Cultic castration may be found, for example, in Babylon, in Lebanon, in Phoenicia, on Cyprus, in Syria, in the cult of Artemis in Ephesus, in the cult of Osiris in Egypt, and in the Phrygian cult of Attis and Cybele, which was widely disseminated in both East and West (cf. Peter Browe, *Zur Geschichte der Entmannung*, 1936, pp. 13 ff.)

In his book, *Das Kreuz mit der Kirche: Eine Sexualgeschichte des Christentums* (1974), Karlheinz Deschner shows how in keeping with age-old belief closeness to the gods requires sexual abstinence. According to Demosthenes (d. 322 B.C.) "a certain number of days of abstinence were to be observed" before every temple visit and before touching the sacred vessels. Tibullus (d. ca. 17 B.C.) writes: "I bid you stay far away, far from the altar, everyone who has tasted the joys of love in the previous night" (*Elegies* II, 11). Likewise Plutarch (d. ca. 120) warns against going to the temple and attending a sacrifice after a sexual contact. There should at least be one intervening night's sleep (*Quaest. conv.* 3, 6). The temple inscription in Pergamum calls for one day of purification after marital sex, two days after extramarital sex.

The Church was solicitous about echoes of celibacy from the ancient world, treating them like reminiscences of a long line of noblemen. Nor was it shy about reinterpreting them to suit its needs. In 1936 Pius XI wrote concerning celibacy: "Even the old Romans had recognized the fittingness of such behavior. One of their laws, which runs, 'One should come chaste to the gods,' was cited by the greatest of their orators" (from the encyclical, *The Catholic Priesthood,* authentic German translation, 1936, p. 18). Thus the Pope had no hesitation in interpreting Cicero, whom he quotes here (*De legibus* bk. 2, ch. 8) as a preacher of celibacy. He does so while equating the ritual purity of the Romans with celibacy, and accordingly identifying marriage with impurity.

It was against the background of hostility to sex and marriage on the part of leading theologians and, in particular, the popes that compulsory celibacy, as we now know it, was foisted upon the Catholic priesthood. The beginnings of the celibate attack on the body can be found as early as the first centuries of our era, but this development was not fixed in law until late in the day, and then in two stages: first in 1139 when Pope Innocent II declared clerical ordination a diriment (i.e., "destructive") impediment. That meant that marriage and ordination were mutually exclusive; every marriage by a priest after this date was invalid. The Church now had an instrument in hand to stop priests from marrying; but later on it got yet another instrument of control: at the Council of Trent (1545–63) a mandatory formal ceremony was introduced for contracting marriage. Up until then marriage had no required forms, that is, people could contract secret, but valid marriages without priests or witnesses. Stipulating that a marriage take place before the local pastor and witnesses prevented men who had been secretly married from becoming priests. Thus after 1139 it was impossible for priests to marry, and after Trent it was impossible for married men to become priests. After the age when priests were allowed to marry came the age of clandestine and persecuted priestly marriages. After Trent concubinage was the only way out, a sad but not infrequently chosen alternative. The history of celibacy was a troubled one, not so much for those who initiated it and pushed it through as for those whom it personally affected. For many of these people, especially women, it meant disaster.

The champion of celibacy, Pope Gregory VII (d. 1085), spoke of "sundering the commerce between the clergy and women through an eternal anathema" (Carl Joseph Hefele, *Konzilienge-*

schichte, vol. 5, p. 22). But long before Gregory this idea had been voiced and found a hearing in the Church. The first important official step can be found in Canon 33 of the Spanish Synod of Elvira, at the beginning of the fourth century. It declared that "the bishops, priests, and deacons as well as all clerics who attend to the service of the altar are commanded to abstain from conjugal relations with their wives and not to beget any more children. Those who violate this order are to be expelled from the priesthood." This is not yet celibacy in the actual sense, priests were not being asked to forgo marriage, nor did they have to dismiss their wives. But the prohibition of further marital relations for priests was the opening round in a long history of repression.

The demands made by the Synod of Elvira had little significance for the Church as a whole. It should immediately be added that the Eastern Church did not join in the swing toward compulsory celibacy, and this development in the West was not the least important factor in prompting the great Schism between the Eastern and Western churches. But Elvira was not the last word. There followed other synods and Church Fathers and, most of all, popes, who increasingly sought to impose celibacy. At the first General Council of Nicaea (325), however, the attempt to force upon the entire Church laws such as those of Elvira went for naught.

It is assumed that the Spanish bishop Hosius of Cordova, who had already led the way in Elvira, was the one who proposed the ban on conjugal relations for priests in Nicaea too. According to an account by the historian Socrates (d. c. 450), the Egyptian bishop Paphnutius, himself unmarried, a man of great prestige, who had lost an eye and a knee tendon in Diocletian's persecution, arose and said that no such heavy yoke should be laid upon the clergy, for marriage was an honorable thing. It was enough if those who entered the clergy unmarried should not get married afterward, but no priest should be separated from the woman whom he had married when he was still a layman. The speech by Paphnutius may be historical or, as some, primarily Western advocates of celibacy, later argued, legendary. That is beside the point, since in either case it is clear that the East followed a different practice, and that there was contemporary resistance to celibacy.

The synods that followed did not lay down a consistent policy. The Synod of Gangra (340/41) took married priests under its wing and stood up against those who refused to take part in masses celebrated by married priests. The so-called Apostolic Constitutions (ca. 380) excommunicated any priest or bishop who repudiated his wife under the pretense of piety. But, on the other hand, the Council of Carthage from the year 390 laid down the same obligation for clerics that Elvira had (can. 2), and a subsequent synod in Carthage eleven years later did the same (can. 4). There were also stricter demands. The Roman Synod of Pope Innocent I (d. 417) from the year 402 stipulated: "Bishops, priests, and deacons must be unmarried" (can. 3). This did not have any consequences in canon law just yet. As before, married men were ordained priests, and later on too many synods, for example the Synod of Arles in 443 (can. 3–4) and the third Synod of Orleans in 538 (can. 2), went no further than calling for marital continence from clerics. Concretely, this meant that, "Priests and deacons are not permitted to share the same bed and the same room with their wives, lest they fall under suspicion of carnal relations" (fourth Synod of Orleans in 541, can. 17). The Synod of Clermont in 535 specified that, "Anyone who is ordained a priest or deacon may not continue to have conjugal relations. He becomes a brother to his erstwhile wife" (can. 12). The Synod of Tours (567) regulated the married life of bishops: "The bishop may look upon his wife only as his sister. Wherever he stays, he must always be surrounded by clerics, and his and his wife's dwelling must be separated from one another, so that the clerics in his service never come into contact with the women serving the bishop's wife" (can. 12). The synod went on to state that: "Since very many archpriests in the country, along with deacons and subdeacons, are under suspicion of continuing relations with their wives, the archpriest should always have a cleric with him who will accompany him everywhere he goes and who must have his bed in the same room with him." This was a system of total surveillance, because "In this connection seven subdeacons, lectors, or laymen can take turns" (can. 19). Thus one ecclesiastical shift replaced another in the supervisor's bed.

The bishop himself was required and permitted to sleep alone. The Synod of Toledo in 633, with St. Isidore of Seville presiding, nonetheless declared: "Since the clergy have caused not a little scandal on account of their way of life, the bishops should have witnesses in their rooms, so that all evil suspicions may be removed from the minds of the laity" (can. 22). On the other hand, the authorities were in a quandary over the bishops. The Synod of Paris decided in 829 that "a priest [is] not permitted to betray the sins of the bishop, because the latter is his superior" (can. 20). Some security could be had in this matter if married priests and their wives lived in separate quarters. The Synod of Lyon in 583 decreed that: "Married clerics may not live together with their wives" (can. 1), a command repeated by the Synod of Toledo in 589 (can. 5).

The Church Fathers in particular entered the lists for celibacy. Cyril of Jerusalem (d. 386) maintained that "a good priest abstains from woman" (*Catecheses* 12, 25). And Jerome wrote against bishops who put up with "pregnant wives of clergymen and children crying in their mothers' arms." In a piece against Vigilantius he charged that, "In the end we are no longer different from the pigs" (ch. 2). Ambrose said of priests who went on having children that they "pray for others with unclean minds as well as unclean bodies" (*On the Duties of the Servants of the Church* II, 249). In North Africa Augustine laid practical stress on the idea of celibacy. When he became bishop of Hippo in 395, he immediately built a monastery. He made all the clergy in the city enter it, and every new candidate for ordination had to bind himself to live in this "clerical cloister" under his supervision.

The crucial factor was the popes' taking up the cause. The first one is Siricius, whom we have already mentioned. In the letter he wrote to Bishop Himerius of Tarragona in 385, Siricius calls the behavior of priests who have sex with their wives a "shame on honorable religion" and a "crime." Such priests were for him "masters of sin," they were "enslaved to lust." In a letter to the bishops of Africa dating from 386 he speaks of "outrage," of "defilement by carnal concupiscence," and applies the words of the Letter to Titus to the priests whom he was attacking: "To the polluted and unbelieving nothing is pure." By the way, either Pope Siricius or his predecessor Pope Damasus (d. 384)—the ascription is uncertain—wrote a letter to the bishops of Gaul enjoining priests to continence vis-à-vis their own wives, and making an admonitory reference to Adam, who was "driven out of Paradise" because of his transgression of the commandment of continence. Pope Damasus (or Siricius) was evidently a partisan of the sexless Eden later rejected by Augustine.

Pope Leo I, the Great (d. 461) was the first to extend the ban on marital intercourse to subdeacons. In a letter to Bishop Athanasius of Thessalonica in 446 he wrote: "While it is permitted for those outside the order of clerics to give themselves to conjugal intimacy and the begetting of children, on the other hand not even the subdeacons are to be allowed carnal marriage, so as to represent the purity of perfect continence, and so even those who have wives should behave as if they did not" Letter 14, ch. 4). On a similar note in a later letter (458 or 459) to Bishop Rusticus of Narbonne, where Leo forbids clerics to dismiss their wives, he nonetheless says: "The law of continence for servants at the altar is the same as for bishops and priests. It was permissible for the latter, when they were laymen or lectors, to marry and beget children. But once they had arrived at the stages mentioned before, that which was formerly allowed to them was allowed no longer. Hence, in order to make their carnal marriage a spiritual one, while they may not dismiss their wives, they must however possess them as if they did not possess them, so that both conjugal love may be preserved and conjugal deeds may stop" (Letter 167, 3).

Pope Gregory I, the Great (d. 604), issued a similar directive in a letter to Bishop Leo of Catana: "May your brotherly spirit watch with all care over those who have just been elevated to this ordination, lest they take the liberty of having relations with their wives, if they have such. But yourself let them know with all severity that everything will be observed just as if it were taking place beneath the eyes of the Apostolic See." Of priests he demanded that from the day of their ordination forward they should "love their wives as if they were sisters and beware of them as if they were enemies" (*Dialogues* IV, 11).

In this context Pope Gregory reports about the exemplary "departure of the soul of a priest from Nursia." The case was related to him by the venerable Abbot Stephanus, "who died not long ago here in Rome." All his life this priest of Nursia had lived up to the motto, "to love his wife like a sister and to flee her like an enemy." Gregory tells us: "That is why this man refused to let his wife do him the smallest service, lest he fall into sin." Having credited this holy man from Nursia with a heroic measure of sanctity far surpassing the perfection normal in clergymen, since the latter gladly permit women to service them in everything and are reluctant to serve themselves, Gregory goes on: "This venerable priest, after having a long life behind him, in the fortieth year after his ordination, was seized by a violent fever and approached his end. When his wife observed how his limbs were collapsing and he lay stretched out as if he were dead, she wished to see whether there was still a breath of life in him, and held her ear to his nose." The exemplary old fellow felt this and cried out: "Woman, go away from me . . . welcome, my lords . . . I am coming, I am coming." And with that he entered into the heavenly men's club of the celibates. Gregory means that the holy apostles (naturally minus their wives) came out to meet this holy priest when he passed away (*Dialogues* IV, 11).

As a result of the West's rigorism on celibacy the world church began to come apart. The break had already been prepared for by events at the first General Council at Nicaea (325); and it grew considerably larger at the Second Trullanum, a synod held in the year 691/692, which took its name from "Trullos," the arched conference hall in the imperial palace in Byzantium. For the Orthodox Church this synod still has crucial importance today and is counted as the Seventh General Council. It was convoked by Emperor Justinian II as an imperial synod. On the question of celibacy the synod took a stance against the Pope, though it also looked for a compromise. Canon 13 reads: "In the Roman Church those who have received the diaconate or the priesthood must promise to stop having relations with their wives. But we allow them to continue their marriages, in accordance with the Apostolic Canons (n. 6). Anyone who aims to split up such marriages will be discharged, and the cleric who dismisses his wife under the pretext of piety will be excommunicated. If he persists, he will be discharged." Canon 48 can be interpreted as a compromise formula vis-à-vis Rome: "If anyone is ordained a bishop, his wife is to go to a rather distant monastery. But the bishop must take care of her. If she be worthy of it, she can also become a deaconess."

As we can see, the notion of the impurity of intercourse, or of the pollution of the priest by marriage, was also alive in Byzantium. But it had milder consequences than with the popes. So it is no wonder that Pope Sergius I would not sign the resolutions that had been signed by the Emperor and 211 patriarchs and bishops or representatives of the bishops. He said he would rather die. Serious complications ensued, until almost two hundred years later Pope John VIII (d. 882) recognized the decisions of the council with an elastic formula: He said he accepted those canons of Trullanum II that "did not contradict the true faith, good morals, and the decrees of Rome" (Hefele, III, pp. 316–17). In this way he let it be known that in his eyes conjugal relations on the part of priests contradicted all three. To this day the Orthodox Church bases its practice in this matter on the resolutions of Trullanum. Priests are allowed to marry before ordination and to remain married afterward. Only for bishops has there been any change: to avoid the expulsion of wives only monks are appointed bishops.

In the West, by contrast, the position sketched out at the Spanish Synod of Elvira had only hardened. In Germany Boniface (d. 754), the so-called apostle of the Germans, considered the struggle against the married clergy of his time as his chief task. Just how harshly St. Boniface pursued his goal can be seen by the penalties assessed "lascivious" priests, monks, and nuns, at the first German Council, which he convoked in 742. A guilty priest was to "remain two years in prison, before which he is to be publicly flogged and after which the bishop may repeat the punishment." Monks and nuns were "to be taken to prison after the third beating to do penance there till a year runs its course." At the same time the nuns were "to have all the hair shaved off their heads" (*Sämtliche Schriften des hl. Bonifatius,* 1859, vol. 2, p. 7). Despite the rigorous treatment from the Church around the year 1000 the majority of clerics seem to have been married.

With Pope Leo IX (d. 1054) the so-called Gregorian Reform began, named after Gregory VII (d. 1085). Reform movements in the Catholic Church always mean, apart from the strengthening of papal power, the repression of women and the campaign for celibacy. At a Roman synod Pope Leo IX had the wives of priests enslaved for the Lateran palace (cf. Kempf, in Jedin, *Handbuch der Kirchengeschichte,* vol. III/I, 1966, pp. 407ff.). It was his legate, Cardinal Humbert, who made the definitive break with the East. It is no accident that the great Schism between the Eastern and Western churches took place at the time of the Gregorian Reform, because the issue of priestly marriage played a decisive role in this reform. Cardinal Humbert, who led the papal delegation to Byzantium and on July 16, 1054, pronounced the anathema over the Eastern Church, described the difference between the two churches on this point as follows: "Young husbands, just now exhausted from carnal lust, serve at the altar. And immediately afterward they again embrace their wives with hands that have been hallowed by the immaculate Body of Christ. That is not the mark of a true faith, but an invention of Satan." In the Latin Church, said the cardinal, only those who promised continence were ordained to the priesthood (C. Will, *Acta et scripta quae de controversiis ecclesiae graecae et latinae,* 1861, p. 126).

Patriarch Petros of Antioch reacted to the prescription of celibacy in the Western church with irony. The Latins, he said, must have lost the authentic documents of the Council of Nicaea when Rome was occupied by the Vandals. He too defended the married clergy of his patriarchate (Georg Denzler, *Das Papsttum und der Amtszölibat,* vol. 1, 1973, 54).

Another spokesman for the Gregorian Reform was the preacher

of penance and opponent of women Peter Damiani (d. 1072). He thought that since Christ was born of a virgin, he also had to be served by virginal souls in the celebration of the Eucharist. Only virginal hands should be allowed to touch the body of the Lord (*De dignitate sacerdotii*). As for the uncomfortable fact that Peter, the first pope, was married, the pious zealot for celibacy replied that "Peter washed away the filth of marriage with the blood of his martyrdom" (*De perfectione monachorum*).

The most relentless combatant for celibacy was Gregory VII (d. 1085). In those days the canon law allowed a priest to enter into a valid marriage even after his ordination, but in so doing he lost his clerical office. But this regulation was in most places mere theory, because many priests had both a wife and a clerical post. In not a few regions this was the general practice. In a letter to Bishop Bernold of Constance Gregory made it clear what he thought of priestly marriage: He called it a "crime of fornication." He called upon the people to boycott married priests, and forbade the laity under pain of excommunication to participate in masses or any church services at all held by them. To Gregory priestly marriage was concubinage.

Among the priests in question Gregory aroused open resistance. Lambert of Hersfeld reports that not a few of them actually held the Pope to be a heretic who had forgotten the words of Christ ("Not all men can receive this saying") and the apostle ("But if they cannot exercise self-control they should marry"). He was trying to force human beings to live like angels. And while he was flying in the face of the ordinary course of nature, he was only promoting fornication. If he persisted in his approach, they would prefer to give up the priesthood than marriage, and then he might see where to get angels to serve the Church (Hefele, V, 23–24). And Sigebert of Gembloux wrote: "Many have seen in the ban on attending the mass of a married priest an open contradiction to the teaching of the Fathers. This has led to such a great scandal that the Church has never been split by a greater schism. Only a few observe continence" (ibid., 24).

Archbishop Siegfried of Mainz took the Pope's lead, but only with great hesitation (ibid., 25–26). He admonished his clergy to do "(voluntarily)" what they had to do, namely renounce either marriage or the priesthood, and assured them at the same time that the Pope was forcing him to take action in this way. The indignation of the priests was so great that some called for the deposition or, in a handful of cases, even the assassination of the archbishop, so as to discourage his successor from similar assaults on their marriages. The archbishop sent messengers to Rome requesting the Pope to be less rigorous. But his plea was destined to go unheard. At the Synod of Mainz held in 1075 Bishop Heinrich of Chur appeared as the Pope's plenipotentiary and ordered the archbishop to force his clerics to give up either their marriage or their office. Once again the protest was so furious that Bishop Heinrich went no further on the matter. There were similar protests in Passau against Bishop Altmann, who called priestly marriage a "vice" for which the penalty was eternal damnation (ibid., 27). The Bishop even became the target of physical attacks.

Bishop Otto of Constance did the exact opposite of what the Pope commanded: Not only did he allow married priests to remain married, he gave permission for unmarried priests to get married. The Pope wrote an encyclical in which he demanded that all priests and lay people in Germany cease obeying bishops unfavorable to celibacy. In 1078 the Pope placed under anathema a letter of St. Ulrich of Augsburg that spoke out in favor of marriage for priests. (ibid., 121).

There were also protests in other countries, for example at the Synod of Paris in 1074. Almost all the bishops, abbots, and other clerics felt the Pope was in the wrong; and when Abbot Galter of St. Martin at Pointoise declared that the flock must follow the shepherd, there was an uproar. The priests spat on and beat the abbot, then threw him out (ibid., 28). And Archbishop John of Rouen, who held a synod in 1074 and threatened the married priests with excommunication, was driven out of the church with a hail of stones. Under his successor, Goisfred of Rouen, fist-fights broke out in church over the question of celibacy during the synod of 1119.

The wives in question bore the brunt of all this, as can be

seen from the following facts: As early as 1089 Pope Urban II, a successor to Pope Gregory VII, had stipulated at the Synod of Melfi that when a subdeacon was unwilling to be separated from his wife, "the prince may enslave his wife" (*Decretum Gratiani*, pars II, dist. XXXII, c. 10; Hefele, V, 175). In 1099 Archbishop Manasse II of Rheims granted permission to the Count of Flanders to imprison the wives of clerics (Hefele, V, 231). A London synod organized in 1108 by the famous Anselm of Canterbury, which attempted to impose celibacy with might and main, declared that the wives of priests were the property of the bishop (can. 10).

Around this time the popes had gotten fixed in their heads the notion that the marriage of a priest was simply invalid, although this idea ran counter to prevailing canon law. In 1130 Pope Innocent II (d. 1143) declared at the Synod of Clermont that, "Since priests are supposed to be God's temples, vessels of the Lord and sanctuaries of the Holy Spirit . . . it offends their dignity to lie in the conjugal bed and live in impurity" (Mansi, *Sacr. conc. collectio* 21, 438). On the basis of such thinking wives were considered merely concubines who had no rights.

The crucial legal step in this struggle was taken by Innocent II at the Second Lateran Council in 1139. Here the marriage of priests was no longer simply forbidden, but it was officially announced that marriages contracted after ordination were invalid. In the eyes of the Church a priest was incapable of marriage. Those who had gotten married after being ordained had to be separated. This was justified by saying that, "In this way the purity that is pleasing to God may spread among ecclesiastical persons and the ranks of the ordained." In other cases marriage in the Catholic Church was indissoluble, but in the interest of priestly "purity" valid marriages were now declared invalid after the fact and the partners were separated.

From 1139 on married men were no longer ordained as priests, insofar as the Church knew they were married. This, however, was not always the case before 1563 (when a formal wedding ceremony was made obligatory). Thus until 1563 there were still, from the standpoint of canon law, some validly, if secretly, married priests. But in the Church's terminology the wives of priests had been, since 1139, labeled without distinction as "concubines" or "whores" by Pope Alexander III (d. 1181), or "adulteresses," as Pope Innocent III (d. 1216) calls them. In 1231 the provincial Synod of Rouen ordered the concubines of priests to have their hair cut off before the assembled community at a charge service and then to be severely penalized.

In 1227 in Germany Pope Gregory IX (d. 1241) directed the much-feared Conrad of Marburg (d. 1233) to take effective measures to get the German priests to dismiss their concubines. Conrad, who was the confessor of St. Elisabeth of Thüringin and since 1227 "papal Inquisitor for all of Germany," a tool of papal centralism, visitator (inspector) of clergy, crusade fund raiser, and an important figure in the preparations for the crusade in 1227, was murdered in 1233, a victim of the resistance to the first great persecution of heretics in Germany, which he had set afoot.

For centuries the Danish clergy protested against compulsory celibacy. In Sweden the practice began to be introduced only in the thirteenth century. In Italy the General Synod of Melfi in 1284 attacked those who "have married as minorists [clerics with minor orders] and then after receiving major orders keep their wives, after the Greek fashion." In Spain the Synod of Salamanca in 1335 reinforced the ban against marriage for the higher clergy. But the large number of medieval synods speaking out against the marriage of priests shows just how widespread it was. Official stands against priestly "concubinage" were taken in the synods of Saumur in 1253, of Albi in 1254, of Cologne in 1260, of Vienna in 1267, of Ofen in 1279, of Bourges in 1280, of St. Pölten in 1284, of Würzburg in 1287, of Grado in 1296, of Rouen in 1299, of Pennanfiel (Spain) in 1302, of Cologne in 1310, of Bergamo in 1311, of Notre-Dame-de Pré near Rouen in 1313, of Bologna in 1317, of Valladolid in 1322, of Prague in 1349, 1365, and 1381, of Padua in 1350, of Benevento in 1378, of Palencia in 1388, etc. The list is incomplete and could be extended.

Just how heartless the Church could be in imposing celibacy may be seen from the Synod of Münster in 1280, which forbade priests to take part in the wedding or funeral of their children (can. 2). The same is true of a regulation to be met with in many places, for example in the Synod of Vallodolid in 1322 (can. 7), that priests' wives could not be given a church burial. The Synod of St. Pölten in 1284 arranged for priests to inform against each other.

The Synod of Bremen, held in 1266 under Cardinal Guido, legate for Pope Clement IV, gives an indication of the difficulties prevalent in Germany at this time: "The subdeacons and higher clergy, who take a concubine under the title of wife and join themselves to her under the name of wife, are for ever deprived of all churchly offices. The offspring of such forbidden unions have no claim to their fathers' property, and whatever those fathers leave behind at their death is to be divided between the bishop and the city. The sons of such priests are for ever disgraced. But because some prelates permit impurity for the sake of money, we excommunicate and anathematize all those, clergy and laity, prelates and their subordinates, who openly or secretly protect such fornicators, as well as those who help to prevent the observance of this statute, which must be read out at all diocesan and provincial synods. But those, whether clergy or laity, who bestow their daughters or sisters on clerics in higher orders, either for a supposed marriage or for concubinage, are barred from entering the church" (Hefele, VI, 84).

The resistance to celibacy continued. But events were slowly pressing toward a reform of a rather different sort from Pope Gregory's: the Reformation. Borrowing the name of the Emperor Sigismund, a document called the *Reformatio Sigismundi* that made the rounds at the Council of Basel (1435) made a case for those who wished to do away with celibacy: Priests, it argued, should live as their counterparts in the Orient or Spain, "where the priests have wives." Besides, Christ had issued no prohibition on the marriage of priests, and then too this law had produced more bad results than good ones (Denzler I, 177–78). The document was rejected.

On the other hand, many priests did not obey the rule of celibacy. Although the same canon law applied to Spain as to other parts of the West, priestly marriage seems to have been practically established there. For example, the third general of the Jesuit order, Francisco de Borgia (d. 1572), who was later canonized, a great-grandson of Pope Alexander VI, spent his childhood in the bishop's palace in Saragossa, where his grandparents Don Alonso of Aragon and Doña Anna Urrea lived together quite officially. And the Basque parish priest Pedro Lopez, brother of St. Ignatius Loyola, the founder of the Jesuits, left four children behind when he died—and he was not an exception.

As for the priests in Germany, in 1525 the Mainz canon Karl von Bodmann noted an "almost unbelievable increase of licentiousness among the German clergy since proclamation of the new, so-called Gospel [of Luther]." That Augustinian monk had taken the problem of clerical marriage in hand; and the effect of his assaults on celibacy and monastic vows was so enormous that a wave of marrying swept over the whole clergy, as well as the monks and nuns. The first Reformers, with the exception of Melanchthon (d. 1560), were all priests. Even the famous humanist and priest Erasmus of Rotterdam (d. 1536), the second son of a priest and a physician's daughter, came down on the side of "transforming concubines into wives" (*De conscribendis episcopis* 47).

In 1542 when the papal nuncio Morone called Archbishop Albrecht of Brandenburg's attention to the urgency of celibacy, the archbishop said: "I know that all my priests are living in concubinage. But what should I do to stop it? If I forbid them concubines, they either want to have wives or to become Lutherans" (cf. Morone's letter to Cardinal Farnese, *Monumenta Vaticana,* edited by H. Laemmer, 1861, p. 412). It was to no avail that Pope Paul IV (d. 1559) commissioned Daniele da Volterra to paint clothes on the naked figures in Michelangelo's giant fresco, "The Last Judgment," in the Sistine Chapel. In 1561 the papal nuncio Commendone reported from the court of the Duke of Cleves that according to the duke in his provinces "there were not five priests who are not living in public concubinage" (August Franzen, *Zölibat und Priesterehe,* p. 82).

The delegate of Duke Albrecht of Bavaria, Augustin Baumgartner, reported to the Council of Trent in 1562 that at the last visitation in Bavaria, "of a hundred priests scarcely three or four could be found who did not live in public or secret concubinage or else had not openly gotten married." In this startling speech to the council Baumgartner stressed that most of the Protestant provinces of Germany would have remained true to Rome if Rome had been more accommodating on the incidental question of marriage for priests (*Concilium Tridentinum,* ed. Görresgesellschaft, 1901ff., VIII, 620ff.).

But the Council of Trent, which has remained to this day the essential foundation of Catholic doctrine, not only showed no flexibility on marriage for priests, it brusquely declared: "If anyone says that it is not better and more godly to live in virginity or in the unmarried state than to marry, let him be anathema." Of the three possible conclusions—but who would dare to conclude anything on this point?—that either marriage had a higher value than celibacy in the eyes of God, or that marriage and celibacy were of equal value, or that celibacy had higher value, the celibate Council Fathers opted for the last. This is understandable, because what they had in mind was their own higher value, which they wanted to establish by a doctrinal principle. But when no married person is allowed to suggest that marriage and the unmarried state are equal before God, without being anathematized, then celibate arrogance has become unendurable.

After the Council of Trent ended, in 1564 Emperor Ferdinand wrote a letter to several cardinals, stressing the idea that if it were possible for priests to marry, then almost all of those who had gone over to the "sectarians" (Lutherans) would remain in the Catholic Church (Denzler, II, 225). But nothing changed. In the eyes of celibates the situation, for example in the diocese of Constance, was quite deplorable. In 1576 Nuncio Bartholomäus of Portia wrote to the suffragan bishop of Constance that priestly concubinage in that city was considered neither shameful nor a vice. The clergy did not shrink from going to serve the altar with impure hearts and hands besmirched by the most disgraceful of beds, and from touching the Body of Christ in the presence of the angels. The nuncio said he could not think about such a sacrilege without breaking down in tears (ibid., 242).

Transgressions against celibacy were often punished with fines. In 1521 the bishop of Constance, Hugo von Landenberg, took in about six thousand gulden in fines for the fifteen hundred or so children of priests born each year—or so his Protestant enemies claimed (*Flugschriften aus den ersten Jahren der Reformation* IV, 7, edited by Schottenloher, 1911, 305–6.) And thus the question of married priests played a substantial role in the spread of the Reformation. Many became Protestants for reasons of economy, such as, for example, the Catholic pastor Samuel Frick from Maienfeld, who from 1515 to 1521 was always punctual in paying the charges to his bishop for his seven children, until he became a Protestant (O. Vasella, *Reform und Reformation in der Schweiz,* 1958, p. 51). For Frick as for many others the Reformation meant financial gain. The visitators could tell whether a pastor was Protestant or Catholic by his designation of the woman resident in his house as an *uxor* (wife) or *famula* (maid-servant). These two terms became keys to confessional differentiation. And in this process of denominational formation and discovery of identity the whole difference, at first, sometimes consisted in the simple fact that the Catholic pastor said his wife was the cleaning lady, and the Protestant said his cleaning lady was his wife. The Catholic vice-curate of Heerdt found an ecumenical formula for his situation and in 1569 told the visitators right to their faces that he could not run his wretchedly poor farm without his housekeeper (*famula*) and his four children (August Franzen, *Visitationsprotokolle,* 1960, pp. 109–10).

But even after the Reformation there were still many Catholic priests who considered themselves married. Bishop Philip of Worms wrote in a letter to the Dean of Wimpfen in 1598 that with the exception of the dean "all the clerical persons are afflicted with the disgraceful, scandalous vice of concubinage." A visitation to Osnabrück in 1624/25 disclosed that the great majority of the clergy lived in concubinage. Nonetheless the Church proceeded with brutal violence. In 1651 the Synod of Osnabrück announced: "We shall . . . inspect the houses of those under suspicion night and day and have the shameful persons publicly branded by the hangman. And should the authorities be lax or negligent, they shall be punished by us" (Decr. 26; cf. Deschner, p. 162). Again in the seventeenth century Archbishop Ferdinand of Bavaria had the priests' wives thrown into prison or driven out of the country (Franzen, *Zölibat und Priesterehe*, p. 97). The bishop of Bamberg, Gottfried of Aschhausen, turned to the secular arm, "so that it might thrust its way into the rectories, fetch out the concubines, publicly whip them, and place them under arrest" (Deschner, p. 164).

Luther's Reformation notions on the marriage of priests and religious led to all sorts of turmoil in England, which broke away from Rome as a result of Henry VIII's divorce. As an example of this take the Augustinian nuns from the monastery of Lacock. The monastery was founded in the thirteenth century and was one of the last to be dissolved by Henry VIII in 1539. It was sold to William Sherrington, a gentleman of Henry VIII's royal household, and remains to this day in the possession of the Sherrington family. Henry first sent the choir nuns home, but—still bound to Catholic tradition on this matter—he insisted that no English nun was allowed to marry. The King would not hear of the newfangled Lutheran ideas from Germany. But then, under his son Edward VI, England became more decidedly Protestant. The nuns were allowed to marry, and many of them did. Shortly after this, Mary, Henry's daughter from his first marriage to Catherine of Aragon, came to the throne. Mary was Catholic; and the nuns who had married in the meantime now had to learn that they were living in mortal sin. They were ordered to put back on their habits as quickly as possible; but that was all they could do, because even Mary could not manage to dislodge William Sherrington from the handsome building for which he had spent so much money. Finally, Henry's third royal child, Elizabeth, was crowned queen; and she determined that the nuns were legally married women. We know of only one nun who succeeded in finding her husband and taking up once again the married life that had been interrupted by the Counter-Reformation (cf. Bamber Gascoigne, *Die Christen*, 1981, VII, 14).

The Enlightenment and the French Revolution did not look on celibacy with a friendly eye. The Declaration of the Rights of Man and Citizen proclaimed in 1791 that nobody should be prevented from marrying. Thousands of French priests got married, among them Bishop Talleyrand. Celibacy was revived in France thanks to Napoleon and his concordat with Pius VII in 1801. With the dogmas of the Immaculate Conception in 1854 and papal infallibility in 1870, the nineteenth century would be a century not only of Mariology and the papacy, but also of celibacy. In the twentieth century, with the Lateran treaties and the concordat between the Vatican and the Italian government, the fascists in Italy did their part to impose the idea of celibacy. The Concordat of 1929 states that priests were not to be hired nor remain in government or public service without the permission of the local bishop. And so the calamity of the married priests was officially programmed.

Even in our century the idea that the human body is something negative, something the person close to God should be liberated from, has decisive importance for the Church's celibates. In his encyclical *The Catholic Priesthood,* from the year 1936, Pius XI stresses: "Since God is spirit, it seems appropriate that everyone who consecrates and devotes himself to his spirit should also in a certain sense free himself from his body" (authentic German translation, 1936, p. 18). And in his modesty he further notes: "When someone has an office that in a way towers even over those of the purest spirits that stand before the Lord, is it not then proper that he must live as much as possible like a pure spirit?" (ibid., p. 20). By their will to live as pure spirits, the Church's celibates have gotten rid of their first and most important responsibility, namely, to live as human beings among other human beings.

On October 25, 1969, Paul VI prayed to Mary in the Basilica of Santa Maria Maggiore in Rome: "Teach us what we already know and humbly and believingly confess: to be pure, as you are; to be chaste, that is, true to this powerful and lofty duty, which is our holy celibacy, in these days when so many discuss celibacy and some no longer understand it." Here, to be sure, we have an appeal only to the holy Mary of the Western Church, who stands on the side of the pure and chaste celibates in the struggle against

an impure and unchaste married priesthood. A few degrees of
longitude eastward Mary lacks the same doctrinal and practical
sphere of influence, because of the immemorial custom of marriage for priests.

Polls of candidates for the priesthood as far back as 1974
show that nowadays too celibacy is often rejected by those destined for it, and consequently it is lived or endured only more
or less unwillingly. "52% of the candidates consider it necessary that the obligation of celibacy be lifted in the future and be
left for the individual to decide. Another 27% consider this idea
worth thinking about, 11% consider it unnecessary, and only
9% rate it out of the question" (*Geist und Leben* vol. 49, 1976,
nr. 1, 65). In the case of priests, at least the younger ones, the
results are similar: "On the question of celibacy candidates for
the priesthood think along altogether similar lines as the
younger priests" (ibid.).

Thus we can understand that many priests are turning their
backs on celibacy. One reads estimates for West Germany that
run as high as six thousand priests (*Christenrechte in der Kirche*,
13th circular, 1987, 61). The figures quoted for Italy are eight
thousand, for France also eight thousand, and for the United
States, seventeen thousand, not including men and women who
belong to religious orders (Ursula Goldmann-Posch, *Unheilige
Ehen: Gespräche mit Priesterfrauen*, p. 12). Worldwide, the Association of Catholic Priests and Their Wives (*Vereinigung
katholischer Priester und ihrer Frauen*), which was founded in
Bad Nauheim in 1984, counts eighty thousand married priests.
That would be approximately 20 percent of the Catholic clergy
in the world. "During the tenure of Pope Paul VI (d. 1978)
around 32,000 priests from all over the world were laicized,
that is, relieved of their office and hence from the obligation to
celibacy. Since the accession of John Paul II the Vatican has
issued practically no laicizations at all. In Rome they talk about
a "laicization-jam" . . . In the meantime unofficial figures show
over 10,000 petitions on ice" (ibid., p. 13).

The number of those who wish to abandon celibacy and get
married would surely be greater, if the priests in question did not

to a great extent find themselves facing a vocational void once they leave their office, since they get neither unemployment insurance nor counseling nor help in retraining.

It should be obvious that in comparison with married priests the number of unmarried priests who have sexual relations with women is substantially higher. And evidently the priests themselves have come to the same conclusion on their own. "A recent poll commissioned by the 'Study Group on Celibacy,' surveying 1,500 priests in the archdiocese of Cologne, found that 76% believed that many of the clergy would live with a woman anyway" (ibid., p. 15).

Thus celibacy has become a fiction, and even artificial respiration from the pope will not save the patient. One of the most pathetic attempts at justifying celibacy came in a letter from John Paul II to all priests on Holy Thursday, 1979: "Those who demand a 'laicization' of priestly life and applaud its various manifestations will certainly leave us in the lurch if we succumb to temptation. We shall then cease to be in demand and popular" (translation by the Secretariat of the German Bishops Conference). If the meaning of the celibate way of life is to be "in demand and popular," in other words to make oneself interesting, then it is time to declare this system bankrupt.

VIII

CELIBATES' FEAR OF WOMEN

J*esus was a* friend of women, the first and practically the last friend women had in the Church. He caused a stir by the fact that he had dealings with women, that he was surrounded by "many women" (Lk. 8:3), which for a rabbi and teacher of Jewish law was absolutely inappropriate and unprecedented for his day and age. We all know that he had twelve male disciples, but he also had many female disciples, including society ladies such as Joanna, the wife of a high official under Herod Antipas. Nowadays these women would be called "liberated," because they did not accept traditional female roles, but on the contrary financed Jesus and his group "out of their means" (Lk. 8:3).

In Jesus' day, the general practice was that if a woman so much as spoke with a man on the street, she could be repudiated by her husband without repayment of the marriage portion—roughly equivalent to our alimony. And, conversely, it was considered outrageous for the student of a rabbi (= disciple), not to mention for the rabbi himself, to speak with a woman on the street. These women gathered around Jesus, his female disciples, were not a passive audience. Women were the first to announce the resurrection of Jesus. Luke (24:10) says, "Now it was Mary Magdalene and Joanna and Mary the mother of James and the other women who told this to the apostles." This was not merely private information but a public announcement, since the Greek word for "told" (*apaggellein*) has an official character.

Jesus' openness with women struck even his own disciples as unusual. He asked the Samaritan woman at the well for a drink and conversed with her, although the Jews were on hostile terms with the Samaritans. "Just then his disciples came. They marveled that he was talking with a woman, but none said, 'What do you wish?' or 'Why are you talking with her?' " (Jn. 4:27).

Jesus' followers, however, have not followed him on this point. His openness to women, the respect he showed them, was replaced after his death, on the part of male church officials, by a peculiar mixture of repressed fear, mistrust, and arrogance. A poetic testimony to pious distance to women can be found in the second pseudo-Clementine letter, "To the Virgins," which was presumably composed in the third century but until very late in the modern period went under the name of Pope Clement I (d. 97) and hence was extremely important in clerical education: "With God's help this is what we do: We do not live with virgins and have nothing to do with them. We do not eat and drink with virgins, and where a virgin sleeps there we do not sleep. Women do not wash our feet, nor do they anoint us. And we positively do not sleep where a consecrated virgin is, indeed we do not even stay over night there" (ch. 1). Where the Pseudo-Clement does stay over night, "there may not be any female, neither unmarried girl nor married woman, neither old woman nor one consecrated to God, neither Christian nor pagan maidservant, but only men may be with men" (ch. 2). This pseudo-papal saying is especially curious because its author evidently wanted to outdo Jesus in chastity. He alludes all too clearly to the scene with the sinful woman who washed the feet of Jesus with her tears, then kissed and anointed them. In his celibate purity the writer would never have allowed anything like this to be done to him. With his peculiar standard of chastity the writer affronts Jesus, who ate and drank with women and took no offense at sleeping in a house where women were sleeping too.

The Church's celibates never managed to deal freely and openly with women. Their status and way of life were too firmly based on differentiation from and opposition to marriage and femininity for them not to view women as the negation of their celibate existence and a threat to it. Women have often struck them as the personification of the snares of the devil. The greatest danger in the world, as they see it, lurks in that direction. Chrysostom makes this clear in his *On Priesthood:* "There are in the world a great many situations that weaken the conscientiousness of the soul. First and foremost of these is dealings with women. In his concern for the male sex, the superior may not forget the females, who need greater care precisely because of their ready inclination to sin. In this situation the evil enemy can find many ways to creep in secretly. For the eye of woman touches and disturbs our soul, and not only the eye of the unbridled woman, but that of the decent one as well" (VI, ch. 8). Obviously celibacy cannot transmute men into sexless beings, and hence the "eye of woman" was a continual danger.

Augustine played a crucial role in the relations of celibates with women. This illustrious saint shaped the ideal of Christian piety more than anyone before or after him, and his negative attitude toward women proved especially fatal. We could hardly imagine a greater contrast than the one we find between Jesus' conduct and Augustine's. Possidius, for many years his friend and fellow lodger, reports of him that, "No woman ever set foot inside his house, he never spoke with a woman except in the presence of a third person or outside the parlor. He made no exceptions, not even for his own elder sister and his nieces, all three of them nuns" (*Vita* 26). Such behavior would suggest that the man was psychically disturbed.

Women were a moral danger that grew all the more formidable the more the Church's leadership insisted on compelling priests to be celibate. The phobia about women, as found, say, in Augustine, could be viewed as a grotesque private aberration only so long as such pathological modes of behavior did not have legal consequences in the Church. But they did have consequences, which meant immense injury to women. The Synod of Elvira forbade priests to allow their own daughters in their house, unless they were virgins who had taken vows of chastity. Countless synods forbade women who were not relatives to stay in the houses of clerics, e.g., the fifth Synod of Orleans in 549 declared that there were to be no strange women in the house, "and even women relatives may not be there at unsuitable hours" (Carl Joseph Hefele, *Konziliengeschichte,* III, 3). The Synod of Tours in 567 decreed that the cleric might have in his house "only mother, sister, daughter . . . no nun, no widow, no maidservant." Mâcon in 581 stipulated that "only a grandmother, mother, sister, or niece may, if necessary, live at their house." Toledo in 633 ordered that, "No woman may live in clerics' houses except their mothers, sisters, daughters, and aunts." Rome in 743 allowed "no women except for their own mother or nearest relative." The third Synod of Toledo in 589 established that all clerics who had strange women in their houses who aroused suspicion were to be punished, while the women were to be sold into slavery by the bishop. Similarly, a provincial synod of Seville (ca. 590) directed secular judges to sell the women found in the houses of clerics. The fourth Synod of Toledo (633) repeated the command of the third: If clerics had dealings with strange females, the latter were to be sold, while the clerics were to do penance. The Augsburg Synod of 952 dictated that "suspicious" women in the houses of the clergy were to be driven out with a whip. The synods of Sens in 1269, of Bourges in 1286, and the German National Council in Würzburg in 1287 forbade clerics to have female cooks.

But strange women (i.e., nonrelatives) in the houses of clerics were not the only ones under suspicion. Even the closest family members were mistrusted. Pope Gregory I (d. 604) wrote to bishops (Letter 60) warning them not to live together even with their mothers or sisters. The Synod of Nantes in 658 reports of wicked relationships among priests and their mothers and other relatives, declaring that, "The cleric should not even allow mother, sister, or aunt to live with him in the house, because horrible acts of incest have already taken place." The Reform Synod of Metz in 888 would not allow a cleric's mother or sister in the house with him; and the Synod of Mainz in the same year says in Article 10: "Clerics may have no females whatsoever in their house, since some have gone astray even with their own sisters." Such pronouncements suggest how much misery many people have suffered from the unfortunate practice of coercing priests into celibacy.

The following regulations illustrate how the Church defined woman's role as temptress: The Synod of Paris in 846 forbade any woman to enter where a priest was staying. In 906 Abbot Regino of Prüm in Eifel issued a directive, prompted by the archbishop of Trier, Ratbod, for the supervision of priests: Check and see whether "the priest [has] a cubicle near the church or if there are suspicious little doors thereabouts" (cf. Karlheinz Deschner, *Das Kreuze mit der Kirche: Eine Sexualgeschichte des Christentums*, p. 160). The Synod of Coyaca in 1050, organized by King Ferdinand I, allowed no women to live in the vicinity of the church. The same synod demanded that women in clerics' houses wear black.

The saintly example of Augustine has found imitators in modern times. La Varende, the biographer of Don Bosco, who died in 1888 and was canonized in 1934, writes in 1951 that this famous priest "was so chaste that he would allow himself to be served only by his mother." (If getting such service is the criterion, many sons have the makings of a saint.) And in 1895 Pope John XXIII, then a fourteen-year-old boy, captured the spirit of Augustine when he wrote in his spiritual diary: "At every time . . . I must avoid having dealings, playing, or joking with women—regardless of what condition, age, or degree of kinship." In 1897 he wrote: "Women of every condition, even relatives or saintly persons, I shall meet with respectful reserve and avoid all familiarity, all gatherings and conversation, with them, especially if they are young. I shall also not raise my glance to their faces, remembering what the Holy Spirit teaches: 'Do not look intently at a virgin, lest you stumble and incur penalties for her' " (Translation in *Geistliches Tagebuch,* Herder, 1969, pp. 26, 36. This translation is skewed. Instead of "avoid" the Italian original has "flee, as if from the devil." A similarly misogynistic note fifty years later, written in 1947 by the man who was now Nuncio Roncalli in Paris, has been simply dropped from the German translation.) The Pope, of course, has completely misunderstood the passage from Sirach 9:5 that he quotes. The text means that one should not seduce any girl, so as not to be obliged to pay the father a fine and to marry the girl.

To this day the Church's celibates believe that danger has a female face, and this belief has been taken into account in the formation of priests. This is attested to by the many priests and theology students quoted in *Klerus zwischen Wissenschaft und Seelsorge,* edited by Leo Waltermann (1966). The voices here are unfortunately anonymous; but the Catholic Church does not cultivate free speech. How spineless clerics are trained to show anxious obedience to their masters would constitute a further chapter in the story of priestly education. Some of Waltermann's informants were nonetheless brave enough to say that seminarians were admonished "not to speak with the sisters and girls in the house" (p. 83). A chaplain reports about the "prohibition against saying hello to the girls who dusted the corridors" (p. 146). A pastor writes: "Actually we were left almost entirely without guidance on the subject of celibacy; for the most part we were advised that the best way to conduct ourselves was to run away from women" (p. 158). Another chaplain tells us: "Priestly life: The topic of celibacy was taboo. Upon asking the director whether he didn't want to use the regular instructional hour to say something to us about celibacy, instead of covering the usual subjects (rubrics, the daily order, deportment, the translation of Latin hymns from the breviary), we got the answer: 'What is there to say about it? You're not allowed to get married, and that's it.' Later he did in fact say something: We should be careful with women and . . . even with blessed candles you can burn your fingers" (p. 167).

In maintaining the proper distance from women the Church's celibates are helped by the consciousness of their own spiritual superiority. When they unexpectedly do condescend to compliment women, their words reveal a comic flavor that can be even more dismaying than the usual everyday belittlement. As a bishop of Essen once wrote me (in 1964): "I am glad that you, a wife and mother, can still be so spiritually active."

IX

THE SUPPRESSION OF WOMEN BY CELIBATES

The churchman's favorite proof text is 1 Corinthians 14:34 ("the women should keep silent in the churches"). The Bible is the Word of God, but sometimes the word of men squeezes its way in; and we evidently have one of those cases here. I shall make no effort to soften the edge of this verse; but one counterquestion is in order: How do those who insist on female silence explain the fact that in the same letter (11:5) Paul talks about women openly preaching in church, and treats it as a matter of course? However Paul's remark about silence is to be understood—there has been an infinite variety of attempts to explain it (a later interpolation not from Paul himself, or just refers to "interruptions," and

|

|

hence disorder, since a few verses before [vv. 28 and 30] the same silence is demanded of men too, etc.)—it must not in any event be read in the simpleminded, one-sidedly misogynistic fashion that some churchmen prefer.

This is not to deny that there are passages in Paul and in other New Testament scriptures that treat women as subordinate. The First Letter to Timothy (2:12) makes no bones about it: "I permit no woman to teach or to have authority over men; she is to keep silent." Thus if First Corinthians (14:34) is not enough, commentators cite the Letters to Timothy, regardless of whether Paul wrote them or not. The Bible is the Bible. Or perhaps that's not always quite true. Just before the verses cited from First Timothy we read that "Women should adorn themselves . . . not with braided hair or gold or pearls or costly attire" (v. 9). Nowadays this directive is not interpreted so strictly. Or at least one doesn't hear of women being stopped at the church door and having to deposit their earrings and broaches in the sacristy for safekeeping, or being checked for braids.

For many people the Bible is a kind of supermarket where you pick up whatever you need. For example, in citing the beloved verse, "Wives, be subject to your husbands" (Eph. 5:22), preachers regularly omit the main clause, where we read, "Be subject to one another" (Eph. 5:21), in other words that husbands should likewise subordinate themselves to their wives. This would square things between men and women—but not quite, because a few verses further on the text says, "Let wives be subject in everything to their husbands" (v. 24), with no mention of husbands' returning the favor. This imbalance is unfortunate, and cannot even be justified by the position of women in Jesus' day, since non-Christian women were doing better than this on many points. As Christianity gained ground women lost even the offices that they had in the Pauline dispensation.

At first women were actively involved in the expansion of the young Church. Paul reports (1 Cor. 11:5) that women preached during the liturgy just as men did. He speaks of women's "prophesying," which means an act of official proclamation, best translated as "preaching." Women such as Phoebe were deacons (Rom.

16:1–2). Paul also calls himself the deacon, or minister, of a community (Col. 1:25); and part of the service rendered by the deacons was teaching (Col. 1:28). In the Letter to the Romans (16:3) Prisca is called a "fellow worker in Christ Jesus," a term that for Paul always carries with it a special official authority. Service in the church is characterized in 1 Corinthians 16:16 as "working hard." In Romans 16:12 three women, Tryphaena, Tryphosa, and Persis are described as "working hard in the Lord." And in First Thessalonians (5:12) people who do such work are equated with "those who are over you."

Paul characterizes a woman named Junia as "outstanding among the apostles" (Rom. 16:7). In the time since he wrote Junia has undergone a sex change, and been renamed "Junias." But the old Church knew better: Jerome and Chrysostom, for example, take it for granted that Junia was a woman. Chrysostom writes: "What brilliance and ability this woman must have had to be thought worthy of the title of apostle, indeed to be outstanding among the apostles" (*In epist. ad. Romanos homilia* 31, 12). Up until the late Middle Ages not a single commentator had seen a man's name in Romans 16:7 (cf. B. Brooten in *Frauenbefreiung: Biblische und theologische Argumente,* edited by E. Moltmann-Wendel, 1978, pp. 148–51. But in the Church's continual repression of women this woman's name was taken over by men. The history of Christianity is likewise a history of how women were silenced and deprived of their rights. And if this process no longer goes on in the Christian West, that is not thanks to, but in spite of, the Church, and it certainly has not stopped in the Church itself.

At the root of the defamation of women in the Church lies the notion that women are unclean and, as such, stand in opposition to the holy. In the assessment of clerics, women were second-class human beings. Clement of Alexandria writes: With women "the very consciousness of their own nature must evoke feelings of shame" (*Paedagogus* II, 33, 2). Though Clement does not explain to women the reason for this intrinsic shamefulness, he does make it clear how they should dress: "Women should be completely veiled, except when they are in the house. Veiling their faces assures that they will lure no one into sin. For this is the will of the Logos, that it befits them to be veiled in prayer" (*Paedagogus* III, 79, 4).

The commandment for women to be veiled applied above all to the realm of the sacred. The Apostolic Constitutions (II, 57— composed ca. 380) laid down that women could take Communion only while wearing the veil. In his famous Response to the Bulgarians in 866 Pope Nicholas I also called for women to wear the veil in church. In the sixth century the Church even demanded that women's hands be veiled: "A woman may not approach the Eucharist with bare hands" (Mansi 9, 915). All this was part of the Church's repressive measures against women.

But the command to wear the veil went beyond the realm of the sacred. Invoking a supposed regulation of the Apostle Paul that actually does not speak of veiling at all, Chrysostom bade women "be veiled not only at the time of prayer, but continuously" (Twenty-sixth Homily on 1 Cor. 11:5). "Paul does not say she should be covered, but that she should be veiled, that is, quite carefully draped" (ibid., 11, 6). Chrysostom is wrong and exaggerates here. Paul is not talking about veiling; indeed, he does not even talk about covering, but about a certain women's *hairdo* prescribed for pious Jewish circles, especially the Pharisees. In Paul "with uncovered head" equals "with hair undone," the sign of a loose way of life. "With covered head" equals "with a decent hairdo." But Chrysostom was not the only one to misunderstand Paul: In some countries women must still borrow a hat or a veil before they will be allowed into church.

A heading for 1 Corinthians 11 entitled, "On the Veiling of Women," was added on later to many Bible translations, but this too is false. The point at issue is hairdos. In Jesus' day the hair of respectable Jewish women was first gathered in braids, then a woolen cloth reaching down to the eyes was laid on the head. The braids were arranged on this cloth, then came a frontlet, and then a little covering over the braids to hold them together, and finally on top of it all a hair net, which gave support to the whole affair.

The story is told of the wife of the famous Rabbi Akiba (d. 135) that she sold her braids to pay for her husband's studies. This shows that some women would spend money for a proper coiffure, if nature had not provided them with enough hair of their own (cf. H. L. Strack and P. Billerbeck, *Kommentar zum Neuen Testament aus Talmud und Midrasch,* III, p. 427 ff.) The "woman of the city who was a sinner" (Lk. 7:37) dried Jesus' feet with her hair let down—which corresponded to her dissolute life. By contrast the Talmud reports of a woman whose seven sons became high priests that she never went about with her hair undone, not even at home (Strack and Billerbeck, III, p. 430). Paul argues that if a woman will not do her hair decently, then she might just as well shave it all off (1 Cor. 11:6). That would be completely shameful. In any case he is talking about hair and not veils or hats. Still, he is already confusing questions of fashion with those of decency and morality.

And it must nonetheless be admitted that Paul does demand a proper coiffure from women and wants to maintain patriarchal order in her life. Still he does not go as far as the Church's celibates claim in their repressive interpretation. It is noteworthy that Paul calls for a woman to cover her head (in the sense explained) during prayer *and public preaching.* Chrysostom typically drops the subject of preaching altogether: The process by which the Church silenced women, covered them up as much as possible, and took them out of the public eye was in full swing. The woman preacher disappeared from the ecclesiastical scene. From the Church's standpoint the best woman is the one least talked about, least looked at, and least heard from. The Pauline hairdo regulation was turned into a magic cap, under which one can make women disappear entirely. Of all the time-bound rules of the New Testament the Catholic Church has most carefully preserved and multiplied those that lower the status of women. As for other dated biblical regulations, such as the injunction, "Take no interest from him [your brother] or increase, but fear your God," (Lev. 25:36), diocesan credit unions and papal banks have long since gotten used to suspending them.

Like Chrysostom, Ambrose too ordered women to go veiled in the streets: "Let the woman cover her head, so as to secure her modesty even in public. Her countenance should not be readily offered to the eyes of a young man, and for that reason she should be covered with the marriage veil" (*On Penance* I, ch. 16). The so-called Apostolic Constitutions (ca. 380) likewise call for the veiling of women on the street.

The Church came up with still more commandments and measures to degrade women. At the beginning of the fourth century Canon 81 of the Synod of Elvira stipulated that women could neither write nor receive letters in their own name. Nor were they allowed to cut their hair (Synod of Gangra, fourth century). This ban was aimed at the female adherents of a certain Eustathios of Sebaste (d. after 377), the founder of a rigorously ascetical sect. Hefele writes: "In the First Letter to the Corinthians (11:10) the Apostle Paul views women's long hair, which has been given them as a natural veil, as a sign of their subjection to man. Since many female followers of Eustathios, as the Synod of Gangra informs us, had rejected this subjection and left their husbands, they also gave up the symbol of that condition and stopped wearing their hair long" (I, 760).

The regimentation of women by the Church's celibates extended into private life. The Apostolic Constitutions warn women not to wash too often: "Furthermore she [woman] should not wash all too frequently, not in the afternoon, nor every day. Let the tenth hour be assigned to her as the right time for bathing" (I, 9). Clement of Alexandria was concerned about women's sports. While he wanted places for the young men to exercise ("The men should either take part in wrestling unclothed or play a ball game" (*Paedagogus* III, 50, 1), he said that, "Women too should not be excluded from physical training. They should not be called upon to wrestle and race, but they should be made to practice spinning wool and weaving, and helping with the baking of bread, when necessary. Women should also fetch from the pantry the things we need" (ibid., 49, 2–3).

Chrysostom (d. 407) heaves a pious sigh about women in general: "The whole sex is weak and flighty" (Ninth Homily on 1 Tim. 2:15). But he knows one possibility of redemption for them: "What then, is there no salvation for them? Yes, there is. What kind? Salvation through children" (ibid.) By contrast, Ambrose (d. 397) sees in children and the troubles they bring, as well as in the mother's carnal pleasure that they make manifest, a reason for rejecting motherhood and recommending virginity: "Let a noble wife boast of her numerous brood of children; as the number of her children increase, so do her troubles. She may count up the consolations that her children bring her, but let her also count the griefs. She becomes a mother, but the burdens waste no time in piling up: Before she can press the child to her heart, she wails in her pangs . . . the daughters of this world marry and are given in marriage, but the daughter of the Kingdom of Heaven refrains from all fleshly lust" (*De virginibus* I, ch. 6).

With such a theology in place women are quickly driven out of the realm of the Church and the sacred. It comes as no surprise that the Apostolic Constitutions did not allow women to fill any posts in the Church. (This text was the most comprehensive collection of material on canon law and the liturgy of the fourth century. It claims the apostles for its authors, and because of this attribution it was very influential. Around 1140 it was largely incorporated into the Decree of Gratian and in this form it has continued to be important up until the present): "We do not permit women to exercise the office of teaching in the Church; rather they are simply to pray and listen to the teachers. For our Teacher and Lord Jesus himself sent only the Twelve to us, to teach the people and the gentiles. But he never sent women, although there was no lack of them. For the mother of the Lord was with us, and her sister, and Mary Magdalen, and Mary the mother of James, and Martha and Mary, the sisters of Lazarus, Salome, and several others. If it had been seemly for women, he would have called them himself. But if the husband is the head of the wife, it is not fitting that the rest of the body rule the head" (III, 6). In keeping with the will of their spiritual lords, women in church had to be quiet, so quiet that they could only move their lips without making a sound. "The virgins should silently read the Psalms or read. They should speak only with their lips so that nothing can be heard; 'for I do not allow women to speak in church.' Women should do just this. When they pray they are to move their lips, but their voices should not be heard," as Cyril of Jerusalem (d. 386) says (*Introductory Catechesis,* ch. 14).

The Apostolic Constitutions argue that since the mother of Jesus did not baptize her son, this proves that women are not allowed to baptize or perform other priestly functions. "But if in the previous section we did not allow women to preach, why would anyone wish to go against nature and permit them to do priestly service? For to take priestesses from among the women is an error of pagan godlessness (the pagan priests were evidently less hostile toward women than the Christian ones). Then too, if women were allowed to baptize, the Lord would surely have been baptized by his mother and not by John" (ibid., III, 9). Tertullian (d. after 220) too demands that women not be permitted to teach or to baptize. On the one hand he stresses that baptism may be administered by "anyone," but on the other hand he strenuously forbids women to do so: "One hopes that the mad insolence of women, who have dared to wish to teach, will not go so far as to claim the right to baptize as well" (*On Baptism,* ch. 17).

Women were also not supposed to serve at the altar. The Synod of Laodicea (fourth century) declares (can. 44) "that women are not allowed to approach the altar." The Synod of Nîmes (394) forbade the "priestly service" of women, thereby taking a stand against the Priscillian sect, in which women were priestesses. Similarly, in a letter to the bishops of Lucania in 494 Pope Gelasius (d. 496) treats women's service at the altar as disrespect: "As we have learned to our anger, such a contempt for the divine truths has set in that even women, it has been reported, serve at the holy altars. And everything that is exclusively entrusted to the service of men has been carried out by the sex that has no right to do it." A similar complaint was raised at the Synod of Nantes in 658.

In the East too, at the Persian Synod of Nisibis in 485, Metropolitan Barsumas and his bishops banned women from entering the baptistery and from looking on at baptisms, because this had led to indecency and forbidden marriages. The Synod of Aachen in 789 said that women were not allowed to enter the sanctuary.

The synodal statutes of St. Boniface (d. 754) prohibited women from singing in church. The Reform Synod of Paris in 829 complained about the following abuses: "In some provinces it happens that women press around the altar, touch the holy vessels, hand the clerics the priestly vestments, indeed even dispense the body and blood of the Lord to the people. This is shameful and must not take place . . . No doubt such customs have arisen because of the carelessness and negligence of the bishops."

The second Pseudo-Isidorian Letter, ascribed to Pope Soter (d. 175), which is a forgery (presumably dating from around 850), but which has a solid basis in the repression of women taught by the Church's leaders, states: "It has been reported to the Holy See that consecrated women or nuns among you have been touching the holy vessels and the sacred linen. No one who knows what is right will doubt that this deserves disapproval and blame. Hence we declare on the ground of the authority of the Holy See that you put a stop to all this as soon as possible, and prevent this plague from spreading over all the provinces." Around 1140 the forgery was cited by Gratian as having papal authority, and in this way it received an importance it has had till the present (cf. Ida Raming, *Der Ausschluss der Frau vom priestlichen Amt*, 1973, p. 9). It has contributed to the fact that not only the "plague" of the nuns, but of all women at the altar, has been opposed down through the centuries to the present day.

Even in the twentieth century the ban on women serving at the altar has been maintained. In 1917 it was anchored in the Church's law book, the CIC (Corpus Iuris Canonici). "A female person may not minister. An exception is allowed only if no male person can be had and there is a good reason. But female persons may in no case come up to the altar, and may only give responses from afar" (can. 813 §1). In a nuns' chapel mass may be celebrated with a sister serving: But if an "altar boy" could easily be had, then one commits venial sin in using a woman. It is forbidden under pain of serious sin, however, for the female person who is serving to approach the altar" (H. Jone, *Katholische Moraltheologie*, 1930, p. 444).

In the new code of canon law in force since 1983 progress

has seemingly been made, since Canon 906 says that "the participation of one of the faithful" at the celebration of mass is called for, which apparently ends the ban on women serving at the altar. But Canon 230 §1 makes it clear that the office of "acolyte" may be entrusted only to men. And before then in 1980 Pope John Paul II ordered, in an Instruction with the fine name of "A Priceless Gift," that "Women are not allowed the functions of a mass-server." Thus Rome banged down the gavel, case dismissed.

From Antiquity all the way into modern times women have been forbidden to sing in church choirs. Even in the twentieth century the ban was repeated by Pius X (now canonized), because women were not allowed to have any liturgical function (*Motu proprio de musica sacra,* 1903). In the *Repertorium Rituum* by Philipp Hartmann from the year 1912 we read: "Only men of known piety and probity should be permitted to be members of the church choir, men who show themselves to be worthy of the sacred service. Since the singers in church occupy a liturgical office, women's voices may not be used in church music. Thus if one wishes to use high soprano and alto voices, boys must be enlisted" (p. 360). Not until 1940 was there a turnabout, when in the new edition of the *Repertorium Rituum* by Johannes Kley, the text reads ". . . boys must be enlisted, but now women too are, for the most part, admitted" (p. 403). Pius XII cautiously permitted women's singing, but only "outside the presbyterium or the altar rail" (*Instructio de musica sacra* AAS 48 [1958] 658). But it's not impossible that reformers such as the present Pope will cleanse church choirs of female infiltrators.

In the past the way to block women here was the choir of castrati. In the *Lexikon für Theologie und Kirche* we read: "The castration of boys to keep their soprano or alto voices intact was practiced especially in Italy from the 16th to the 18th century. In contrast to Germany and France in Italy the castrati quickly made their way into the Church. In the Sistine Chapel they came in during the reign of Clement VIII (1592–1605) to replace men singing falsetto in the soprano parts (they were never generally accepted in the alto parts). At the beginning of the 19th century they disappeared from secular music, while at the beginning of the 20th century castrati were still singing in the Sistine Chapel" (VI, 1961, 16). Perhaps, if things go the popes' way, and the way the popes understand the holiness of the liturgy, the castrati may once again be singing by the end of this century.

All in all, considering the repression, defamation, and demonization of women, the whole of church history adds up to one long arbitrary, narrow-minded masculine despotism over the female sex. And this despotism continues today, uninterrupted. The subordination of woman to man has remained a postulate of the theologians throughout the history of the Church; and even in today's male Church it goes on being treated as divinely willed dogma. The male Church has never understood that the reality of the Church is based on the shared humanity of man and woman. The apartheid practiced toward women by the Church's rulers violates justice, much as political apartheid does. The fact that the Church invokes God and Christ in the process does not make things any better; that simply adds blasphemous accents to its unjust procedure. But above all, a merely masculine Church, despite the name that it awards itself, has long since ceased to be a church in the full sense, because out of male arrogance it has renounced a crucial aspect of the catholicity it must live out. It has long ago exchanged its catholicity for a conceited sexism.

This virile Church has degenerated into a vestigial Christianity. The Christian faith has dried up into a celibate creed; and for that reason the spiritual lords of the Church have largely lost their sense of what Christian faith actually is. A typical instance of this is the statement made by Cardinal Hengsbach of Essen on the occasion of an ordination. According to the *Westdeutsche Allgemeine Zeitung* of May 24, 1988, he called the "current spectacular demands for removal of the link between celibacy and the priesthood" a "crisis of faith." Still worse, he described this crisis as the "real religious emergency of the present." Thus a crisis of faith in this view is doubting compulsory celibacy, while faith is clinging to such compulsion. Such prelatic axioms in fact only show blindness to the actual emergency of the present. The pastoral outlook needs to be broadened into a vision of real human emergencies, of the real crisis of faith; and here women—if they were permitted—could be of real service to the gentlemen of the Church.

X

LAY PEOPLE INTO MONKS

W*e now turn from* the process of monasticizing priests, which was legally complete in the West but not always practically successful, back to the laborious and never completed task of "turning lay people into monks" through "bachelor theology" (Friedrich Heer, *Gottes erste Liebe: Die Juden im Spannungsfeld der Geschichte*).

Although at the end of his life Augustine had conceded to the Pelagians a controlled, quasi-joyless pleasure in Paradise, in the period that followed theologians opted for the position that Augustine had taken in his prime: There was no lust in Eden. They constantly emphasized a verse from the Psalms (50:7 [Protestants 51:5]): "Behold, I was brought forth in iniquity, and in sin did my mother conceive me." This verse was used as the source for Augustine's teaching that the pleasure which resonates through every act of generation is the vehicle of original sin. Many of the theologians who came after Augustine condemned sexual pleasure even more than he had. While Augustine had described sex for the purpose of procreation and performing one's marital duty as guilt-free, in a Christmas sermon by Pope Leo the Great (d. 461) we meet for the first time the statement that *all* conjugal intercourse is a sin. Leo praises Mary as an exception—after all, it was Christmas—because she conceived without guilt, "whereas with all other mothers on this earth conception is not without sin" (*Sermons* 22, 3).

The most important theologian of his day, Fulgentius of Ruspe

(d. 533), did not go quite as far as this famous pope. He adheres more strictly to Augustine and his two exceptions from the rule of the sinfulness of married sex. Fulgentius had been converted to the monastic way of life by the writings of Augustine, and later he was appointed a bishop. He fully shared Augustine's views, for example, the notion that in every act of generation the pleasure involved stains the child with original sin, and that hence unbaptized children cannot enter eternal bliss. While he borrows from Augustine without changing him, he improves on the Apostle Paul. Fulgentius says: "It is a great good not to touch any woman" (1 Cor. 7:1). Here, apart from the fact that, like almost all theologians to this day, he puts words into Paul's mouth that actually express the view of the people posing a question to Paul, Fulgentius escalates "it is good" to "it is a great good" (*magnum bonum est*) (*Epistle* I, 6–9, 20.22; *De veritate praedest.* I, 10). The absence of pleasure thus becomes the supreme good of a misdirected Christianity, as Fulgentius admonishes the faithful to strive for this higher form of life.

Pope Gregory the Great (d. 604) marks the end of the period of the "Church Fathers," who occupy a special place in theology. Gregory too strictly follows Augustine and his ideal of paradisiacal marriage: God originally made man in such a way that children were begotten "without the sin of carnal lust" and born without sin, just as earth brings forth its fruits without lust (*In VII Psalm. poenit.*, on Psalm 5 [101], n. 26). Now marital sex is guiltless only when performed with the purpose of procreation. If the couple seek pleasure, however, then "they besmirch the fair form of the conjugal bond through the admixture of lust." Like Augustine, Gregory refers to Paul as saying that such people will be pardoned, because they stay within the framework of marriage. Thus, satisfying one's sexual drive is sinful even in marriage, though, in keeping with 1 Cor. 7:6, this sin finds forgiveness (*Moral.* 32, 29; *Reg. past.* 3, 27).

All these speculations by monk-theologians on the sinfulness (or innocence) of sex need not have disturbed married couples too much, if such ideas had not brought on altogether concrete consequences. First of all, three passages from the Old Testament had an influence on the rules of abstinence. As a preparation for the divine revelation on Sinai Moses demanded that the Israelites abstain for two days from relations with their wives (Ex. 19:14–15). The priest Abhimelech handed over the loaves of the holy bread to the hungry David only when he knew that David and his men had not had intercourse for several days (1 Sam. 21:1–6). Finally, according to Leviticus 15:18, after intercourse married couples were unclean till evening. The Church had to go looking for these three Old Testament passages with the magnifying glass, since Judaism is far from desexualizing married people; but from the fourth century onward Christianity increasingly viewed such desexualization as its most important mission.

During the entire Middle Ages the questions of *when* one was allowed to have intercourse and *when not,* what sort of punishment (along with a diet of bread and water) one had to inflict on oneself and for how long, for having sex at the wrong time, were enormously important. (We can disregard the ban on sex during menstruation and after delivery, since in these cases physicians mistakenly believed that the blood of a menstruating woman or one who has just given birth was poisonous, which makes the prohibitions somewhat understandable.) The subject here is the ban on intercourse at the so-called holy times: on all Sundays, all feast days (of which there were very many), in the forty-day fast before Easter, at least twenty days before Christmas, often twenty or more days before Pentecost as well, three or more days before receiving Communion. That was why people generally took Communion only at the great feasts—Christmas, Easter, and Pentecost—since one had to fast and abstain from sex at such times anyway. The spectrum of abstinence required varied from region to region. But the times of continence always added up to a minimum total of five months. Then there were the individual periods of time out for menstruation, childbirth, and as we shall see, nursing. Many of the faithful complained that there was not a whole lot of time left over.

But the theologians knew how to impose such demands. Pope Gregory the Great, for example, in one of his many miracle stories, recounts the following cautionary tale of divine punishment:

A newly married noblewoman was invited by her mother-in-law to attend the consecration of the Church of St. Sebastian. "On the night before she was overcome by fleshly lust and could not abstain from relations with her husband. Because she feared shame in the sight of men more than God's judgment, she went to church despite her conscientious scruples. Just as the relics of the holy martyr were being carried in, the evil spirit entered her and despite many efforts it could not be driven out for a long time." Finally the saintly Bishop Fortunatus of Todi managed to subdue it (*Dialogues*, I, ch. 10). Pope Gregory's mother-in-law tale was told over and over again by preachers and pious writers for centuries afterward.

Bishop Caesarius of Arles (d. 542) had even worse examples to report in his sermons to the people: "Everyone who cannot abstain before a Sunday or any other feast day will have leprous or epileptic or diabolically possessed children born to him. All the lepers come not from the people with understanding, who observe chastity on feast days, but for the most part from the peasants, who cannot control themselves. If irrational animals come together only at certain proper times, how much more should human beings made in God's image do the same" (Peter Browe, *Beiträge zur Sexualethik des Mittelalters*, p. 48).

In this same sermon, by the way, Caesarius prophesies similar handicaps for children conceived during menstruation. "As often as you come on a feast day into church," he lectures believers, "and wish to receive the sacraments, maintain chastity for several days in advance, so that you can approach God's altar with a peaceful conscience. You should also do this during all of Lent and up until the Sunday after Easter, so that the most holy feast may find you chaste and pure. Whoever is a good Christian will not only observe chastity for several days before Communion, but he will have relations with his wife only out of longing for a child" (Browe, p. 51).

A woman once showed St. Gregory of Tours (d. 594) her blind and crippled child, "and confessed in tears that she had conceived it on a Sunday . . . I told her that this had happened to her because of the sin of violating that Sunday night. Pay heed, you men, it is quite enough for you to indulge your lust on other days. Leave this day undefiled to the praise of God, otherwise the children born to you will be cripples, epileptics, or lepers" (Browe, p. 48). And in his famous letter to the newly converted Bulgarian prince Boris in 866 Pope Nicholas I (d. 867) did not fail to proclaim the good news of continence on all Sundays, either. "If we must abstain from worldly labor on Sundays, how much the more must we be on our guard against fleshly lust and every bodily defilement" (n. 63). Of course, Nicholas also speaks in the letter about refraining from sex during Lent, etc., etc. (n. 99).

For transgressing these laws the penalties imposed by the priests generally varied between twenty to forty days of strict fasting on bread and water. Readers may think that these bans on intercourse were only advice to married couples, that violating them was not a serious sin, which brought drastic penalties along with it. But this is to wipe away a thousand years of tyrannizing married couples and to replace them with later, milder times. Preachers and writers from the Merovingian (500–751) and Carolingian (751–987) periods, Gallican bishops and councils, penitentials (list of sins with a table of penalties), synods, and confessors all agreed that married couples had to abstain from sex, the only questions were for how long and what was the punishment for disobedience. Sometimes the demands were extreme, as in the synodal ordinance of Bishop Ratherius of Verona in 966: In addition to the usual times (all Sundays, etc.) he added all Fridays. A collection of canons from Ireland speaks, in addition, of all Wednesdays and three forty-day periods of fasting in the year (Browe, p. 42).

Needless to say, no weddings could take place during the times of abstinence. "For at this time the bride and groom are not allowed to have relations with each other," explained the Burgundian abbot Henry of Vienne at the end of the fourteenth century (Browe, p. 46). Many episcopal regulations enjoin priests to teach the people about the prohibitions, and to preach about them, especially during Lent. It is clear from many penitentials, for example the Decree of Burchard of Wurms (d. 1025; XIX, ch.

5) that the confessors had to question married people about abstinence. During the visitation the bishop was supposed to ask his clergy, "whether they have taught the faithful on which days the husbands must refrain from relations with their wives," as it says in the penitential of Abbot Regino of Prüm (d. 915). Regino formulates the questions as follows: "Have you engaged in conjugal relations on Sunday? Then you are to do three days of penance . . . Have you sullied yourself with your wife during Lent? Then you are to do a year of penance or give 26 soldi in alms. If you did it while drunk, then you are to do penance for only forty days." The priest must also watch out that the husband stays away from his wife twenty days before Christmas and Pentecost, on all Sundays, and after conception is certain. (Browe, p. 47). In the twelfth century such strict obligations were still in force almost everywhere. Gratian, the father of churchly jurisprudence, incorporated Regino's regulations into his collection of canon law around 1140, thanks to which they enjoyed a long and influential career. St. Elizabeth of Schönau (d. 1165) admonished married couples to practice continence unless they wished to call down God's retribution upon themselves and their children (*Liber viarum Dei,* ch. 13).

There is a letter on this subject that has been quoted countless times since the eighth century: the famous rescript (*Responsum Gregorii*) of Pope Gregory I to Bishop Augustine in England. This document did not have any mollifying influence on the strict regimentation of marital life, on the contrary it only confirmed the notion that every act of sex was a sin. One of the questions, the tenth, from England, that Gregory's letter responded to was: "May a man enter the church or even take communion after marital relations?" Recently, the *Responsum* has been viewed (perhaps unfairly) as a later forgery (composed no earlier than 731). But its impact was nonetheless powerful, since until the twentieth century it was steadfastly quoted as coming from the great Pope Gregory I. His answer declares: "Sexual pleasure can never be without sin. The Psalmist was not born from adultery or fornication, but from a legitimate marriage, and yet he said, 'Behold, I was brought forth in iniquity and in sin did my mother conceive me' (Ps. 50:7 [Protestants 51:5])." Augustine's complicated schizophrenic distinction between feeling pleasure but enduring it (sinless) and seeking pleasure and enjoying it (sinful) is discarded, to the detriment of married couples—if things could get any worse for them after Augustine. The only perfect man, Gregory's rescript teaches, is "the one who manages not to burn amidst the fire." And for that reason, Gregory (or his forger) advises the man from England not to go to church.

The German Albert the Great (d. 1280) thought that Gregory's prohibition against entering the church could be justified in this way: In coitus the mind is stifled under the weight of the flesh (*In IV sent.* d 31 a. 28 soll.). Which makes Albert wonder why purely spiritual sins, which are much more serious, do not incur the ban on churchgoing. He answers that this is because the serious spiritual sins do not paralyze the mind by the rush of sensual pleasure, and they also arouse no feelings of shame. Sexual intercourse, on the other hand, enervates the spirit, and hence a person who has engaged in it should refrain from the contemplation of sacred things (ibid., ad 5).

Back to Gregory's rescript, which prompted Albert the Great to the above profundities. What if the husband had sex only for procreation? Answer: "If the man had relations only for the purpose of begetting children, then he may enter the church." Thus procreation is allowed on Saturday and Sunday. There is only one problem: One has to presuppose that the person continually keeps his mind fixed on procreation and knows how "not to burn amidst the fire." Gregory thought that the man from England should himself decide whether this was the case with him. But that decision was taken from him by the celibate theologians. They determined that he and all other married people were not graced with Gregorian frigidity, and without exception they barred couples from taking Communion after intercourse.

Gregory also goes into the question of how long after the birth of a child a man may resume relations with his wife. We have already seen that the same rule holds for the time right after childbirth as for menstruation (Gregory writes that "God's law punishes with death the man who has commerce with his wife during menstruation"). But Christian theologians, including Gregory, go further. "The husband should abstain from cohabitation until the weaning of the child." Gregory condemns the use of wet nurses: "Among married people an evil custom has become habitual, namely that the women no longer wish to nurse their babies themselves, but hand them over to other women for this purpose. The sole cause of this evil custom seems to be incontinence. Because they refuse to be continent, they wish to withhold the mother's milk from their children." The medical error that intercourse spoils a mother's milk had a major influence on the use of wet nurses all the way into modern times (see the interesting book on this topic by Elisabeth Badinter, *Die Mutterliebe,* 1982).

As for Sundays, feast days, and fasts, steps were taken toward abandoning the rigid old-time scheme by Scholastic theologians from the eleventh to the thirteenth centuries. They shifted the accent from times to motives, with respect to individual acts of intercourse. They distinguished—again with Augustine as their guiding light—between the spouse who demands sex and the one who engages in it on request; and again they asked what motive a spouse had for intercourse. Best of all was the desire to have children, which must not however be equated with joy in the child or heir, but must be joy in a new servant of God. It further depended upon what role pleasure played in intercourse, whether it was borne unwillingly, grudgingly, and with regret, or sought for, exclusively sought for, immoderately sought for, or sought for in an unnatural way. Beyond that, the "very first stirrings" toward the sexual act have to be assessed, what thoughts the individual had at the beginning, in the middle, and at the end of intercourse. In this way theology carved out for itself a rich new field of activity. Since they were predominantly interested in motives, many of these new theologians looked upon violations of forbidden times as *per se* only venial sins.

But belief in the reprehensibleness of intercourse at certain times survived for a long time in episcopal ordinances and sermons, and in the confessional. In the thirteenth century in Lausanne five women had slept with their husbands before the feast of Patrocinium. When they entered the cathedral, they had a kind of epileptic seizure, which did not stop until they confessed their guilt before the people and promised not to do such things before high feasts in the future (*Cartulaire du Chapitre de N.D. de Lausanne; Mémoires et documents publ. par la Soc. d'hist. de la Suisse Romande* I, 6 [1851], 576).

In the case of the great popular preacher Berthold of Regensburg (d. 1272) the differentiation of intercourse according to motive made its way, at least in outline form, into the strict time scheme. In one of his marriage sermons he says: "On the night before holy days of obligation one should keep chaste. Likewise during the whole day being celebrated, until the night time. You women know well that you follow me more than the men do. We often see that women are chaster than men, who want to be free in everything, and with eating and drinking want to have their will, and on account of that they become so free that they would pay no heed to any time. Woman, then you should dissuade him from it as best you can. But if he gets so devilish that he curses and wants to leave you and go to another, and he is serious about this, and you cannot stop him from doing this, before you let him go to another, look, woman, even though it be on the holy night of Christmas or the holy night of Good Friday, then give in with a sad heart. For you are innocent, if only your will is not in it. But all the saints whose time you have not respected will cry out over you at the Last Judgment" (Franz Pfeiffer, *Berthold von Regensburg*, 1862, vol. I, p. 324).

Thus while Berthold of Regensburg in his sermons makes distinctions while passing judgment on the motives for intercourse, in the pastoral directives given to his clergy, Bishop Guilelmus Durandus (d. 1296) indiscriminately forbids intercourse at holy times. The same thing occurs in a decree of the diocesan Synod of Nîmes in 1284 and in a Castilian confessors' guide dating from the thirteenth century (Browe, pp. 76–77). In 1443 St. Bernardine of Siena preached in Padua that it was "swinish irreverence" and a mortal sin when married couples did not abstain from sex for several days before Communion (Browe, pp. 77–78). For proof he cites Gratian. Thus, in contrast with almost all the theologians of his day, Bernardine held these canons to be emphatically binding. And, likewise, in the manual for the clergy of the diocese of Salisbury in 1506 continence before receiving Communion as well as on feast days and during fasts was strictly prescribed for married people—which was again exceptional for the period. It is true that the catechism of the Council of Trent (1566) still issued a general call for abstinence from sex at certain times, while invoking the practice of the past. But this was no longer understood as an obligation, only as an "admonition." The synods after this (of Besançon in 1571, Bourges in 1584, and Würzburg in 1584) only "admonish" the faithful to observe continence, but they no longer lay down any obligation.

Thomas Sanchez (d. 1610) provides a survey of the opinions held by theologians: Some considered it a venial sin to demand sex on the night before receiving Communion; others, though only a few, did not consider taking Communion after intercourse a sin at all. He himself, Sanchez, thought it most appropriate not to take Communion after intercourse, except when relations had occurred for the purpose of procreation. In that case the physical pollution and the sexual pleasure were outweighed by the good of having offspring. The same was true for sex engaged in out of duty or to avoid one's own incontinence. But if one had sex to enjoy the pleasure, then one could not receive Communion on the same day without venial sin. The spiritual enervation caused by intercourse was not an appropriate state for the reception of Communion. Even in this case, to be sure, receiving Communion might not be a sin, if staying away from Communion would attract unpleasant attention (Dominikus Lindner, *Der Usus matrimonii*, p. 222).

The Jansenists, who will be discussed later, take a noticeably harder line. Alphonsus Liguori (d. 1787), who was less strict than the Jansenists on this point, shared the opinion of Thomas Sanchez. In the course of the nineteenth century, sexual relations for the sake of pleasure ceased to be labeled as sinful (provided, of course, no contraception was used), and so receiving

1 4 5

Communion after intercourse came to be considered free from sin. But as late as 1923 in the twentieth edition of the *Treatise on the Sixth Commandment and the Use of Marriage* (*Abhandlung über das 6. Gebot und den Ehegebrauch*) by the authoritative moral theologian H. Noldin (d. 1922), we find an admonition to married couples not to go to Communion after venially sinful intercourse (sinfulness being mostly a question of the percentage of sexual pleasure in the couple's motivation), unless there is an important reason to do so. In the twenty-first edition of Noldin/Schmitt in 1926 this admonition has been dropped. Still in 1929 Dominikus Lindner would write in his book *Der Usus matrimonii:* "Nobody disagrees that refraining from carnal commerce on the day of communion is extremely commendable" (p. 224). And even today there are many women still living who once used to go to confession because they had had sex with their husbands on the day before Communion.

XI

PENITENTIALS AND PUNISHMENT TABLES

I*n the period after* Augustine, opposition to birth control took on a still sharper edge. Caesarius (d. 542), bishop of Arles (the Rome of Gaul), an erstwhile monk, was commissioned by Pope Symmachus (d. 514) to look after "the matter of religion in Gaul and Spain." Caesarius initiated thirteen synods in the sixth century; his influence extended to the bishops of the Ostrogoths and the Franks.

In a letter to all the bishops and priests in his sphere of influence about pressing moral problems he urges his confrères to impart Christian customs to the people. After speaking about abortion as murder, he comes to contraception: "Who could omit to point in warning to the fact that no woman may drink a potion that makes her incapable of conceiving or that impairs the power of nature in her, which is designed by the will of God to be fruitful. As often as she would have been able to conceive or give birth, she will be held accountable for that many murders. And should she not subject herself to a suitable penance, she will be damned to eternal death in hell. If a woman does not wish to have children, let her arrange that piously and conscientiously with her husband, for a Christian woman is unfruitful only by means of chastity" (Letter, among the *Sermones* 1, 12). The handy formula, "So much contraception, so many murders," pleased Caesarius, and he repeated it in two later sermons (44, 2 and 51, 4).

Thus Caesarius lets women choose between Hell after death or penance in this life or, as the Synod of Agde in 506 (can. 37), led by Caesarius himself, defines it, between excommunication and church penance. The latter was something quite different then from what it is now. People enrolled in the "penitential state" were, like monks, obliged to a life of complete renunciation of the world. That meant years of refraining from sex. For this reason the Synod of Agde warned against imposing church penance too readily on young people. Caesarius himself noted in his sermons that young married couples who took penances on themselves should not be bound at all to renounce intercourse, unless they had committed a serious crime that had to be atoned for in this way.

Pope Leo I likewise, in a letter written in 458 to the bishop of Narbonne, had asked that young penitents be allowed to get married and make use of their marital rights (*Epistle ad Rusticum* 13). The councils of Arles in 443 and Orleans in 538 ruled that married persons were permitted to take church penance upon themselves only with the consent of their partner (Peter Browe, *Beirtäge zur Sexualethik des Mittelalters*, p. 44). Because it was so severe, church penance was in general chosen only by old and dying people.

Martin (d. 580), archbishop of Braga in Spain, who had also been a monk before he became a bishop, prescribed ten years of penance for practicing contraception. He equated birth control with infanticide: "When a woman has committed fornication and then killed the child that resulted from it, or when she has tried to have an abortion and to kill what she has conceived, or to take precautions so that she will not conceive, whether she does this in adultery or a legitimate marriage, the earlier canons stipulate that such women could not receive communion until they were on their deathbed. But out of compassion we decide that such women or others who are accessories to their crimes, should do ten years of church penance" (*Capitula Martini* 77).

The regimentation of the sex life of lay people by monk-bishops (Caesarius, Martin) and popes such as Gregory I found expression in a unique literary genre: the penitentials. These books contained catalogues of sins and a list of penances for each one. They show that contraception was classified as an especially grave matter, a mortal sin with no exceptions. The oldest penitentials come from the monasteries of Ireland, where they were composed by the abbots. (Irish monks played a major role in the proselytizing of Europe.) Other widely disseminated penitentials were those of Regino of Prüm (d. 915) and of Bishop Burchard of Worms from 1010. At that time Worms was an important church center, the site of seventeen imperial synods, which met over the years from 764 to 1122.

One text from the penitential of Regino of Prüm, which was later picked up by Burchard of Worms, had an enormous effect on the Church's teaching about birth control, because in the thirteenth century it was made part of canon law. Speaking of the questions that the bishop should ask during his visitation, Regino says: "If anyone (*si aliquis*) in order to satisfy his lust or out of deliberate hatred does any harm to a man or woman, so that he or she does not have children, or if anyone gives them something to drink, so that he cannot beget or she cannot bear, then he shall be considered a murderer." This principle, which was a component part of Catholic canon law until 1917 and which labeled contraception as murder, had a great influence on the dramatization of contraception.

The Church condemned as birth control not only the potions people took, but also various kinds of intercourse in which conception was avoided: coitus interruptus as well as anal and oral sex. The penances for these three forms of intercourse were enormous. The sentences meted out by the individual penitentials vary widely, but one is struck by the fact that anal and oral intercourse (coitus interruptus is mentioned less frequently) were often punished more severely than abortion, indeed more severely than premeditated murder. The authors of these books evidently thought that certain sexual practices were more reprehensible than killing a human being. It is no accident that in its struggle against sin, sometimes only the putative sins from the sexual realm, the Catholic Church to this day displays more commitment than it does against the crimes against human life in war, mass murder, and the death penalty. Rejecting the perversion that the morality of the Christian West has suffered at the hands of such false values, Ernst Bloch wrote bitterly in 1936: "Women with bare arms are not allowed into church, but they let naked Jews dig their own graves."

The Anglo-Saxon penitential (put together between 690 and 710) of Theodore, a Greek monk from St. Paul's hometown of Tarsus, who became the archbishop of Canterbury and is considered the actual organizer of the English church, sets the penalty for oral intercourse at seven or fifteen years or even a lifetime of penance, for abortion three times forty days, and for premeditated murder seven years. The Anglo-Saxon penitential of the Pseudo-Egbert (ca. 800) lays down seven years (or lifelong) penance for oral intercourse, ten years for anal intercourse, seven or ten years for abortion, and seven years for premeditated murder. The *Canones Gregorii* (690–710, also considered the work of Archbishop Theodore) require fifteen years of penance for anal intercourse, seven years for premeditated murder. The Anglo-Saxon penitential of Egbert, archbishop of York (d. 766), punishes anal intercourse with seven years penance, murder with four to five years. The Frankish penitential of St. Hubert (680–780), named after the monastery in the Ardennes where it was discovered, demands ten years of penance for coitus interruptus, likewise ten years for birth control by means of potions, and ten years for premeditated murder. There were also church penances—though considerably milder ones, lasting only days or weeks—for deviating from the "monastic position": The female-superior position was thought to be peculiarly lustful and an obstacle to conception. If the deviation from the prescribed position was regularly used by the couple for birth control, then the penalties were harsh. The penitential of Egbert provided three years of penance for such cases, that of the Pseudo-Theodore (ninth century) one to three years (cf. John T. Noonan, *Contraception*, p. 152ff.).

From the eighth century on confessors were directed to ask expressly about birth control. The most detailed evidence of such questioning comes from the Decree of Burchard of Worms. Burchard instructs confessors to ask the questions "gently and kindly." He has a great many questions, "which concern the women in particular." The key points were abortion and contraception. In the questions posed to the husbands he asks: "Have you coupled with your wife or another woman from behind like dogs? If so, then ten days of penance on bread and water. Have you coupled with your wife during menstruation, then ten days of penance on bread and water. If your wife went to church after having a baby, but before being purified, then she is to do penance for as long a time as she should have stayed away from church. And if you have coupled with her during this time, then you will do twenty days of penance on bread and water. If you have coupled with your wife after the child stirred in her womb or during the forty days before delivery, then you will do twenty days of penance on bread and water. If you coupled with your wife after conception was certain, then you will do ten days' penance on bread and water. If you coupled with your wife on the Lord's Day, then you have to do four days' penance on bread and water. Have you stained yourself with your wife during Lent? Then you have to do forty days' penance on bread and water. If it happened while you were drunk, twenty days' penance on bread and water. You have to keep chaste twenty days before Christmas, on all Sundays, during all fasts that the law ordains, on all feast days of the Apostles, and on all major feast days. If you have not kept this rule, you are to do forty days' penance on bread and water."

The penitentials also forbid intercourse with a pregnant woman and between sterile or older partners. However, intercourse with pregnant women often has no assigned penalty, and sex between sterile persons never does. This is surprising, since Augustine was so vehement about having sex exclusively for procreation. The oldest Irish penitential, that of Finnian (sixth century), forbids intercourse during pregnancy and between sterile individuals, but prescribes no penalty for transgressions. The second Irish penitential book, that of Columban (end of the sixth century), doesn't even mention the subject (cf. Noonan, p. 163ff.).

Perhaps this overly gentle attitude (in papal eyes) of the Irish penitentials is the reason why Pope John IV felt impelled to write to the bishops of Ireland in 640, castigating the "poison of the Pelagian heresy," which "has again revived among you." He refers to Psalm 50:7, "Behold, I was brought forth in iniquity, and in sin did my mother conceive me." (The letter may be found in Bede's *Ecclesiastical History* 2, 19.) Actually, none of the penitentials (the Irish ones were not alone in this) assigned a penalty for desiring pleasure from the sexual act; hence they were following the Pelagians more than Augustine—and that caught the Pope's attention.

While the Irish prescribed no penalty for intercourse with pregnant women, the Frankish penitential of Pseudo-Theodore (ninth century) ordered forty days of penance for intercourse during the last three months of pregnancy. The penitential of the churches of Germany (eleventh century) assigned ten days on bread and water for sex after conception was known, twenty days if it occurred after the first quickening. Some penitentials do no more than forbid intercourse in the last three months of pregnancy. A major factor in such regulations was concern for the embryo. Back in the second century the physician Soranus of Ephesus had maintained that intercourse should cease completely during the first stage of pregnancy, for just as the stomach brings up food when it is shaken, so the womb will eject the embryo. On the other hand, Galen (second century) argued that there could be intercourse in moderation even during the first stage of pregnancy.

The Church Fathers forbade intercourse with a pregnant woman mainly because conception could no longer occur, and so there was no justification for relations. But as time went on, concern for the embryo was increasingly mentioned as the reason for the ban. From the thirteenth century on this was cited as the only reason. Albert the Great (d. 1280) writes that sexual pleasure creates the danger that the uterus may open and the embryo fall out. This danger, he thought, was especially acute in the first four months of pregnancy (*Commentary on the Sentences* 4, 31, 22). Thomas Aquinas (d. 1274) believed that intercourse with a pregnant woman was a mortal sin only when there was a danger of miscarriage (*Commentary on the Sentences* 4, 31, 2, 3). In the centuries that followed, this remained the Church's official teaching.

Intercourse with a menstruating woman was also forbidden. In the Anglo-Saxon penitential of Bede the Venerable (d. 735) and in the *Canones Gregorii* a penalty of forty days is prescribed. Pseudo-Theodore calls for thirty days of penance, and an old Irish penitential (ca. 780) only twenty days. It is not stated whether the authors agreed with Isidore of Seville (d. 636) that conception could not take place during menstruation or with Jerome, who assumed that children conceived then were born with handicaps. As mentioned in the previous chapter, none of the penitentials fails to enjoin the obligation of continence during times of prayer, penance, and religious feasts.

XII

EARLY SCHOLASTICISM, PART I:
MARRIAGE OF THE LASCIVIOUS AND
JOSEPHITE MARRIAGE

Augustine's sexual pessimism, which was for the most part intensified by the *Responsum* of Pope Gregory the Great ("Sensual pleasure can never be without sin"), dominated the eleventh to the thirteenth centuries, the time of Scholasticism, "the Golden Age of theology," as it is called. The zenith of Scholasticism is thought to have been reached in Thomas Aquinas (d. 1274), who to this day ranks with Augustine as the second grand authority on sexual issues. But with Aquinas Christian theology of marriage reached its nadir, setting the stage for the demonization of sex. The blame for the "Witches Bull" (1484) of Pope Innocent VIII, two hundred years after Thomas's death, cannot be laid at his door, but without Aquinas' superstitious belief in sexual intercourse with the devil and his call for the destruction of heretics, that document would not have been conceivable.

The theologians of what is called Early Scholasticism (eleventh to the early thirteenth centuries) distinguish, as Augustine does, between two purposes in marriage: a) the procreation of children in accordance with the command of Genesis, "Be fruitful and multiply," and b) the avoidance of fornication (in keeping with 1 Cor. 7). Like Augustine, the Early Scholastics felt that in pre-Christian times mankind had multiplied enough to complete the number of the saints in heaven. Now, in the post-New Testament period, celibacy, or virginity, was the divinely chosen program.

While Augustine stressed procreation as the purpose of marriage and pushed its so-called remedial character into the background, the Early Scholastics emphasized the latter. For them marriage is now chiefly intended to prevent fornication. But, quite as Augustine would have it, they grant a moral preeminence to reproduction. That is, the remedial feature of marriage runs up against its limits when reproduction is affected or contraception is practiced. In the eyes of these theologians marriage is the hospital for those who because of their weakness cannot handle their proper assignment, virginity. For, as Augustine had shown, the punishment for the Fall struck man "not in the eye or in any other member, but only in the sexual organs, which are supposed to serve reproduction" (William of Champeaux [d. 1121], *sent.*, q. 26).

The Early Scholastics saw in all married people potential fornicators, whose sickness—"consisting in one's inability to refrain from sexual intercourse" (Peter Lombard, IV *sent.* 26, 2)—is, in the final analysis, sexual pleasure, which did not exist in Paradise, as Augustine showed. The sickness couples suffer from finds its remedy and its pardon in marriage. That, too, had been demonstrated by Augustine with his grounds for excusing sex in marriage. The medicine they take is copulation, which must therefore always be at their disposal. Stephen Langton, archbishop of Canterbury (d. 1228), went so far as to demand that conjugal sex be provided even at the risk of one's life: "The wife must rather let herself be killed than her husband sin." And so she must do her marital duty even while in childbed, should she think it "very" likely that her husband will not be able to contain himself (Michael Müller, *Die Lehre des hl. Augustinus von der Paradiesesehe und ihre Auswirkung in der Sexualethik des 12. und 13. Jahrhunderts bis Thomas von Aquin*, p. 173). In such a case the wife is obliged to engage in sex even during Lent and the other periods of continence.

Woman as nurse breaks through the temporal grille with which the theologians had surrounded marital sex. The error committed by celibate theologians in dictating to married couples when they could exercise their rights was slowly replaced by another error. This one was that married people—or actually married men, since male theologians generally think only about men—that married men were like mortally ill patients headed for eternal damnation, unless their nurse-wives sacrificed themselves for them, even risked their lives to fulfill their conjugal duty, to supply the medicine against incontinence at all times. Practically speaking, this meant the sexual enslavement of women.

The notion of women as men's nurses was not always stated explicitly, but it was the prevalent idea in these masculine minds. It did not, however, work the other way around, as we see in a rule laid down by Odo, the chancellor of the University of Paris (d. ca. 1165). Odo says that if it is the woman who demands sex at the holy times, her husband should not grant her wish, but rather "keep her impudence down with fasts and beatings" (*In IV sent.* 32, 3). He does not say anything about the wife beating her husband for *his* untimely requests.

Proof for the fact that the medicine of intercourse cures sexual desire was discovered by William of Auvergne (d. 1249), bishop of Paris. His motto for married couples was, "Flee all physical pleasure," because pleasure hinders the soul's development. In conversations with married people he had learned the happy news "that sometimes young men remain cold with their wives, even when they are beautiful, and almost icy toward other women, even when *they* are beautiful" (*De sacramento matrimonii,* ch. 8 and 9). Around the year 1200 an anonymous theologian made the same joyful discovery. He writes that young men have testified to the real efficacy of the remedy, saying "that they are for all practical purposes cold with their beautiful wives, and almost cold toward others" (Müller, p. 203). While the penitentials sought to cut down human sexual desire by temporal limitation, theologians in the Early Scholastic era were more in favor of homeopathic methods: Marital sex was the remedy for marital sex.

Albert the Great later mentions an objection raised by some theologians: A weakness is not cured by what it desires, but only by the opposite remedy, namely complete continence and strict physical discipline. To this Albert answers that sexual concupiscence lies at too deep a level in humanity, which is stricken with original sin. It is a chronic condition, so that radical asceticism would only do damage to nature (*In IV sent.* d. 26 a. 8). Fortunately the monks did not plan a complete monasticization of married people; they were content to lessen the amount of marital lust.

In the twelfth century theologians fixed the number of sacraments at seven. At this time marriage was one of the sacraments, but it was given a separate classification. In the eyes of the Early Scholastics marriage had an inferior position within the sacraments because of its medicinal function. In his *Sentences,* which was *the* textbook for academic theology all the way up to the sixteenth century, Peter Lombard (d. 1164) writes that there are three kinds of sacraments, 1. those that confer grace, such as the Eucharist and holy orders; 2. those that are a remedy against sin and confer grace, such as baptism; and 3. lastly, marriage, which is a remedy against sin, but confers no grace (IV, 2, 1). The Spanish Dominican Raymund of Peñafort (d. 1275) thought that the first five sacraments were intended for everyone, the sixth, holy orders, was for the perfect, and the seventh, marriage, was for the imperfect (*Raymundiana* 3, 24, 2).

In High Scholasticism (thirteenth century) many theologians did talk about grace with references to the sacrament of marriage, but in the case of Thomas Aquinas, for example, that ended up sounding like this: "Wherever full power is given by God, help to use it rightly is also given. Now since full power in marriage is given to the husband to use his wife for procreation, so too that grace is given him without which he could not do this appropriately (*convenienter*)" (*Summa Theologiae. Suppl.* q. 42 a. 3). What "appropriately" means with regard to sexual relations was defined by pleasure-hating celibates, of which Thomas Aquinas was one, much as some people would like to dispute that nowadays. And so Thomas also writes: Through this grace "concupiscence is suppressed at its root" (*In IV sent.* 26 q. 1 a. 4). Or, as his teacher Albert the Great said: The effect of the "medicinal grace" of marriage is the lessening of concupiscence (ibid., 26 a. 8).

Some theologians today see great progress from the Early Scholastic view that marriage confers no grace, but is only a remedy, by which lust is suppressed to the High Scholastic position that marriage does confer grace, which consists in the suppression of lust. But such progress exists only in the eyes of these religious rhetoricians. They want to see an advance in the work of Thomas

Aquinas, who has remained a great authority to this day, although in reality Thomas only aggravates Augustine's sexual hostility with Aristotle's biological errors and patriarchal assumptions. No Early Scholastic spoke more offensively about the sacramental character of marriage than Thomas, who wrote: "It was necessary to apply a remedy for sexual desire by means of a sacrament. First of all, because through sexual desire not only is the person corrupted, but nature as well; secondly, because sexual desire with its instability paralyzes reason" (*Summa Theologiae III* q. 65 a. 1 ad 5). Given this notion, it goes without saying that Thomas ranks the sacrament of marriage last, "because it has a minimum of spirituality" (ibid., a. 2 ad 1).

The Church had a program of grace, or frigidity, for married people, and to reach this goal even sex itself was brought in as an instrument. This effort, as we have heard, was already bearing fruit, the monasticization of the laity was making progress: Christian husbands had already cooled off toward their own beautiful wives; it was only vis-à-vis alien lovelies that the chilling process had not yet quite succeeded. But coldness toward one's own wife was the most important thing, since the Christian husband is forbidden to commit adultery anyway. His freedom from lust has to be preserved in marriage, which is the emergency option for Christians, and in the final analysis the whole point of marriage is children. But even for the children's sake, the theologians argued, continence is useful and necessary. William of Auvergne (d. 1249) maintained that the most thorough continence possible would lead to a larger number of children and higher quality children, because the "heat" of the sexual act not only contravened the lofty virtue of continence, but also had the disadvantage "that those who burn most with concupiscence have only a few or no children" (*De sacramento matrimonii,* ch. 8). With restraint on the parents' part the children become "bigger, stronger, and in every way more praiseworthy" (ibid., ch. 9). The less passion reigned in marital sex—this was the moral quintessence—the larger would the number of children be, and so much the better would they turn out.

Despite the attempt by the Church's celibates to repress it, pleasure remained and kept turning up in each act of generation. How married couples should deal with this was a problem for which the Franciscan monk Odo Rigaldus (d. 1275) had a helpful model. Odo believed that an even stronger feeling could suppress the sinful pleasure. For example, a horse with an injured hoof could be forced by the rider wearing spurs to trot along without limping. So too a perfect husband could forestall sexual excitement through the right intention and could direct it by the command of reason toward its goal in such a way that the sexual connection would be sinless (*In II sent.* d. 20 q. 6). Naturally, before intercourse one had to be on the lookout lest sexual stirrings come first (these, according to Odo and many others, were sinful). Instead things should take place in this sequence: First of all, the couple should have the intention to procreate. Then the first sexual excitement should be unleashed by this thought. Then with good intentions leading the way all later acts would be a priori oriented toward the right goal. That is why there would be no sin even in the approaches to intercourse, whereas otherwise the first sexual impulses would be sinful, that is, when they first occurred by themselves and were not directed by reason toward procreation or doing one's duty until afterward (ibid., d. 31).

The breakdown of the conjugal act into many individual acts so as to filter out the sinful element properly became the fashion among theologians. Simon of Tournai (d. 1201) said that the act might begin without sin (i.e., without pleasure), but could not be completed without it (*Disp.* 25 q. 1). He owed this idea to his teacher, Abbot Odo of Ourscamp (d. after 1171). Cardinal Robert Courçon, who died as a preacher to the Crusaders before Damietta in 1219, found the sin of intercourse lay rather in the middle: "When anyone knows his wife for the purpose of procreation or to do his duty, then the first and last parts of doing that duty, during which he seeks God, are meritorious. But the middle parts, in which the whole man is mastered by the flesh and becomes wholly carnal, are a venial sin" (*Summa theologiae moralis* c. 128). There were, to be sure, some husbands who were capable of morally rehabilitating even those critical middle sections or the conclusion of the act. William of Auxerre (d. 1231) maintained that, "When a holy man . . . has carnal knowledge of his wife and the pleasure that befalls him in the course if it . . . in no way pleases him, but rather is hateful to him, then such commerce is without sin. This, however, seldom happens." (Müller, p. 185). The Dominican Roland of Cremona (d. 1259) liked this theological discovery so much that he borrowed William's presentation of it (Müller, p. 194).

Anselm of Laon (d. 1117), who has been honored as the "Father of Scholasticism," defended the thesis that the magnitude of the sin is determined by the amount of pleasure (Müller, p. 114).

This gave rise to a controversy among theologians over whether the sin was greater with a beautiful woman or with an ugly one. Petrus Cantor (d. 1197) opined that intercourse with a beautiful woman was a greater sin than with an ugly one, because it gave more delight. Once again, the greater the pleasure, the greater the sin. Accordingly, he sought to downgrade beautiful women in men's eyes, speaking of them as sixteenth-century Spanish ascetical literature would often do: "Consider that the most lovely woman has come into being from a foul-smelling drop of semen, then consider her midpoint, how she is a container of filth; and after that consider her end, when she will be food for worms" (Müller, p. 151).

Alain de Lille (d. ca. 1202) came to a different conclusion in this dispute. He thought that the man who had sex with a beautiful woman sinned less, "because he was more compelled by the sight of her beauty," and "where the compulsion is greater, the sin is slighter." Bazian (d. 1197), a distinguished canonist from Bologna, advanced the same argument (Müller, p. 138).

One vigorous supporter of the view that the sin was greater with a beautiful woman was the famous jurist and cardinal of Ferrara, the Camaldolese monk Huguccio (d. 1210), the teacher of Pope Innocent III. With these two theologians the Augustinian-Gregorian notion that all sexual pleasure is evil reached its apogee. Huguccio continually repeats the axiom from Pope Gregory's rescript, "Pleasure can never be without sin." Hence he rejects the idea of the holy husband who hates the pleasure he gets during intercourse with his wife and for that reason is supposedly free from sin. This husband sins too, because pleasure is always bound up with the ejaculation of sperm. Only "he who feels nothing does not sin" (Müller, p. 111). Every sensation of venereal pleasure is a sin, regardless of the reasons for, or the occasion of, its appearance. It makes no difference whether it comes to a virgin being raped or a husband begetting a child, or a man having a nocturnal emission. Pleasure can never be without sin. Huguccio methodically carries this abstruse Augustinian-Gregorian idea to its logical limit.

It may be noted in passing that the peculiarly celibate problem of whether the nocturnal "pollutions" of priests and monks were sinful, and to what degree, kept moral theologians extremely busy. Their comments on the subject fill entire libraries. Was it the fault of excessive eating and drinking? Of erotic fantasies during the day? Huguccio gives the earlier solutions short shrift. It was not overeating or the fantasies—these were sins in themselves—that served as the criterion for the degree of sinfulness of nocturnal emissions. The crucial factor was the degree of pleasure involved. The man who merely felt the pleasure sinned venially, the man who surrendered complacently to it sinned mortally (Müller, p. 112).

Since all experience of sexual pleasure was a sin, Huguccio, like Augustine before him, thought that Jesus did not wish to be begotten through sexual intercourse. In accordance with the continuously repeated verse from Psalm 50:7 (Protestants 51:5), "In sin did my mother conceive me," the parents' sin during the sexual act is the reason for original sin's being passed on to the child (Müller, pp. 110–11). So consistent was Huguccio's condemnation of pleasure that he had a conceptual collision with the theologian who gave pleasure a dirty name, Augustine himself. In fact he clashed with an opinion of Augustine's shared by almost all theologians, i.e., that marital sex for procreation or the performance of one's duty was sinless. For Huguccio such intercourse *was* sinless, but not the pleasure one necessarily felt in the process. On God's command in creation, "Increase and multiply," he writes: "One can assert that God commands and does many things that neither are nor can be without sin." Thus, for example, God commands man to care for his wife and children, which can hardly be done without sin. The duty of spouses to provide one another with sex is not an obligation to sin but to an action that cannot be carried out without sin (Müller, p. 113). It's not easy to embarrass a theologian. Huguccio does concede a certain difficulty in his position, but it only spurs him on, and makes him the herald of a new kind of marital sex, one that was sinless even by his strict standards. This was the "reserved embrace," as it would later be called (*amplexus reservatus* or *coitus reservatus*—not to be confused with *coitus interruptus*), a topic that has kept moral theologians busy to this day and that will be discussed in Chapter 14.

Cardinal Huguccio sets the motives for marital sex in order. Theologians had gradually settled on four main motives: 1) intercourse for procreation, 2) intercourse to perform one's duty (these two alone considered sinless by Augustine), 3) intercourse because of incontinence (held to be sinless by some, but viewed by most, including Huguccio, as a venial sin), and 4) intercourse to satisfy one's lust (considered mortally sinful by most, including Huguccio). Many authors were unclear about the difference between motives three and four, but Huguccio clears the whole thing up. He says that in sex prompted by incontinence, sexual excitement first occurs and then one decides to have intercourse with one's wife. Such intercourse is (for the husband) a venial sin. It is sinless (ever since Augustine) only for the partner who performs (her) duty on demand. In sex for satisfying lust Huguccio maintains that the man himself provokes sexual excitement through thoughts, touches, or stimulants designed to enable him to have intercourse more often. Such intercourse is a mortal sin. In the next few centuries, as it happened, theologians would have their hands full giving precise descriptions of this lustful intercourse, with the mortally sinful, or not always mortally sinful, husband, as well as answering the question of whether number-three intercourse was perhaps not sinless after all.

Like many Early Scholastics, Huguccio was caught up in the contemporary trend of seeing the husband (male theologians were mostly concerned with male spouses) as a patient in constant danger of succumbing to an attack of mortally sinful fornication, unless the remedy of sex was available at all hours, day and night, to be dispensed by his nurse-wife. Huguccio no longer viewed the ban on sex at holy times as a strict obligation, but only as a suggestion. Thus he rejected the claim that any kind of intercourse at Easter, for whatever motives, was a mortal sin. For him the mortally sinful thing was lustful, or libidinous, intercourse, as well as the unnatural kind; and these were wrong at all times. What exactly "unnatural" meant for the theologians we shall see later on. But Huguccio even allowed intercourse with a pregnant woman (which many penitential books had forbidden) out of regard for the greater dangers of incontinence, fornication, and adultery.

On the issue of constantly providing the remedy of conjugal sex, Huguccio thought out the following extreme case: Assume that a husband was elected pope, against the wishes of his wife. Even then he would be bound to perform his marital duty to his wife. If her husband failed to persuade her to continence, the wife could even demand her husband back from the council and the cardinals. Of course, his papal career would be finished. But the danger of fornication ranked above all other considerations, the supply of marital sex had to be guaranteed. This was one of the few cases, by the way, in which a theologian talked about the rights of the wife. But such a preferential treatment occurred only because of her disadvantaged position in the Church, i.e., because she could not be a popess. Otherwise Huguccio would have spoken about the husband's reclaiming his wife from the council and the cardinals.

Huguccio's disciple was Innocent III (d. 1216), the most important pope in the Middle Ages. The defamation of pleasure and the stress on the sinfulness of every act of intercourse, adopted by Huguccio from Gregory the Great ("sexual pleasure can never be without sin"), reached a climactic point with Innocent III. He writes, for example: "Who could not know that the consummation of marriage never takes place without the flames of lasciviousness, without the pollution of lust, through which the seed that has been received is defiled and destroyed?" Like all the

Church's pleasure-haters he cites Psalm 50: "The parents commit an actual sin, . . . the child contracts original sin. That is why the Psalmist says: 'Behold, I was conceived in unrighteousness, which my parents committed at my conception.' " As for Augustine's idea of the goods that excuse marriage, for Innocent they excuse intercourse from mortal, but not from venial, sin (*Commentary on the Seven Penitential Psalms* 4).

A series of Early Scholastic theologians sharply condemned the consumption of sexually stimulating foods and, above all, any deviation from the normal position as mortally sinful, insofar as it occurred out of lust. The anonymous "Summa" from the thirteenth century (*Codex latinus Monacensis* 22233) asserted that the wife's agreeing to depart from the normal position was as serious a sin as murder. Similar notions were advanced by the Dominican Roland of Cremona (d. 1259), a professor in Paris, and his follower, another Dominican, Hugh of St. Cher (d. 1263), as well as the Dominican William of Rennes (d. ca. 1250). The anonymous "Summa," along with Roland of Cremona and William of Rennes, allows a deviation from the normal position in certain cases, namely for medical reasons, such as obesity, when intercourse will otherwise be impossible and when attempts at slimming down have failed. In such instances Roland enjoins corpulent persons to "come together in the manner of the beasts," but "always with pain in the soul." As a diet for overweight individuals he recommends work, sweating, little sleep, little meat, millet bread, and vinegar to drink (*Summa de matrimonio solutio*). Any position except the normal one was considered "unnatural," and hence among the gravest sins. Among other reasons for this, the author of the anonymous "Summa" mentions that it makes conception almost impossible. We know better nowadays— which makes it all the more grotesque that in this century T. H. van de Velde's book *Ideal Marriage* (1926) was put on the Index, although its only heterodox position was the abandonment of the missionary position.

This unhealthy fixation of the Church's celibates on the conjugal act as at once a sin and a remedy for sin, this simultaneous abhorrence of sex and insistence on it (even if it meant mortal danger to the wife) brought on, as early as the twelfth century, a sharp reaction from the German Hugh of St. Victor (d. 1141), who had earlier been the count of Blankenburg. He recommended pure, spiritualized Josephite marriage, a union of souls without union in the flesh. The true, the real, the perfect marriage is consummated in the spirit and only in the spirit. Hugh was fascinated by the marriage of Mary and Joseph, the celibate dream couple of the pleasure-haters. He wanted all other marriages to be modeled on Josephite marriage.

Like Augustine, Hugh was convinced that Mary and Joseph had a true marriage, from which he concludes, as Augustine did (see the passages in Müller, p. 32), that the physical act does not belong to the ideal essence of marriage. According to Hugh's older contemporary, Anselm of Laon (d. 1117), at the time of her marriage Mary agreed to conjugal intercourse, but was convinced that Joseph would never ask her to do her duty as a wife. Hugh indignantly rejects such a view, because it is based on a false concept of marriage. He argues that sexual intercourse is not part of the essence of marriage, because otherwise Mary would have had to acquiesce in sexual relations—but that would be a criminal accusation against the most blessed Virgin (*De b. Mariae virginitate*).

The difficulties that the clerical celibates got into with their invention of a sexless Josephite marriage are still with us. Although the fact that Mary was married is not denied, pious ecclesiastical usage prefers to speak of Joseph not as her husband but as her "bridegroom," thus practically suppressing the marriage. Hugh, by contrast, saw in Joseph the ideal husband and in Josephite marriage the authentic marriage. For pious minds today, however, the term "marriage" has evidently been so corrupted by normal married people that they no longer like to use it for the ideal picture of marriage and hence prefer to call Joseph Mary's bridegroom, which sounds purer. After thus rescuing true marriage from the "evil" of sexual excitement, he finds lofty, exquisite words about married love, which other theologians thought it difficult to talk about—or to whom it never occurred to talk about—because they always had in mind lust-besmirched marital sex. Only after separating body and mind in this way, did Hugh succeed (as had Augustine) in speaking about married love and in supplementing and transcending the crude view of marriage as primarily an institution for reproduction or a cure for fornication. Hugh delivers a harsh verdict on the notion of marriage as a remedy for incontinence, since the experience of sexual pleasure is for him an evil: Marriage, he says, confines "the heat of excessive lust" to the conjugal alliance. It "pardons" by means of its goods this evil thing, "lest it be reckoned unto damnation." But "it does not cause this evil not to be evil, it simply makes it not damnable."

Instead of rehabilitating pleasure and the body, and sweeping away the whole system of "pardoning" launched by Augustine, Hugh prefers to distance himself from marriage that is carnally consummated and sets up a purely spiritual marriage, thereby only defaming physical love all the more. For example, unlike many Early Scholastics, Hugh strictly forbids sex at holy times, equating it with "unnatural intercourse" (*De sacramentis* 2, 11, 7. 9. 10).

According to Hugh, God's main reason for instituting marriage is not the procreation of children, nor the prophylaxis of vice, but rather—as shown by Adam's words, when God brought him Eve—for the cleaving together of souls. Adam says: "Therefore a man leaves his father and his mother and cleaves to his wife" (Gen 2:24). Not until after this does he cite the "task" of marriage, which consists in becoming one flesh. But spiritual love takes priority over this.

Marriage is not based on carnal union, but on a union of hearts (Müller, pp. 81ff.). And if the first thing, namely, this "alliance of love," were lacking, then the marriage would be "invalid," even if it had been consummated (Müller, p. 83). Conversely, the ideal of marriage would be more perfectly realized with no intercourse. Then there would be the holiness of love, and nothing would happen "that chastity must blush at" (Müller, p. 79). Sexual relations, which are necessary for procreation and the performance of marital duty, do not belong to the essence of marriage, but only to its "task," which is subordinate to that essence. Thus to contract a valid marriage the spouses need only desire the fellowship of spiritual life and love, not the fellowship of sex (cf. Müller, p. 78). "Rather I believe that marriage is more fully, more truthfully, and more holily present, where the alliance was forged with the chain of love alone and not in the concupiscence of the flesh and of desire . . . Is it not more when two become one in the spirit than when they become one in the flesh?" (Cf. Müller, p. 81).

Hugh's altogether tender-minded words about marriage and love sound unusual and agreeable for a time when theologians were offensively fixated on the sexuality of married couples, and saw sex primarily as the threat of fornication and adultery. But Hugh did not succeed in making physical union a part of his spiritualized vision. He became instead one of the most extreme spokesmen for the so-called consent theory of marriage and the harshest opponent of the cohabitation theory.

For centuries a controversy raged in the Church over these two theories. The question was, did marriage come about through cohabitation or consent or both? Roman law advanced the principle that it was consent and not cohabitation (*consensus facit matrimonium et non concubitus*). Catholic marriage law followed the Roman principle, as we see, for example, in the letter written by Pope Nicholas I to the newly converted Bulgarians in 866. But the question of the application of the law and where to place the accent in interpreting it gave rise to the two conflicting theories.

The issue first became concretely important in a case that raised quite a stir in its day (the ninth century). A nobleman from Aquitaine named Stephanus married the daughter of Count Regimund and then sent her back to her father immediately after the wedding, without having consummated the marriage. Count Regimund brought a complaint to the Synod of Touzy in 860, particularly to the Frankish bishops. They in turn commissioned the most prominent theologian of the period, Hincmar of Rheims (d. 882) to investigate the matter. In the piece he wrote on "The Marriage of Stephanus and the Daughter of Count Regimund" Hincmar defended the cohabitation theory: Sexual consummation was so essential to marriage that without it one could not even speak of marriage. He cited a supposed passage from Augustine: "A wedding is no image of the marriage of Christ and the Church, unless the participants make use of their marital rights," that is, unless there is cohabitation.

In the twelfth century the two theories were sharply opposed to each other. The consent theory was advanced mainly by the University of Paris, the cohabitation theory by the University of Bologna. The leading jurist in Bologna, the monk Gratian, saw the constitutive element of marriage in cohabitation, *copula*. Because of its consequences for Josephite marriage (Mary would not have been married then), Hugh of St. Victor saw the constitutive factor exclusively in the consent to the marriage, from which he excluded—in the interests of Josephite marriage—all connections with sex.

The dispute was settled by a compromise that has held to this day: Pope Alexander III (d. 1181) essentially endorsed the consent theory. Thus a marriage is already valid before it is consummated, but not until then is it indissoluble. This means that an unconsummated marriage can be dissolved, but a consummated one cannot. Even today, according to canon law someone who has not had intercourse after the wedding can have the marriage dissolved and get married again.

XIII

EARLY SCHOLASTICISM, PART II: ABELARD'S OPPOSITION—A TALE OF WOE

A*round the end* of the twelfth century and the beginning of the thirteenth, there was, as we have seen, almost universal agreement among theologians that every act of marital intercourse was sinful. This view reached its high point with Huguccio. Opposition to it came from the only married theologian, Peter Abelard (1079–1142), who became famous because of his unfortunate love affair with Héloise (1101–1164) and his great success as a teacher in Paris. Abelard was the only dissenter in the mass of lust-hating theologians who were always rehashing the same arguments. Abelard was also one of the few to criticize the great slaughter of the Jews during the Crusades of the twelfth century. During his life he was defamed as a heretic by St. Bernard of Clairvaux (d. 1153). Bernard finally managed to get Pope Innocent II to impose eternal silence on Abelard, shortly after which he died.

When Abelard was still teaching in Paris, he already had an international reputation. In 1118 his university career was interrupted by his affair with Héloise. At the time Abelard was living in the house of the Canon Fulbert, whose beautiful and clever niece Héloise spoke Latin as fluently as French and was even learning Hebrew. Abelard, who was not yet a priest then, gave Héloise private lessons. He later wrote about these tutorials in his *Historia calamitatum mearum,* in other words, his tale of woe: "Thus I agreed with Fulbert that he would take me into his house, setting the price at his discretion . . . And so Fulbert reached the goal of his wishes: My money for himself and learning for his niece . . . During the lessons we had abundant time for our love . . . and there were more kisses than words. My hand often had more searching to do in her bosom than in the book, and instead of reading scholarly texts, we read longingly in each other's eyes" (ibid., 17ff.). Héloise became pregnant; Abelard abducted her and brought her to his sister in Brittany. He promised her infuriated uncle to marry Héloise, provided Fulbert would keep the marriage secret. Because of the reforms of Pope Gregory VII all married men were excluded from the priesthood, unless their wives entered a monastery. But Héloise did not want to enter a monastery; on the other hand neither did she want to stand in the way of Abelard's academic career, which at that time was possible only for priests. Hence she decided to remain his mistress. He convinced her, however, to get married, which was supposed to be known only to a few trusted friends. They left their son Astrolabe with Abelard's sister and got married in Fulbert's presence. Once again Héloise moved back to Fulbert's house, Abelard returned to his bachelor quarters, and they saw one another only occasionally. Fulbert found this secrecy a blot on Héloise's reputation and spread the news of their marriage. Thereupon Abelard abducted Héloise and brought her to a monastery in Argenteuil, where he ordered her to put on a nun's habit, but not to take vows. When Fulbert and his people learned this, they viewed it as "a quite contemptuous fraud and an attempt to get rid of Héloise in this way. These people became so embittered that they decided on my destruction. My servant took a bribe and led them one night to my chamber, where I was sleeping peacefully. And now they took their revenge on me, so cruelly, so shamefully that the world froze in horror: They cut off my body the organs with which I had troubled them. Two of the fellows were caught in flight, they were blinded and castrated as well" (ibid. 28).

All of Paris, all the clergy were on Abelard's side. His students sought him out to console him. Abelard convinced Héloise to take the veil; later she became an abbess, and he himself became a monk in St. Denis. At the urging of his students and his abbot he went back to lecturing. The story of Abelard and Héloise remains for all time the story of a celebrated couple, first lovers and then married, who fell victim to the laws of celibacy.

Abelard chided his contemporaries for allowing marital intercourse to take place only in a way that can never happen. It was not tradition, but reason that had to decide the correctness of a thesis. Abelard argues: "No natural pleasure of the flesh may be declared a sin, nor may one impute guilt when someone is delighted by pleasure where he must necessarily feel it." For "from the first day of our creation, when man lived without sin in Paradise," sexual intercourse and the consumption of good-tasting foods were naturally bound up with pleasure. God himself has established nature in this way (*Eth.* 3). The teaching of Augustine that sexual pleasure is the consequence of, and punishment for, sin is something Abelard does not even mention, though he is naturally familiar with it. He reproaches his contemporaries for their unreasonableness in allowing sexual intercourse for procreation and the fulfillment of duty, while forbidding the pleasure necessarily bound up with it. Abelard also opposes the usual interpretation of 1 Cor. 7:6, that Paul "forgives" marital intercourse, in other words looks upon it as a sin. Paul, he says, leaves it up to married people to have intercourse or not to have it. And the continually repeated verse from Psalm 50 (v. 7): "I was brought forth in iniquity, and in sin did my mother conceive me," does not imply that the pleasure experienced by the parents in generation besmirches the child, but simply speaks of original sin, which everyone has.

As a result of his attempt to rehabilitate sexual pleasure, Abelard also affirmed the Immaculate Conception of Mary, that is, the doctrine that Mary was conceived without original sin, while his opponent Bernard of Clairvaux vehemently attacked it and called Abelard a heretic for supporting it. Since it was assumed that Mary was begotten through normal sexual intercourse—the legendary names of her parents were Joachim and Anne—neither Augustine nor the tradition that followed him absolve her of original sin. Bernard stressed that there was pleasure (*libido*) in sexual intercourse, and pleasure is sin, and where sin prevails the Holy Spirit is not present. Hence it is impossible that the soul of Mary received sanctifying grace at the moment of conception (*Epistles* 174, 1. 5. 6. 7. 9). Pleasure and sin, pleasure and the transmission of original sin were seen as linked together. Abelard, the defender of pleasure, was the first one to break up this false connection.

As sensational as such theses may sound, Abelard was also in many things a prisoner of tradition, for example, when he claimed that the ideal motive for marital intercourse was the desire to have a child, and that the holy women, such as Anne, might have renounced sex all together if there had been another way to have children (*Eth.* 3). Abelard too considered the celibate life of continence as a more perfect and meritorious way than marriage in the eyes of God.

The pleasure-hating theory of Augustine was so dominant that it suffered no damage from the appearance of Abelard's argument for the naturalness of pleasure. Rather it maintained its authoritative influence and only after Abelard did it reach its first apex in Huguccio, to whose perverted proposal for sinless marital sex we now turn our attention.

XIV

COITUS RESERVATUS: THE RECIPE FOR SINLESS SEX

The *method of* intercourse favored by Cardinal Huguccio (d. 1210), the great expert on canon law and teacher of the even greater Pope Innocent III, works only for the man. It is out of the question for anyone interested in procreation and for that reason it was later discussed as a form of contraception. It must be differentiated from coitus interruptus (which for Huguccio was a mortal sin, as it is for all strict Catholics to this day). Huguccio's theological problem was this: How should intercourse for duty's sake (which the husband is obliged to perform at his wife's request) be carried out so as to be sinless for the man, since pleasure will undeniably set in when he ejaculates, and thus he will become liable to sin, though only venial sin.

Huguccio found a way out: "I can do my duty to my wife and wait until she has fulfilled her pleasure. In fact, in such cases women are often accustomed to feel the pleasure before their husbands, and when the woman's pleasure in the physical act has been sated, I can, as I wish, withdraw without fulfilling my pleasure, free from sin and without letting the seed of generation flow forth" (*Summa* 2, 13). One had to have a certain amount of concentration to hold in the semen, but the trouble was worth it:

1 7 1

The husband striving for holiness remains without sin here because he has gone without pleasure. He has withdrawn his member from the vagina and even after that he has not permitted an
ejaculation to occur (which would have been a mortal sin).

The orgasm of the wife, who demanded intercourse out of incontinence in the first place, is a venial sin, because, according to
Augustine, when intercourse is demanded only the demand for
procreation is sinless. Huguccio, who exceeds even Augustine in
hatred of pleasure, seems to prefer his coitus reservatus to Augustine's sinless intercourse for procreation or duty. For Huguccio
only coitus reservatus is really sinless, because it alone is without
sensations of pleasure. Huguccio does not go into the question of
to what extent a man can feel pleasure even without ejaculating.

Some have wondered how the monk Huguccio ever thought of
this method. He himself mentions that it was "frequently" practiced. John T. Noonan conjectures that it was a contraceptive
method of the Cathars and widespread in northern Italy (*Contraception*, 1986[2], p. 297). The method is likewise mentioned in
the courtly love literature of the troubadors. First introduced into
theology by Huguccio as a means of excluding sexual enjoyment
from marital intercourse, it was later to become a bone of con-
tention because of its contraceptive side effect.

The theological dispute that will now be presented, with its
various twists and turns, might be summed up as the story of
"how married people were tyrannized by hatred of pleasure and
the taboo on semen." The ideas behind coitus reservatus and the
centuries-long theological controversy over them are so abstruse
that one doesn't know whom to shake one's head over more, the
monk-theologians who recommended it or those who forbade it.
Those who forbade it did so because even as it was, too much
pleasure occurred or might occur, and those who recommended it
did so in order to permit as little pleasure as possible. There were
contradictory policies, with the same motive behind them.

To this day no Catholic theologian has failed to label coitus
interruptus as a serious sin, but the judgment on coitus reservatus has been and is often positive. The question arose as recently

as 1960, after Cardinal Suenens recommended it as a contraceptive method for couples who for legitimate reasons had to avoid pregnancy (*A Crucial Problem*, 1960, pp. 81–82).

For a hundred years after Huguccio first made his suggestion nothing was said about it. Then Archbishop Petrus de Palude (d. 1342) voiced his opposition to a husband's practicing coitus interruptus out of a desire not to have any more children when he could no longer support them. On the other hand, he conceded the use of coitus reservatus under certain conditions: "But if the husband withdraws before the act is completed and does not ejaculate, then he evidently commits no mortal sin, unless his wife happens to be aroused to ejaculation" (*Commentary on the Sentences* 4, 31, 3, 2). He means orgasm, in which case there is mortal sin.

The expression "female seed" derives from the Greek physician Galen (second century). Galen describes this supposed seed as colder and moister than the male variety; he considers it necessary for procreation, unlike Aristotle, who thought male seed alone had generative properties. From the time of Albert the Great and Thomas Aquinas onward theologians had chiefly followed Aristotle's biology. Insofar as they mention this "female seed," and whatever they mean by the term, they had no doubt that its ejaculation was connected with orgasm, like the male ejaculation. In Cardinal Huguccio's case the woman's orgasm was part of the plan, and coitus reservatus went under the heading of husbandly duty, but without the sin of feeling pleasure on his part. With Archbishop Palude the wife was now not allowed to have an orgasm either, because coitus reservatus for him went under the heading of contraception.

The method found a still wider public thanks to St. Antoninus (d. 1459), a Dominican and the archbishop of Florence. In his *Summa* (3, 120) he adopts the presentation of Archbishop Palude verbatim. And two manuals for confessors, also from the fifteenth century, stick precisely to Palude's wording. These were the *Summa of Cases of Conscience*, under the entry for *debitum* (marital duty), by the Franciscan Trovamala (d. after 1494) and "The Moral Leprosy of the Misuse of Sex by Married People" by the

German Dominican Johann Nider (d. 1438). During the period from 1450 to 1750 coitus reservatus was increasingly mentioned by the theologians as a permissible method of birth control.

But there were dissenters. The first of these was the Dominican Sylvestro Prierias (d. 1523), who from 1517 onward was busy trying to refute Luther's theses on indulgences. He found Palude's viewpoint "utterly unreasonable" (in his *Summa* under *de debito coniugali*). Others followed him in this, and stressed that a sexual act which did not serve procreation always deserved to be condemned. The Inquisitor Bartholomaeus Fundo (d. 1545), a Dominican, viewed the method as mortally sinful. This opinion was shared by the Italian Dominican Ignatius Conradi (d. 1606) and the Spanish Jesuit Henriquez (d. 1608).

Archbishop Palude's position, that coitus reservatus was permitted as a contraceptive act only to be condemned in cases where it led to the wife's orgasm, was supported by Luther's adversary, Cardinal Cajetan (d. 1534) and the Jesuit Thomas Sanchez (d. 1610). Sanchez thought that if the couple was poor and had many children, whom they could not feed, then that was a legitimate reason for allowing this method (*The Holy Sacrament of Marriage* 9, 19).

Alphonsus Liguori (d. 1787) considered coitus reservatus a mortal sin when it induced an orgasm ("ejaculation") in the woman, otherwise it was a venial sin. The German Jesuit Paul Laymann (d. 1635), confessor to Emperor Ferdinand II, in his standard work on moral theology, rated it a venial sin, as did Charles Billuart (d. 1757). The moral theologian Diana (d. 1663), whom Pascal attacked for his laxity, claimed the method was "frequently" employed.

The foolish controversy over coitus reservatus went on through the nineteenth and twentieth centuries. Lehmkuhl (d. 1918) judged the method to be "scarcely practical," since it stimulated sexual desire rather than satisfying it. Others forbade the method since they suspected that most couples were in reality practicing coitus interruptus. In this century Bishop de Smet of Bruges recommends the method as a "lesser evil" for couples who would otherwise use contraceptives. Arthur Vermeersch (d. 1936) maintains that for most people it was a sin, because they would not escape the danger of coitus interruptus. He is prepared to allow couples only occasional ejaculations, provided they were not intentional. Two books by the Catholic layman Paul Chanson, which appeared with the *imprimatur* of the archdiocese of Paris in 1947, were pulled from circulation in 1950 by order of the Holy Office. Chanson had recommended coitus reservatus as an act of self-control, "the humanization of the flesh." The act, as he described it, lasted from ten to thirty minutes, and was designed to promote married love.

In 1951 there occurred the most massive attack ever launched against this method, led by the Dominican H. M. Hering. He called the whole thing "immoral," because, as opposed to, say, kisses, it involved the sexual parts that according to Canon 1081 §2 were intended for the generation of offspring. Hence the entire process was "most serious sin, which actually belongs to the un-natural vices." Chanson, Hering charged, had forgotten the first purpose of marriage (procreation), and with many married persons the whole thing amounted to coitus interruptus, since they did not know how to control themselves. Chanson had left out of the account a whole series of dogmatic truths, e.g., "the doctrine of original sin and its consequences" (*De amplexu reservato*, 1951).

In 1952 the leading Jesuit moralist, Franz Hürth, entered the lists against the Dominican Hering, defending coitus reservatus as *not* unnatural. A compromise was reached on June 30, 1952, when the Holy Office issued a *monitum* stating that priests ought not to speak about coitus reservatus as if there were no objections to be raised against it.

More recent moral theologians allow the practice, disagreeing only on exactly to what extent they allow it. Bernhard Häring wishes neither to recommend nor forbid *copula sicca*, or dry intercourse, as it is sometimes called. He would not forbid it, if the married couple could control themselves and persist "in reverence before the creator and one another." "The positive feature of it is the determination not to misuse the seed of new life, in case procreation is not intended" (*Das Gesetz Christi*, 373). Needless to say, Häring strictly forbids coitus interruptus.

1 7 5

The Jesuit Josef Fuchs follows the Jesuit Franz Hürth in positively assessing coitus reservatus. A great advocate of the method is the Belgian Cardinal Suenens, who has already been mentioned. He recommends it as a solution in cases where for good reasons pregnancy must not occur (on the whole controversy, cf. Noonan, pp. 296ff., 303, 336ff., 447ff.) The entire debate illustrates the disaster of Catholic sexual morality, whose supreme guideline is the imperative not to spill semen and forcing couples to dismantle their pleasurable feelings, a process invented by theologians but presented as "reverence before the creator."

Meanwhile some of the latter seem to have given up the warning about the female orgasm, although for centuries it was for many theologians the crucial point. The female orgasm, as these theologians saw it, took place in the ejaculation of a "female seed." As late as 1930 Heribert Jone spoke in his textbook on moral theology about the ejaculation of the woman (p. 615), and the Dominican Hering does the same as late as 1951 ("De amplexu reservato," in *Angelicum*, 1951, 323). Since over the years the biological knowledge of theologians has drawn somewhat closer to the facts (the ovum was discovered in 1827), some of them have abandoned the religious notion of the female seed, and in so doing have swept the female orgasm under the rug with it, consigning it to theological oblivion. But for this reason the whole business of the "reserved embrace" is all the more focused on the man and his seed.

The supreme point is that the man should not practice coitus interruptus. By dropping the idea of the female seed and the orgasm thought to be bound up with it, pastoral care concentrated on male semen. It has been declared taboo, it must not be misused, may not be discharged. On it depends eternal salvation, on this substance that is not allowed to come to light, whose only proper place is the vagina, where, on the other hand, it cannot always be, since under certain circumstances there are legitimate reasons against its presence. But if it is not wanted there, it is not wanted anywhere. If not indicated there, it is contraindicated everywhere else, and all this amid stress and expenditure of a great deal of energy in self-control—out of reverence for the creator of the whole arrangement.

Such absurdities are the result of a mistaken sexual morality that after almost two thousand years is still not ready to give up its usurped dominion over the bedrooms of married people. It is astonishing how abundantly down through history one generation has intellectually begotten another generation of incompetent self-styled experts, surrounded them with a divine halo, devoting substantial portions of their lives to utter nonsense. This pseudo-theological waxworks would make us laugh out loud, if we didn't know that its owners and operators have a lot of marital tragedies to answer for.

XV

THE THIRTEENTH CENTURY:
GOLDEN AGE OF THEOLOGY—
AND PEAK OF MISOGYNISTIC SLANDER

M*any writers nowadays* would like to view the great theologians of the High Scholastic period, especially Albert the Great (d. 1280) and his student Thomas Aquinas (d. 1274), as a turning point in the tradition of Augustinian hatred of pleasure. This shift is supposed to have occurred when Albert incorporated Aristotelian biology into the structure of church dogma. Since Aristotle characterized the pleasure taken in a good action as good and natural, this brought détente to the Church's cold war against sex. Unfortunately, none of this is true.

The only ones to profit from Aristotle were Adam and Eve, insofar as Albert and Thomas argued that in Paradise sexual pleasure was greater than it is today—although on the other hand it was also lesser than it is today, since in those days pleasure was entirely regulated by reason. Augustine had already conceded a similar point to Julian the Pelagian at the end of his life, but during the early Middle Ages and Early Scholasticism this had slipped into the background. Otherwise bringing Aristotle into theology brought nothing but mischief. First of all—because of the abstruse Aristotelian biology—it led to an increase in contempt for women, and secondly it generated still more hatred of sex because Albert and particularly Thomas managed to add Aristotle's remarks on the ecstasy and mental numbness of orgasm as one more negative feature of Augustine's sexual pessimism. Thirdly and lastly, Aristotle's characterization of sexual intercourse as a "natural act," common to mankind and animals (which actually might have led to an easing of the Church's suspicion of pleasure), only helped to thrust the whole sphere of sex down to the animal, or the bestial, level. "In sexual intercourse the human being becomes similar to the beast (*bestialis efficitur*)," said Thomas (*Summa Theologiae* I q. 98 a 2). In classifying sex as bestial Thomas went further than his teacher Albert. On the other hand there are venomously misogynistic passages in Albert of a sort one does not find in Thomas's dry system.

Albert the Great was a great despiser of women. He claimed that, "Woman is less qualified [than man] for moral behavior. For the woman contains more liquid than the man, and it is a property of liquid to take things up easily and to hold onto them poorly. Liquids are easily moved, hence women are inconstant and curious. When a woman has relations with a man, she would like, as much as possible, to be lying with another man at the same time. Woman knows nothing of fidelity. Believe me, if you give her your trust, you will be disappointed. Trust an experienced teacher. For this reason prudent men share their plans and actions least of all with their wives. Woman is a misbegotten man and has a faulty and defective nature in comparison with his. Therefore she is unsure in herself. What she herself cannot get, she seeks to obtain through lying and diabolical deceptions. And so, to put it briefly, one must be on one's guard with every woman, as if she were a poisonous snake and the horned devil. If I could say what I know about women, the world would be astonished . . . Woman is strictly speaking not cleverer but slyer (more cunning) than man. Cleverness sounds like something good, slyness sounds like something evil. Thus in evil and perverse doings woman is cleverer, that is, slyer, than man. Her feelings drive woman toward every evil, just as reason impels man toward all good" (*Quaestiones super de animalibus* XV q. 11).

One can see from such quotations how celibacy can corrupt and dehumanize even its most eminent spokesmen. Every kind of slander against women was all right with them if it furthered the monasticization of society. Albert offers us still more insights into his father confessor's wisdom: "As I heard in the confessional in Cologne, delicate wooers seduce women with careful touches. The more these women seem to reject them, the more they really long for them and resolve to consent to them. But in order to appear chaste, they act as if they disapprove of such things" (ibid., XIII q. 18). This is an old male theory, now given the blessing of St. Albert: The more a woman resists, the more she wants it. Albert the Great should be given the title "Patron of Rapists."

It may be mentioned in passing here that Albert also played an important role in the history of Christian anti-Semitism. He mercilessly suppressed and destroyed Jewish scholarship. He belonged to the leaders of the investigatory commission that in 1248 sanctioned the burnings of the Talmud (240 wagonloads) in 1242. He corroborated this disastrous miscarriage of justice with his signature. This resulted in still more burnings of the Talmud and the destruction of important centers of Jewish learning.

In his letter to King Louis IX (St. Louis) of France (d. 1270) dated May 9, 1244, Pope Innocent IV (who convoked the Albert commission in 1247 because of complaints from the Jews) cited as a reason for the Talmud burnings of 1242 "fabrications about the most blessed Virgin." He meant the Jewish contesting of the Virgin Birth. We are well informed about St. Louis IX of France, under whose rule the burnings took place. Sire Jean de Joinville, his friend and companion on the Seventh Crusade (he had no stomach to join Louis on the Eighth and stayed home in his castle), is considered a reliable reporter and careful biographer of the king. No layman, declared Louis IX, should dispute with Jews over the Virgin Birth; but when someone calumniates the Christian faith, the believer should thrust his sword into the

Jew's body, "as far as it can go." Joinville relates in this context the fate of a Jew who was severely beaten in the monastery of Cluny because he could not believe in the Virgin Birth.

Albert, who was Louis' contemporary, glorified Mary at the expense of all other women. He thought that Eve, by contrast, had left all women a double and triple "woe"—quite apart from the woe of the hardships of pregnancy and birth pangs—first, the woe of the temptation to concupiscence, second, the woe of depravity in the sexual act, and third, the woe of excessive lust in conception (*In Lc.* 1:28).

Albert is supposed to have introduced a less biased attitude toward sexual pleasure. That is untrue, because Albert (and Thomas) stick closely to the Augustinian line and incorporate Aristotle's affirmation of pleasure only insofar as it doesn't interfere with Augustine's hatred of pleasure. Albert and Thomas emphasize that pleasure is good insofar as it is a means to maintain the species. Albert means that, in Aristotle's sense, nature put pleasure in intercourse so that it would be desired for the upkeep of the species (*In IV sent.* 26, 2 and 31, 21 n. 3). Pleasure, therefore, is good only as a means to an end. Striving for pleasure is now, as it was before, a sin.

No High Scholastic made even the slightest concession on this point. On the contrary, whatever tiny gains were made from the Aristotelian loosening up with regard to pleasure were invested by the Scholastics in a still sharper accentuation on procreation as the actual, natural purpose of marriage: Pleasure was only the means ensuring the accomplishment of procreation. But anyone who was *prompted by* pleasure was turning the means into the end, which was against the God-given order and hence a sin. It is a mortal sin, i.e., incurring eternal damnation, when one has intercourse "for pleasure alone."

This does not represent any change from Early Scholasticism. Albert and Thomas merely avoid the formula of Gregory the Great ("Pleasure can never be without sin"), in accordance with which from the fifth to the twelfth centuries all sexual pleasure in marital sex was considered at least a venial sin. Albert and Thomas stay rather closer to Augustine, who labeled intercourse sinless when engaged in for procreation and the performance of one's duty at the request of another. For Albert and Thomas pleasure is not a sin in both these cases, although it is in Albert's eyes (as it was in Augustine's) an "evil," a "punishment," "filthy," "defiling," "ugly," "shameful," "sick," a "degradation of the mind," a "humiliation of reason by the flesh," "common," "debasing," "humiliating," "shared with the beasts," "brutal," "corrupted," "depraved," "infected" and "infecting" (with original sin) (cf. Leopold Brandl, *Die Sexualethik des hl. Albertus Magnus,* pp. 45, 61, 73, 79, 80, 82, 83, 95, 96, 216).

It is only appropriate that, given this torrent of suspicion of pleasure that Albert (in association with Gratian, the father of canon law) should demand thirty nights of chastity from newlyweds, the idea being that it should still be possible, at first, to enter a monastery (*In IV sent.* d. 27 a. 8). Even on the wedding night, indeed even on the honeymoon the monks won't give up hope. In fact, after the time has passed for entering religious life, one can still strive for perfection. The husband who "unwillingly" does his conjugal duty is more perfect (ibid., d. 32 a. 3), although not quite perfect, because only the celibate, like Albert, is that.

Albert also says that it is indecent to have sex on feast days and days of fasting and processions (ibid., d. 32 a. 10). And couples are permitted to receive Communion after intercourse only when it has taken place from morally unobjectionable motives, i.e., for posterity's or duty's sake, though this usually applied to the consenting party alone. If the motive of the person requesting intercourse is not procreation but desire for pleasure, then the confessor should advise him or her to stay away from Communion (ibid., d. 32 a. 13 ad quaest. 1). One sees how important confession is for the confessor to learn from his penitents such fine moral distinctions in the motivation of married couples.

One of the mainstays of Augustinian sexual ethics, which can still be found in the most recent textbooks of Catholic morality, is the great difference between doing one's duty and demanding that one's partner do his or hers. Albert stresses the distinction when he says: Whoever does his duty does not approve but deplores the sexual craving of his spouse. He does not intend to promote the other's lust, but to cure the spouse's sickness. To be sure, both are operative together, but the moral attitude of the spouses is thoroughly different. "The spouse who demands acts out of lustful desire, the spouse that does his duty acts on the basis of the virtue of marital fidelity. Thus the demand is sin, and the fulfillment of duty is merit" (ibid., 32, 9; cf. the passages in Müller, *Die Lehre des hl. Augustinus von der Paradiesesehe und ihre Auswirkung in der Sexualethik des 12. und 13. Jahrhunderts bis Thomas von Aquin*, p. 254).

One sin, of course, is not the same as another sin. Albert cites the standard axiom of the pleasure-haters, which, as we saw, made its way into the celibate repertoire thanks to Jerome: The "all too passionate [burning] lover of his wife" commits mortal sin. The "not all too passionate lover of his wife" commits a venial sin. The latter receives the apostolic "pardon," which Albert, like Augustine, reads into 1 Cor. 7:6 (*In IV sent.* 31, 5).

Albert has more than theological arguments for directing and regulating marital sex, he also has a scientific case: Overly frequent intercourse leads to premature aging and death (*de animalibus* 1. 9 tr. I, 2 and 1. 15 tr. 2, 6). Too much sex thins out the brain, the eyes become sunken and weak. And Albert has proof for this: "A Master Clement from Bohemia told me that a certain monk, already graying, had gone to a beautiful woman, like a ravenously hungry man. Up until the ringing of matins he lusted for her sixty-six times. But in the morning he lay sick in bed, and he died on the same day. Because he was a nobleman, his body was opened up. And it was found that his brain had been quite drained out, so that what was left was only the size of a pomegranate, and the eyes were as good as destroyed" (*Quaestiones super de animalibus* XV q. 14). Frequent intercourse makes one bald sooner, because sex dries you out and cools you off (ibid., XIX q. 7–9). Albert also noticed that people who have sex often are followed around by dogs. He explains this by saying that, "Dogs love strong smells and run after cadavers, and the body of a person who has a great deal of intercourse approaches the condition of a cadaver because of all the rotten semen" (ibid., V q. 11–14).

As far as semen goes, Albert also believes that women emit seed during intercourse, and he addresses this matter in great detail. The woman's ejaculation, he thought, is most often linked with orgasm, but sometimes the orgasm also derives from a "ticklish animal spirit" (*De animal.* XV, 2, 11). Female semen is whitish. Black women have more semen because they are more passionate. Dark-haired women have the most semen. Thin women have more than fat ones. Albert follows Aristotle's biology in opposing writers who attribute generative power to female semen. A woman's seed is watery and thin and "not suitable for reproduction" (*Quaestiones super de animalibus* XV q. 19). For that reason Albert thinks that the term "woman's semen," which goes back to Galen, is incorrect (*De animal.* IX, 2, 3). The man's semen is like the artist, like the master that gives the form, the female semen receives it (*De animal.* III, 2, 8). This formation by male semen, a process that always strives to achieve the perfect masculine form, can fail owing to unfavorable conditions, in which case a woman is born. This is the old Aristotelian defamation of women, which Albert made a component part of celibate theology. Michael Müller writes that, "The greatest damage done to women, after the threat from Gnostic dualism in Antiquity, came in the 13th century from the unqualified acceptance of Aristotelian biology" (*Grundlagen der katholischen Sexualethik*, p. 62).

XVI

THOMAS AQUINAS: LUMEN ECCLESIAE ("THE LIGHT OF THE CHURCH")

B*asically Thomas Aquinas* (d. 1274) did no more than weave together, in a systematic fashion, the views of the High Scholastics as a group. And as far as the adoption of Aristotelian biology goes, he said nothing that his teacher, Albert the Great, had not already presented in a more detailed but less organized way. Nevertheless, we must investigate Thomas's sexual ethics more closely, because his arguments have had enormous influence right up into our own time. In sexual morality Thomas has remained *the* authority, along with Augustine.

In his standard treatment of "St. Augustine's teaching on pre-lapsarian marriage and its impact on the sexual ethics of the twelfth and thirteenth centuries up until Thomas Aquinas" (*Die Lehre des hl. Augustinus von der Paradiesesehe und ihre Auswirkung in der Sexualethik des 12. und 13. Jahrhunderts bis Thomas von Aquin*, 1954), Michael Müller calls the teaching of Aquinas "surprisingly—as far as the subject matter of the individual questions goes—little more than a repeat of the usual more hard-line scholastic opinions, fortified with didactic bits from Aristotle" (p. 255). Except for the fact that there is nothing surprising about this, Müller's characterization is on target. Only someone who believes that there has been any essential change in the Catholic Church's defamation and contempt of women from Augustine in the fourth and fifth centuries to Thomas in the thirteenth, or that there could have been any change, given Thomas's towering influence, from the thirteenth to the twentieth centuries—only such a naive observer would be "surprised" to note that basically everything remains stuck in the old groove.

Thomas writes: "Perpetual continence is necessary for perfect piety . . . That is why Jovinian, who put marriage on the same level as virginity, was condemned" (*Summa Theologiae* II/II q. 186 a. 4). And Thomas repeats several times what Jerome had already calculated in the fourth and fifth centuries, namely, that virginal individuals receive a 100 percent heavenly reward, while widows and widowers get 60 percent, and married people 30 percent (ibid., II/II q. 152 a. 5 ad 2). Anyone who tries nowadays to raise marriage to the same rank as virginity will be viewed, as he or she would have been back then, as dragging virginity down to the lowly level of marriage and as slandering the Virgin Mary herself. And as for the position of women in the male-dominated Church there has not been the slightest change.

Augustine wrote long ago that all of humanity's troubles began, so to speak, with woman, namely Eve; that the expulsion from Paradise was her fault. And until the turn of the century the Vatican was still reading the story of Creation and the Fall in Genesis more or less as a literal documentary account. Why did the devil speak not to Adam, but to Eve? Augustine asks. And his answer: Satan turned to "the inferior of the human pair . . . supposing that the man would not be so easily gullible, and could not be trapped by a false move on his own part, but only if he yielded to another's mistake." Augustine acknowledges mitigating circumstances for Adam: "We cannot believe that the man was led astray . . . because he believed that the woman spoke the truth, but that he fell in with her suggestions because they were so closely bound in partnership . . . Eve accepted the serpent's statement as the truth, while Adam refused to be separated from his only companion, even if it involved sharing her sin" (*The City of God* XIV, 11, translated by Henry Bettenson). Love of woman brings man down to ruin.

The nun Hildegard of Bingen (d. 1179) borrowed Augustine's explanation and made it still clearer: "The devil . . . saw that Adam was inflamed with so violent a love of Eve that he would carry out what she told him" (*Scivias* 1, *visio* 2). All this is the same old damning of women, for woman is the metaphorical Enemy of all celibate theology, and women themselves all too often accepted the notion of their sex as a divinely chosen plague.

With this old Augustinian contempt for woman as a background, in the thirteenth century Scholastic theologians, notably Albert and Thomas, reinforced by Aristotle, made their contribution. Aristotle opened the monks eyes' to the deepest reason for woman's inferiority: Woman owed her existence to a mistake, to a slipup in the process of birth. She was, in other words, a "misbegotten or defective man." Although this discovery by Aristotle fit in smoothly with the thinking of the Augustinian male Church, it was not accepted without a few hitches. William of Auvergne (d. 1249), *Magister regens* of the University of Paris, argued that if woman were labeled a defective man, then man could also be labeled a perfect woman, which sounded disquietingly like the "sodomitical heresy" (homosexuality) *De sac. matr.*, ch. 3).

But the churchmen's fear of adopting, along with Aristotle, a misogynistic Greek admiration for homosexuality was weaker than their desire to find at last a convincing explanation of woman's subordination to man. The Christian theologian-patriarchs got a tutorial on this point from the pagan philosopher-patriarchs. After the men (pagans and Christians) had driven woman back to her children in the kitchen and had requisitioned all other interesting-looking activities for themselves, it occurred to them (pagan and Christian males) that man is "active" and woman is "passive." And this fact of masculine activity, Albert thought, gave men greater worth than women. Augustine's principle that "The active is more valuable than the passive," is purely and simply "correct" (*Summa Theologiae* ps. 2 tr. 13 q. 82 m. 2. obj. 1; cf. Michael Müller, *Grundlagen der katholischen Sexualethik*, p. 62).

Aristotle connected this masculine activity and feminine passivity to the act of generation: The man "begets," the woman "conceives" (= receives) the child. Our linguistic habits have been untouched by the discovery (in 1827) of the ovum by K. E. von Baer, which proved that women contributed their half to the process of generation. The notion that semen is the only active principle in procreation has remained so firmly in place, thanks to Thomas Aquinas, that even today the Church's hierarchy ignores the theological consequences of von Baer's discovery, e.g., for the conception of Jesus. We can no longer simply say that Mary conceived Jesus from the Holy Spirit. Accepting the existence of the ovum means denying that God was the sole force effecting the Incarnation, and admitting that Jesus' conception was only 50 percent the work of the Holy Spirit (cf. U. Ranke-Heinemann, *Widerworte,* Goldmann Paperbacks, 1989², pp. 287ff.)

The idea that the male was the sole cause of generation was not invented by Aristotle. It fits the image men had of themselves. Even Aeschylus (525–456 B.C.), the father of Western tragedy, saw the man as the one and only begetter of life. Hence the fact that Orestes has murdered his mother, Clytemnestra, is not as serious as if he had murdered his father. As Apollo says, "The mother is no parent of that which is called/ her child, but only nurse of the new-planted seed/ that grows." Pointing to Pallas Athena, who was born without a mother from the head of her father, Zeus, he continues, "There can/ be a father without any mother. There she stands,/ the living witness, daughter of Olympian Zeus,/ she who was never fostered in the dark of the womb." And Athena, her father's daughter, says: "There is no mother anywhere who gave me birth" (*Eumenides,* 11. 658–60, 662–65, 736–40, translated by Richmond Lattimore).

These belittling notions of woman as a kind of flower pot for the male's semen were worked up by Aristotle into a theory that lasted for thousands of years. Aristotle, Albert, and Thomas see things this way: According to the basic principle that "Every active element creates something like itself," only men should actually be born from copulation. The energy in semen aims of itself to produce something equally perfect, namely, another man. But owing to unfavorable circumstances women, i.e., misbegotten men, come into existence. Aristotle calls woman *"arren peperomenon,"* a mutilated or imperfect male (*On the Generation of Animals* 2, 3). Albert and Thomas translate the Greek phrase as *"mas occasionatus."* Albert writes that *"occasio* means a defect that does not correspond to nature's intentions" (*De animalibus* 1, 250). And for Thomas that means "something that is not intended in itself, but originates in some defect" (*In II sent.* 20, 2, 1, 1; *De veritate* 5, 9 ad 9).

Thus at her birth every woman already has a failure behind her: Woman *is* a failure. Thomas writes that the adverse circumstances causing a man to beget something not as perfect as himself include, for example, moist south winds, which bring to birth a person with a high water content (*Summa Theologiae* I q. 92 a 1). And he knows what this inconvenient situation can lead to: "Because there is a higher water content in women, they are more easily seduced by sexual pleasure" (*Summa Theologiae* III q. 42 a. 4 ad 5). Women find it all the harder to resist sexual pleasure since they have "less strength of mind" than men (II/II q. 49 a. 4).

Albert too credits the influence of the winds, among other things, with producing males or females: "The north wind strengthens the power, and the south wind weakens it . . . The north wind leads to the generation of males, the south wind to the generation of females, because the north wind is pure and dries out the exhalations and stimulates the natural force. But the south wind is moist and heavy with rain" (*Quaestiones super de animalibus* XVIII q. 1). Thomas takes a similar position (*Summa Theologiae* I q. 99 a. 2 ad 2).

Woman, therefore, is a product of environmental pollution, a miscarriage. In his characteristically philosophical and abstract, rather than ecological or graphic, style, Thomas says that women do not correspond to "nature's first intention," which aims at perfection (men), but to "nature's second intention, (to such things as) decay, deformity, and the weakness of age" (ibid., q. 52 a. 1 ad 2). Thus woman is a substitute that comes into existence when nature's first intention, the creation of a male, comes to grief. She is a developmentally retarded man. Still, even this female failure is part of God's plan, not in a primary but a secondary (or whatever) sense, since "woman is intended for procreation" (ibid. I q. 92 a. 1). But from Thomas's monkish standpoint that exhausts woman's usefulness.

Thomas cites Augustine without naming him: The help for which God created woman for Adam refers simply to help in generation, since in all other activities a man would be of more help to the man. Albert had said the same thing before this (*In II sent.* 20, 1 and *IV sent.* 26, 6). The male theologians internalized Augustine: For male intellectual life woman had no meaning. On the contrary, Thomas thought that through a woman's touch a man's soul—as Augustine taught—descended from its lofty heights, and his body fell under her domination and thereby into "a slavery more bitter than any other" (*In 1 Cor. 7:1*). Thomas quotes Augustine: "Nothing drags the mind of man down from its elevation so much as the caresses of woman and the bodily contacts without which a man cannot possess his wife" (*Summa Theologiae* II/II q. 151 a. 3 ad 2).

Women have less physical and intellectual strength than men.

Men have "more perfect reason" and "stronger virtue" than women (*Summa Contra Gentiles* III, 123). Because of the "defect in her reasoning ability," which is "also evident in children and mentally ill persons," a woman is not allowed to serve as a witness for testamentary matters (*Summa Theologiae* II/II q. 70 a. 3). (Canon law rejected evidence from women in testamentary matters and criminal trials, but in other cases they were permitted to testify.) Children too had to observe the superiority of their father: "The father should be loved more than the mother, because he is the active principle of generation, while she is the passive one" (ibid., II/II q. 26 a. 10).

Such differences may be found even in the conjugal act: "The husband has the nobler part in the marital act, and hence it is natural that he needs to blush less when he requests the debt of marriage than when his wife does" (*Summa Theologiae Suppl.* q. 64 a. 5 ad 2). For intercourse "always has something shameful about it and causes blushing" (ibid., q. 49 a. 4 ad 4). Women are also more inclined to incontinence than men are, Thomas says, invoking Aristotle (*Summa Theologiae* II/II q. 56 a. 1). *The Hammer of Witches* (*Malleus Maleficarum,* 1487) claimed this was the reason why there were more witches than warlocks (I q. 6).

As a defective creature, still somehow on the level of the child, woman is capable of bearing children but not of educating them. The intellectual training of the children can come only from the father, since he is the intellectual leader. Thomas largely grounds the indissolubility of marriage on the fact that "the woman is in no way adequate" to the task of educating the offspring. On this score the father is more important than the mother. Because of his "more perfect reason" he can better "instruct" the children's understanding, and thanks to his "stronger *virtus*" (= both "strength" and "virtue"), he can better "hold them in check" (*Summa Contra Gentiles* III, 122).

Thomas has yet another reason for making marriage indissoluble: "For the woman needs the man not only for generating and educating the children, but also as her personal master (*gubernator*)," for the man, Thomas repeats, is of "more perfect reason" and "stronger virtue." Many men imagine that because they have more physical strength (*virtus*, literally "manliness"), they also have more virtue. Hence the Latin word "virtus" can be translated as "virtue" or "power" or simply as "masculinity." For as far back as the Romans virtue was derived from the notion of masculine strength. There is a great deal of evidence that the first virtues to appear in the human race and to gain an advantage over the others, men over women, churchmen over women in the Church, were the virtues through which the stronger made themselves masters of the weaker and in this way won glory and honor for themselves. Thus strength and masculine, warlike bravery (virtus) came to mean the same thing as "virtue." When Thomas says that the wife is subject to her husband because of his "greater *virtus*," he probably means both the strength to keep her in line and the virtue to correct her. In any case the wife has the same advantages as her children of being "instructed and held in check" by their father (*Summa Contra Gentiles* III, 123; 122).

Thomas maintains that "because women are in a state of subordination," they cannot receive Holy Orders (*Summa Theologiae Suppl.* q. 39 a. 1). This subordination to men is for Thomas the actual reason for denying women any churchly office. But he contradicts himself when, on the other hand, he speaks of women who do not exist in a state of subjection to men: "By taking the vow of virginity or of consecrated widowhood and thus being betrothed to Christ, they are raised to the dignity of men (*promoventur in dignitatem virilem*), through which they are freed from subordination to men and are immediately united with Christ" (*In 1 Cor.*, ch. 11, lectio 2).

But then why may such women not become priests? Thomas has no answer to that. Perhaps the cause lies more with men than with women. Long before this, by the way, Jerome had voiced the crazy idea that "a woman ceases to be a woman" and may be called a man, "when she wishes to serve Christ more than the world" (*Commentary on Ephesians*, Book III, ch. 5).

We may note in passing that as bad as this degrading of women by the Church was, it must be made clear that the worst accusation—that the Church doubted women had a soul or were human at all—is untrue. One often hears and reads that at the second Synod of Mâcon (585) the participants disputed whether women had souls, but that never happened. Souls were not the issue. Gregory of Tours, who was there, reports that a bishop raised the question, "whether woman could be called 'homo.' " Thus it was a philological question (though raised because of the higher value that men placed on themselves): *homo* in Latin means "person" as well as "man," as do cognate words in all the Romance languages, and as "man" does in English. The other bishops, Gregory reports, referred the questioner to the story of Creation, which says that God created man (*homo*), "male and female he created them," and to Jesus' title "Son of Man" (*filius hominis*), although he was the son of a virgin, and hence the son of a woman. These clarifications settled the issue: the term *homo* was to be applied to women as well as to men (Gregory of Tours, *Historia Francorum* 8, 20).

Thomas felt he had the support of Aristotle not only in the disparagement of women but in the matter of hostility to sex and pleasure. Aristotle's remark that sexual pleasure interferes with thinking (*Nicomachean Ethics* 7, 12) was grist for his mill, strengthening his Augustinian sexual pessimism. He borrowed the saying that Aristotle cited from Homer, that Aphrodite "bewitches the senses even of the most judicious," and stressed the notion that "sexual pleasure totally suppresses thought" (*Summa Theologiae* II/II q. 55 a. 8 ad 1). Thomas keeps returning to his belief that "sexual pleasure completely checks the use of reason," that it "stifles reason," and "absorbs the mind."

Today we can no longer reconstruct the thought processes behind the fanatical rejection by Thomas (Thomas in particular, but also by all Augustinian-based theology) of sexual intercourse, on the grounds that it "darkens," indeed "dissolves" the mind. Thomas maintains that frequent intercourse "enervates the mind" (*In IV sent.* 33 expos. text). Thus the roots of his thinking are not primarily theological, and no one can share his primitive biological anxieties unless one still believes, in this day and age, that frequent sex causes stupidity and disintegrates the brain cells. Something like this is what Thomas seems to mean by "enervate." And thus he makes a point of adding in his description of virginity ("the fairest of the virtues," *Summa Theologiae* II/II q. 52 a. 5) that it liberates its practitioners from the "damage to reason" (*corruptio rationis, In IV sent.* 33, 3, 1 sol. and 4) that occurs in sexual life. Evidently the Church's celibates were not claiming merely that because of their way of life they had more divine grace (100 percent in comparison with the 30 percent of married persons), but that they also had more rationality (because it was undamaged) at their disposal. Along with their salvation quotient, unfortunately, they make no mention of their intelligence quotient, though this would surely be of general interest too.

The connection between sexuality and original sin and this dragging down of the mind by lust were the main reasons why Augustine developed his doctrine of the compensatory goods that excuse marriage. Thomas took over this doctrine. Like Augustine, he described sexual pleasure not as unconditionally sinful, but as a punishment resulting from the Fall. Whence the need for compensatory goods, the principal one of which is children. Thinking altogether along Augustinian lines he argues: "No rational man may take any loss upon himself, if this is not canceled by an equal or greater value." But marriage is the sort of situation in which one experiences losses: Reason is swept up by pleasure, as Aristotle says, and then there are the "afflictions of the flesh," as Paul says. Hence the decision to marry may be seen as proper only when this "damage is matched by a compensation that makes the marital union honorable: And this is achieved by the goods that excuse marriage and make it honorable." By contrast Thomas cites eating and drinking: Since there is no pleasure bound up with them so vehement that it overwhelms reason, eating and drinking require no corresponding counterweight. As opposed to eating and drinking, "the power of sex, through which original sin is passed on, is infected and corrupted" (*Suppl.* q. 49 a. 1 ad 1). Thomas sees "the resistance of the flesh to the spirit that sometimes becomes noticeable in the organs of generation as a greater punishment than hunger and thirst, since the latter are purely physical, while the former is also intellectual" (*De malo* 15, 2 ad 8). Even the Jesuit

Josef Fuchs considers this idea of Thomas's "somewhat onesided" (*Die Sexualethik des heiligen Thomas von Aquin*, p. 40).

If sexual pleasure transmits original sin, this does not mean that someone who feels nothing also transmits nothing. Otherwise the children of the frigid would be sinless. But the theologians have thought of that too. Thomas explains: "If by the grace of the God someone has the gift of not feeling any inordinate pleasure in the act of generation, he would nevertheless pass on original sin to the child." For the sexual pleasure in question is not the actual pleasure (experienced in the moment of generation) but the habitual pleasure (based on the human condition), which is the same in all people (*Summa Theologiae* I/II q. 82 a. 4 ad 3). Thus even the frigid are out of luck, because they are latently lustful, they have a *propensity* to mind-absorbing pleasure, and that is enough. Even God's grace, which spares them the concrete pleasure that would otherwise darken their minds during sex, can do nothing about that.

No parents can escape the theologians' pitfalls. Mary's father and mother are the only exception, and that was not established until 1854 in the dogma of the Immaculate Conception. As far as Thomas is concerned, only Jesus and not Mary was free from original sin. He argues that since every act of intercourse means a "corruption" and "pollution" of the womb, in Mary's case Jesus was conceived without intercourse "for reasons of purity and to avoid defilement" (*In Matth.* 1 [19:247]). According to Thomas, only Jesus was pure, i.e., conceived without being infected by sex, without contracting the contagion of original sin from the parental act of generation. Josef Fuchs, the expert on Aquinas, observes here that, "How Thomas understands this 'impurity' of the sexual cannot be precisely determined" (ibid., p. 52). The theologians are inclined, especially in the case of the prince of theologians, to put the best interpretation on things. And when that is no longer possible, then they prefer stressing that they cannot understand Thomas to frankly admitting that he was talking nonsense and fell prey here to the nonsense of that other great theologian Augustine.

At this point we might briefly itemize the unholy terms supplied by the holy medieval theologian for the act of marital sex, terms that Josef Fuchs thinks "might surprise" the reader (ibid., p. 50). The only readers to be surprised, however, will be those who refuse to see that the whole corpus of Catholic sexual morality has been skewed from the beginning. Aquinas' terminology includes: "filthiness" (*immunditia*), "staining" (*macula*), "disgustingness" (*foeditas*), "shamefulness" (*turpitudo*), "disgrace" (*ignominia*). Clerics, Thomas says, maintain "bodily purity" through celibacy (passages cited in Fuchs, pp. 50–51). By way of excuse, Fuchs adds: "Thomas was part . . . of a long tradition . . . Thus it would have been hard for him to present a more liberal teaching" (ibid., p. 51). Nobody has to repeat nonsense, and since then the tradition, strengthened by Thomas, has become still longer, and the nonsense is still repeated, and the more liberal doctrine becomes increasingly harder to present because of the increasingly greater weight of tradition.

Here are a few more descriptions of intercourse provided by Thomas, who has been canonized as a saint and is called *doctor angelicus* ("the angelic teacher"): "degeneration" (*deformitas*), "sickness" (*morbus*), "corruption of integrity" (*corruptio integritatis*) (*Summa Theologiae* I q. 98 a. 2), a reason for "aversion" and "loathing" (*repugnantia*). Thomas says that those ordained to the priesthood feel such aversion to marriage "on account of the conjugal act," because it "impedes the acts of the mind" and stands in the way of "greater integrity" (*Summa Theologiae Suppl.* q. 53 a. 3 ad 1). Thomas spends more time than the other medieval theologians presenting and interpreting Pope Gregory I's teaching about the "eight daughters of unchastity." One of the worst effects of unchastity is the "feminization of the human heart" (*Summa Theologiae* II/II q. 83 a. 5 ad 2). Male pagans elevated *virtus* (= masculine strength) to mean "virtue" in our sense. Christian celibates, or at any rate Thomas Aquinas, degraded "woman" to mean "infamy." Celibate hatred of sex is hatred of women. Fuchs notes that "Thomas gladly repeats what Paul says in 1 Cor. 7:1: 'It is good for a man not to touch a woman' " (Fuchs, p. 261).

The fact that the Gnostic principle (which Paul cited in order to refute it) has been represented to this day as Paul's own principle has caused all sorts of mischief for two thousand years. The supposed Pauline axiom became the chief proof text for celibacy. And Thomas repeats the "salary scale" that had been accepted for centuries, namely that the heavenly reward for virgins amounts to 100 percent, 60 percent for widows, and only 30 percent for married people, with the celibates counting themselves as virgins (*Summa Theologiae* II/II q. 152 a. 5 ad 2; I/II q. 70 a. 3 ad 2; *Suppl.* q. 96 a. 4).

For Thomas, as for Augustine and all of tradition, "a marriage without carnal relations is holier" (*In IV sent.* d. 26, 2, 4). The fact that not only Thomas, but theologians in general, go into detail about vows of continence taken by married people shows that there were more than a few couples who lived like monks. Both Gratian and Peter Lombard deal in their standard works with such marriages and the questions of what the partners have to do, are allowed to do, are no longer allowed to do, etc. The model here is always the marriage of Mary and Joseph.

Besides this, married women, even though they shared a place with their husbands on the lowest level of celestial remuneration, for the most part also formed a still more poorly compensated group. This can be seen from an observation by the Jesuit Peter Browe, an expert on the Christian Middle Ages, who wrote in his book *Die Häufige Kommunion im Mittelalter* (1938): "Married women were never allowed to take communion frequently. They were considered not pure or worthy enough. Only if their husbands had died or if both husband and wife had taken a vow of continence could the actual quest for perfection begin and, if their situation was right, communion be received more frequently" (p. 120).

But not all married couples could reach this monkish goal of widowhood or total sexual abstinence. For them the point was that if they couldn't be perfect, at least they shouldn't fall into sin. To that end Augustine and Thomas offered them two modes of intercourse: 1) sex for procreation and 2) sex as fulfilling one's duty to the spouse requesting it, the latter "being designed to avert danger" (*Summa Theologiae Suppl.* q. 64 a. 2 ad 1; ad 4), that is, "to prevent fornication (by the other person)" (*Suppl.* q. 48 a. 2). All other motives, as good and noble as they might be (for example, love, which is never mentioned), will get one no further than sinful intercourse, venially sinful at the least (*Summa Theologiae Suppl.* q. 49 a. 5).

Some Early Scholastic theologians had argued that intercourse for the sake of avoiding fornication by *oneself* was sinless too, as we see even in a work written for confessors around the middle of the thirteenth century and attributed to Cardinal Hugh of St. Cher (d. 1263). According to him, the confessor should ask his penitent: "Have you had knowledge of your wife only for the sake of pleasure? For you should have knowledge of her only for procreation or to avoid your own fornication or to do your duty" (Noonan, *Contraception*, p. 272). But Thomas sticks closely to Augustine and rejects such a lax approach. He writes: "If someone has the intention of using intercourse to avoid fornication on his own part . . . then this is a venial sin, for marriage was not instituted for that." To be sure one may engage—sinlessly—in intercourse to prevent fornication by one's spouse, since that is a matter of performing one's duty (*Summa Theologiae Suppl.* q. 49 a. 5 ad 2).

When we read the centuries-long theological discussions about the danger of fornication, by oneself and by one's spouse, which one must avert by intercourse, or of fornication only by the other person (Thomas and others say that one's own leaning to fornication is best handled with prayer and fasting), we can take this view of sex as only one thing: an insult to married couples. Once the maximum number of children has been arrived at, the only chance for sinless sex is when the other person is on the verge of stumbling into fornication, and one is then obliged to prevent this by doing one's duty to him or her. The continual threat of fornication and adultery that the Church's celibates impute to married people and concede as a motive for intercourse is a piece of intolerable nonsense.

Even the Second Vatican Council, which has been wrongly described as a step forward in sexual morality, says that "often enough fidelity runs into danger, when the number of the children—at least for the time being—cannot be increased" and no "immoral solutions" (meaning birth control) may be employed. The danger of infidelity is the first thing that occurs to the council on the subject of contraception. The only other danger the council sees is that "the child as a good of marriage will suffer, and the brave readiness to have more children will be endangered" (*Gaudium et spes*, Pastoral Constitution on the Church in Today's World, 51).

Let's begin with the second point: The second *danger* that the Church sees when one can have no more children is that one would like to have no more children. The first *danger* is that married people may commit adultery. With their imagined *danger* of adultery the Church's celibate theologians have missed the true danger, namely that married people are slowly turning their backs on the celibate monastic Church because they are sick and tired of such nonsensical, incompetent, patronizing treatment, and would like to have sex not to ward off any sort of dangers, but for motives that obviously transcend the imagination of clerical celibates. The "exercise of the virtue of conjugal chastity," which Vatican II recommends instead "of following ways to regulate birth that the Magisterium . . . rejects" constitutes interference by the Church in the private concerns of married people that couples are no longer willing to put up with.

Back to Thomas. Deviation from the missionary position, he believes, is one of a series of unnatural vices that were classified, in a system going back to Augustine, as worse than intercourse with one's own mother (more about this in the next chapter). This ban on other sexual positions does not quite fit into Thomas's schema, because the other unnatural vices he catalogues have the common feature of excluding generation. In exceptional cases he does allow other positions, when couples cannot have sex any other way for medical reasons, e.g., on account of their corpulence (*In IV sent.* 31 exp. text). Thomas holds that the other most seriously sinful—because they are unnatural—vices, worse than incest, rape, and adultery, are masturbation, bestiality, homosexuality, anal and oral intercourse, and coitus interruptus (*Summa Theologiae* II/II q. 154 a. 11). Thomas appears to put deviation from the missionary position on the list of the most serious sins because he thought that like the other acts on this list, which prevented contraception, this one, if nothing else, made conception more difficult.

Albert, Thomas's teacher, had taught that when a woman lay in the lateral position the semen would have a hard time getting into the uterus, and that when the woman lay on top of the man the uterus would be "upside down" and the contents would spill out (*De animal*. 10, 2). In any case Thomas and all the theologians who followed him rated deviations from the "normal" sexual position, insofar as this was motivated by lust, as among "the most serious sins of unchastity." This folly continued even into the twentieth century (cf. the banning of Van de Velde's *Perfect Marriage* which had been published in 1926), even though in the meantime biological studies had shown that the notion of these positions being a hindrance to conception was a mistake.

The early medieval penitentials and manuals of theology treat the "unnatural positions" in great detail. Albert the Great attempts to demonstrate with physiological-anatomical arguments that the missionary position is the only natural one: "Whether the man should lie underneath or on top, whether he should stand or lie down or sit, whether copulation should take place from behind or from in front . . . this sort of shameful questions should actually never be dealt with, unless singular things, or the kind one hears nowadays in the confessional, make it necessary to do so" (*In IV sent.* 31). (If only the Church's celibates would stop using the confessional to meddle in matters that don't concern them . . .)

For Thomas, conjugal sex is a goal-directed secretion of semen to breed children. That is the only purpose of the sexual act (*Summa Contra Gentiles* 3, 122). And sex is moral only when it corresponds to correct order. The expressions "orderly manner" (*Summa Theologiae* II/II q. 153 a. 2) and "order" (ibid., II/II q. 125 a. 2) keep coming up. They mean the way that best matches the purpose of procreation, a specific form, in other words, which may not be deviated from. Deviation from the Church's prescribed method of ejaculating semen is *contra naturam,* unnatural. Thomas writes: "The manner of intercourse is prescribed by nature" (*In IV sent.* 31, exp. text). The act must proceed in proper order, even when in the case of a sterile woman conception cannot take place. Deviation from this natural method is always a serious sin, always unnatural.

Thomas's theory has implications today for artificial insemination, which was forbidden in 1987 by the Vatican Congregation for the Faith: "*Homologous artificial insemination* (italics mine) within marriage cannot be allowed." There is one exception, however: Semen can be obtained from intercourse by means of a condom, if this condom is perforated, so that the form of a natural act of generation remains intact, and no impermissible mode of contraception occurs. The conjugal act must take place as if it were leading to procreation, as if it were possible for conception to take place through the holes in condom (cf. *Publik-Forum,* May 29, 1987, p. 8). And only by this roundabout path, by an infertile conjugal act proceeding as if it were fertile, can fertility be helped along. The supposedly natural act has become the first commandment and it has kept that status even when its original goal, as prescribed by the Church, procreation, cannot be reached at all, and when obtaining semen through masturbation would be just as good a method, or a better one, because it is less complicated. But masturbation still ranks with the most serious, unnatural sins of contraception, even here when it is precisely being used to make conception possible. The standardized procedure has become more important than the goal, namely procreation. What is "natural" is determined by old traditions, and such traditions are carefully protected by old male celibates.

Breeding in the manner prescribed by the Church may not take place outside of marriage. This, says Thomas, is a law that nature too has laid down. In certain species, birds for example, Thomas observed (with Aristotle as his proto-Konrad Lorenz) that males and females stay together after breeding in order to raise their young together, "since the female would not suffice by herself to rear them." Thus the indissolubility of marriage is ordained by nature, for as with the birds (dogs are a different story, Thomas thought) the human female cannot raise her children all alone, since, among other things, this lasts "a long time" (*Summa Contra Gentiles* 3, 122). Accordingly, *heterologous artificial insemination* (from anyone but the husband) would be out of the question for the Catholic Church and is flatly rejected. It does not correspond to the proper order of sex for procreation.

Thomas maintains that "it is in keeping with nature for the honorable habits of animals to recur in man, but in a more perfect form" (*Suppl.* q. 54 a. 3 ad 3). There is no reason, therefore, to hope for new methods of generation unless we find them first in the animal kingdom. Josef Fuchs says about Thomas: "Again and again Thomas looks for the way into the animal kingdom" (p. 115). "He . . . draws comparisons between human and animal sexual life as a methodical approach far more than other theologians do" (Fuchs, p. 277). According to Thomas, whatever nature teaches all creatures has a binding force, and this can best be discovered from animal behavior. The most important message from the animal kingdom even today is one that the Catholic Church still considers binding: Animals have intercourse only for procreation (as the theologians see it, anyhow), which shows us the meaning of the sexual act. Animals do not use contraceptives, which shows us that contraceptives are unnatural. Thus pseudotheological study of animal behavior can lead to permanent ecclesiastical truth.

XVII

THE HEIGHTENED CAMPAIGN AGAINST CONTRACEPTION ("UNNATURAL SEX") AND ITS LEGAL CONSEQUENCES IN THE CHURCH, FROM THE MIDDLE AGES TO THE PRESENT

The *medical knowledge* about contraception available in medieval Europe came from the Arabs. The first two medical schools in Europe were founded in the eleventh century in Salerno and in the twelfth century in Montpellier. At these medical centers information about birth control from the Greco-Roman world and new findings by the Arabs were passed on to medieval Europe through Muslim textbooks. The most important text was the *Canons of Medical Science* by Ibn-Sīnā, written in Damascus in the eleventh century and translated into Latin, under the name of Avicenna, in Toledo a century later. Until the mid-seventeenth century it remained the most significant standard reference work for European physicians.

In his pharmacology, Avicenna lists the contraceptive qualities of various plants. "Oil of cedar destroys the semen, and if one anoints the penis with it before intercourse it prevents pregnancy" (2, 2, 163). Aristotle had already referred to this quality of cedar oil in his *On the History of Animals*. Avicenna also cites ancient prescriptions of Hippocrates, Soranus of Ephesus, and Pliny, along with more recent ones. Avicenna, following the line of Soranus, recommends contraception especially when pregnancy would endanger the life of the mother.

Albert the Great looks to Avicenna for most of his medical knowledge, for example, the idea that in the female superior position the uterus is twisted, "so that which is in her flows out again." Albert describes the causes of sterility primarily in his work *De animalibus,* with the guiding purpose of "enabling medicine to treat sterility." In dealing with everything that must be avoided lest one be sterile, he explicitly sets forth the knowledge of the Arabs and ancient Greeks and Romans about what must be done *in order* to become sterile. But as soon as he leaves his scientific presentation of Avicenna and speaks as a theologian, like all the Scholastics, he uses the Augustinian *"aliquando"* text referring to artificial methods of contraception as "poisons of sterility."

Not all theological writers treat the drugs used for birth control and abortion with as much breadth as Albert. The Dominican bishop Vincent of Beauvais (d. ca. 1264), reports in his *Encyclopedia* (the first substantial work of its kind in the Middle Ages) about plants, for example, rue: "It checks and suppresses evil desires, reduces and wholly dries out the semen" (*Speculum naturale* 10, 138). He claims that lettuce has similar qualities. In only one case of lust-suppressing drugs does he mention that it is also a contraceptive. St. Hildegard of Bingen (d. 1179), abbess of Ruppertsberg, wrote a book about natural medicine, in which she makes no reference at all to contraception and abortion, but, in keeping with the Catholic ideal of piety, recommends remedies, for example wild lettuce, "to stifle sensual lust in men and women" (*Subtilitatum* I, 92). To this day contraception in the Catholic sense by and large has to be practiced in this nunlike fashion, namely by combating one's lust.

From the standpoint of modern science most of these drugs had no effect one way or the other. And so those who took them would not have noticed that in about 1300 the physician Magnino of Milan, from the school of Salerno, in his book *Regime for Health* recommended that people "who wish to be continent" (and whom he found "admirable" for doing so) should "subdue their sexual drive" by using the very same plants that Avicenna prescribed as aids to potency. Another piece of advice from Magnino was that eating a bee "makes a woman sterile, but eases birth" (*Regime for Health* 2, 7). Magnino dedicated his work to the bishop of Arezzo. Medicine and theology in those days both made heavy demands on people's faith.

With the eleventh century the Catholic Church's struggle against birth control entered a new phase. The confrontation with the Cathars (= the pure ones, a sect whose name is the root of the German word for heretic, *Ketzer*), who condemned all procreation, fired up the Church's commitment against contraception. Secondly, in Scholasticism theology became the object of earnest scholarly endeavor, which led to a revival of the thought of Augustine. In the fourth century Augustine's opponents had been the Gnostic Manichaeans, who rejected breeding as diabolical. Augustine himself had belonged to this sect before he became a Christian, only to turn into its most formidable foe. Around the beginning of the eleventh century once again a wave of hostility toward reproduction began sweeping over Western Europe. It consisted of individual groups and ideologies that agreed on this one point of rejecting all generation: Bogomils, troubadours, Cathars, Albigensians. This is not the place to go into the difficult question of the extent to which (if at all) these groups are interrelated and whether, for example, the troubadours, with their glorification of love and sexual pleasure without childbearing, were reacting to the impoverishment of Christian teaching about sex. (Alluding to the purpose of procreation, which was given a one-sided emphasis by the theologians, many minnesingers declared that love did not exist among married people.) In any event, it is clear that in the Middle Ages the Augustinian struggle against Manichaean contraception recurred or grew stronger in the battle against birth control, especially among the Cathars.

Three texts in particular were destined to play a great role in the campaign against contraception, two from Augustine and the text *"si aliquis."* The two Augustinian texts, which are cited as *"aliquando"* and *"adulterii malum,"* were first brought into prominence by Ivo of Chartres (d. 1116). Noonan has called Ivo "one milestone in the formation of the canonical approach to contraception" (*Contraception*, p. 173). He was an adherent of the Gregorian Reform. He was not satisfied with the *Decretum* of Burchard of Worms, and adopted as the most important item in his own collection of laws (*Decretum* 10, 55) a text that had fallen into oblivion, in which Augustine speaks about the "poisons of sterility" and labels the wife who uses them "her husband's harlot." This text was called *"aliquando,"* after the first word. Secondly, Ivo incorporated into his collection three Augustinian texts on "unnatural intercourse in marriage," which conclude that, for example, coitus interruptus is a worse sin than fornication and adultery (*Decretum* 9, 110, 128), indeed worse than sex with one's own mother, since such incest is "natural," because it is open to procreation. These three texts were later grouped together under the heading, *"adulterii malum."* Ivo wanted this anthology to document a harsh condemnation of every kind of contraception.

The texts *"aliquando"* and *"adulterii malum"* acquired an importance that endured for centuries thanks to two standard works that were still more important than anything Ivo did. In around

1140 the first of these appeared: the unofficial, but generally recognized collection of laws made by the monk Gratian in Bologna under the title *Concordantia discordantium canonum* (= Concordance of the Discordant Laws), also called in brief the "Decree of Gratian." Until 1917, when the Code of Canon Law was introduced, Gratian's *Decree* was considered the most significant piece of fundamental legislation that the Western Church had. For centuries Gratian was the daily bread of canonists. Thanks to Gratian, every student of canon law was familiar with *"aliquando,"* with its heading, "Those who procure the poisons of infertility are fornicators, not spouses" (*Decretum* 2, 32, 2, 7).

In connection with Ivo's quotations from Augustine, Gratian sets up a "scale of indecency," which goes like this: "The evil of adultery [*adulterii malum*] is greater than that of fornication, but still greater is that of incest; for it is worse to sleep with one's mother than with the wife of another. Worst of all, however, is everything that takes place against nature, for example, when a man wishes to use a part of his wife's body that is not permitted for such use." Included in this "unnatural intercourse" are coitus interruptus and any kind of contraception. This apex of unnatural behavior is raised even higher over one issue: "It is more shameful when a wife has this done to herself than when her husband does it to another woman" (*Decretum* 2, 32, 7, 11). In the immediate context Augustine was speaking more about anal and oral intercourse, but in Gratian's *Concordance* that prohibition is tightened into an unheard of criminalization of birth control in marriage, which is now the absolute limit of vice, beyond even incest or "safe sex" with a prostitute.

Also in about the middle of the twelfth century, Peter Lombard (d. 1160), the bishop of Paris and a highly esteemed theologian, put together a second theological anthology, known as *The Sentences*. This would be the standard textbook for students of theology (including Martin Luther) all the way into the sixteenth century. If Gratian was the Father of Canon Law, Peter Lombard was the Master of Dogmatic Theology, until in the sixteenth century his *Sentences* were replaced by Aquinas' *Summa Theologiae,* which retains its authority to this day.

Peter Lombard often follows Gratian; and he cites *"aliquando"* against the practice of birth control. Under the heading, "Those who procure poisons of sterility are not spouses, but fornicators," he says: "She is her husband's harlot, and he an adulterer with his own wife" (*Sentences* 4, 31, 4). He also adopts Gratian's "scale of indecency" (ibid., 4, 38, 2), in which "unnatural" intercourse (contraception), especially with one's own wife, constitutes the summit (or the abyss) of vice.

Both Gratian and Peter Lombard are rooted in Augustine. Peter Lombard brings up again the old Augustinian connection between original sin and marital sex: "The cause of original sin is a defilement that [the begotten child] contracts from the ardor of the parents and their lustful desire." The transmission of original sin, once again, produces in the "members the law of deadly desire, without which sexual relations cannot take place." For this reason "sexual intercourse is reprehensible and evil, insofar as it is not excused by the goods of marriage" (ibid., 2, 31, 6; 4, 26, 2). Gratian and Peter Lombard thus take Augustine for their foundation, but go beyond him, first, by incorporating into their collections the rescript of Pope Gregory the Great, with its fatal axiom, "There can be no sexual pleasure without sin," and secondly, by placing a particularly negative stress on contraception.

The practical consequences of their strict ban on birth control can be seen in the following example: A woman had suffered an umbilical hernia because of childbirth, and the doctors insisted that she would not survive another delivery. Some people argued "that the women should get a sterilizing poison, and thus she would be able to continue fulfilling her marital duty, if she was sure that she would not get pregnant." The theologian Petrus Cantor (d. 1197) opposed this opinion and decided, in accordance with *"aliquando,"* that under no circumstances could the woman get herself such "poisons" (*Summa de sacramentis* 350; *quaestiones et miscellanea*).

In general, however, confidence in contraceptive potions was not widespread. Only with the invention of the pill (which moral theologians today call an "infertility drug") did this situation change. And so less importance was accorded in the Church's pastoral practice to *"aliquando"* than to the second classical Augustinian text on the question of birth control, namely the "scale of indecency." The methods of contraception that it excoriates are what Bernhard Häring, the best-selling German moral theologian in this century, nowadays calls "the disfiguring of conjugal relations" (*Das Gesetz Christi,* p. 355). What the medieval writers chiefly had in mind was coitus interruptus. This, as we have seen, was considered worse than intercourse with one's own mother. In the language of the theologians at that time coitus interruptus was usually called ejaculation "outside the proper vessel," although Thomas prefers the word "organ" (*instrumentum*) to "vessel." In the thirteenth, fourteenth, and fifteenth centuries theologians devoted more attention to the "sins against nature" than to the "poisons of infertility." Marriage sermons were sermons about "the sins against nature." Confessors were directed to ask their penitents whether they had committed them.

We can see how thoroughly the condemnation of birth control had penetrated the Christian mind-set from some remarks by St. Catherine of Siena (d. 1380), who was herself the twenty-fifth child in her family. She saw in her visions a group of sinners in Hell "who sinned in the married state." Her confessor and biographer, Raymond of Capua (d. 1399), later general of the Dominican order, asked her "why those sins, which are not graver than others, are punished so gravely." She answered, "Because the sinners are not so aware of them, and hence do not feel as much remorse as for other sins. Furthermore, they commit these sins more regularly and frequently than other sins" (Noonan, p. 227). Even back then married couples apparently had a hard time discovering sins where the theologians and their pious parrots, male and female, wished to see them. St. Catherine followed the same party line as Gratian, Peter Lombard, and Thomas Aquinas, all of whom saw contraception as a "sin against nature" and consequently classified it as the worst kind of unchastity.

The famous popular preacher Bernardine of Siena (d. 1444), whose goal in life was to foster devotion to Mary and Joseph, was another one who evidently was under the impression that married people needed to have their eyes opened to their sins, which only the celibate clergy were not blind to: "Married people have sunk into miserable ignorance, like a pig in his dirt-filled trough" (*The Christian Religion* 17, ante 1). "You will see that you have many sins in this married state that you have never confessed nor realized that they were sins . . . It is wicked when a man has intercourse with his own mother, but it is much worse when he has unnatural intercourse with his wife" (*Seraphic Sermons* 19, 1). "It is better for a woman to have relations in the natural manner with her own father than with her husband in an unnatural manner" (*The Christian Religion* 17, 1, 1). Bernardine can also cite exact figures: "Of a thousand marriages nine hundred and ninety-nine are the devil's," all because of the "sins against nature." These, Bernardine says, are every act of ejaculation "wherever and in whatever way that procreation cannot take place" (*Seraphic Sermons* 19, 1). "Every time that you came together in such a way that you could not conceive and beget children, it was a sin" (*Le prediche volgari,* Milan, 1936, p. 433).

In his sermons against unchastity that he gave at the French court John Gerson (d. 1429) even invoked a decree of the Christian Emperor Valentinian from the year 390 that punished homosexuality with burning at the stake (*Codex Theodosianus* 9, 7, 6). Gerson equates every action that thwarts the fertility of marital sex with homosexuality. He attacks the "inventive indecencies of sinners" in marriage. Such deeds "often deserve death by fire, and are worse than if they had been committed with women who were not the sinners' wives. May a person have intercourse at all, if he prevents the fruit of marriage from being conceived? I say that such is often a sin that deserves the flames . . . Every imaginable conduct that hinders the union of a man and woman from producing issue must be condemned" (*Sermon against Unchastity,* 2nd Sunday in Advent, Works, vol. III, 916).

The Dominican Girolamo Savonarola (1452–98), who drove the Medici from Florence, proclaimed Christ as King, and had all worldly baubles consigned to bonfires, and who himself was later burned at the stake, told confessors: "You should ask about this sin . . . whether it was in the vessel, or in an unseemly vessel or outside a vessel" (*Confessor's Guide,* Sins Against the Sixth Commandment). What he meant was 1) use of a pessary, 2) anal or oral intercourse, 3) coitus interruptus.

The sacrament of penance provided the best opportunity for calling people's attention to their marital sins through cross-questioning. The early medieval penitentials and the Decree of Burchard (d. 1025), which was generally recognized until late in the twelfth century, put their questions squarely. The problem, however, was that to many penitents such querying suggested undesirable (to the Church) ideas. For this reason, at about the end of the twelfth century confessors began steering away, to some degree, from explicit questions. The penitential of Bartolemy of Exeter (d. 1184) says that sins against nature by married couples should not be described too precisely, "for we have heard that men and women, because of the detailed mentioning of crimes they were previously unfamiliar with, have fallen into sins they had not known" (*Penitential*, ch. 38). Clearly, questions in the confessional sometimes fulfilled a function nowadays reserved to pornographic literature. Anyhow, lay men and women were usually just dilettantes on the fine points of sex, the confessors were the experts. Even today one wonders about the source of this detailed knowledge, which far exceeds the information level of the ordinary citizen.

Alain de Lille likewise recommends caution in his penitential. He writes that if the penitent confesses a forbidden kind of cohabitation, the priest should ask whether it was fornication, adultery, incest, or a sin against nature. This is important, since the sin against nature is the gravest among all these. But the priest "should not go too much into particulars." Otherwise he might be providing the penitent with an opportunity to sin (*Penitential* PL 210, 286ff.) Robert of Flamesbury, an Englishman and confessor to students from the Abbey of St. Victor in Paris, took a similar position in the penitential he wrote shortly after 1208.

In the year 1215 the Fourth Lateran Council ordered all Christians to go to confession and receive Communion at least once in the year. This led to the composition of many guides for thirteenth-century confessors. Cardinal Hostiensis gives a clear account of how to question the penitents: "What questions can or should be posed by the one hearing confessions?" For questions about unchastity the confessor should explain the sin against nature with the following words: "You have sinned against nature if you have had carnal knowledge of your wife in ways other than nature calls for." The confessor should not, however, go into the different ways that coitus can violate nature. He might question the penitent "carefully," as follows: "You know very well what way is the natural one. Have you ever had an ejaculation in a different way? If he says no, then ask no further questions. If he says yes, you could ask, while asleep or awake? If he says awake, you can ask, with a woman? If he says, with a woman, you could ask, outside of the vessel or inside it, and how?" (*Summa* 5, "Penance and Forgiveness" 49). And in a work usually ascribed to Cardinal Hugh of St. Cher (d. 1263), the direction for confessors under the heading of "adultery" reads: They should ask, "Or have you sinned with your own wife against nature? If the sinner asks, What is that, against nature? the priest may say, The Lord has allowed only one way, to which all men must adhere. So if you have done it in any other way but this, you have committed a mortal sin" (cf. Noonan, pp. 271–72).

Despite the caution recommended to confessors, unsuspecting women in particular must have sometimes pricked up their ears or gotten irritated in the confessional. This emerges from a remark by Bernardine of Siena (d. 1444): "Foolish women often come to their husbands and say, to give themselves the air of respectability, 'The priest asked me about this dirty business, and wanted to know what I do with you,' and the simpleminded husband always gets furious with the priest." Bernardine means that for this reason the priests were restrained in their questioning. But he, Bernardine, wished to be alert, and not a "silent dog." So he demanded that confessors express themselves clearly in their questions (*Seraphic Sermons* 19, 1). Evidently Bernardine's clarity resulted in some women's ceasing to come to his sermons. Because of that he criticized husbands for leaving their wives at home when he preached, so that they "would not learn these necessary truths" (*The Christian Religion* 17, ante 1). We may conclude that some married people found that what was unnatural and shameful was not so much their own sexual practices as their confessor's interrogation and Bernardine's sermons.

Harsh penances were dictated for contraceptive practices such as coitus interruptus. One important penalty was the denial of conjugal relations. The innocent spouse (usually the wife) was responsible for enforcing the penalty against the guilty one. Thus the wife had to deny her husband sex as a condition for not sharing her husband's guilt. The *Summa* of Alexander of Hales (d. 1245) lays down the rule: "The wife may under no circumstances yield to the sin against nature, and if she does consent, she commits a mortal sin" (*Summa Theologiae* 2/2, 3, 5, 2, 1, 3). John Gerson preached that if one spouse desired something "unseemly" during marital relations, the other should resist, "even unto death" (*Works,* Antwerp, 1706, Vol. 3, 916). And Bernardine of Siena made it clear in his sermons that "You wives should die rather than give in" (*Seraphic Sermons* 19, 1; similarly in *Le prediche volgari,* Milan, 1936, p. 435). All three, Alexander, Gerson, and Bernardine, explicitly included coitus interruptus in their definition of the sins against nature (cf. Noonan, pp. 261–62).

The absolutely ultimate condemnation of contraception—in case the Church had any further to go here—came at last in the third classical anticontraceptive text. This is found in a third important Scholastic anthology, which was drawn up on commission from Pope Gregory IX (d. 1241) by his chaplain, the Dominican Raymund of Peñafort. It was a collection of papal decretals, which, like Gratian's *Decree,* prepared or provided the contents of the Code of Canon Law, issued in 1917; and it incorporated the text already mentioned apropos of the penitentials: "Whoever [*si aliquis*] uses sorcery or administers sterilizing poisons is a murderer." When contraception was labeled as murder in a universally binding code produced on orders of the Pope, the summit of Mt. Everest had been reached in the campaign against contraception.

The canon *"si aliquis"* was consonant with the violent rhetoric of both Jerome and Chrysostom, and made a serious contribution toward outlawing contraception in the Catholic Church. But on the other hand it was alien to canon law from the beginning, since the Church's code assumed the theory of the successive animation of the fetus and penalized as murder, not contraception, but only the abortion of an animated fetus. Gratian and Peter Lombard held the same position. A letter from Pope Innocent III (d. 1216) shows that only abortion and then only after a certain point in time (ca. eighty days) was considered murder. The case at issue involved a Carthusian monk who had arranged for his lover to get an abortion. The Pope decided that the monk was not guilty of homicide, provided the embryo was not yet "animated," in the sense of Aristotelian biology. Augustine saw things Innocent's way, and so did Jerome, when he expressed himself in legal, not rhetorical, terms.

Thomas, the master of hairsplitting, alludes to *"si aliquis"* when he says that the use of poisons for infertility is a grave sin "and against nature, since even animals do not prevent themselves from conceiving young, but not as grave as murder, since conception might possibly not have taken place for other reasons." We can speak of murder, he says, only when someone aborts an already formed embryo (*In IV sent.* 31. 2 exp. text). Ignoring the inconsistency, the papal decretals characterize contraception as murder and place it at the top of the list of sins. Meanwhile in his critique of *"si aliquis"* when Thomas describes the taking of sterilizing poisons as a "sin against nature," he is departing from the usual language, since this in general only meant intercourse that did not properly advance the semen into the right "vessel," the vagina. "Murder" was applied to the taking of poisons that brought on sterility.

Even today canon law distinguishes between the two groups: on the one hand there is the pill and on the other coitus interruptus and intercourse with a condom. The new code of canon law, in force since 1983, says in Canon 1061: "A valid marriage between baptized persons, if it has not been consummated, is merely contracted (*ratum*). It is 'contracted and consummated' (*ratum et consummatum*) when the spouses have consummated the marital act with one another in a way befitting human dignity.

That act is intrinsically intended for procreation, to it marriage is oriented by nature, and through it the spouses become one flesh." This means, as we have seen, that a merely "contracted" marriage can be dissolved, and both partners can marry again; but a "contracted and consummated" marriage is indissoluble, and for as long as the other lives the spouses cannot remarry. And, in particular, intercourse with the woman on the pill counts as consummation of the marriage, but with coitus interruptus it does not. If the wife takes the pill, the marriage is indissoluble. If the husband always withdraws before ejaculating, the marriage can be broken up because according to canon law it was never consummated.

Canon law gets into difficulties with the use of condoms. The Church's legal experts argue about whether ejaculation *into* the vagina is necessary, or ejaculation *in* the vagina will suffice. For the men and women involved in the issue, of course, the celibate nitpicking is of no interest. Because even if the canon lawyers decided that there had to be ejaculation *into* the vagina for the marriage to be consummated and indissoluble, nobody could get a dissolution on the grounds of having used condoms. All previous attempts to use this argument have been rejected by Rome for lack of a guarantee that "a drop might not have gotten into the vagina." Condoms don't offer absolute security, and so the question of the indissolubility of marriage is a problem for the rubber industry.

The importance of semen has been carried to extremes here. We have already seen that holes in the condom have advantages for some married couples, since without such holes Catholics would be forbidden to practice any kind of artificial insemination. The point of canon law raised by the perhaps-not-leakproof condom leaves its users, if not a dissoluble marriage, an insoluble problem: To be safe, or not to be safe, that is the question.

Another way not to consummate one's marriage was through coitus reservatus, where there was no ejaculation. Once again we see the importance of semen. Unlike intercourse with a condom, coitus reservatus presented theologians with a clear and simple situation, because the semen was ejaculated neither in nor into the vagina. Unfortunately, not all problems in the Catholic theology are so easy to settle.

Intercourse with a diaphragm, it might be added, counts as consummation. This is connected with—among other things—the Aristotelian view that the man is the actual procreator, which has left its imprint on Catholic marital legislation. For the Church, ejaculation into the vagina is the crucial thing, the disposition of the woman's internal organs is of less concern. We shall meet this unequal treatment of men and women once again on the question of impotence.

Back to Thomas's position on the *"si aliquis"* canon. Although, as we saw, he rejected the word "murder" for contraception, and restricted its use to the abortion of an animated fetus, he was nevertheless the one who encouraged and consolidated the Church's legal notion of contraception as quasi-murder. The criminalization of birth control, as promoted by the twentieth-century popes, can be largely traced back to the theories of Thomas Aquinas.

For Thomas, every sexual act has to be a marital act, and every marital act has to be an act of procreation. A violation of the sexual commandments is a violation of life itself. For the semen already contains the potential for the whole person (or, more precisely, the whole man, for women come into being only when something goes awry in the process of development; *De malo* 15 a. 2). The unregulated ejaculation runs counter to the well-being of nature, which lies in the preservation of the species. "Therefore, after the sin of murder, through which human nature, which already exists in reality, is destroyed, the sin of preventing the generation of human nature comes in second place" (*Summa Contra Gentiles* III, 122). Contraception is thus not the same thing as murder, but is very close to it. Along with Aristotle, Thomas calls semen "something divine" (*De malo* 15, 2). "A person can be generated from a single cohabitation, and hence bringing disorder to cohabitation, which hinders the welfare of the offspring to be generated, is a mortal sin" (*Summa Theologiae* II/II q. 154 a. 2 ad 6).

While Thomas rejected the *"si aliquis"* canon, others went beyond it and labeled as murder not just contraception by means of medicinal poisons, but also, for example, coitus interruptus. Petrus Cantor (d. 1197; *Verbum abbreviatum* 138, "the sodomitical vice") argued for applying the term "murder" to contraception, by which he particularly meant the sin of Onan, who "spilled his seed upon the ground." The Franciscan Bernardine of Siena (d. 1444), the most prominent preacher of his day, made the same case. In the fifteenth sermon of his cycle of sermons on "the eternal Gospel," dedicated to "the horrible sin against nature," he quotes a line that he erroneously believed to be Augustine's: "Those who are infested with this vice are murderers of human beings, not with the sword but in deed." In fact, he adds, "They must be characterized not only as murderers of men, but what is still more terrible to think, truly as murderers of their own children." This sin is committed by men and women, "and most of all by those who are in the holy state of matrimony" (15, 2, 1), cf. Noonan, pp. 236–37.

The incredible, senseless inflation of contraception into murder through *"si aliquis"* was in itself meant only to evaluate behavior in the realm of confession and penance. But it left its mark on secular penal legislation, and for many people its consequences were dreadful. Thus *"si aliquis"* found an echo both in the "Bamberg criminal law" of 1507 and in Emperor Charles V's "Penal Rules" of 1532: Article 133 of the latter imposed the death penalty for contraception and abortion of the animated fetus. This meant beheading for the men and drowning for the women. For abortion of a "child that was not yet alive" (in other words, before animation) the penalties were lighter.

There were still more victims of the Church's madness. In 1215 at the Fourth Lateran Council Pope Innocent III, who was the uncle of the *"si aliquis"* Pope Gregory IX, had called on the Church to do battle against the Cathars and promised that all Catholics who took part in a crusade to eradicate heresy would have the same privileges as the Crusaders who went to the Holy Land. A terrible, centuries-long persecution of the Cathars was launched. In their struggle for fictitious life the warriors against contraception had evolved into murderers who had no mercy on the living. The punishment for the heretics who opposed the true faith was burning at the stake.

But the fires that began to burn then were only the beginning. In 1326 Pope John XXII equated the witches with the heretics, after theologians had stirred up mass hysteria with the idea of sexual relations between the witches and the devil. And in 1487 the authors of *The Hammer of Witches* pleaded for the application of the *"si aliquis"* canon to the "witch midwives," so as to punish them with death. Thus after the burning of heretics came the burning of witches, events that in Germany were destined to reduce to ashes a nontrivial percentage of the female population and a large portion of the midwives.

XVIII

INCEST

As *bad as unnatural* intercourse (e.g., contraception) is, it could have its advantages from the standpoint of canon law, particularly on the complicated subject of impediments to marriage. The connection is not immediately clear at first glance, but it can soon be recognized. For example, a man was not allowed to marry his female in-laws, not even very distant ones. If a man had had relations with any woman before his wedding, his brothers were barred from marrying her—by the impediment of affinity arising from illicit intercourse. At this point the question arises as to whether contraception had been used during the illegal intercourse or not. Pope Urban II (d. 1099) was asked to solve the following problem: Assuming that one of two or more brothers had unnatural relations with a woman, did that create a marital affinity so that none of the brothers could marry the woman? The Pope's answer: No. An improper ejaculation was not the kind of intercourse that led to that sort of impediment. The brother could marry the woman.

But from another point of view this advantage was a disadvantage, because the brother could no longer separate from his wife by invoking the impediment to marriage on the grounds of forbidden cohabitation, whereas a husband's careful investigation of his own or his wife's past had often been rewarded with a decree of nullity. Marriage despite such affinity was incest. The simplest way to get a divorce in the Middle Ages was to go looking for incest along this tangled network of relations. That was the course followed by the most famous would-be divorcé in Church history, Henry VIII.

This whole structure was invented by the Church's celibates, and extended to a downright grotesque extreme (people within the seventh degree of kindred could not marry, although since the time of Innocent III [d. 1216] this has been limited to the fourth) in order to make it harder to marry and to promote the monasticization of the laity. The system also turned out to be an opportunity to shed one's spouse on account of 1. blood relationship, 2. affinity by marriage, 3. affinity by forbidden cohabitation, 4. public integrity (prior betrothal), and 5. spiritual relationship (with godparents, sponsors at confirmation, and their families).

In the Old Testament (Leviticus and Deuteronomy) relatively few marriages between relatives and in-laws are forbidden. A man may not marry: his mother, sister, granddaughter, aunt, stepmother, mother-in-law, daughter-in-law, stepdaughter, stepgranddaughter, daughter of a stepmother by a previous husband, wife of one's father's brother, or brother's wife. On the other hand, a man was actually obliged by the custom of levirate marriage to beget children on the widow of his brother if she had no children. Otherwise among the Jews to this day marriage among relatives is not only not forbidden, but recommended. It was said that "a man should not take a wife until his sister's daughter was grown up; only if she did not please him, should he look for someone else" (H. L. Strack and P. Billerbeck, *Kommentar zum Neuen Testament aus Talmud und Midrasch* II, 380). Marriage between cousins was common: Isaac married Rebecca, Jacob married Leah and Rachel.

John the Baptist was beheaded because he reproached Herod Antipas: "It is not lawful for you to have your brother's wife" (Mk. 6:18). Herodias had abandoned her husband, "Herod the landless." John was speaking for Old Testament law, as found in Leviticus (18:16 and 20:21). John forbade marriage with the wife of a brother who was still living, but not because he was defending the indissolubility of marriage and attacking the remarriage of divorced persons. These are notions that were developed later by Christianity. John the Baptist was merely repeating the Old Testament law that permitted divorce and even polygamy but banned marriage with one's brother's wife while he was still alive. Pope Gregory the Great was wrong to invoke John the Baptist in his rescript to England and to make him a martyr to the Christian prohibition against marrying one's in-laws.

In contrast to the relative moderation of the Jews, Christians worked up a whole mass of legal technicalities for prohibiting marriages that no religion hitherto had been even theoretically capable of contriving and that can be explained only by Catholic hostility to sex and pleasure (cf. G. H. Joyce, *Christian Marriage*, 1948, pp. 507ff.: the forbidden degrees of kinship and affinity by marriage).

In 314 the Council of Neocaesarea decreed that if a woman married two brothers in succession she was to be excommunicated for five years. The Spanish Synod of Elvira, in the early fourth century, prescribed that if a man married the sister of his deceased wife, she was to be excommunicated for five years. Only if she was gravely ill could she be allowed to make amends, but then she must promise to give up the relationship. The Old Testament did not forbid marriage with the sister of one's deceased wife, but marriage with the wife of one's living brother. St. Ambrose was wrong too when in 397 he forbade a man from marrying his niece, arguing that in the Book of Leviticus marriages between first cousins are banned, which would include marriages between uncles and nieces (*Letter to Paternus*). Ambrose was mistaken on both counts. Augustine admits that the Old Testament saw things differently. He thought that in those days marriages between first cousins had been allowed, but now they were forbidden as unseemly because, "There is in human conscience a certain mysterious and inherent sense of decency . . . which ensures that if kinship gives a woman a claim to honor and respect, she is shielded from the lust (and lust it is, although it results in procreation) which, as we know, brings blushes even to the chastity of marriage" (*The City of God* XV, 16).

In the sixth century the ban on incestuous marriages reached all the way to third cousins. Pope Gregory the Great in his rescript to the newly converted English made some small concessions for more distant degrees of kinship. But he strictly forbade marriage between first cousins: "Experience has taught us," he said, "that such marriages are barren."

The idea of justifying bans on incest by citing the hereditary damage to the offspring did not become fashionable among theologians until recently. Two examples of this would be Fritz Tillmann in his *Handbuch der katholischen Sittenlehre,* which appeared during the Nazi period, and Bernhard Häring in his much-reprinted *Das Gesetz Christi.* Yet the health of the children born depends not on the degree of relationship but on the hereditary material. Gregory the Great forbade Englishmen to marry their brother's widow. "That is why St. John the Baptist was beheaded." To the question of whether those who were already living in such marriages before the arrival of the Christian missionaries would now have to be separated, the Pope announced these glad tidings: "Since it said that there are many among the English people who at the time when they were still pagans were living in such reprehensible marriages, if they accept the faith, they must be admonished to observe continence. They are to fear God's dreadful judgment, lest they incur eternal pains and torments for the sake of carnal lust." In any case, they did not have to dismiss their wives from pagan days. The newly converted Latvians in the thirteenth century had a harder time of it, as we shall see.

In the eighth and ninth centuries the Church demanded that couples who had married within the sixth degree of kindred separate and take other spouses. Thus, for example, the synods of Verberie in 756 and Compiègne in 757 issued such orders. In the year 800 Pope Leo III exhorted the bishops of Bavaria not to permit any marriage with blood ties even if they were seven generations back, because on the seventh day the Lord rested from all his words (Wetzer/Welte, *Kirchenlexikon*, XII, 847). Proof that the couple were not related in the seventh degree was practically impossible to obtain, and if such a connection showed up afterward, the marriage was annulled. A Council of Cologne in 922 went only as far as the fifth degree.

As for affinity from forbidden cohabitation, the Synod of Compiègne laid down for the first time in 757 that if a woman married the brother of a man with whom she had previously had an immoral relationship, the marriage was invalid. In the ninth century the previously mentioned Count Stephanus, who sent his young wife back to her father, Count Regimund, after the wedding but before the marriage night, and who was the occasion for the famous judgment delivered by Hincmar of Rheims (d. 882), claimed that before his marriage he had had intercourse with a woman related to his wife and hence incurred an impediment because of the forbidden cohabitation. He refused to give the lady's name, and with Hincmar's help he got the Frankish bishops to concede that such an affinity constituted a "diriment impediment" to the marriage.

Emperor Henry III (d. 1056) violated the laws of the Church by marrying Agnes, the daughter of William of Aquitaine, for Agnes and he were great-grandchildren of two stepsisters, Albreda and Mathilde, and thus related in the fourth degree. It was not until the Gregorian Reform in the eleventh century that the Church consistently managed to suppress incestuous marriages, which along with the eradication of priests' marriages was a key point of the reform. St. Peter Damiani (d. 1072) zealously proclaimed that the sacred canons forbade all marriages between relatives, so long as the faintest memory of their connection endured. In 1066/67 Pope Alexander II forbade a marriage because the woman was related in the fourth degree to a person with whom the man had earlier had an affair.

It had become difficult to find any marriage partner at all. No married couple could be sure that someone motivated by envy and malice might not accuse the marriage of being incestuous before the Church's tribunal. If the children were suddenly declared illegitimate, that would have legal consequences for their inheritance, etc. The whole situation caused understandable unrest, and so Pope Alexander III (d. 1181) decreed that if a marriage in the fourth degree of kinship had lasted from eighteen to twenty years it could no longer be challenged. And Pope Lucius III (d. 1185) allowed the archbishop of Spalato to leave a marriage in the fifth degree of kindred undisturbed.

In 1215 Pope Innocent III reduced the forbidden degrees of relationship by blood and marriage from the seventh to the fourth. But this didn't mean that the door had been slammed shut forever on papal marriage rulings. Innocent III informed a woman who had petitioned for the annulment of her marriage because she was related to her husband in the fourth degree that the ban on such marriages was a human, not a divine law. Hence it was possible, with a papal dispensation, to tolerate such a marriage— and the woman failed in her attempt to get rid of her husband. In addition, the bishop of Riga inquired of Innocent III how he should deal with the newly baptized Latvians, who had a custom whereby a man would marry his brother's widow. If these people were not allowed to keep their wives once they became Christians, many of them would refuse to be baptized. With an eye to the Old Testament levirate marriage, the Pope decided as follows: If the widow had children from the first marriage, then the subsequent marriage had to be annulled before the husband or wife could be baptized. If the wife had no children from the first marriage, then the marriage could continue, by exception. But no baptized person was allowed to enter a new marriage with his sister-in-law. Practically this meant that a widow with children from her first marriage had to part with her current husband, because he had been her brother-in-law; otherwise she could not become a Christian. If her husband wanted to convert, he had to dismiss his sister-in-law/wife, whether she was young and with small children or older with grown children. And so a good number of people must have become Christians out of marital discord, at least in Latvia.

Dispensations were granted on an occasional basis. Some people who wanted, not a dispensation to preserve their marriage, but an annulment to end it, like the woman who turned to Innocent III, got one anyway. Some who wanted dispensations couldn't have them. Cardinal Turrecremata (d. 1468), a renowned canon lawyer, told Pope Eugene IV (d. 1447) that it was not in the pope's power to give the Dauphin, later Louis XI of France, a dispensation to marry the sister of his deceased wife. It may be noted in passing that this impediment was not dropped until 1983, although long before this dispensations had been customarily granted from the rule, despite the cardinal's verdict.

The first dispensation to marry the sister of a deceased wife was provided in the year 1500 by Pope Alexander VI for King Manuel of Portugal (d. 1521) to marry Maria of Aragon, the sister of his deceased wife, Isabella. In 1503 a dispensation was issued to permit Maria and Isabella's sister, Catherine of Aragon, to marry the brother of her late husband, namely Henry VIII. This dispensation would later become the occasion for England's breaking away from Rome. The Council of Trent, by the way, decreed that dispensations in the second degree of kinship could be granted only to princes for reasons of public welfare (Sess. 24 Chap. 5 *de reform. matr.*).

Henry VIII's efforts to annul his marriage with Catherine of Aragon came to naught. Since Pope Julius II had given Henry the dispensation to marry the widow of his brother Arthur, the King could scarcely hope that Clement VII would do an about-face. And so he finally took matters into his own hands. Memoranda from *his* canon lawyers certified the correctness of what he intended to establish, namely that Julius had not had the right to give him the dispensation in the first place. The Pope had violated a divine commandment. Henry even had (quasi-)proofs that his cause was just from his own personal experience: He thought that the series of miscarriages and the birth, in the end, of only a daughter (Bloody Mary) were to be traced back to the threat in Leviticus 20:21: "If a man takes his brother's wife, it is impurity; he has uncovered his brother's nakedness, they shall be childless." The Church Assembly of Canterbury decided in the

King's favor by a vote of 244 to 19, the Assembly of York approved by 49 to 2. Henry also won support from the Protestants, who said that the degrees of kinship forbidden by Leviticus were as binding as the Ten Commandments. And so the Pope had no say in dispensing from them.

With his second wife, Anne Boleyn, the King succeeded—by now he was himself the head of the English Church and no longer made inquiries in Rome—in declaring his daughter Elizabeth a bastard with the help of the impediment of marital affinity through forbidden cohabitation. Anne was gotten out of the way by decapitation. But before he had married Anne, he had had relations with her older sister Mary (normal intercourse, and so the impediment did not collapse, as it had in the controverted case of the brothers settled by Pope Urban II). Thus according to the expert opinion of his canonists, Henry had never been validly married to Anne Boleyn. Elizabeth was an illegitimate child and so had no claim to the throne—until the times changed again and she ascended it after all.

Despite many calls for reducing the forbidden degrees of kindred and affinity by marriage, the Council of Trent (1545–63) stood by the fourth degree. Not until 1917 did the Church admit a reduction, but only to the third degree. Hence from 1917 onward one could marry the child of a second cousin—roughly the position that had prevailed in the fifth century. In 1983 new reductions were announced, e.g., before then a woman could marry her father's cousin only with a dispensation, afterward the impediment was dropped and no dispensation was needed.

In 1983 the impediment arising from a spiritual relationship was dropped altogether. In 530 the Emperor Justinian had forbidden the marriage of godchild and godparent. At the Second Council of Trullanum in 692 (can. 53) and at the Roman Synod of 721 the marriage of a godparent to one of the parents of his or her godchild was forbidden. Pope Nicholas I (d. 867) banned the marriage between the children of a godparent and his or her godchild. The Frankish Synod of Verberie (756) called for the separation of spouses if the husband had become spiritually related to his wife by standing as sponsor at the confirmation of his wife's child. So women who wished to separate from their husbands used this confirmation trick, which put them into an incestuous relation with their husbands. That led the Synod of Châlons to declare in 813 that in this case there should be no separation, but that the guilty party should be condemned to lifelong penance.

The *Kirchenlexikon* of Wetzer/Welte (1901, volume XII) has an article on "spiritual relationships," which shows how thoroughly the leaders of the Church had thought everything through and bound it up with regulations. Thomas too—especially Thomas—devoted such pains to spiritual relationships that one has to marvel at the precision with which he explains such nonsense to himself, so that he can move on to justifying it in particular instances (*Suppl.* q. 56 a. 4 and 5). Here is Wetzer/Welte's historical overview of the whole crazy situation: "In the period that followed (from the ninth century onward) the notion of impediments received its broadest extension. On the ground of *paternitas spiritualis* marriage was banned between the baptizand and the priest who baptized her, and then between the baptizand or confirmand and the godparent or sponsor, but also between the spouse of the baptizer or godparent and the baptizand or confirmand, in case the baptizer or godparent were married and the marriage had been consummated (*paternitas indirecta*) . . . Owing to the *compaternitas* or *commaternitas spiritualis* marriage was forbidden between the baptizer and the godparent, on the one hand, and the physical parents of the child on the other. The impediment also existed between the spouse of the baptizer or godparent in the case of a consummated marriage and the parents of the godchild (*compaternitas indirecta*) . . . Finally because of *fraternitas spiritualis* marriage was forbidden between the baptizand or confirmand and the children of the godparent as well as of the baptizer" (XII, 851).

In the work of Alphonsus Liguori (d. 1787) we find page after page about where and when the godparent has to touch the godchild, so that between whom and whom else from then on an impediment to marriage may exist, and which spouse may not thenceforward request his or her marital duty from which spouse or may perform it only upon request, because he or she by touching during baptism the child they had or did not have together suddenly became spiritually related to his or her marriage partner and thus from that point on was living in incest, because he or she inadvertently or maliciously did it (lift the child out of the font, that is)—or maybe did not (*Theologia moralis* 6, n. 148ff.). Still things are greatly simplified in Alphonsus, since the Council of Trent had discarded much of clutter involved in the impediments to marriage from a spiritual relationship.

Luther, by the way, had thrown this whole issue out of court as early as 1520 when he wrote: "And so these lies about godfatherhoods, motherhoods, brotherhoods, sisterhoods, and daughterhoods ought to be a completely dead letter . . . Just see how Christian freedom has been subjugated by human blindness" (*On the Babylonian Captivity of the Church*). But it was not until five hundred years after his birth, in 1983, that this impediment was removed from canon law.

In 1522 in his sermon on married life Luther upbraided the Catholic Church for the abuses it fostered: The Old Testament prescriptions ought not to be extended. They related to explicitly mentioned persons, not to degrees of kinship. Calvin contested that. He thought that the Old Testament laws had to be completed by analogy. For example, if a woman was not allowed to marry two brothers one after the other, then neither could a man marry his wife's sister. But anything else that went beyond such parallel situations was a diabolical deception by the popes. The Council of Trent attacked the thinking of both Reformers and excommunicated everyone who said that "only those degrees of kinship and affinity by marriage that are named in Leviticus could prevent the contracting of a marriage or, if it had already taken place, annul the contract, and that the Church could not issue a dispensation from the impediment for some of these degrees or could not ordain that other degrees were capable of banning and breaking up a marriage."

The Eastern Church spared itself many complications by never recognizing the impediment of affinity from forbidden cohabitation, which sprang up in the West in the eighth century. Otherwise the regulations concerning blood relations and affinity by marriage were not essentially different from those in the West. When Patriarch Markos of Alexandria pointed out to the famous canon lawyer and patriarch of Constantinople Theodore of Balsamon (d. after 1195), that the Christian community of Alexandria had dwindled so much that it had become difficult to avoid incestuous marriages, Theodore replied that this did not justifying the committing of sins.

Josef Fuchs, the expert on Thomas, bestows special praise on Aquinas because, among other things, he provided a thorough justification for the ban on incest. Fuchs writes: "Thus although Thomas kept a body of traditional teaching that was simply passed on by other theologians, he thought it through in a completely new and independent way. Compare, for example, the careful substantiation of the ban on incest in Thomas with the nonproblematic handing down of tradition in the other theologians. For instance, the otherwise quite independent William of Auxerre is unaware of any intrinsic justification for his case" (*Die Sexualethik des heiligen Thomas von Aquin*, pp. 277–78). Where all justifications are ridiculous, no justification is surely more sensible than a lame one. The praise Fuchs gives Thomas is identical with the blame he deserves for justifying where there is nothing to justify, for uncritically accepting nonsense and then proceeding to rationalize it.

Thomas has a particularly easy time doing this, because it fits in, so to speak, with his motto on the repression of marriage. One reason that he borrows from Augustine is "the increase of friendship" (meaning the friendship that comes into being through kinship and marital affinity). The bonds of friendly relations are increased, Thomas argues, by limiting marriage to nonrelated persons. Another reason that he thinks he finds in Aristotle— though Aristotle would be amazed to learn how he had validated such farfetched taboos—is this: If the love of kinsfolk is added to sexual love, there is a danger of excessively passionate love, "since by nature man loves his blood relatives, if the love that derives from the sexual connection supervenes, there would be too much passion in the love and a maximum of sexual desire, and this goes against chastity" (*Summa Theologiae* II/II q. 154 a. 9).

Thomas explains Christianity's broad extension of the Old Testament's very few forbidden degrees of kinship by arguing that through "the new law of the spirit and of love" more degrees of kinship were forbidden and it was also necessary "that men withdraw more from carnal things and devote themselves more to spiritual things." What we have, in other words, is the process of turning lay people into monks. For this reason Thomas finds it "reasonable" that the ban on marriage was extended all the way to the seventh degree of kinship and marital affinity—reasonable because beyond that a husband and wife could no longer easily recall their common origin, and also because it "is in keeping with the seven gifts of the Holy Spirit."

More recently, Thomas notes, this has been reduced to the fourth degree (by Innocent III at the Fourth Lateran Council in 1215). Thomas finds four degrees "appropriate," because through the prevalence of sexual desire and carelessness the failure to observe the many forbidden degrees of kinship has turned into a "pitfall for the damnation of many." Thus, whether four or seven, Thomas can justify any number of degrees. No doubt he would have found reasonable and God-given reasons for the fourteenth degree, all under the monkish motto of more friendship and less passion.

XIX

SPELLS FOR IMPOTENCE, SATANIC LOVES, WITCHES, AND CHANGELINGS

The importance of Thomas Aquinas for sexual ethics comes not from his having changed the course of theology in this area, but, on the contrary, from the fact that he was the great conformist in tune with his time, who took its doctrine, especially the conservative variety, gave it a permanent shape, and defended it against liberalization. His gravest mistake, which owing to his authority was destined to have the most devastating consequences, was his opposition to those who doubted (even in the credulous thirteenth century) that devils were particularly busy and effective in the realm of sex, that they had, for example, the magical power to make men impotent. Such doubts, he thought, contradicted the Catholic faith: "Catholic faith teaches us that the demons have some importance, that they can harm human beings and even prevent sexual relations." He criticizes "those individuals who have said that such bewitchment does not exist and is nothing but a product of unbelief. As these people see it, the demons are only human imaginings, that is, humans imagine the demons and then suffer harm from their terror at such fantasies" (*Quaestiones de quodlibet* X. q. 9 a. 10).

Here too Thomas was not the inventor but the most influential preserver of prejudices. The idea of magically induced impotence can be found as far back as a letter written in 860 by Archbishop Hincmar of Rheims. According to Burchard of Worms (d. 1025) the confessor should question the penitent as follows: "Have you done what amorous women are accustomed to do? When they see that their lover wants to enter upon a lawful marriage, they kill his desire through magical arts so that he cannot have relations with his wife. If you have done this, you must do penance for forty days on bread and water." This superstition was then incorporated into the collections of laws made by Ivo of Chartres in the eleventh century and Gratian in the twelfth, as well as by Peter Lombard (twelfth century) in his *Sentences*.

But not until the thirteenth century, the "Golden Age of theology," did this belief make unimaginable strides toward acceptance. Still there were other opinions. The Jesuit Peter Browe, an expert on the medieval Church, writes: "Thus power of the devil over the male procreative drive was, however, apparently contested by a few theologians and laymen. At least in a very large number of textbooks one finds the recurring objection that this thesis was only an attempted explanation of effects whose causes were unknown and were hence ascribed to the demons and their instruments. But this objection was . . . refuted and rejected by Thomas Aquinas as freethinking and un-Catholic" (*Beiträge zur Sexualethik des Mittelalters*, p. 124). Thomas's teacher before him, Albert the Great, likewise berated those un-Catholic free thinkers: "No one may doubt that there are many(!) who have been bewitched by the power of the demons" (*Commentary on the Sentences* IV d. 34 a. 8).

On the question of why the devil should prevent men particularly from having intercourse but not from eating and drinking, St. Bonaventure (d. 1274), the great Franciscan theologian, noted that, "Because the sexual act has been corrupted (through original sin) and has become, so to speak, stinking, and because human beings besides are for the most part too lustful, the devil has so much power and authority over them. One can prove this by an example and the authority of Scripture, for we are told that a devil named Asmodeus slew seven men in bed, but not at the table" (ibid., d. 34 a. 2 q. 2). Bonaventure is referring to the Book of Tobit, which through the additions to, and deletions from, the text made by its translator, St. Jerome, was falsified to express hostility to sexual pleasure, and as such is cited to this day by Catholic theologians as biblical proof that God intended the conjugal act purely for procreation (e.g. Bernhard Häring, *Das Gesetz Christi*, 371–72). All the way into the eighteenth century the text was also quoted as proof of the fact that, while the devil cannot bring death to the marriage bed, he can certainly cause impotence.

The Book of Tobit tells about the marriage of the young Tobias to his relative Sarah, who had already been engaged to seven men, all of whom were killed by the demon Asmodeus on their wedding night. The archangel Raphael gives Tobias the following advice (actually from Jerome): "The devil has power over those married people who exclude God and abandon themselves to lust like horses and mules that have no understanding. But you refrain from her for three days and pray with her during this time . . . when the third night is past take the virgin unto yourself in the fear of the Lord, more out of love of children than out of lust." And after three days and nights Tobias says: "And now, Lord, you know that I am not taking this sister of mine out of lust, but only out of love of offspring" (Tob. 6:14–22 and 8:9). In the original text of Tobit (second century B.C.) Tobias has relations with Sarah on the very first night, and both the lecture by the archangel and the bridegroom's fine words come from the ascetical St. Jerome.

From the beginning of the thirteenth century onward countless synods attacked the sorceresses "who put spells on married people so that they cannot engage in conjugal relations." These included the synods of Salisbury in 1217, of Rouen in about 1235, of Fritzlar in 1243, of Valencia in 1255, of Clermont in 1268, of Grado in 1296, of Bayeux in 1300, of Lucca in 1308, of Mainz in 1310, of Utrecht in 1310, of Würzburg in 1329, of Ferrara in 1332, of Basel in 1434 (cf. Browe, p. 127).

In his notorious "Witches Bull" of 1484, Pope Innocent VIII appointed two German Dominicans, Jakob Sprenger (a professor of theology in Cologne) and Heinrich Institoris (later the authors of *The Hammer of Witches*), as inquisitors, since he had heard that in the dioceses of Mainz, Cologne, Trier, and Salzburg a very large number of people of both sexes were engaging in sorcery so as "to prevent the men from begetting and the women from conceiving, and to make the conjugal act impossible." On the grounds of the *"si aliquis"* canon, which labels contraception as murder, Institoris and Sprenger in their *Hammer of Witches* (1487; I q. 8) demanded the death penalty for those who practiced the kind of sorcery, as mentioned by the "Witches Bull," that caused impotence and sterility. God himself, the authors believed, looked after the death penalty for another kind of contraception, making short work of the sinners: "No sin has God avenged so often through sudden death," they said, as the vices aimed "against the nature of reproduction," for example, "coitus outside the ordained vessel" (ibid., I q. 4). For Sprenger and Institoris contraception even without witchcraft was worthy of death.

The belief in impotence by enchantment and the mass hysteria about witches were given authoritative direction from on high. Thomas had attacked those freethinkers who denied that impotence was the result of bewitchment and challenged the role of the devil in sexual intercourse. Similarly the Pope's "Witches

Bull" was aimed against the many people, "regardless of what dignities, offices, honors, privileges, titles of nobility, rights or prerogatives of sovereignty they might possess," those "clergy or laypeople who claim to know more than behooves them," and those who "hindered, resisted, or rebelled against" the witchcraft trials instigated by the two inquisitors (the Pope called them "my beloved sons"). The penalties against these know-it-alls—there seem to have been a lot of them in Germany in those days—were supposed to be "made harsher."

The Hammer of Witches also launches its first assault against the skeptics. It begins with the question, "whether the claim that witches exist is so thoroughly Catholic that a stubborn defense of the opposite must be considered heretical." The answer, of course, is yes. The chief source and guarantee for such Catholic doctrine is Thomas Aquinas. "This error [that there were no witches who 'prevent the power of generation or the enjoyment of love'] may be rejected in its simple falsity by all other scholars; still it is combatted even more vehemently by St. Thomas, since he condemns it as a heresy, when he says that this error has arisen from the root of unbelief; and because incredulity in a Christian is called heresy, these people are rightly suspect of heresy" (I q. 8).

Germany became the country with the most witch trials. The resistance of the Germans to these trials was broken by the "Witches Bull" and *The Hammer of Witches*. Before the "Witches Bull" there were only scattered witch trials in Germany; afterward the number rose so enormously that about one hundred and fifty years later the Jesuit Friedrich von Spee, who despite the danger that he himself might be burned to death, argued against the trials in his *Cautio criminalis* ("Warning About the Trials," 1630), said that, "in Germany especially the smoke from the stake is everywhere" (q. 2).

Spee thought the reason why the witch trials raged more in Germany than in all other countries of the world was "Jakob Sprenger and Heinrich Institoris, who were sent at that time into Germany as inquisitors of heresy by the Apostolic See. . . . I begin to fear, no, the anxious thought has already come to me before this that those inquisitors brought to Germany the whole host of witches with their artfully contrived and wisely spread out tortures" (q. 23). Spee alludes here to the most gruesome stipulation of *The Hammer of Witches,* namely the introduction of spread out—i.e., endlessly repeated—torture. With the help of this method it was possible to extort all the confessions and denunciations one wanted.

The Hammer of Witches examines in detail the question "why God gave the devil greater power of bewitchment over coitus than over other human actions." The two criminal and sexually pathological authors of the book keep coming back to this question (I q. 3; q. 6; q. 8; q. 9; q. 10; II q. 1; q. 1 c. 6) and they answer it by referring to Thomas Aquinas: "For he says that the first corruption of sin, through which man has become the slave of the devil, entered into us through the act of generation. Hence the power of witches was given to the devil by God in this act more than another" (I q. 6). In fact Sprenger and Institoris were right to invoke Aquinas. Josef Fuchs writes in 1949: "In view of the role played by the sexual power in passing on original sin Thomas proclaims that the realm of sex is in a special way a realm of the devil" (*Die Sexualethik des heiligen Thomas von Aquin,* p. 60) For this conviction, Thomas, in turn, appeals to Pope Gregory I (*De malo* 15, 2 o. 6). This recurrent question as to "why the devil is permitted to exercise sorcery precisely in the sexual act and not in the case of other human acts," and the answer, "because of the loathsomeness of the act of generation, and because through it original sin is transmitted to all men" (I q. 3; q. 10) make up the leitmotif of *The Hammer of Witches.*

Another question that especially exercises both authors is why among women "the witch-midwives exceed all other witches in deeds of shame" (III q. 34). Sprenger and Institoris write from their experience as inquisitors: "Repentant witches have often confessed to us and others, saying that no one harms the Catholic faith more than the midwives" (I q. 11). In Cologne from 1627 to 1630 nearly all the midwives were wiped out. One out of every three women executed was a midwife. These trials in Cologne prompted Spee, who had accompanied many witches to the stake, to write several chapters of his *Cautio criminalis.*

In their book *Die Vernichtung der Weisen Frauen* ("The Destruction of the Wise Women," 1985, p. 131), Heinsohn and Steiger claim that Spee "saw many real witches . . . at work," but how they can say such a thing is incomprehensible. The sentence in Spee's book that they refer to is a rhetorical question: "What could seem more senseless nowadays than to believe that the number of real witches is small and getting smaller. And yet, . . . truth has no greater enemy than prejudice" (q. 9). To characterize as Spee's opinion what Spee himself calls prejudice makes no sense. A few pages later he writes: "Thus I have to confess that in various places I accompanied a good many witches to their death, women whose innocence I have just as little doubt about even now as I expended every effort and enormous diligence to discover the truth . . . but I could find nothing but guiltlessness everywhere" (q. 11).

The main reproach that Institoris and Sprenger level at the "witch-midwives" is that they kill unbaptized infants (II q. 1 c. 2). "For the devil knows that such children are excluded from entering the Kingdom of Heaven because of the punishment of damnation or because of original sin" (II q. 1 c. 13). As for the connection between dead newborns and the devil, that idea is a consequence of Augustine's insane teaching that God condemns unbaptized infants to hell. But there is nothing to justify *The Hammer of Witches'* blaming midwives for the death of newborns. The second reproach made by the authors against the witch-midwives is that they "prevent conception in the womb by various means" (II q. 1 c. 5). It's likely that the midwives passed on information about contraception, or what was taken to be such. But it is equally clear that they cannot be made responsible for all cases of sterility. The crazy traditional theological claim (adopted by Institoris and Sprenger, who invoke *"si aliquis"*) that contraception is murder is the second crucial reason for "incinerating" the midwives. And "incinerate" was the dreadful word that they constantly used in their campaign to exterminate women and midwives.

In the High Middle Ages experts were familiar with some fifty or sixty methods used by the devil to prevent the marital act from taking place. *The Hammer of Witches* cites a whole series of these, for example, "directly causing the power of the organ serving fertilization to wilt" (I q. 8). The authors believed that chastity in the sense of frigidity prevents the devils "in their habit of casting spells on the male organs" (I q. 1 c. 7), and on this score they regularly cite the Book of Tobit, with the passage doctored by Jerome: "The devil has won power over those who are given to lust" (I q. 8; q. 9; q. 15; II q. 1 c. 7; q. 1 c. 11; q. 2 c. 2; q. 2 c. 5).

Especially feared was the so-called "lace knot," which the French called *nouer l'aiquillette*. This consisted in the witch or warlock's tying a knot or snapping a lock shut during the marriage ceremony. Depending on the kind of formula spoken the effect would last for a longer or shorter time. It would be impossible for the couple to have intercourse until the spell had been broken. Francis Bacon (d. 1626), the keeper of the great seal and lord chancellor, says that such lace knots were widespread in Saintes and Gascony (*Sylva sylvarum seu historia naturalis*, n. 888).

But there were also voices of reason. In his essay on "The Power of the Imagination" Montaigne (d. 1592) deals in detail with the phenomenon of lace knots, "for people are no longer talking about anything else." He describes how he helped his friend the duke of Gurson get over his fear of being hexed into impotence on his wedding night. Montaigne's sympathetic prescription for the newlyweds, designed to get rid of the fixation of impotence, is patience and indulgence toward one's own imaginative capacity. He thinks this will be more successful than the obstinacy of those who get it into their heads that they must conquer themselves.

Unlike this humane skeptic, the Church in its superstitious fashion condemned magicians and witches. A provincial synod held by St. Charles Borromeo in Lombardy in 1579 instituted penalties against sorcery that prevented conjugal intercourse. Similar action was taken by the synods of Ermland in 1610 and Lüttich in 1618. And the Synod of Naumur in 1639 renewed an earlier ordinance against these bewitchments, "because we know that every day marriages are thrown into confusion by enchantment" (Browe, pp. 128–29). The Synod of Cologne in 1662 likewise took up the matter of impotence through magic spells. The Bavarian Jesuit Gaspar Schott (d. 1667), who was for a long time professor of physics in Palermo, explained that "No other kind of magic is more widespread and feared nowadays. In some places married couples no longer dare to be married publically in church before the pastor and witnesses, but they do it at home the day before and then go to church on the following day" (Browe, p. 129). Some couples were married behind closed doors or at night and consummated the marriage before the break of day, so that they would not be seen by magicians and witches (Browe, p. 129). Some Italian and French provincial synods, such as those of Naples in 1576, Rheims in 1583, and Bourges in 1584, forbade such superstitious weddings. The Synod of Rheims advised couples to use an antidote that the Book of Tobit, alias Jerome, advised as an aid against the demons, namely, "to come together out of love of offspring and not out of lust." Belief in magically induced impotence gave countless couples neurotic anxiety attacks all the way into the eighteenth century—Alphonsus Liguori was thoroughly engrossed by it and had no doubts about its reality.

This diabolically caused impotence had legal consequences. Hincmar of Rheims said that in cases where the marriage was not and could not be consummated because of bewitchment he favored separation and the possibility of remarriage. At first Rome did not recognize such divorces and demanded that the partners live together as brother and sister. But once Hincmar's opinion was accepted into Gratian's collection of laws and into Peter Lombard's *Sentences* almost all theologians decided that magically induced impotence was an impediment to marriage. In 1207 Pope Innocent III decided that the marriage of Philip II Augustus of France with Ingeborg should be dissolved for this reason, if a new attempt that the king was to make, with auxiliary measures such as almsgiving, prayer, and masses, should not be successful. Similarly in 1349 the marriage of John of Tyrolia and Margaret of Carinthia was dissolved because of impotence due to magical spells. Even today so-called relative impotence (operative vis-à-vis only one's wife), if it proves lasting and incurable, is a diriment impediment. The marriage can be declared invalid (can. 1084, CIC, 1983), and both partners can remarry. But nowadays questions of impotence are no longer treated in the context of the devil and bewitchment, but with medical or psychological counseling.

At the beginning of the "Witches Bull" the Pope asserts that apart from causing impotence witches of both sexes carried on another monstrous activity, namely fornication with the devil: "Not without distress has the word reached our ears that in some parts of Upper Germany and likewise in the provinces, cities, regions, villages, and dioceses of Mainz, Cologne, Trier, and Salzburg a great number of persons of both sexes, unmindful of their own salvation and apostatizing from the Catholic faith, are practicing fornication with the demons in the shape of men or women . . ." At the bottom of all this lies the theological idea of the missionary position, which evidently the devils adhere to as well: male devils lie on top, female devils lie on the bottom, which is why the Pope calls the devils with whom the witches or warlocks commit fornication simply *incubi* (lying on top) or *succubi* (lying beneath). The main source for the "Witches Bull" and *The Hammer of Witches,* which is intended to be a commentary on the "Witches Bull," is Thomas Aquinas's notion of diabolical amours with the *incubi* and the *succubi.* The wretched *Hammer of Witches* cites no one so abundantly as Thomas, who spells out how sex with the devil and the begetting of diabolical children take place when he develops a theory of how the semen is obtained: One and the same devil can produce semen by taking the form of a woman and having intercourse (as a succubus) with a man and then taking the form of a man and having intercourse (as an incubus) with a woman. The diabolical children begotten in this fashion (they are usually distinguished by their extraordinary size) are thus actually human children, because they are generated by human semen (*Summa Theologiae,* I, q. 51 a. 3 ad 6). Individual details, such as how the semen obtained by the devil from a man is kept fresh and fertile until intercourse with the witch, are something Thomas doesn't go into. Such gaps are filled by *The Hammer of Witches.* The devils, it seems, have a heating-and-refrigerating apparatus for the transfer of semen (I q. 3).

And so Thomas Aquinas, the greatest Catholic theologian, was the man who explained the system of diabolical amours. This is attested to by Sigmund von Riezler, who studied the *Geschichte du Hexen Prozesse in Bayern* (*History of the Witch Trials in Bavaria*): "The persecutors based what they were doing on his [Thomas's authority]. Wherever one checks the proof passages cited as evidence of their position, one finds that only the one from Thomas has the character of a clear doctrinal principle. The 'angelic doctor,' the celebrated saint and scholar of the Dominican order, must therefore be identified as the one who contributed most to the establishing of the witchcraft hysteria. For this reason, as the authors of *The Hammer of Witches* report, their colleague (among others), the inquisitor of Como, in the county of Bormio or Wormserbad, in the *one* year 1485 had forty-one women burned at the stake, while many others avoided the same fate only by fleeing across the border into Tyrolia" (1896, pp. 42–43).

The authors of *The Hammer of Witches* are absorbed by the question of why men don't have intercourse with *succubi* as much as women do with *incubi* (I q. 2 c. 1), in other words why more women are witches than men. This issue gives both writers an opportunity to develop at length their vision of women, joining in the Church's theological chorus with all the defamers of women, of which they found an abundant supply in Catholic tradition. We find here the old Aristotelian argument about women's greater water content, which according to Albert and Thomas makes women inconstant and unreliable, and which had become such a commonplace of theology that direct quotation of it was superfluous (I q. 6). The authors do quote Chrysostom on Matthew 19: "It does not profit a man to marry. For what is woman but an enemy of friendship, an inescapable punishment, a necessary evil, a natural temptation, a desirable misfortune, a domestic danger, delectable mischief, a fault in nature, painted with beautiful colors?" (I q. 6). The authors cite "experience" as proof that there is more profligacy among women than among men. In any case, women are "deficient in all powers of the soul as well as of the body . . . for in what concerns reason or the understanding of spiritual things, they seem to be of a different species from men, as indicated by authorities, one's reason and various examples in Scripture."

Authorities are dug up for everything. The authors of *The Hammer of Witches* find Terence and Lactantius with their misogynistic sayings. They strike it rich too in the Bible, especially in Proverbs: "Like a gold ring in a swine's snout is a beautiful woman without discretion" (11:22). And there is that "reason": "The reason is one taken from nature, because she [woman] is more carnally minded than man, as can be seen from the many filthy things about her."

Institoris and Sprenger even cite slanderous sayings about women's tears. "For Cato says, 'When a woman cries, she is surely thinking of spiteful deception.' And it is also said, 'When a woman cries, she means to deceive man' " (I q. 6). On the other hand, not crying is a sign of guilt and witchcraft. The physiological fact that during torture a person is incapable of shedding tears was construed by the two inquisitors as damning witches and brought women still more grief in the form of torture: "Experience has taught," they write, "that the more they were entreated, the less they could cry . . . it may be that later, in the absence of the judge, and outside of the place and time of torture they are capable of crying in the presence of the guards. If one asks why witches are prevented from crying, it may be said that it is because the grace of tears in the repentant is reckoned among the outstanding gifts of God." But just in case the witch should cry, our two sadists know what to make of it. "Yet what should we think if through the cunning of the devil, and with God's permission, it should happen that a witch cried, since crying, contriving, and deceiving are all parts of woman's peculiar nature? To this the answer can be given that since God's decrees are hidden . . ." etc. etc. (III q. 15).

The inferiority of woman (*femina* in Latin) can be seen in her very name: "For the word *femina* comes from *fe* and *minus*. Fe = fides, faith, minus = less; femina, therefore, means she who has less faith; because she always has and maintains less faith, and that from her natural inclination to gullibility, although thanks to both grace and nature the faith of the most blessed Virgin never wavered, while that of all the men at the time of Christ did waver" (I q. 6). Like almost all great Christian defamers of women the authors of *The Hammer of Witches,* especially Sprenger, who did particularly meritorious work in promoting the rosary, were also great venerators of Mary.

The authors of *The Hammer of Witches* have still more objections to bring against women: "If we look into it, we find that almost all the kingdoms on earth have been destroyed by women. The first one that was a happy kingdom, namely Troy . . ." They opine that "If it were not for women's evil tricks, not to mention the witches, the world would be free from countless dangers." And while they're on the subject of women, another idea occurs to them: "Let us hear about yet another quality: the voice. For just as woman is mendacious by nature, so we see the same thing with her speech. For she stings and delights at once. That is why her voice is compared to the song of the sirens, who allure passersby with their sweet melodies and then kill them. They kill them because they force them to empty their purses, rob them of their powers, and make them defy God . . . Proverbs 5:3–4: 'For the lips of a loose woman drip honey, and her speech is smoother than oil; but in the end she is bitter as wormwood, sharp as a two-edged sword' " (I q. 6).

But it was not just woman's voice, but her hair as well, that predestined her to intercourse with the devil: "Guilelmus too observes that the incubi seem to cause more trouble for those women and girls who have beautiful hair . . . because they wish or are wont to inflame the men with their hair. Or because they vainly pride themselves on it; or because heaven's kindness permits this in order to deter woman from inflaming men by the means that the demons too would have men inflamed" (I q. 2 c. 1). In any event, beautiful hair in women has something to do with proximity to the devil.

The answer to the question, why there are more witches than warlocks, culminates in the following determination by both authors: "We conclude that everything happens because of carnal desire, which is insatiable in them. In the next to last chapter of Proverbs we read, 'Three things are insatiable (etc.) and the fourth, which never says, It is enough, . . . namely the opening of the womb.' Therefore they have dealings even with the demons, so as to quiet their desires.—We could go into more details

here, but a word to the wise is sufficient . . . Logically, therefore, the heresy to be named is that of female witches, not
male. . . . praised be the Most High, who has to this day so
preserved the male sex from such shamefulness: It was in this sex
that he wished to be born and to suffer for us, and hence he has
thus shown his preference for it" (I q. 6).

After this thorough presentation of the essence of woman one
can understand that both authors feel a deep intellectual kinship
with Thomas Aquinas, about whom they say the following: "No
less do we read that St. Thomas, the teacher of our order, was
given this sort of grace. Because of his having entered this order,
he was imprisoned by his relatives and subjected to fleshly temptation by a harlot, who tried to seduce him. His relatives sent her
to him in a splendid dress and all adorned. When the Doctor
caught sight of her, he ran to the fireplace, seized a firebrand, and
chased out the seductress to fiery lust out of the prison. Then he
fell immediately on his knees to pray for the gift of chastity and fell
asleep. Thereupon two angels appeared to him and said: 'See, we
gird you according to God's will with the girdle of chastity that can
never be loosened through temptation later on; and what cannot be
reached through human virtue or merit will be brought by God as
a gift.' He felt the girding, that is, the touch of the girdle, and
awoke with a cry. He felt he had been blessed with the gift of such
chastity that from this very time on he started in terror from all
voluptuousness, so that unless he were forced he could not even
speak with women, but possessed perfect chastity." In this way,
as Institoris and Sprenger see it, Thomas had the good fortune to
belong to the "three kinds of human beings," outside of which no
one "is safe from witches," "so that they would not be bewitched
or seduced and misled into sorcery in the eighteen ways, described
below, which will be dealt with in turn" (II q. 1).

Alphonsus Liguori, once again, discusses diabolical amours in
detail in a chapter on, "How the Confessor Must Treat Those
Troubled by the Devil." Invoking Thomas, Alphonsus describes
how the children of the devil are born from intercourse of the
devil with a woman, although such a child is not really the devil's
but the offspring of the man from whom the devil previously
collected the semen.

Alphonsus turns to confessors: "Thus if someone who has been attacked by the evil enemy comes forward, the confessor must take zealous pains to provide the penitent with weapons in his fearful struggle . . . Let him enjoin the penitent to refrain as far as possible from sensual pleasure . . . Further let him ask the penitent whether he ever called upon the wicked enemy or ever made an alliance with him . . . Let him ask him in what form the devil appears to him, whether as a man or a woman or in the shape of an animal, because then, if sexual relations have taken place, the sin against chastity and religion is compounded by the sin of fornication or sodomy or incest or adultery or sacrilege . . . Let him ask too in what place and at what time this intercourse took place . . . Let him seek to move the penitent to a complete confession, for such lost individuals readily leave out sins when making their confession" (*The Practice of the Confessor* VII, 110–13). As late as 1906 the moral theologian Franz Adam Göpfert was giving instructions to confessors about how they should deal with penitents who confessed to having had sex with the devil (see Chapter 29 of this book, "The Moral Theology of the Twentieth Century").

The idea of diabolical amours had dreadful consequences not only for the witches but also for many children (supposed children of the devil). In his book *Das unselige Erbe des Christentums: Die Wechselbälge—Zur Geschichte der Heilpädogogik* ("The Unholy Legacy of Christianity: The Changelings—On the History of Therapeutic Pedagogy," 1985) Walter Bachmann describes the effects of the theory of diabolical amours on many handicapped children all the way into the twentieth century. *The Hammer of Witches* reports in 1487 concerning these "substituted" children: "There is still another terrible thing that God has permitted human beings to endure, namely that sometimes women have their own sons and children stolen away, and strange ones are substituted by the demons. And these children are usually called *campsores,* or in German *Wechselkinder* [changelings] . . . Some are always skinny and scream" (II q. 2 c. 8). Luther recommended that changelings be drowned, since "such changelings [are] only a piece of flesh," and "no soul is in them" (Bachmann, pp. 183, 191, 195).

The first German to take a stand against the witchcraft hysteria and the inhuman treatment of the mentally ill and handicapped was the Calvinist doctor Johann Weyer (d. 1588). His book, *Von den Blendwerken der Dämonen, von Zauberei und Hexerei* ("On the Delusions of the Demons, on Magic and Sorcery," 1563) was promptly put on the Index of Forbidden Books. Weyer was personal physician to Duke Johann Wilhelm of Jülich and Cleve. He was ultimately accused of having caused the duke's melancholia by witchcraft and had to flee Düsseldorf. His voice went unheard.

In the *Naturwissenschaftliche Untersuchung über die untergeschobenen Kinder (Scientific Investigation of Substituted Children)* by M. G. Voigt (Wittenberg, 1667), we read that, "Substituted children have no rational soul," and "substituted children are not human" (Bachmann, pp. 38, 45).

One sad chapter of this story concerns the deaf and dumb, even though they were not ranked with the changelings. A whole series of theologians maintained that the deaf and dumb were excluded from faith, indeed that they were damned to hell. To prove this, theologians invoked Augustine, who had said: "This defect [of being born deaf] also hinders [*impedit*] faith itself, as the Apostle attests with the words: Faith comes from hearing (Rom. 10:17)" (*Contra Julianum* 3, 4). Thus the fate of the deaf and dumb was a grim one, "because curing them was considered not just impossible but a presumptuous invasion of divine authority. In the eighteenth century, Chief Pastor Goeze, in Hamburg, immortalized by Lessing, thundered in sermons . . . against the irreligious arrogance of wanting to get the deaf and dumb to speak" (Georgens and Deinhardt in Vol. I of their *Heilpädagogik mit besonderer Berücksichtigung der Idiotie und der Idiotenanstalten*, Leipzig, 1861, cf. Bachmann, pp. 230–31). It is true that a Protestant minister in Hamburg who took care of the hard of hearing, Dietfried Gewalt, alludes to the fact that it was not Pastor Goeze but Pastor Granau from Eppendorf near Hamburg who issued this negative judgment on the deaf and dumb ("Samuel Heinicke and Johan Melchior Goeze," in *Hörgeschädigtenpädagogik*, 1989, vol. 1, 448ff.). But there is no contesting the fact that the deaf and dumb had to suffer from a gloomy, bitter-end Augustinian theology. Thus we still find in the Brockhaus Encyclopedia (Jubilee Edition, 1903, vol. 15, 635):

I

I

"Even the Church did not take their [the deaf and dumb] part, since St. Augustine had laid down the principle: People born deaf and dumb can never receive faith, for faith comes from preaching, from what is heard" (Bachmann, pp. 29ff.).

The French abbé de l'Épée (d. 1789) is considered the "Redeemer of the Deaf and Dumb." Of him Georgens and Deinhardt write: "The abbé, a pious, compassionate man with an independent mind—an independence that he demonstrated more than once—was, as we know, so deeply moved and touched, first of all by his acquaintance with two deaf and dumb sisters, well-mannered and well-educated persons, whom a clergyman had tried (but no more than tried) to teach with the help of pictures, that he decided to help the whole race of such unfortunates." "When he launched into his effort, he had to contend with the most violent resistance, with derision and persecution, but he continually followed his path, and only in his declining years, did he get general recognition and admiration, and—this meant more to him than fame—did he know that the destiny of his children, the deaf and dumb persons in the Institute, was secure" (Bachmann, p. 233).

Bachmann offers a bitter summary: "In the course of human history the handicapped could hardly have experienced more prejudice, or as much disdain, intolerance, and inhumanity as they did in the Christian world" (ibid., p. 442).

XX

THE COUNCIL OF TRENT AND POPE SIXTUS THE MOMENTOUS

In the seven hundred years since the death of Thomas Aquinas (d. 1274), who is often considered the zenith of Catholic theology, in their unrelenting war of pros and cons the theologians actually solved only two marital problems—although a married person can only shake his head in bafflement at their findings. Augustine had decided that intercourse is sinless only for procreation or out of duty at the request of one's partner. In about 1300 the idea that intercourse to avoid committing fornication *oneself* was not a sin, although it had some support, was contested by Thomas, who followed Augustine in this. Such sexual relations were categorized by Thomas (and Augustine) as venially sinful. The fourth motive for intercourse, sexual desire, was generally viewed in about 1300 as at least a venial sin, and under some circumstances a mortal sin. Heinrich Klomps, a moral theologian from Cologne, summarizes the whole situation: "The concrete result in moral theology of these subjective existential reflections is the excuse theory and the indulgence theory. The first claims that Christian spouses are completely excused if their ethical striving is aimed . . . at procreation . . . or performance of marital duty, in which case the good of offspring and the good of fidelity outweigh the negative effects of concupiscence and sexual pleasure. The indulgency theory, by contrast, allows the goods of marriage to intervene and lessen guilt, if intercourse is motivated by the wish to prevent fornication on one's own part or by the will to satisfy sexual desire" (Klomps, *Ehemoral und Jansenismus,* p. 209).

The very absurdity of binding marital love to a Procrustean scale of values with children at the top, lust on the bottom, and the avoidance of fornication in between, is unrealistic, disconcerting, downright ridiculous. Anyhow, in the seven hundred years since Thomas's day it was finally concluded that type 3 and type 4 (conjugal) intercourse qualify, as do types 1 and 2, as free from sin. However, apropos of type 4, long the most controversial, it must be noted that according to a decision reached by Pope Innocent XI in 1679 "intercourse out of lust *alone*" may not be considered sinless.

The Dutch Carthusian monk Dionysius (d. 1471) from Roermond wrote a book in Latin for his "greatly beloved" educated married friends on *The Praiseworthy Life of Married People.* In it he raises the question, among others, of whether married people may love one another "with sensual lust." He thinks this is permissible, but as a precautionary measure he points to the fact that St. Brigid of Sweden (d. 1373) speaks in her visions about a man who was damned for loving his wife too sensually. Thus, Dionysius opined, married men with beautiful wives and women with attractive husbands should be careful (John T. Noonan, *Contraception,* p. 305).

In the fifteenth and sixteenth centuries we meet three theologians who, evidently unimpressed by St. Brigid's terror-stricken visions, reached the position held by the twentieth-century Church. They did not, though, go beyond it, because while they decriminalized intercourse as a means of avoiding fornication and taking pleasure they believed that contraception through coitus interruptus or medications was a mortal sin.

The first of the three is Martin Le Maistre (d. 1481), a celebrated professor in his day, who in 1464 was Rector Magnificus of the University of Paris. Le Maistre abandoned the standard four-tiered Augustinian model of minimum to maximum lust. He tried to get rid of the Augustinian distinctions in the motives for the conjugal act, and to give it unlimited legitimization. He claimed that the notion that intercourse for the sake of pleasure could be a mortal sin was "much more dangerous for human morality" than his own view. Here he appealed to reason: "Clear reason tells me that it is permitted to seek conjugal union for the sake of pleasure." He attacked his theological opponents: "I ask in how many dangers do they involve the consciences of overscrupulous spouses, for many a one finds that his wife has become pregnant immediately after sexual union, and once that happens they expose every such person to the danger of mortal sin if he desires the debt of marriage unless it is certain that he does this only to avoid fornication." To this he opposed his own, previously unheard-of opinion: "I say that anyone can have the wish to enjoy pleasure, first out of pure joy in this pleasure, and second, to escape the *taedium vitae* and the pain of depression that come about from a lack of sensual joys. Conjugal intercourse that seeks to brighten up the dark mood that ensues when sexual pleasure is lacking has nothing wrong with it."

As for the two authorities who were always being thrown in his face, namely, Augustine and Aristotle, he maintained that Augustine was only against "unbridled" and "unnatural" sex. Thomas Aquinas did continually invoke Aristotle's idea that the intelligence suffered damage from conjugal intimacy, which thus had to be compensated for by the "goods that pardon marriage," but Le Maistre tries to mitigate this position: even if it was true—which did not strike him as evident—this loss of reason would be immediately balanced out by the good effects of marital relations, And besides Aristotle permitted the use of pleasure when it served "the health and wellbeing of body and soul."

This critical thinker even wondered how coitus interruptus actually was unnatural, "if the thing itself is not unnatural, the organ is not unnatural, and the copulation is not unnatural." But when he answers he at once turns back into the Church's prescribed path. He says that the semen is not ejaculated "into the organ that nature has intended for receiving it," and "that is a grave sin against nature." For his authority on this he cites the Old Testament story of Onan. And as he sees it, coitus interruptus and the use of contraceptive medications fall under the category of homicide.

Le Maistre also never tried to press his rational questions on the traditional false answers. He shows the dilemma that the present-day popes and Catholic theologians now face five hundred years after him and most especially when they also cling to the supposed unnaturalness of contraception for no other reason than that theologians always have clung to it and that in their eyes duration guarantees correctness. But no matter how many centuries pass, an error does not turn into truth.

The motive that Le Maistre imputes to married couples seeking to prevent conception is the very same one and the first one cited again by Pope Pius XI in his encyclical *Casti connubii* (1930). Le Maistre knows only one motive for contraception: It is practiced, he says, by those who lead a loose life . . . so as to have greater enjoyment in the sexual act." *Casti connubii* (lit. "Chaste Marriage") says: "Some individuals lay claim to such criminal freedom because out of aversion for the blessing of children they want to avoid the burden but enjoy the bliss."

The encyclical then mentions a second category of birth control practicing, criminally liberated married couples—one sees the progress in theological reflection in the five hundred years since Le Maistre—"others, because they supposedly cannot observe any sort of continence." In other words, apart from those

|

|

seeking pleasure, there are now those who refuse to do without it." Before going on, like Le Maistre, to speak of Onan, the bogeyman of the bedroom, whom "God killed," *Casti connubii* sets the record straight: "But however serious it may be, there is no reason whatever that could make something intrinsically unnatural into something in conformity with nature and morally good. And since the conjugal act is intended by nature to waken new life . . ." etc., etc. The celibates and monks have once and for all conceded intercourse exclusively for reproduction, and hence procreation can under no circumstances be eliminated from it (on Le Maistre cf. Noonan, 306ff.; 357ff.; 367).

Le Maistre was ahead of his time. His liberal views were continued at the University of Paris by the Scot John Mayor (d. 1550). His disciple, the later Scottish reformer John Knox, writes of him that he was "considered an oracle on matters of religion." He criticized the Early Scholastic canon lawyer Cardinal Huguccio (d. 1210), who accepted the famous sentence from Pope Gregory the Great's rescript, "There can be no sexual pleasure without sin," and hence viewed every act of intercourse as sinful: "See how this otherwise so reasonable man is ready, because of these few words, to throw a rope around everyone's neck. If no other answer occurred to me except that one, I would rather totally ignore ten authorities of Gregory's stature than make such assertions. I would say: To be sure, he does claim that, but he doesn't prove it. And where something contradicts probability, it needs bold testing. Whatever one may say, it is quite hard to prove that the husband sins when he goes to his wife for the pleasure of it" (*In IV sent.* d. 31 q. un. concl. 7).

Even the already mentioned chaste elephant, which some theologians propose as a model for married people, makes no impression on Mayor: "If reference is made to the fact that the elephant, for example, avoids the pregnant female or that other animals no longer mate after fertilization has occurred, and the conclusion is reached that wives too are no longer allowed to request conjugal relations during pregnancy or in the barrenness of old age, one must answer: The inference is invalid. For the various creatures also have various capacities . . . Whether a sensation of pleasure is strong or weak has no significance" (*In IV sent.* d. 31 un. fol. 204).

Mayor's disciple, Jacques Almain (d. 1515), who was called "the sharpest thinker" (*disputator acutissimus*) of the University of Paris and died when he was only thirty-five, defended positions like those of Le Maistre and Mayor. "To say that every one seeking intercourse in order to be pleased commits sin seems hard" (Noonan, p. 311). "To wish to have no passion would imply stupefaction" (Klomps, p. 57).

After these three theologians the voice of reason is mute for centuries. And where it is not, it is quickly silenced. We shall hear nothing like this among the reformers of the sixteenth century, nor still less among the Jansenists of the seventeenth century, nor from Thomas Sanchez (d. 1610), one of the "lax Jesuits" fought by the Jansenists, nor from Alphonsus Liguori, who dominated Catholic ethics in the eighteenth and nineteenth centuries.

After the Council of Trent the sort of openness one finds in Le Maistre, Mayor, and Almain was no longer possible. The Roman Catechism, published at the behest of the Council of Trent in 1566 for the use of pastors, which had and still has great prestige, contains only one executive order about the conjugal act: "Believers are to be taught mainly about two things: 1. not to have relations for the sake of lust or sensual desires, but within the boundaries prescribed by the Lord. For it is becoming to recall the warning of the Apostle: 'Let those who have wives live as though they had none,' and further remember the saying of St. Jerome: 'The wise man should love his wife with reason and not with passion, let him master the stirrings of lust and not allow himself to be tumultuously swept away into cohabitation. Nothing is more shameful than to love one's wife as if she were an adulteress,' and 2. to refrain from intercourse now and then, and to pray." (It should be noted that the Roman Catechism also has a few other things to say, not about marital sex but marriage as a whole; for example, it quotes the saying from Ephesians, "Husbands, love your wives" [*Catechism* 2, 8, 16].)

Whoever is troubled by point one, namely that he is not allowed to have relations out of lust, can adhere to point two, that he can always refrain from sex, "above all for at least three days before receiving the Holy Eucharist, but more often during the solemn forty day time of fasting, as our fathers have rightly and holily written." After these two points have been clarified—no others are mentioned under this heading of "What Should Be Taught About Conjugal Duties"—those who comply with the two-point program are promised an increase in divine grace, and finally they "will receive eternal life through God's kindness" (2, 8, 33). St. Brigid's vision of the man who was damned for loving his wife too passionately takes on ominous overtones in the Roman Catechism, especially since it makes a point of enlisting that specter of the nuptial couch, Tobias. The Roman Catechism doesn't fail to bring up the subject of Tobias with his new lines from St. Jerome, according to which Tobias's seven predecessors did not survive their wedding night with Sarah, "because they were the slaves of lust" (2, 8, 13).

It is worth noticing that the Roman Catechism lacks the Augustinian stress on procreation among the motives for sex in marriage. More important than constantly thinking about children during sex is constantly not thinking about pleasure. This, to be sure, preserves Augustine's essential program because he was no lover of children, only a hater of lust. His opponent Julian of Eclanum calls him the "persecutor of the newborn" because of his damnation of unbaptized children. For Augustine it is more important that people live virginally than that children be born. Section Eight of the Roman Catechism, "On the Sacrament of Marriage," begins by saying that it would actually be desirable that all Christians remain unmarried, "that all would wish to strive after the virtue of continence, for believers can find nothing more blessed in this life than that their spirit, distracted by no worldly cares and after quieting and subduing every pleasure of the flesh, should rest solely in the zeal of godliness and in the contemplation of heavenly things."

Despite this harmony with Augustine the Roman Catechism makes a long overdue departure from the four Augustinian motives for intercourse, and points in the direction of the twentieth century: Procreation need no longer be the motive for every act of marital sex, but it may not be excluded. The Roman Catechism equates contraception with murder: "Whoever in married life either prevents conception through medications or aborts the fruit of the womb commits a crime of the gravest kind, for such things are to equated with a wicked conspiracy to commit murder" (2, 8, 13).

After the Council of Trent a process of strict regulation of religious life began to gain ground. This is shown by a second decree from Rome that was still more severe than the Roman Catechism, although it was only in force for a short time. This ordinance suspended a ruling that had been valid until then and that later remained in effect until into the nineteenth century, namely, that the abortion of a male fetus up until forty days after conception and of a female fetus up to eighty days after conception carried no penalty with it. In practice this meant—since there was no way of determining the sex of the fetus—that abortion was exempt from punishment for the first eighty days of pregnancy.

That rule was now suspended by the fanatical Pope Sixtus V, who in 1588 in the bull "Effraenatam" attempted to convert the *"si aliquis"* canon into penal practice. Up to that point *"si aliquis"* (and its equation of contraception with murder) had for the most part been limited to the realm of confession and penance. Sixtus V now threatened with excommunication and the death penalty those who gave others or themselves took contraceptive potions ("cursed medicines"), as well as those who carried out an abortion, from the moment of conception on. After the death of Sixtus V "Effraenatam" was revoked by his second successor, Pope Gregory XIV, in 1591, as soon as he took office. This meant that once again abortion was not punished with excommunication until after the eightieth day.

Sixtus had made it his goal to reform the Church and above all to eradicate sexual sins. He threatened adulterers with the noose, and had a woman executed for procuring her own daughter. In his *History of the Popes,* Ludwig von Pastor remarks: "There is no denying that Sixtus V went too far." But this doesn't cast any shadows on his positive judgment of this Pope: "Historians of the most diverse sympathies agree that Sixtus was one of the most powerful of the many important popes who produced the era of Catholic Reformation and Restoration . . . Posterity has unfairly . . . deprived this pope the name of Great" (X, 6–7).

Pastor describes the case of the hanged procuress: "General disapproval also greeted the execution in early June, 1586 of a Roman woman who had sold the honor of her daughter. The carrying out of the judgment was made even harsher in this case by the fact that the daughter, adorned with her lover's jewelry, had to attend the execution and stand for an hour under the gallows on which hung her mother's corpse. In a contemporary account excusing the event we are told that procuring had become so widespread in Rome that girls were less protected with their mothers than with strangers" (ibid., 70). "In the same month Sixtus V had a priest and a boy burned at the stake for sodomy, although both had voluntarily confessed their guilt" (ibid., 71). "The death penalty was inflicted not only for incest and crimes against budding life, but also for spreading oral and written calumnies" (ibid., 69). We have already seen in the chapter on incest how broadly the Church interpreted that crime (pp. 215ff.).

"In August 1586 the execution for adultery of a noble Roman lady along with two of her accomplices was deplored far and wide. Sixtus V was so unaffected by this that he ordered Cardinal Santori to draw up a bull threatening the death penalty for adultery. His advisors tried to make the Pope abandon his idea, arguing that the Reformers would exploit such a document for their own purposes, as proof of the corrupt morals in the Curia, but it was all in vain. The bull was published on November 3, 1586, ordering adulterers and adulteresses, as well as parents who procured their daughters, to be put to death. Married couples who divorced on their own initiative were to be given similar punishment at the discretion of the judges . . . The number of the accused was so great that the ordinance could not be rigorously enforced" (ibid., pp. 71–72).

In 1587 this fearsome Pope issued a regulation that has meant tragedy for many of the people concerned: A man had to have real semen (i.e., from the testicles), otherwise he could not marry. This order was not revoked until 1977. On June 28, 1587, Sixtus wrote to the apostolic nuncio of Spain and bishop of Novara about the capacity for marriage of those who lacked both testicles, yet could have erections and ejaculate a semen-like fluid that, however, "is no good for procreation and for marriage." They could not secrete "real seed" (*verum semen*). According to Sixtus, these eunuchs or *spadones* nonetheless mingled with women "with filthy lasciviousness" and "impure embraces," and even had the arrogance to contract marriages, indeed to fight "stubbornly" for this right. The fact that women knew about the "defect" of these men made this offense even worse in the eyes of the Pope.

Sixtus commanded the nuncio to see to it that such husbands be separated from their wives, and that their marriages be annulled. He found it unbearable that these people slept in the same bed with women, and instead of living chastely together with them, gave themselves over to "fleshly and libidinous acts." He therefore forbade marriage to men who lacked the capacity for procreation (*potentia generandi*) and declared them unfit for marriage. In this he was drawing the logical consequence from the fact that according to Augustine and Thomas Aquinas procreation is the first and essential purpose of marriage. Sixtus continued to tolerate sterility when the reasons for it were unknown, but he pronounced that the sterility whose cause was known (lack of testicles) constituted impotence and made one incapable of marriage. Obviously it was easy to check for testicles.

Harder to verify were the causes of barrenness in women. Some biblical women had even borne children in their old age. In any case this uncertainty gave rise to peculiar, muddled legislation. In several decisions by Rome (of February 3, 1887; July 3, 1890; July 31, 1895; April 2, 1909, December 10, 1916), the Church determined that women were not to be denied marriage although they were completely lacking the internal organs of generation (e.g., after surgical removal). In the case of such a *mulier excisa* ("cut-out woman") the reason for the decision was that doubts remained "whether the operation undertaken actually excluded every possibility of conception" (Cf. Klaus Lüdicke, *Familienplanung und Ehewille*, 1983, p. 175). On the other hand, a ruling of February 3, 1916, declared a marriage invalid on account of the wife's "impotence," because there was no connecting tissue between the vagina and the post-vaginal organs (Lüdicke, p. 83). Apparently here the sterility was considered to be undoubtable and manifest. But in general, rulings about women practically demanded of women only the capacity for intercourse (*potentia coeundi*), unlike the situation with the men. Given that until 1977 the Church demanded more of men than of women, one wonders if this were not an aftereffect of Aristotelian biology, of the notion that the man alone did the generating.

Thus for men the capacity to engage in intercourse was not enough, they also had to be able to produce "real semen." It is true that in response to a question from Aachen as to whether a man who had been forcibly sterilized through an irreversible vasectomy could be allowed to marry, the Holy Office decided on February 16, 1935, not to stop the marriage, since the case dealt with an unjust coercive measure by the state. But on January 22, 1944, the Roman Rota explicitly disavowed this judgment, invoking an address given by Pope Pius XII on October 3, 1941. The man from Aachen, who had been forced to undergo sterilization under Hitler, did not meet the demands made by Sixtus V in 1587. Just like the libidinous sixteenth-century eunuchs, he could not produce *verum semen*.

Since 1977, however, the man from Aachen need no longer do this. The decree on impotence of the Sacred Congregation of the Faith that seeks to end the long controversy begins with the words: "The Sacred Congregation of the Faith has *always held the position* that those who have suffered a vasectomy or find themselves in similar circumstances should not be hindered from marrying." Claiming that it *always was this way* is a striking peculiarity of the Catholic Church, which it practices even when this means standing the historical truth on its head, because in fact things were *not* always this way. Look at the new Code of Canon Law (1983, can. 1084), which does not simply follow the ruling of the previous Code (1917, can. 1068) that impotence makes a marriage invalid, but limits it by adding the little word *coeundi*, meaning that only the inability to engage in intercourse, not to have a normal ejaculate, invalidates a marriage.

There has been movement here, as we can see from the dismay of the well-known Italian canonist Pio Fedele, who wrote in 1976, apropos of the fact that in the future "real semen" would no longer be required of men: "Thus it was not worth the trouble of wearying the mind so much, of enduring hunger and sleepless nights, if the endless and dangerous sea voyage through so many reefs is destined to end with the conclusions that a majority of the commission [about to issue the decree on impotence] has unexpectedly arrived at." Fedele then bemoans the fact that such a decision would mean abandoning the Second Vatican Council and the encyclical *Humanae vitae*. He continues: "Where in fact do we hear in these conclusions . . . the echo of the notion that marriage and married love are oriented by nature to the procreation of offspring?" (quoted in Lüdicke, pp. 247ff.).

People who have gotten as far away from the realities of human sexuality as the high-ranking celibates of the Catholic Church, people who cast the procreational purpose of marriage in bronze this way because they are suspicious of pleasure, are just manufacturing pseudo-problems that then prove too hard to handle. Even if the majority of the Roman gentlemen take comfort in the thought that things were always decided as they were in 1977, there are still those who at the first sign of progress toward rationality suddenly find the world unintelligible.

Despite the laments of Pio Fedele, just how far even the 1977 impotence decree is removed from the real life of the men and women concretely involved in these issues can be seen from reports that appeared in almost all German newspapers on December 3, 1982. The *Westdeutsche Allgemeine Zeitung* described the case as follows: "Two young handicapped persons were not allowed to be joined in marriage in a Catholic church in Munich. According to the couple's account, the pastor refused to marry the 25 year old man, who suffers from muscular atrophy, and his nearly blind girl-friend without a certificate of potency. The pair—the bride, who is the same age as the groom, is a Protestant—were then married in a Protestant church. According to Catholic marriage law sexual incapacity is considered a natural legal impediment to the contracting of marriage, from which the Church can provide no relief, as the archbishop's office explained in Munich on Thursday." On December 9, 1982, under the headline "Youth Union in Munich Against 'Penis-Test' " the *Westdeutsche Allgemeine Zeitung* reported that: "The Youth Union in Munich sees the refusal of a Catholic priest to marry a handicapped couple in a church ceremony as a 'violation of the commandment of humanity and an infringement of human dignity.' As reported, the reason cited by the priest was the husband's 'procreative incapacity.' In an open letter to the archbishop's office the Youth Union labels this 'penis-test' as the crowning point of the Catholic Church's 'unrealistic and reactionary' approach to questions of sexuality."

Let us assume that it was not the Church authorities but the young couple who were mistaken in giving *procreative incapacity* as the grounds for the pastor's refusal to marry them. The archbishop's office would have known that now only the inability to have intercourse is an impediment to marriage. Still for some paraplegics—including the couple in question—Catholic marriage law is as unbearable now as it ever was. The change made in 1977 can't help the man who for lack of an erection cannot engage in intercourse, although under certain circumstances he would certainly be able to procreate. The Church dictates the precise form of the conjugal act to everybody and does this in a way that demotes a paraplegic and his partner to the level of infants, because according to Catholic sexual morality intimacies are allowed only in marriage and only in connection with the standardized intercourse conceded by the Church. This sort of interference in everyone's right to marriage is intolerable and shows once more that the celibates running the Church would be better advised not to get mixed up in such matters.

Sixtus V's decision in 1587 to forbid marriage to castrati brought many personal tragedies to the individuals concerned. From the twelfth century on the use of castrati as choristers in the Greek church had become widespread. In the Western Church castrati probably first appeared in sixteenth-century Spain (they were the occasion for Sixtus's fateful decree). But other countries emulated Spain. The Spanish castrato Francesco Soto was accepted into the Sistine Chapel choir in 1562. The first Italian castrato who sang in the Sistine Chapel (beginning in 1579) was Girolamo Rossini (d. 1644). The presence of castrati in the court chapel of the Gonzagas in Mantua is attested to as early as 1563. Sixtus V himself promoted the increasing practice of castration when in 1588 he forbade, for the first time, the appearance of women on the stages of the public theaters and opera houses of Rome and the Papal States. (Women had been forbidden to sing in church no later than the fourth century). The Pope's expulsion of female singers and actresses was soon copied by other states in and outside of Italy. Pope Innocent XI (d. 1689) reiterated the ban, which was in force all during the seventeenth and eighteenth centuries. Goethe heard castrati in Rome and found the custom a good one, but the French Revolution put an end to Sixtus's gagging of women. In 1798 females reappeared for the first time on the stages of Rome.

In 1936 the Jesuit Peter Browe accused the popes of being "the first, at the end of the 16th century, to introduce castrati into their chapels or to tolerate their presence there, when they were still unknown in the theaters and in the other Italian churches." After they had forbidden the appearance of female singers and actresses on the stages of the Papal States, "[the popes] must have been entirely out of touch with life, if they didn't learn that castrati took over the women's roles." Therefore the "defence of the popes" is incorrect (*Zur Geschichte der Entmannung*, 1936, p. 102).

In 1748 Pope Benedict XIV issued a decisive "no" to inquiries about whether the bishops at their synods ought to issue a decree against choirs of castrati. The Pope stressed that otherwise there was a danger that churches without the castrati would be empty. "The pope's conviction, which was dominated . . . by the fear of empty churches, naturally encouraged castrato singing. It slowed down the process of suppressing castration, and it was one of the reasons why no provincial or diocesan synod in the 18th and 19th century issued an ordinance against it. Benedict's ideas promoted castration and impeded its abolition" (ibid., pp. 115ff.).

The Sicilian Jesuit Tamburini (d. 1675) was a particular advocate of castration because in this way "the praise of God [is] sweeter to hear in the churches." Alphonsus Liguori admittedly writes that the opinion that such mutilation for maintaining the soprano voice is forbidden is "more probable" than the opposite opinion of Tamburini and many other theologians whom he lists. But he points out that the theologians can appeal to the tolerance shown by the Church toward this custom (*Theologia moralis* IV n. 374). The last castrato to sing in St. Peter's died in 1924.

These castrati often led the much feted life of stars and popular idols. They were surrounded by women, but the Church forbade them to marry. Bartolomeo de Sorlisi, who secretly married Dorotea Lichtwer, fought all his life long to stay by her side, and died of a broken heart when he failed. The castrato Finazzi had better luck. He fell in love with a Protestant woman, Gertrude Steinmetz from Hamburg, who felt bound by no ecclesiastical marriage laws and who proved a good wife.

Sixtus V elevated semen to the alpha and omega of married life, as if it were a sort of dispenser of the sacrament. Whoever was incapable of showing that he possessed semen that conformed to the Pope's specifications was forbidden to marry. Since 1977, however, the ban applies only when semen, whether the genuine variety or "just a fluid similar to semen," cannot proceed along the path prescribed by the Church's regulations.

Sixtus V's scandalous brief about the "lasciviousness" (*tentigo*) of the eunuchs who had to be separated from their wives because of their "filthy embraces," since this was a "scandal" leading to the "damnation of souls," shows us that the voices emanating from the University of Paris in about 1500, voices more favorable to pleasure even if they didn't really like it, had now, in the wake of the Council of Trent, given way to a different tune.

On February 4, 1611, the Holy Office in Rome announced that where sex was concerned there was "no such thing as a trivial matter." On April 24, 1612, the general of the Jesuits, Claudio Acquaviva, sent a directive to all members of his order, telling them neither to teach nor advise that any sin of unchastity could be minor. That is, every directly willed sexual pleasure outside of marriage is always a serious sin. Acquaviva threatened all those who contravened the directive with excommunication and removal from every teaching post. As opposed to, say, theft, where pennies do not mean much, the stirrings of sexual pleasure felt by an unmarried couple when they hold hands is a mortal sin, insofar as it is deliberate—the pleasure, that is, not the sentence to Hell that they incur. And that's how it is in the Church, even today.

XXI

LUTHER AND HIS INFLUENCE ON CATHOLIC SEXUAL MORALITY

Thus, *as we have noted,* some rather harsh voices made themselves heard after the Council of Trent. On the other hand, however, the confrontation with Luther—especially on the part of the Jesuits—led to a certain anti-Augustinianism and hence to some negligible liberalization in sexual morality. These two trends in the second half of the sixteenth century were ultimately destined to collide in the form of strict Augustinian Jansenism, on the one side, and what the Jansenists called "lax Jesuit morality," on the other. Alphonsus Liguori (d. 1787) worked out something of a compromise, and his moral theology is still considered valid in the Church today: stricter than the "lax" sixteenth- and seventeenth-century Jesuits, but less strict than the Jansenists.

As for Luther, Catholic theologians like to point to the fact that he had been an Augustinian monk (a Hermit of St. Augustine), who in no way left Augustinian sexual morality behind him. On the contrary, they say, he overstressed the damage done to man by original sin, and to that extent he not only didn't mean any progress, but rather a step backward in this area. Thus, for example, in his standard life of Luther (1911) the Jesuit Father Grisar wrote: "It is tragic enough that Luther . . . in his supposedly so lofty concept of marital relations . . . nevertheless characterizes the conjugal act, because of concupiscence, as a serious sin. In the piece he wrote from the Wartburg, *De votis monasticis,* he declares: 'It (the marital act) is a sin according to Psalm 50:7, in no way to be distinguished from adultery and fornication, insofar as sensual passion and hideous lust come into play. But God does not in the least hold it against married people, and for no other reason than his compassion, since it is impossible for us to avoid it, although we are obliged to do without it' " (II, 499).

Grisar is right: Luther did repeat all the pleasure-hating nonsense of the Christian past, mostly in its Early Scholastic, i.e., especially pleasure-hating, form. But nevertheless he discarded it. Grisar himself alludes to this, when he continues, somewhat querulously: "We are already familiar with his strange, essentially impossible 'accountability' theory, according to which God is able not to see a sin that is, however, really there." Despite his Augustinian roots and his stress on original sin, Luther did introduce some essential progress in sexual morality. His doctrine of justification "by faith alone" brought about a leveling in the classification between venial and mortal sin, so painstakingly differentiated by Catholic theologians, and thereby paved the way for liberalization. The distinction between venial and mortal sin disappears from the language of Protestantism; the concept of the individual mortal sinner gives way to the idea that we all are simultaneously just and sinful.

Whatever one may think of the Protestant doctrine of justification, it was a blessing for sexual morality. For whereas Catholicism produced the consciousness of sin without sins being committed, the Protestant notion of sins not being counted is always appropriate. The tangled undergrowth of motives and compensating values that makes carnal pleasure sometimes acceptable, sometimes tolerable, deserving indulgence, forgivable, unforgivable, allowed, etc., now disappears. The dizzying structure of phantasms about pleasure, which supposedly violated human dignity, was struck by Luther's "by faith alone," and came tumbling down, at least at first. The prudery of Puritanism is a swamp blossom of reformed Protestantism.

Luther's trailblazing achievement in this area—graphically symbolized by his wedding with a nun—was the fact that he did away with the unnatural subordination of the married state to celibacy. In his sermon, "On Grateful Estimation of the Married State" (1531) he says: "Under the papacy marriage was thought to be inferior, and all praise was heaped on the unmarried state, into which almost everyone was forced."

Luther's Augustinianism, i.e., his emphasis on man's forlornness owing to original sin and his need for redemption—which was immediately buffered, in Luther's case, by his still greater stress on forgiveness and grace—brought forth in reaction on the

Catholic side a certain anti-Augustinianism, which shed a few rays of enlightenment on Catholic sexual morality. This decline in sexual pessimism was connected to the controversies with the Reformers over original sin. While the great significance Augustine had for Protestantism did not make him suspect to Catholics, it did give rise to some criticism of his ideas. Cardinal Bellarmine (d. 1621) of Rome, the most influential Jesuit theologian of his day, maintained that Augustine's notion that original sin was passed on through sexual pleasure could not be taken literally. Augustine had never found a sure answer about precisely how original sin was transmitted. Nor does Bellarmine provide any solution for the problem, but settles for exonerating sexual pleasure (*Controversy on the Loss of Grace* 4, 12).

For Bellarmine and then especially for many seventeenth-century Jesuits who were influenced by him, the controversy with Luther led to a cautious optimism in their view of human nature and, hence, of human sexual inclinations. They leaned on Thomas Aquinas, who, following Aristotle, had characterized pleasure as something natural. Starting in the sixteenth century Thomas's *Summa Theologiae* took over from the *Sentences* of Peter Lombard (d. 1164) as the Church's chief training manual, a position it still holds today.

One of the moderately progressive Jesuits who went a few steps beyond Augustine was Thomas Sanchez (d. 1610) from Cordoba, who was the supreme authority on marital issues. One small bit of progress by Sanchez was his treating the third kind of marital sex (to prevent oneself from committing fornication) as sinless, provided of course all other legitimate means of resisting temptation, such as fasting, vigils, and works of piety promised no help (*The Holy Sacrament of Marriage,* lib. 9, dist. 9). Sanchez was preceded in this move by three Dominicans, Cardinal Cajetan (d. 1534), Sylvestro Prierias (d. 1523), both known as opponents of Luther, and the court theologian of Emperor Charles V, Dominicus Soto (d. 1560).

Sanchez can sound rational and modern, for example, when he argues that there is actually no reason to classify a couple's motivation for sex in one of the categories of purpose. It is no sin, he says, "when spouses wish to be joined together simply because they are spouses" (ibid., 9, 8). The fact that such simple truths strike the reader as pleasantly touching shows just how much tension the Church's celibates worked themselves into with their technical grids for analyzing sex. But then Sanchez immediately reins in his progressive, if obvious, statement. He does *not* think intercourse for sheer pleasure is sinless, and he distances himself from Mayor and Almain, who are practically the only ones he quotes as supporting such an extreme view. He thus joins the majority in rating intercourse for pleasure's sake as a venial sin (ibid., 9, 11, 2).

Here is one more of his progressive statements: He poses the question whether married couples are allowed to "embrace, kiss, and indulge in other touches, as are customary among spouses, in order to attest their love for one another," even if there is a foreseeable danger of ejaculation. "In many teachers," he writes, "I have seen the assertion that it is a mortal sin for those subject to the danger of pollution." He cites these experts one after another and tries to refute them. He himself believes that to do something that can lead to an unintentional ejaculation is not always bad, an urgent reason can justify the risk. For a spouse an "urgent reason" is the desire to "bear witness to and strengthen mutual love . . . It would be extremely harsh, and love would suffer greatly if the spouses refrained from these touches." Thus he defends sexual contact (in marriage) outside the context of intercourse, although "the danger exists," that semen will be spilled and will not arrive where Catholic morality says it is uniquely intended for: the standardized conjugal act that in no way hinders procreation (ibid., 9, 45, 33–37) (cf. Noonan, *Contraception*, pp. 324ff.).

The progress achieved by Sanchez becomes clear when measured against the steps backward taken in our century. Thus, for example, Bernhard Häring writes in 1967 that if pregnancy may not take place because of mortal danger to the mother, then "in my opinion, the expression of love must contain itself within the bounds of mere tenderness, so long as there is *no danger of gratification*. Whatever goes beyond that . . . may not be actively participated in" (*Das Gesetz Christi*, p. 357). On this notion Häring follows Alphonsus Liguori, the founder of his own order, the Redemptorists. From the time of Alphonsus down into the twentieth century unmarried, engaged, and married couples have less freedom, because of the "danger of gratification," that is, of pleasure, than they were given by Thomas Sanchez in the sixteenth century. (St. Alphonsus' position, which Häring presents and which is still valid today, can be found in his *Theologia moralis* III, n. 416; VI, n. 854; VI, 934). Sanchez hastens to add that, of course, married people are not allowed to aim at provoking an ejaculation with their caresses; but with Alphonsus/Häring they can't do anything should there be a *danger* of *gratification.*

Thomas Sanchez, like all theologians, calls coitus interruptus a mortal sin against nature (*The Holy Sacrament of Marriage,* 9, 20, 1). On the other hand, he takes a progressive stance on the question of whether a woman who has been raped may remove the semen. Sanchez says yes, arguing that this is an act of self-defense against the semen as an unjust assailant (ibid., 2, 22, 17). He presupposes that fertilization has not yet taken place. Roughly one hundred and fifty years later Alphonsus Liguori, the moral pope even in this century, attacked Sanchez's opinion. He maintained that the semen may never be removed "without doing injustice to nature or to the human race, whose reproduction [by rape!] would be impaired." Besides, the semen now was in "peaceful" possession, that is, it was behaving peacefully. In the course of the rape the woman was allowed to defend herself, so that the rapist's semen would be spilled outside the "vessel" intended for it, but after the rape this was no longer the case (*Theologia moralis,* VI, n. 954). Thus the rapist's semen has been promoted to the status of a quasi-person; nothing may be done to harm it. It enjoys the same protection that a peaceful citizen would.

A series of seventeenth-century theologians who came after Thomas Sanchez differed from him in holding that even marital intercourse for pleasure (Nr. 4) was sinless: the Spanish Augustinian Ponce de Leon (d. 1629), the Spanish Jesuits Gaspar Hurtado (d. 1647), Martin Pérez (d. 1660), and the Spanish secular priest Juan Sanchez (d. 1624), a sharp-witted writer and known as a "laxist," who in his work on the sacraments quotes page after page of Mayor and Almain, noting enthusiastically, "These are beautiful words, these are golden words" (Heinrich Klomps, *Ehemoral und Jansenismus,* p. 71). Thus all four of the motives for intercourse devised for married people by the Church's celibates are sinless. This puts us more or less at the stage where we are now: Current Catholic teaching holds that in the marital act the motives, with procreation at their head, no longer need be given so much thought. What's important is rather that nothing be done to check the course of the conjugal act as laid down by nature; that would be against nature and a serious sin. In other words: Thou shalt not practice contraception. One need not be constantly thinking of a child, so long as one doesn't exclude the possibility.

Heinrich Klomps writes that with this an "entirely new kind of argument in the history of conjugal morality is launched . . . Instead of a morality of intention a morality of action prevails, and the concept of the *natura actus* (the nature of the marital act) takes on central importance" (ibid., p. 72). And "This put the slow-moving, back and forth discussion about motivations on a wholly new foundation" (ibid.). But on closer inspection the situation of married people has not changed in any crucial way. They are admittedly free from the old Augustinian four-point grid, but now they have been locked into a new one-point program. In a system as muddled as Augustinian sexual morality, every step forward leads into a new dead end. The only help for married people here comes from saying good-bye to the dictatorship of the monks and celibates and relying instead on their own intelligence and their own conscience.

On March 2, 1679, the Supreme Magisterium intervened in the controversy over pleasure in the conjugal act; Pope Innocent XI condemned the principle espoused by Juan Sanchez (and others) that intercourse purely for pleasure was wholly sinless. The Pope thus became one more voice—and not even the most forceful—in a whole series of protests. Still more massive was the outcry against the whole development of the lax Jesuits, including Thomas Sanchez, on the part of the Jansenists. They wanted to lift Augustine, whole and uncurtailed, back onto his pedestal. They were disturbed by the word "alone" in the papal condemnation. Pleasure in any form, whether "alone" or "not alone," was repugnant to them. And they could foresee how the Jesuits would handle the papal ban, thanks to the word "alone": They would say something such as, intercourse prompted by pleasure was not affected by the Pope's prohibition, only intercourse prompted by pleasure alone. And that in fact is what the Spanish Jesuit Fuente Hurtado (d. 1686) immediately did.

Hardly anyone was satisfied with this condemnation. The strict enemies of pleasure were bothered by the "alone," and others, ranging from rather lax to lax, were bothered because any condemnation of intercourse for pleasure had occurred at all. In any case the "alone" provided a new and exciting theological topic for the next two hundred years: What distinguished intercourse "for pleasure" from intercourse "for pleasure alone"? For the Pope had objected only to "pleasure alone," and therefore . . .

XXII

THE JANSENISTS AND JESUIT MORALITY

Jansenism takes its name from the Dutch-born bishop of Louvain, Belgium, Cornelis Jansen (d. 1638) (for what follows see Heinrich Klomps, *Ehemoral und Jansenismus*, pp. 97ff.). In his book *Augustinus*, Jansen tried to bring strict Augustinian sexual morality to bear against all the recent trends toward leniency, and to confront the "very splendid advocates of lust." Jansen traces the low moral level of his time, which he labels *saeculum corruptissimum*, "the most corrupt age," to the "more recent theology," which has deviated from Augustine and the Church Fathers. (He reckons Thomas Aquinas among the unadulterated theologians still faithful to Augustine.)

For Jansen, the motivation for marital sex has to be entirely concentrated on procreation, in no way prompted by pleasure. "The physical connection is bestial if it is sought not for the sake of children but under the pressure of sensual desire." For this reason all intercourse with pregnant, sterile, or post-menopausal women must be condemned. Intercourse to avoid falling into fornication or sheerly for pleasure is, to use Jansen's term, "Pelagian," that is, laxism. As with Augustine, the only kind of conjugal intercourse he recognizes, apart from sex for procreation, is sex as performance of one's duty. The ideal is lust-free relations. Even the clouding of the will to procreate by the expectation of pleasure is culpable. Jansen reports that he spent his whole life with the works of Augustine, that he read some sections twenty, others thirty times. And he was outraged that Augustine's teaching, which he had spared no pains to understand, had been distorted by the new doctrines.

Here is the upshot of his effort: "Truly, this is the ideal way to lead a Christian married life, which resists the sexual desire of coupling with the menstruating woman, the pregnant woman, the wholly barren woman, or the woman too old to bear children. And I say further that one should not do the least thing for the sake of sexual pleasure. Indeed, if offspring, on account of whom married people unite, could be conceived in another way without the experience of desire, they would have to refrain from conjugal union." Jansen views sex during pregnancy as immoral and sinful, not because of possible damage to the fetus (that was one more aggravating factor) but because generation was no longer possible. On this point all Jansenists were agreed. They appealed to Augustine, Ambrose, Jerome, Clement of Alexandria, etc. (Klomps, pp. 184, 186ff.)

Jansen keeps coming back to 1 Corinthians (7:6), according to which (in the false Augustinian interpretation) Paul characterizes marital sex that does not serve procreation as in need of pardon, and hence sinful. For Jansen sexual desire was imposed upon us as a penalty through the sin of Adam and Eve. It can be morally coped with only as a punishment one submits to. "Thus *delectatio carnalis* (fleshly enjoyment)," Klomps writes, speaking of Jansenist theologians, "must appear as an impairment of human dignity. Had artificial insemination been possible back then, given the basis they were working on, our authors would have had to establish it as the norm" (ibid., p. 203).

At a time when other theologians were trying to escape a system of compulsory motivation affecting every single act of marital sex, the Jansenists returned to it. No moral theologian could deny that Jansen's interpretation of Augustine's sexual morality was perfectly accurate. Five statements from Jansen's book *Augustinus* were condemned by Pope Innocent X in 1653 as heretical, but they referred to dogmatic questions about grace and predestination and not to conjugal morality. The sexual morality of *Augustinus* corresponded so completely to Augustine's views that not only did the Church not condemn it then, it has never condemned it since. The Catholic Church has yet to realize, much less acknowledge, that its greatest "Doctor" got it off onto the wrong track on an issue that has concrete, everyday repercussions on most men and women, unfairly burdening the consciences of innumerable people, then and now. In 1679, Pope Innocent XI, at the urging of the Jansenists, did condemn the "lax" principle that intercourse simply for pleasure was not a sin.

Frequent Communion (1643), a book by the prominent Jansenist Antoine Arnauld (*"le grand* Arnauld"), which laid down stringent requirements for receiving the Eucharist, had a great deal of influence all the way into the twentieth century. Married couples were advised to abstain from intercourse before and after Communion. The book was occasioned by a dispute between two noble ladies (the marquise de Sablé and the Princesse de Guéméné) about how often they should take Communion. Arnauld attacked the "lax Jesuits," who called for frequent Communion even if people did not exactly meet all the requirements for necessary Communion. As a result of this book people seldom went to Communion until the decree on Communion by Pius X in 1905.

Still more effective in spreading Jansenism were the "Letters to a Friend in the Country," the famous *Provincial Letters* by Blaise Pascal (d. 1662). Jansenism is a complex phenomenon, but all Jansenists shared an aversion to the Jesuits. Pascal succeeded in casting the Jesuits in a dubious light that for many people still hovers over them. In *Augustinus,* Jansen had not only resurrected Augustine's marital morality, but above all his doctrine of grace. The *Provincial Letters* deal with this Augustinian-Jansenist doctrine and criticize the Jesuits for their wrongheaded notions of grace and morality. Pascal scarcely touches on sexual morality. He reports to his fictitious friend in the country about a conversation with a Jesuit priest, who has presented to him, among other things, the views of Jesuit theologians on married and engaged couples. Pascal writes: "Then he told me the strangest things one could imagine. I could fill several letters with this, but I don't even want to reproduce the quotations, since you show my letters to everyone you can. I wouldn't like anyone to read them who was simply looking for diversion in them" (Letter 9). Thomas Sanchez, the Jesuit specialist on sexual ethics, whom Pascal mentions by name in Letters 5, 7, 8, and 9, with reference to other aspects of ethics, was likely one of those whom Pascal refuses to quote. His deviation from strict Augustinian sexual morality was minimal, but too much for Pascal.

Pascal wrote these letters to help his friend Antoine Arnauld, who had been expelled from the Sorbonne. In Letters 15 and 16 he praises Arnauld's book on frequent Communion. Pascal thinks that, by contrast, the Jesuits "profane the sacrament" (Letter 16) with their loose requirements.

When Pascal died at thirty-nine, a hairshirt with little iron hooks was found on his body. Pascal had worn it to punish himself for the tiniest faults. The geniality and wit of Pascal's letters that enabled him to make his Jesuit opponents look ridiculous obscure the fact that on questions of sexual morality the "lax Jesuits" were closer to the truth than he was. On the other hand, Pascal was right on target in denouncing the evolution of Catholic moral theology from the sixteenth century, with its endless microscopic distinctions and casuistic minutiae, which go far beyond Augustine and Thomas Aquinas and often lead to absurdities. Pascal wittily pulls such nonsense to pieces, but prefers to pass over in refined silence the subject of sexual morality. He correctly sensed that especially in this area the obsessive concern with details, regardless of whether one finds these theologians too lax (as Pascal did) or too strict (as we do today), is out of line. The further history of Catholic moral theology in the eighteenth and nineteenth centuries with its assiduous eye for sexual questions, above and beyond all else, would prove Pascal right.

Pascal managed, in the judgment of many, to make the Jesuits lose their credibility on ethical issues. One of the results of this was that, although he himself had discreetly bracketed the topic of sex, other Jansenists, who made rigorous demands on married people, made more of an impression on many believers than the Jesuits with their "lax" demands. Not least of all thanks to Pascal, Jansenism had a profound effect, and, particularly in France, Belgium, and the English-speaking Catholic world, was a determining factor far into the nineteenth century.

Laurentius Neesen (d. 1679), the Jansenist rector of the seminary in the Belgian city of Mechlin, went so far as to draw the following comparison: Just as the state does not actually approve bordellos, but reluctantly permits them in order to avoid a greater evil, so married couples may not affirm sexual pleasure internally, but simply tolerate this pleasure, let it happen to them, when there is a just cause for it, namely, the procreation of children and the performance of one's duty. With nature corrupted as it is, we have no other way of arriving at the good goal of begetting offspring (Klomps, pp. 182ff.).

Louis Habert (d. 1718), who was one of the leading French theologians of the seventeenth century and the adviser of several bishops, maintained that humanity had already been destroyed once—in the Flood—because of sins committed in marriage. The Flood was brought about by "the defilement, the pollution, the desecration [what else?] of the conjugal bed." Through the grace given by the sacrament of marriage married people are enabled to share in the mind-set of Tobias ("to come together only for love of offspring, not out of lust"), which was of vital importance to humanity, since it "protects the human race from a new Flood" (ibid., p. 160) and makes spouses capable of rightly using "the evil of sexual pleasure," as opposed to loving like pagans "in the sickness of desire" (ibid., p. 158). The Jansenists continually trot out the Book of Tobit, which in the guise of Jerome's translation has inspired fear in Christian married people, as a sort of Dracula of the bedroom (Sarah's seven husbands carried off by Asmodeus), for the past fifteen hundred years.

Needless to say, the Jansenist hatred of pleasure also led to Augustinian conclusions in the field of Mariology, as we see in the work of the Belgian William Estius (d. 1613), a professor in Douai and one of the pioneers of Jansenism. He argued that because of the "dirtiness" of the carnal drive Jesus wished to be born of a virgin and not from the marital act (Klomps, p. 78). And Estius's successor in Douai, Sylvius (d. 1649), demonstrated how Mary's purity could be imitated by normal married people. They must, he said, eliminate every internal assent to the excitement befalling them in the act of generation, just as a lame man welcomes the forward progress he makes, but not the limp that accompanies it (ibid., p. 80). Although we no longer use the word "filth" in reference to the conjugal act (not least of all thanks to "lax" Jesuit morality), the filth is still there. It is what the Church's leading celibates want to protect Mary from when they refuse to let Mary near normal wives and normal marriages in the matter of conception and childbirth.

XXIII

CONTRACEPTION FROM 1500 TO 1750

While *Antiquity and* the Middle Ages dealt scientifically with contraception and a woman's infertile periods, the belief in demons and the persecution of witches led people to view these topics as the domain of the devil. Especially after the promulgation of the "Witches Bull" (1484), the publication of *The Hammer of Witches* (1487), and the subsequent intensifying of the campaign to burn the so-called witch-midwives, the question of contraception had become suspect and dangerous. Scientific progress in this area was blocked by the superstition that the popes and theologians were always delving into. The "Witches Bull," with its denunciation of the arts of sorcery, which "prevent men from begetting and women from conceiving," and the centuries of witch-burning that followed it—especially in Germany—did not create an environment in which unbiased scientific study could develop.

Thus Christian married couples had only two methods of contraception at their disposal. The first was the most Catholic one, namely continence, suitable when both partners desired it. This is what Jonathan Swift (d. 1745) advised in *Gulliver's Travels* (1726). The perfect, wholly rational Houyhnhnms (horses) behave in such a way as "to prevent the country from being over-burdened with numbers": The upper-class Houyhnhnms stop having intercourse as soon as they have produced one of each sex . . . But the race of inferior Houyhnhnms bred up to be servants . . . are allowed to produce three of each sex, to be domestics in the noble families. Noonan writes about this method of birth control in his *Contraception* (1982[2]): "No major theologian denied that continence, to avoid too many children, was lawful" (p. 336). From this standpoint there was at least something married people were authorized to do. We may presume that this sort of Columbus's egg was probably never forbidden, even by the minor theologians.

Noonan's words are symptomatic of a situation in which married couples have a group of clerocrats leading them around by the nose: Their every activity, provided it is not forbidden, requires the approval of moral theologians. Continence by mutual agreement was a Christian marital ideal that had been recommended since ancient times. As far back as the Middle Ages there already were a series of monastic herbs available for help in obtaining continence, for example *agnus castus* (literally, "chaste lamb"), which Pliny (d. 79) mentions in his *Natural History,* and about which Francis de Sales (d. 1622) says in his ever popular *Introduction to the Devout Life:* "Whoever sleeps on the herb agnus castus will himself become modest and chaste" (3, 13).

But if the couple disagreed about abstinence, the issue became complicated. The first answer given the question, may a woman in oppressive poverty refuse to do her marital duty, was no. Le Maistre (d. 1481) thought that a woman who would not engage in intercourse "can be legally compelled to grant it [to her husband]" (*Moral Questions* II, fol. 49r). Not until the sixteenth century did theologians decide otherwise. For example, Dominicus Soto (d. 1560) wrote that the refusal to have sex was not a mortal sin, "Especially when they suffer under crushing poverty and thus cannot feed so many children." This was an innovation, a major concession on the part of Soto, who was court theologian to Emperor Charles V.

Thomas Sanchez came to a similar decision. And the Jesuit Paul Laymann (d. 1635), whose book on moral theology was the standard work for a hundred and fifty years in the Catholic theological faculties of Germany, staffed mostly with Jesuits, decided that "in extreme poverty" wives should be allowed to refuse their husbands (5, 10, 31, 16).

All these generous gentlemen were agreed, however, that such refusal was a mortal sin if it caused the husband to fall into mortal sin, e.g., commit adultery. One could hardly give clearer expression to the fact that conjugal sex here has nothing to do with love, since the threat of adultery on the husband's part would scarcely increase a wife's willingness to have intercourse.

Contrary to many of his predecessors, Alphonsus Liguori (d. 1787) was inclined to think that refusing sex under conditions of great poverty was *not* permitted, precisely because of the threat of fornication. This means that the husband's latent infidelity gets rung up against the overtaxed wife as her own sin, if she does not have sex with him. On the other hand, to deny a kindly, faithful, loving husband for a much less serious reason than extreme poverty would be no sin at all, Alphonsus says, as long as the husband doesn't insist (*Theologia moralis* VI, n. 940–41). The precedence given to potentially fornicating husbands has been a basic motif of the Church's sexual morality up to and including the Second Vatican Council. Theologians have devoted their greatest attention to avoiding fornication and adultery, putting in second place any serious harm that might come to the mother. Catholic sexual morality is largely a master-race morality and a pitiless exploitation of women.

To date the Church's celibates have not given a single positive thought to intercourse prompted by love (which simply does not exist in the classical theological taxonomy of sex) and to the responsible contraception this may require. As they see it, marital relations are designed exclusively for avoiding fornication and procreating children, or avoiding fornication while accepting the possibility of children. Despite some fine words here and there the situation today has not changed in the least. If the theologians, beginning with Augustine, had thought as much about marital love as they did about the danger (above all to the husband) of fornication and infidelity, they would have built a more humane ethical system, unlike the brutal one now in place. The bottom line remains that the concerns of married Christians, managed exclusively by unmarried clerics, have suffered harm.

Apart from continence by mutual agreement, then, Christian couples had a second method available under serious circumstances, coitus reservatus. All other methods of contraception were considered mortally sinful, notably coitus interruptus and so-called potions (medications). Coitus interruptus was condemned as a serious sin by, among others, Cardinal Cajetan (d. 1534). Francis de Sales (d. 1622) writes: "Onan's deed was worthy of God's detestation." He criticizes "certain modern teachers of error, who think that not the deed, but only Onan's evil intentions displeased God" (*Introduction for the Devout Life*, 3, 39). By the modern innovators who evidently defended coitus interruptus as a birth control method Francis de Sales did not mean the Reformers, who had brought no progress at all on that point, since they clung to the Augustinian teaching.

On the subject of coitus interruptus, one question has always especially interested the theologians, namely the behavior of the wife. If she knows that her husband is going to practice coitus interruptus, must she resist her husband to the death, as St. Bernardine of Siena (d. 1444) thought? Like Le Maistre and Thomas Sanchez before him, Alphonsus Liguori saw it this way: The wife may, indeed should, go along with intercourse if a greater evil may be anticipated from her refusal. In so doing she is not formally cooperating with sin. In fact, she may herself request intercourse, if she would otherwise fall into incontinence (*Theologia moralis* VI, n. 947). Here we find once again the Church's care for the potential adulterer and its neglect of those who don't see marital sex as a substitute for adultery. Alphonsus's twentieth-century mouthpiece, Bernhard Häring, also allows wives to cooperate in coitus interruptus to "guard against adultery." He does not, however, talk about requesting such intercourse (*Das Gesetz Christi* III, 357).

Häring was wrong, by the way, when, writing in honor of the founder of the Redemptorists (1982), he said: "It will come as a surprise, especially to those who think of Alphonsus as an archconservative, that he applies this basic principle to an issue that is particularly controversial today, namely coitus interruptus: 'Marital relations can allowably be interrupted, provided that a proportionate reason exists' (*Theologia moralis* VI, n. 947). The rigorists thought this was exclusively sinful" (Häring, "Moral für die Erlösten," in *Theologie der Gegenwart,* 1982, 1, 2).

There is nothing of the sort in this passage in Alphonsus. At issue is simply the question of whether the innocent wife sins gravely if she has intercourse with her gravely sinning husband. Even in another passage in Alphonsus, which is evidently the one Häring had in mind and which he cited in 1986 (*Theologie der Gegenwart,* 1986, 4, 214), namely, *Theologie moralis* lib. VI, c. 2, n. 882, Alphonsus by no means permits the use of coitus interruptus for birth control. Rather he expressly says that "neither the threat of poverty nor the danger of childbirth excuse" it, that it is a "violation of the first purpose of marriage." He merely discusses the question of whether one is forced to continue having intercourse, if that would mean a threat to one's health, or if one is being slain by an enemy, or if someone else comes into the room. And as a matter of fact not a single Catholic theologian, even of the deepest conservative dye, has ever claimed that one is forced to let oneself be struck down by the enemy, have a heart attack, put up with the intervention—appearance, disturbance, hindrance, interruption, or interference—of a third person, and despite all this go on having intercourse. And yet one may under no circumstances interrupt coitus for the sake of contraception— that was a mortal sin for Alphonsus and remains one today. The Catholic theologian who has Rome's approval in decriminalizing coitus interruptus has yet to be begotten.

Thus although Alphonsus Liguori was not the progressive decriminalizer of coitus interruptus that Häring, his fellow Redemptorist, would nowadays cautiously make of him—at least until the Church puts a stop to his endeavors—it is remarkable, in any case, that Alphonsus does not, as does Bernardine of Siena, demand that the wife die rather than go through with intercourse with a husband who she thinks is probably going to commit coitus interruptus. In the nineteenth and twentieth centuries the Vatican would judge more harshly than Alphonsus did on the matter of contraception, for example, in the official responses from Rome in 1822, 1823, and 1916, as we shall see.

The other birth control method, namely by potions, was equated by the Roman Catechism of the Council of Trent with homicide. And in 1588 Sixtus V, as already mentioned, threatened anyone who practiced it with the death penalty. The Jesuit theologian Father Laymann (d. 1635) called such contraception "quasi-murder" and a mortal sin (3, 3, 3, 2). He asks: "Can a woman take a medication to prevent conception, if she has learned from her physician or suspects from her own experience that the birth of a child will bring her death?" Answer: No. Contraception goes against the main purpose of marriage. And here is his justification: "If women were to be allowed to prevent conception in such cases, this would be an astonishing abuse and great damage would be done to human reproduction." And he immediately adds the other kind of contraception, coitus interruptus: "For a similar reason the doctors of divinity agree that in no case is it permitted to bring about an ejaculation of semen" (5, 10, 3, 1) (cf. Noonan, *Contraception*, p. 370).

The notion of birth control as equivalent to murder—not shared, though, by all theologians—was confirmed in 1677 by the discovery of mobile spermatazoa in the ejaculate. The "potential person" that Thomas spoke of had now been graphically demonstrated in human semen. In the seventeenth and eighteenth centuries many writers compared the husband with a sower who casts his seed into the furrow, and saw him as placing a little person inside his wife. Contraception was thus brought still closer to murder than it had already been, thanks to *"si aliquis."* But starting in about the middle of the eighteenth century, however, attitudes changed, and people no longer saw contraception as equivalent to murder. The crucial figure here was Alphonsus

Liguori. Noonan remarks: "A tradition as old as Regino of Prüm and Burchard, indeed as ancient as St. Jerome, had fallen into disuse. With St. Alphonsus the homicide approach ended its theological life" (ibid., pp. 364–65).

In about the middle of the seventeenth century the condom was invented, but it was too expensive and too unreliable to be very significant. Men customarily used it only for extramarital affairs. Madame de Sévigné probably had these unreliable condoms in mind when she wrote in a letter (1671) to her daughter, the Comtesse De Grignan, that they were "a bulwark against pleasure and a cobweb against danger." In any case the seventeenth-century condom was not a resounding success.

Pastors had two possible ways of making the ban on contraception known to their flocks: the pulpit and the confessional. In sermons on birth control most people were more careful than St. Bernardine (d. 1444). It seems that only a few of the priests inclined to Jansenism did not put into practice the aristocratic restraint shown by Pascal. One of those who did not was Philippe Boucher, who in about the beginning of the eighteenth century preached against the "abhorrent crime of Onan," against sodomy (anal intercourse), and against the use of contraceptive herbs. Boucher stressed that poverty was no justification for an overstrained wife's denying a husband his marital rights (Noonan, p. 373). In general preachers stuck to the directive of the Council of Trent as formulated by the Roman Catechism. In the section "What Should Be Taught About Conjugal Duties," it reads: "Here pastors should express themselves in such a way that no word slips from their lips that could strike the ears of believers as unworthy or offend pious souls or give rise to laughter" (II, 2, 8, 33). On the question of how the pastor should handle the Sixth Commandment ("Thou shalt not commit adultery") it was hinted: "But let the pastor be careful and prudent in handling this matter, and let him mention it with veiled words" (3, 7, 1). "On this subject many other and various kinds of licentiousness and lust may go unmentioned. The pastor must admonish each person in private, as the circumstances of time and the individuals in question require" (3, 7, 5). The only topic to be clearly mentioned was contraception through medicines, "for this must be considered a godless scheme of murderers" (2, 8, 13).

As for examining penitents about contraception in the confessional, the policy before the Council of Trent was likewise less self-conscious and embarrassed. After the Council of Trent the only advice given to confessors on sexual matters by the *Rituale Romanum* (the authoritative book on the administration of the sacraments) was to omit "careless questions to the young people of either sex, or to others about things they were not familiar with, lest they be scandalized and in this way learn to sin." Charles Borromeo (d. 1584) advised confessors to exercise "extreme caution" with sins of lust (*Instruction on the Right Administration of the Sacrament of Penance,* 12). And Alphonsus Liguori told confessors, "In general, the confessor is not obliged, and it is not fitting for him, to inquire of married people about sins concerning their marital duty, unless he asks wives, as discreetly as possible, whether they have fulfilled their duty, by asking, for example, if they have obeyed their husbands in all things. About other matters he should be silent, if he is not asked first" (*The Practice of the Confessor* II, 41).

This wise reticence on the part of confessors about birth control did not last long. Questions about contraception were destined to be the main theme of confessions by married people in the nineteenth and twentieth centuries. Alphonsus' words about a wife's total obedience to her husband is in keeping with the unbroken tradition of deprecating women in the Catholic Church.

Although Alphonsus gives confessors the wise directive to ask no questions about contraception in marriage, the questioning he recommends for children and unmarried people is all the more impertinent and importunate. The Council of Trent's instruction to discuss these issues with "veiled words" leads in Alphonsus' case to a shady concealment that makes matters even worse: "Children must be treated as lovingly and gently as possible. Let the confessor have them say all the sins they remember. After that one can pose the following questions . . . Did they commit an ugly sin? But on this topic the confessor must question carefully. Let him begin from a distance with general language, asking first whether they used bad words, whether they played games with other boys and girls, and whether they played these games in secret. Afterwards let him ask whether they did dishonorable things. Often, even when the children say 'no,' it is useful to pose suggestive questions to them, e.g.: 'And now tell me, how often did you do that? Five times? Ten times?' Then they should be asked with whom they sleep and whether they played with their fingers in bed" (ibid., VII, 90).

XXIV

JOHN PAUL II AND SEX FOR PLEASURE

When *Pope Innocent XI* declared in 1679 that "marital relations for pleasure alone" were not sinless, he guaranteed that theologians would be kept busy studying sexual morality for the next two centuries. While the Jansenists rejected every pleasurable motivation for intercourse, thereby agreeing with Augustine and the Roman Catechism (1566), moderate theologians tried to concede a little room for pleasure and looked into the distinction between sex for pleasure and sex for pleasure *alone*, since only the latter was affected by the papal decree.

Alphonsus Liguori set the standard for Catholic ethics during the nineteenth and, to a large extent, the twentieth century too. He was canonized in 1839 and made a Doctor of the Church in 1871. Alphonsus solved the sexual problem in a thoroughly circumstantial fashion. He said that intercourse for pleasure alone had been generally considered a venial sin—it was a mortal sin only under certain preconditions—because the pleasure intended by nature as a means for reproduction was made the purpose of the marital act. It is not a sin when the husband chiefly aimed at procreation and used the pleasure by striving for it in a moderate way, so as to excite himself for the conjugal act (*Theologia moralis* VI, n. 912). Pleasure, therefore, may be sought for, but not solely or primarily. The nineteenth century finally reduces the problem to a short formula: Intercourse prompted by pleasure alone is intercourse that *excludes* other conjugal purposes—we find this argument, for example, in the Jesuit Ballerini (d. 1881). This means exclusion from the *motivation* for sex, not the exclusion of offspring by birth control, which would be not a venial but a mortal sin.

The controversy over whether some sexual enjoyment was a morally permissible motive for intercourse was thus decided in the affirmative, although Augustine and the Roman Catechism were against the idea.

But the Church's higher-ups also defined their position by showing what happens to an author who argues for finding greater pleasure by varying the standard missionary position. At about the time when the German bishops almost without exception saw Hitler as "the bulwark against bolshevism and the plague of filthy literature," one of the things they meant by the latter phrase was one specific dirty book that by 1930 had already reached its fifty-first edition, and had been both put on the Index of Forbidden Books and confiscated by the Nazi regime. Pope Pius XI himself took notice of the book in his encyclical *Casti connubii*, where he twisted its title from *Perfect Marriage* into *Perfect Whoredom*. In this way the Pope created a new perfect state and guaranteed the book a still broader distribution. Originally published in 1926, its author was a Dutch gynecologist and former director of the women's clinic in Haarlem, Theodor Hendrik van de Velde. *Perfect Marriage* was an abbreviation of its rather pedantic title, *Marriage Brought to Greater Perfection from the Physiological-Technical Standpoint* (author's foreword).

For many married couples, especially in the Christian West, where sexual pleasure is suspect and hence the culture of the sexual act is underdeveloped, Van de Velde became a sort of Galileo of the conjugal bed. He removed taboos from the physical relations of couples simply by speaking about them, even though he preferred to use Latin expressions in doing so, "because they are most familiar in the language of the physician and they spare people's feelings in the discussion of many subjects" (p. 46), thus elevating them from the level of animalistic dumbness to the realm of the person.

Van de Velde wanted to bring variety into the bedroom, a variety that previously seemed "possible [to the man] only by changing his sexual object." In the final analysis he was concerned about fidelity and love between the spouses; and, especially since he shared Catholic thinking about divorce, contraception, and coitus interruptus, he felt that "my views do not contradict Catholic morality" (p. 269). On that he was deeply wrong. The sexual pessimism and hostility to pleasure typical of Catholic sexual morality forbade this sort of work about the intimate free space for married couples, a space that the Church's celibate overseers consider it their essential task to manage, control, and plan for.

In 1911 the most prominent moral theologian of his day, the Jesuit Hieronymus Noldin (d. 1922), expressed a view of sexual pleasure that was no longer quite so negative as Augustine's, but was positive only in appearance: "The Creator has placed pleasure and the longing for it in nature, in order to attract man to a thing which is in itself dirty and troublesome in its consequences" (*De sexto praecepto et de usu matrimonii*, p. 9).

From the standpoint of such theology Van de Velde just wouldn't do. He not only tolerated the dirty business for the purpose of those troublesome children, he saw meaning and purpose in the dirt itself. No wonder the Church's Magisterium tried to smash him with its full weight. In *Casti connubii* (1930), which was aimed principally at married people who "out of aversion to the blessing of children wish to avoid the burden but enjoy the bliss," Van de Velde too is dealt crushing blows—which is utterly inappropriate, since he has the old-fashioned belief that motherhood constitutes "the highest thing any healthy-minded woman could wish for" (p. 222). This is because he focuses on pleasure as such and does not leave it in the shadowy status of a means to the end of procreation, which Christian marital ethics says is the only thing one should concentrate on. And so with his "idolatry of the flesh," with his "inglorious slavery to the desires," with his "godless thoughts," Van de Velde, as the Pope sees it, contributes to the "affront against human dignity" (*Casti connubii*).

Van de Velde turns the poison cabinet of the confessors into a pharmacy for couples. What had been described for thousands of years as entailing eternal death for the smallest dose taken, he now prescribes in concentrated form, in the opinion that perversity is not a question of sexual position but of intellectual attitude. Nowadays the storm over Van de Velde has quieted down. Since his book was published the Church has intensified its focus on the ban against contraception, in which it infallibly and unteachably drowns out the real questions and pains of the human race.

In his *Law of Christ* (1967) Bernhard Häring issues his own personal condemnation of Van de Velde's book, which he rejects as "instructions that go into repulsive detail." Instead of particulars he has a universal prescription to offer. In his chapter on "The Technique of Love" he recommends "listening together lovingly to the Word of God" and "praying together" (Häring, *Law of Christ*, III, 363).

Häring also provides information about how much pleasure there should be. On the subject of "intercourse from mere desire for sensual pleasure" he writes: "If in this case, however, the consummation of marriage keeps its form as service to life [he means, if there is no birth control], then the fault lies merely in the lack of comprehensive motivation and should therefore—as far as the individual act is concerned—'only' be a venial sin" (ibid., 371). Häring's quotation marks around "only" tell us the matter should not be taken lightly. And, in fact, he continues: "But if this is not the judgment of a single act as such, but an overall attitude toward marital relations that sees only pleasure and has only pleasure for its goal, then in this separation of mere instinct from genuine love and readiness to do service to life we see laid bare one of the most dangerous roots of unchastity, an utterly unchaste attitude." And Häring makes his point still clearer: "The sentiments of Tobias must undergird all that happens in marriage, even though they need not trigger every individual conjugal act: 'Thou knowest, o Lord, that I did not take my sister unto wife out of lust, but out of love of offspring' (Tob. 8:9)." Thus one must always keep one's eye on the child during intercourse, and while some pleasure may be intentional, it should be, according to Häring, "an occasion for activity that

stays within the correct order of motives. Then there is . . . no
sin" (ibid., 371–72).

Even Pope John Paul II accepted a certain amount of desire for
pleasure on the part of married couples when in *Familiaris consortio* (1981) he allowed periodic continence as a method of birth
control. He thereby abandoned the Augustinian motive of procreation as the most important factor in every marital act, and by
making this concession to pleasure the Pope is in open opposition
to Augustine's condemnation of rhythm as a "pimp's method."
Nevertheless John Paul II is still right on the old Augustinian
course. Granted, the motive of procreation as a requirement for
every conjugal act has been dropped, but the hatred of pleasure
has not. And since at bottom Augustine loathed pleasure more
than he liked procreation, Catholic tradition has been preserved.
Procreation may be avoided, so long as pleasure is too: through
continence. One has in any case the impression that the continual stress on children as the first purpose of marriage is really
aimed at the favorite activity of the Church's celibates: keeping
married couples away from sex.

Thus John Paul II, despite his disagreement with Augustine,
has brought out the actual, though hidden driving force behind
Augustine's sexual morality, namely, hatred of pleasure. He is
not primarily concerned with children. As needed, children will
be prevented by birth control, Catholic or otherwise. What he is
concerned with is curtailing pleasure. Here the Church is trying
to save what's savable. Fortunately the rhythm method is still
quite complicated and the period of continence it calls for fairly
long. With great satisfaction John Paul II quotes from Pope Paul
VI's encyclical *Humanae vitae* (1968): " 'Mastering the instinc-
tual life through reason and free will undoubtedly calls for a
certain asceticism, so that the manifestation of marital love by the
spouses may take place in the right order, especially as regards
observing periodic continence.' " How good that we don't have to
fear that science will soon be able to calculate a woman's capacity
to conceive down to the day or even to a certain number of
precisely predictable hours. Otherwise what would happen to the
right order for the manifestation of married love—and to asceti-

cism? And many other things would come to grief too. The Pope quotes a further passage from his predecessor's encyclical: " 'This discipline and order, which belongs to marital chastity, in no way detracts from married love, but rather lends it a higher human value. True, it does call for continual exertion, but thanks to its beneficial influence married people develop their personalities fully and completely, while they become richer in spiritual values. The fruits it bears for family life are peace and happiness, and it alleviates the solution of the other problems. It promotes attention to one's marriage partner, helps spouses overcome self-seeking, which is the enemy of true love, and deepens the sense of responsibility. Through it parents become capable of exercising a still more profound and effective influence on the upbringing of their children.' " in short, continence is a spiritual bonanza. It brings to father, mother, and children (and surely in an indirect way to grandfather and grandmother as well) everything one could ever wish. It is the key to solving all the problems of marriage, child-rearing, and life in general.

Given the wondrous effects of periodic continence, John Paul II has charged the theologians of the future with the task of answering a question. He has addressed "an urgent appeal to the theologians to stand by the Church's magisterium with concerted strength . . . to elaborate and probe more deeply into the difference, at once anthropological and moral, between contraception and recourse to the rhythm method." Since Augustine challenged such a moral-theological distinction, the task will not be an easy one. Strictly speaking, it is an insoluble problem, because where there is no moral difference, none can be discovered. The only difference in fact is not theological but papal: The rhythm method enables the Pope to force married couples under the yoke of continence for at least several days each month, while with other methods he fails to do so.

The theologians, presumably, will not go out on strike, they will discover that difference. After all, John Paul II has already pointed to the solution of the puzzle: "We have here a difference that is greater and deeper than is usually thought, and that in the final analysis is linked with two mutually exclusive notions of the person and of human sexuality." We would never have come up with this idea on our own, but now at least we know in what direction we have to look. The Pope continues: "The decision for the natural rhythms implies an acceptance of the time of the person, of woman, and with that an acceptance of dialogue, of mutual respect, of common responsibility, of self-control." If it weren't for self-control—the only thing the Pope is really interested in—we would have no choice but to agree that the Pope cares about the person, about woman. And any observer would approve of dialogue with one's wife and respect for her, except for the catch that the Pope stipulates, of all times, a woman's fertile period and therefore regular abstinence from sex as *the* opportunity for a morally loftier time in married life and a condition for all the good and lovely blessings he mentions.

This papal hymn to married continence is found under the heading of "Service to Life," within the apostolic letter *Familiaris consortio* (1981). "Service to life" seems to be in contradiction to the de facto birth control being discussed here, but the Pope has a different, higher service to life in mind, along the following lines: By practicing abstinence married people come close, for several days at least, to the state of virginity and become qualified, though once more only periodically, for a higher level of existence. Their "service to life" no longer consists in procreation but in abstinence. In this situation the Pope has modified and transformed the idea of contraception. He considers periodic continence as a kind of marital exercise. He simply refuses to acknowledge the fact that through such abstinence couples are trying to get around the woman's fertile times, that is, to avoid having a child. That is why the Pope doesn't call periodic continence "contraception"—a word that never occurs in this context—but "regulation of births," which straightens everything out. This way we are still talking about birth—sort of.

The theologians, never ones to be at a loss, will surely be helpful in the search for the great difference between contraception and birth regulation. Cardinal Ratzinger has already come to the Pope's aid. In connection with the Roman Synod of Bishops in 1980 he wrote a twenty-seven-page pastoral letter to the priests, deacons, and pastoral care-providers of the archdiocese of

Munich-Freising that gives detailed attention and praise to the results of the synod on the subject of "Marriage and the Family." In it he writes concerning *Humanae vitae*: "Precisely from this point of departure [women's experience], purely from the experiential standpoint, something becomes convincingly clear that our previous theological argumentation failed to show: that in the case of the alternative between natural methods and contraception we do not have a morally meaningless question of different means to the same end, but that there is an anthropological gulf between them, which for that very reason is a moral gulf. But how am I to indicate this in a few lines when our common consciousness simply bars the door to understanding?" In fact, a few lines will not be enough to cope with the ignorance of married people. Theologians will have to go on working for generations to convey enlightenment to the blind common consciousness, which is neither able nor willing to recognize the difference, and to become a light to married people, who are one and all groping about in darkness.

Fortunately the cardinal gives a hint as to how one can work one's way further into these difficult ideas: "With the pill a woman's own sort of time and thus her own sort of being has been taken from her. As the technological world would have it, she has been made continually 'utilizable.' This is a point that Christa Meves has recently emphasized in impressive fashion. She refers in this context to the meaning and beauty of continence, something that our sick civilization scarcely dares to talk about any more.—All this and much else has, as we all know, led to a weariness with the pill that we should look upon as a chance for reconsidering the whole subject."

Thus if in Cardinal Ratzinger's eyes the pill constitutes a burden placed on women, by way of evening things out we should cite a burden placed on men, as described by Christa Meves in an essay, "Does Christian (Catholic) Marriage Still Have a Future?" in the *Pastoral Bulletin for the Dioceses of Aachen-Berlin-Essen-Cologne-Osnabrück* (1976): "Owing to the increased life expectancy for women, who in the 19th century lived for an average of only 35 years, often dying after being weakened by childbirth, often dying in childbed itself, there was also an increase in the number of people who live together for thirty, fifty, even sixty years. This length of time means an additional trial, especially for the husband. For while earlier he could, after the death of his (often still young) wife, remarry a (usually younger) wife, today he is forced to put up with a wife who often ages more quickly than he does." As we see, everybody has his own set of troubles. Women are limited in their freedom and made "utilizable" by the pill, and men lose their freedom through the increasing age of their wives. Besides this, the pill may have done its share to burden men in that not so many women today are weakened by repeated childbirth, nor do they die in childbed and vacate a place in the marriage bed for a younger woman. But fortunately there is help in these burdensome situations, namely continence as recommended by the Pope. Christa Meves continues: "Don't the pope's directives to women also have a practical justification? Don't they protect women from becoming a new kind of fair game for male sexuality? Don't they give the man, through the command of chastity, of consideration for women, greater possibility of a necessary spiritual compensation for his animal instincts?"

The Pope, with his gospel of continence, is the only one protecting wives from the freebooting mentality of their animalistic husbands. A wife's taking the pill would unleash her husband's sex drive in such a way that she would be helplessly surrendered to his clutches. The only protection she can find is with the Pope, who forbids her the pill in her own interest, in order to save her from an existence as fair game. Animalistic husbands justify the Pope's taking this step to block their instincts. The Pope is doing nothing more than standing in front of the wife as her protector and helping her to refuse the pill, because with it she would be helpless in the fact of her lustful husband. The Pope is the mighty fortress of women and the Vatican a kind of women's shelter. And the Holy See promptly works a miracle. While a woman's taking the pill makes her husband behave like a lecher, not taking the pill makes him act chastely and continently. As Christa Meves sees it, the Pope has a Dr. Jekyll and Mr. Hyde notion of the pill: Depending on whether his wife takes or doesn't take the pill, the husband is now a beast, now an angel.

Apart from such miraculous transformations there is something else to consider: All the glorifiers of marital continence from John

Paul II to Christa Meves refuse to see that the unbridled sensualist is not the only one who degrades the other into a mere object for his instincts. There can be a more sublime form of degradation in making the other into the object for controlling his instincts. This says nothing for the pill (Christa Meves: "There is a new kind of pituitary tumor that only appears in women who have been on the pill a long time") or against rhythm, nothing for the condom or against coitus interruptus—or the other way around. The only claim made here is this: All these questions are not directed to theologians and popes, but to medicine and the married couples themselves, to their responsibility and consideration for their partner. In *Familiaris consortio* John Paul II protests against the "severe affront to human dignity" that occurs when governments "try to limit the freedom of spouses to decide about having children." He forgets to say that many Catholic spouses see in the Pope's style of limiting their freedom on this point an equally "severe affront to human dignity." In addition they perceive it as hypocrisy when the Church insists upon freedom *against* contraception, but outlaws freedom *for* it, because at bottom the Church doesn't really defend the freedom of a single couple. It merely strives to impose its own moral dictatorship without regard to the welfare of married people, a dictatorship based on pleasure-hating celibate contempt for marriage and a maniacal cult of virginity.

XXV

THE NINETEENTH AND TWENTIETH CENTURIES: THE AGE OF "BIRTH REGULATION"

The *Enlightenment and* the French Revolution did not at first offer any support for contraception. And when a young Anglican priest named Thomas Malthus presented his idea on overpopulation in 1798, pointing to the fact that population tended to grow faster than food production, he warned against "sullying the marriage bed" and "unhealthy arts designed to hide the consequences of forbidden relations, which clearly must be characterized as vice." He called instead for "moral continence." Nevertheless it was Malthus's work that provided the impetus for the idea of birth control that took hold of the consciousness of the nineteenth and twentieth centuries.

In Europe at the time coitus interruptus was the most widespread contraceptive method; and it remained such even when the vulcanization of rubber in 1843 brought the condom into broader popular use. In 1850 the French Jesuit Father Gury (d. 1866), the most widely read Catholic moral theologian of the nineteenth century, wrote: "In our days the horrible plague of onanism [coitus interruptus] has spread all over" (*Manual of Moral Theology* II, 705). Gury thought that "A woman sins gravely if she leads her husband astray, even indirectly and tacitly, into the misuse of marriage (contraception) by lamenting about the number of children they have, the toils of bearing or raising them, or by declaring that she will die the next time she gives birth" (ibid., II, 824).

Thus the wife may not make her husband practice coitus interruptus because of her fear of dying, but does she have to resist him when he practices it on his own? In November 1816 Rome informed the vicar of Chambéry that a woman was allowed to go along with intercourse, if a serious detriment was to be expected from her refusal. Indeed, the woman might herself request intercourse if she would otherwise fall into incontinence. (Once again we have the Church's concern only for the potential adulterers, and its neglect of those who do not desire marital sex as a substitute for adultery.) This decision by Rome practically repeated the position of Alphonsus Liguori.

On April 23, 1822, in answer to another inquiry, Rome said that a woman could "passively surrender," if she anticipated blows, death, or other severe cruelties if she didn't. Similar responses were given on February 1, 1823, and April 3, 1916. The tone, it will be noted, had grown harsher. There had been no mention of the threat of death in either Alphonsus or the response to the chaplain of Chambéry in 1816; and now nothing was said about a woman under certain circumstances being allowed to request intercourse herself.

In 1853 for the first time Rome delivered a response about the use of condoms. The question was: "May a woman passively surrender to this sort of intercourse?" The answer: No. Thus if there was danger of death she might submit to coitus interruptus, but evidently not to sex with a condom. On June 3, 1916, Rome declared that in the latter case the wife must resist her husband, "as she would a rapist."

The Church's battle against contraception was still not fully underway by the middle of the nineteenth century. This can be seen in the following response from Rome: In 1842 a French bishop named Jean-Baptiste Bouvier had asked Rome how to handle the confessions of those ("almost all the younger couples in the diocese") who practiced coitus interruptus because they didn't want too many children. The answer from Rome was that, in keeping with the advice of St. Alphonsus Liguori ("a learned man and very skilled in this area"), the confessor should keep quiet about these things, unless he was explicitly asked (John T. Noonan, *Contraception*, pp. 400ff.). Father Gury also argued, invoking Alphonsus, that no questions should be posed in the confessional about coitus interruptus.

However, in the last quarter of the nineteenth century, the Catholic Church's embittered struggle against contraception began in earnest. The occasion for it was, on the one hand, the worldwide, increasing public interest in birth control and the spread of contraceptives among the masses, as well as, on the other, the Franco-Prussian War, both viewed in the light of a newly reawakened Thomism, which accepts the sexual act only as an act of marital procreation. On Bastille Day in Beauvais in 1872 the Swiss Cardinal Gaspard Mermillod addressed the French people: "You have turned away from God, and God has struck you. In an abominable calculation you have shoveled graves instead of filling cradles with children. That is why you lacked soldiers" (ibid., p. 414). In 1886 for the first time Rome issued a directive that it was the duty of confessors, in the case of "well-founded suspicion," to ask their penitents about the practice of contraception.

Then in this century the last obstacle to the confessor's duty of asking questions, namely, the requirement of "well-founded suspicion," fell away. In 1901 an unnamed French pastor turned to Rome with a problem. While hearing the confession of Titius (pseudonym), whom he describes as "rich, honorable, and cultured," and a "good Christian," he had asked him about contraception. Titius answered that he practiced coitus interruptus so as not to lower his standard of living—he had a boy and a girl—nor exhaust his wife through repeated pregnancies. The pastor disapproved of this conduct and refused him absolution, but Titius replied that another confessor, a professor of moral theology at a seminary, had approved what he was doing, insofar as he was seeking to quiet his desires and not to have an ejaculation. Titius then left the confessional and spread the word that the pastor was ignorant and arrogant. The answer from Rome, dated November 13, 1901, backed up the pastor, saying it was impossible to give absolution to a penitent who would not disavow his unequivocal onanism (coitus interruptus).

Around the turn of the century Belgian theologians led the way in attacking the system of "tolerant silence." They maintained that even the mothers of newly married girls had to be asked whether they had advised their daughters to "be on their guard." In particular, the leading moral theologian of his day, the Belgian Arthur Vermeersch (d. 1936), sounded the battle cry. If her husband proposes to use a condom during intercourse, the wife is obliged to resist until she is physically overpowered or until she sacrifices "a fair equivalent to life." The wife is obliged to defend herself against her husband as if he were a rapist. She must be prepared to put up with the consequences, namely "no joy or happiness in the family, breakdown of the marriage, wilful desertion, divorce." As Vermeersch said, "Why should one find it terrible that marital chastity, like all Christian virtues, demands its martyrs?" (ibid., p. 432). Vermeersch's directive to wives was included in the previously mentioned Vatican decision of June 3, 1916.

In 1909 at Vermeersch's suggestion, the primate of Belgium, Cardinal Mercier, published a pastoral letter on "the duties of married life." This was followed in the same year by a directive "against onanism" from the Belgian bishops for priests and confessors. It claimed that the "very wicked sin of Onan" was practiced in Belgium by rich and poor, in the city and countryside. "In this public danger," they, the bishops, would be neglecting their duty, if in the face of this vice against nature they did not raise their voices to oppose a sin that cried out to heaven. People should be admonished to have greater trust in Providence, which would see to it that no one died of hunger. The struggle against this evil should be carried on with special severity in the confessional. Silence by the confessor could be construed as approval (ibid., p. 420).

In 1913 the Bishops Conference of Fulda followed the example of the Belgian prelates. They maintained that contraception was a "consequence of a life of pleasure . . . But it is a serious sin to wish to prevent an increase in the number of children by misusing marriage for mere pleasure and thereby frustrating its main purpose through knowledge and desire. That is a grave, very grave sin, however and with whatever means it may be committed." It was the duty of married couples, the bishops said, "to assure the continued existence of Church and State" (ibid., p. 421).

Needless to say the battle over contraception was not interrupted for the First World War. In 1915 Professor A. J. Rosenberg from the diocesan philosophical-theological faculty in Paderborn wrote a piece for the magazine *Theologie und Glaube* that argued: "Modern wars are wars in which the masses play an extremely important role. Thus the deliberate limits placed on the number of children [in France] meant renouncing the same national strength as that attained by Germany . . . Thousands of parents bemoan the loss of their only son . . . There must be punishment . . . The war has shed new light on the problem of deliberate avoidance of children." The macabre idea of threatening parents with the premature death of their children as a punishment for contraception already had the stamp of approval from the Belgian bishops' directive to confessors in 1909. And during the Second World War the notion was echoed in the *Quaestiones de castitate et luxuria* (Questions about Chastity and Debauchery, Bruges, 1944) by the Belgian Dominican and moral theologian Merkelbach (d. 1942).

Not quite so bad, but bad enough were the remarks of Father H. A. Krose in the prestigious Jesuit journal *Stimmen der Zeit* (1915): "In the lively discussion stirred up by the threatening drop in the German birth rate, repeated reference has been made to the danger this poses to the Empire's position as a world power . . . The difficult time that we are forced to live through shows with terrifying clarity just how justified that reference was. How could the German Empire be resisting the onslaught of powerful foes from all sides, if the high birth rates of the first decades after the founding of the Empire had not increased the numbers in precisely those groups of young men who are now old enough for military service? Our enemies cannot get over their astonishment at the nearly inexhaustible human reservoir that allows the German Reich . . . not only to fill the gaps made by the war, but continually to raise the level of manpower."

After the war the battle against contraception went on with undiminished zeal, in the same nationalistic, militaristic spirit as before. In 1919 the bishops of France declared: "It is to sin seriously against nature and against the will of God to frustrate marriage of its end by an egotistic or sensual calculation. The theories and practices which teach or encourage the restriction of birth are as disastrous as they are criminal. The war has forcefully impressed upon us the danger to which they expose our country. Let the lesson not be lost. It is necessary to fill the spaces made by death, if we want France to belong to Frenchmen and to be strong enough to defend herself and prosper" (ibid., p. 422).

The end of the First World War also provided the bishops of Austria with the occasion for a pastoral letter arguing that the profanation of marriage was "the worst moral scourge of our time." The American bishops took a similar line (Noonan, p. 422).

The vigorous emphasis on the ban against contraception was

escalated step by step with the wars in 1870–71 and 1914–18. And to this day the Church gives fictitious potential children more protection than it gives the real, half-grown children from the death and hell of the battlefields, in keeping with the intolerable, perverse Catholic doctrine that the actual crimes of humanity are committed in the bedrooms of married couples and not in the theaters of war and the mass graves. Catholic moral theologians have talked a great deal about just wars, but never about just contraception. This is logical and consistent, because the battlefields are not the least reason why the Church thinks it has to guarantee conception. And contraception is unjust not least of all because it makes just wars more difficult, because low birthrates in draft call-up years are a military handicap. One might also say that rearmament and the struggle against contraception are interconnected: Children are necessary to waging the war. War and contraception don't mix. A person whose conception is prevented is one less weapon available. The preparations for war must therefore be shifted to the bedroom. Contraception is unilateral disarmament. Thus it is no accident that the rejection of contraception swelled to a crescendo in this century of world wars and the arms race.

The ban on contraception admittedly goes back to a long pleasure-hating tradition, but there is a difference between keeping silence or giving answers only to explicit questions from married people, as in Alphonsus Liguori's advice passed on by Rome to Bishop Bouvier in 1842, and drowning out the whole world with dogmatic pronouncements, in season and out of season, as John Paul II does. Even granting that the Pope doesn't realize how the accent he is imposing on Christian morality carries echoes of the politics of nationalistic rivalry and military superiority, this difference remains.

At the culmination of the worldwide debate on birth control, on August 15, 1930, at the Lambeth Conference the Anglican Church abandoned its previous condemnation of contraception. Then on December 31, 1930, Pius XI issued his encyclical *Casti connubii,* the forerunner of Paul VI's *Humanae vitae* and John Paul II's *Familiaris consortio.* One of the co-authors of *Casti con-*

nubii was Arthur Vermeersch. Ever since it was published, the popes have seen it as one of their main duties to speak out continually against birth control. *Casti connubii* repeats the words of the militant French bishops after World War I who spoke of the "criminal freedom" of couples practicing contraception, motivated by the desire, to quote their old refrain, of "avoiding the burden, but enjoying the bliss." The encyclical declares that there is no reason, "no matter how momentous," that could justify contraception. And so, after raising the specter of Onan one more time, the Pope turns to confessors, whom, he orders, "by virtue of our supreme authority," not to leave the faithful in error about "this gravely binding divine law," or to strengthen them in that error "through wilful silence."

The quiet times of 1842 when answers were given only to those who asked questions were definitively over. It was now clear that under no circumstances was anyone allowed to prevent the conception of a human being. It was also clear that under certain conditions—namely war—one was allowed to kill human beings. Those in doubt as to who may legitimately be killed should seek guidance from a declaration made a generation later (1957) in Bangalore by the bishops of India. They solemnly warned the people about three things: communism, immoral films, and contraception.

Admittedly, *Casti connubii* does not present, or even suggest, the connection between contraception and preparations for war. The Pope cannot speak as a nationalist—sexual pessimism is wholly sufficient for his case. But that makes the question all the more urgent: Why doesn't the Catholic Church give living persons the same protection that it lavishes on potential, fictitious persons? Why doesn't it forbid war just as emphatically as it forbids birth control? Why does Catholic morality occasionally embellish war, but never contraception, with the adjective "just"? Doesn't the Church seem to have gotten its values mixed up? If one makes a decision for children, one must also decide against war. Otherwise one is deciding for cannon fodder. Whoever presses concern for potential children so far that he never allows contraception, "no matter how momentous" the reason, ought to press his concern for living children still further and call for a ban on all wars, so that the bishops' and cardinals' motto, Because of war we must have children, can finally turn into the truly Christian motto, Because of children we must never have wars again.

Casti connubii makes only passing reference to the rhythm method. Intercourse in this way is allowed, "provided that the inner structure of the act and therefore its subordination to the first goal of marriage [children] is not infringed upon." In 1930 the rhythm method got nothing like the amount of attention or praise heaped by John Paul II on the Knaus-Ogino system of continence in *Familiaris consortio* (1981). Two researchers, Ogino from Japan in 1924 and Knaus from Austria in 1929, had discovered the method that would not become world famous until the early 1930s. Pope Pius XI's remarks referred to the Pouchet method, named after the Frenchman Archimedès Pouchet, who thought that conception could take place only during menstruation and a period of from one to twelve days after menstruation. It was still believed in 1920 that a woman was infertile in the third week after menstruation, and as late as 1929 Dominikus Lindner wrote in his book *Der usus matrimonii:* "Conception is easier at this time (menstruation) than at any other" (p. 219). The moral theologian Heribert Jone said much the same thing in 1930 (*Katholische Moraltheologie,* p. 617). Thanks to his method, Pouchet had won the prize of the French Academy of Science for experimental physiology in 1845. With the academy's help people who didn't want children had them, and people who wanted them didn't. Thus there was no reason for Pius XI to contest the "right" of married couples to use this method of birth control, about which the *Nouvelle Revue Théologique* wrote back in 1900: "Who has not heard penitents who consistently observed the times prescribed and still could not prevent conception?"

So when at the beginning of the thirties the Knaus-Ogino method became known, and married people cited Pope Pius XI's approval of the rhythm method, some theologians objected that he had approved an unreliable method, but not approved a reliable one. Arthur Vermeersch led the choruses of lamentation over "the heresy of the empty cradles"; and the Belgian Jesuit Ignatius Salsmans claimed that the Pope only meant intercourse after menopause when he approved the use of the infertile period. Oginoism, he said, was not much better than onanism (coitus interruptus). He was right on this—and Augustine would have agreed—but Salsmans drew the wrong conclusions from the situation, by forbidding couples to employ either method. Bishops, too, for example, the provincial councilor of Mecheln, Cardinal van Roey, warned about rhythm. In 1937 it was declared that use of the infertile periods conjured up dangers, such as the spread of selfishness and the cooling off of married love (Noonan, p. 444).

Compared with this viewpoint, John Paul II sounds completely different. In *Familiaris consortio* he writes that, "The decision for natural rhythms . . . [means] living married love in its demand for fidelity, and that marital union is enriched by those values of tenderness and affectivity that make up the soul of human sexuality."

Given such contradictory statements on one and the same method, which was held to impoverish conjugal love in 1937 and to enrich it in 1981, one can conclude only that the bishops and popes have proved each other's incompetence, and that the documented ignorance on either side ought to reduce both to silence, if they care about their credibility with married people.

Other fruits of theological imbecility include: the only children of parents who practice contraception are selfish and sickly, the only children of parents who practice continence are not that way at all (Bishop Rosset in 1895, Noonan, p. 520); coitus interruptus causes nervous disturbances and pelvic disorders in women (ibid., p. 521); Bernhard Häring speaks of "disastrous effects . . . on the nerves and the mental health of spouses, especially wives" (*Das Gesetz Christi*, 357). Wherever the supply of theological arguments fails, there are, fortunately, medical errors ready to take their place.

The Church was strained to the limit with the task of sorting out, labeling, defaming, and even, in some cases, tolerating coitus interruptus, the use of condoms, and marriages run by the calendar, when around midcentury a new misfortune struck the hierarchy in the form of the pill. For Pius XII it was a bitter pill indeed. On September 2, 1958, he declared: "It is inducing a direct and illicit sterilization when one eliminates ovulation, so as to protect the organism from the consequences of a pregnancy that it cannot endure."

This principle is a unique intellectual stunt, but not so much because Pius XII condemned the pill. Since his predecessor Pius XI had condemned any kind of sterilization for the purpose of preventing conception, the pill had to be banned as well. No surprise there; we cannot expect a pope to deviate from the opinions of his predecessor. Papal infallibility serves as a brake on independent thinking. But Pius XI was unable to provide Pius XII with a special justification for rejecting the pill, because there was no pill in 1930. Here Pius XII had to be creative. But his justification meant turning all logic upside down, since here he sets an intention of nature over against the possibility of nature, thereby calling for something like a rape of a powerless nature in the name of nature, which in this case comes down to a rape of woman. Thus the Pope means that nature's intention, procreation, may under no circumstances be thwarted, even when nature cannot bear this procreation, and the woman will die on account of the pregnancy. The Pope, then, is defending a morality that marches over corpses. When the biological laws of nature are made the supreme moral norm and guideline, displacing the spouses' consideration for one another, then one should not argue that nature wants something, even when it cannot perform it, and that its will must be observed by sacrificing human life. Rather, in the case of such an overstrain on nature one should look on contraception as natural. In truth, behind the Pope's guiding star of a nature that is at once driven by God and physically driven past its limits, of a fundamentally unnatural nature, there lies nothing but the old hatred of pleasure.

Even in Rome they don't listen unconditionally to such "nature," as can be seen by the fact that the princes of the Church do not run around in their birthday suits, and their attire, in any case, is still more unnatural than that of the rest of the population. The intelligence that seeks help in clothes when the organism cannot endure the cold and that prevents pregnancies, "whose consequences the organism cannot endure," is probably part of nature as correctly understood. In another area where its hatred of pleasure is not so directly involved, the Church has already shown some more penetrating insight. In 1853 English theologians brought charges against Queen Victoria's personal physician, reproaching him for anesthetizing the Queen during childbirth. The theologians saw in this a violation of Gen 3:16: "In pain you shall bring forth children."

Apart from the sacrosanct laws of nature that forbid the pill, Paul VI brings yet another argument to bear against this form of contraception in *Humanae vitae* (1968). He writes: "Reasonable men can convince themselves still more of the truth of the Church's teaching, if they direct their attention to the consequences of the method of artificial birth control. One should keep in mind above all how such a way of acting could open up a broad and easy path to conjugal infidelity" (no. 17). Adultery is an idea that popes and moral theologians love to bring up, but one has the impression that the continual talk about it has more to do with theologians' desire to threaten and intimidate than the real conditions of married life.

A third reason against contraception cited by Paul VI is this: "Men who have become accustomed to using contraceptives could lose their respect for woman" (no. 17). A Church that understands human rights chiefly as men's rights and human dignity chiefly as male dignity, especially that of the celibate-clerical "dignitaries," should show some restraint when the topic is woman's dignity, and not impute their lack of respect for women to husbands. In any case the churchmen didn't have to wait for the pill to respect women less than themselves. Even as the Pope takes action to increase the dignity of women, the pill is only a new occasion to make all of marriage more ascetical and sexless, to turn lay people into monks and celibates. Anyhow, the Church's celibates have no notion of why a husband loves his wife not just physically, but spiritually. Fortunately, the love and respect married people have for one another are not affected by whether or not contraception is practiced in a way the Pope approves or "artificially."

In *Familiaris consortio* John Paul II asserts that all salvation, both the soul's eternal salvation and marital happiness on this earth, is essentially based on the right method of practicing contraception. In Augustine's eyes this would be an unthinkable heresy. Married people hearing it today only shrug their shoulders: They have already stopped believing the Church's celibates. It is not the prestige of women that the pill has jeopardized, as the Church teaches us, but rather its own authority, which is in the process of being lost if it continues to presume to control completely the autonomous territory of married people. It is finally time for the Church to stop usurping the conjugal act as a kind of celibate act, for married people to lay claim to sex for themselves alone, and to extricate married love from the voyeuristic sphere of a clerical bedroom police force. Why should they be willing any longer to have to give an account to incompetent overseers about things that are none of their business?

The Church does not, in fact, fear any diminution in the respect paid to women, as it pretends when campaigning against the pill.

In the battle over the pill the Church is afraid of losing its own prestige and its own power, besides the loss of money. In October 1977 the conservative *Offertenzeitung für die katholische Geistlichkeit Deutschlands,* a periodical for the German Catholic clergy, wrote: "In fact, it is quite certain that in the next ten to twenty years the 'pill' will crush the growth of the Church, with all the consequences this will have for the next generation of priests and religious, as well as for the yield on church taxes. No more new church buildings will be needed . . . What will happen is precisely . . . why people were warned against the propaganda for the 'pill,' namely: an alarming drop in the birth rate, a demoralization of society, a sexualization of public life, open propaganda for pornography and nudism . . . Public contempt for chastity, resulting in a *decline in the social prestige of priests and religious . . .* all in all a pollution of the spiritual environment on a scale hitherto unknown."

Thus, particularly on the grounds of the clergy's diminished social prestige—not to mention pornography and nudism—as well as of Church income and new building programs, Catholics are obliged not to take the pill.

The biggest bomb that Paul VI dropped on birth control in *Humanae vitae* was the claim that contraception "is to be condemned just as much [*pariter damnandum est*]" as abortion (nr. 14). This meant a huge dramatization of contraception. Some women concluded that it was better to be on the road to damnation at rare intervals because of abortion than constantly on it because of birth control. Thus a certain number of abortions must be credited to the popes, especially since by equating contraception with abortion they helped to trivialize abortion. If, as Paul VI says, contraception counts as much as abortion, we can infer that abortion counts as little as contraception.

With the International Congress of moral theologians held in Rome in November 1988, the papal campaign against contraception reached new heights. If the Pope weren't the Pope, his position might put him at odds with the state penal code. According to John Paul II and his spokesman, Carlo Caffarra, head of the Pontifical Institute for Marriage and Family Matters, a hemophiliac with AIDS may not have intercourse with his wife, *ever*, not even after her menopause, because God has forbidden condoms. And if the hemophiliac husband can't manage to abstain, it's better for him to infect his wife than to use a condom. Catholic sexual morality has turned into a morality of horror.

XXVI

ABORTION

Until recently women having babies in Catholic hospitals in Germany could find themselves in mortal danger because, under certain circumstances, they would be refused care. Wherever official Catholic teaching is observed, they still find themselves in such danger, because it is more important, doctrinally speaking, that the child be baptized quickly before his imminent death than that the mother be allowed to live after the death of an unbaptized child. This is a macabre chapter in our story, and a chapter that is by no means closed. It is true that for Germany, ever since May 7, 1976, the danger for the mother has been somewhat mitigated, insofar as on that date the German bishops declared their intention of "respecting the conscientious decision of physicians" (which doesn't mean that they actually endorse such a decision) "in situations of hopeless conflict where a choice must be made between the loss of the life of both the mother and the child and the loss of only one life." In plain English: In case both mother and child are dying, the doctor's choice will be respected if he saves the mother's life while sacrificing the life of the child. In other words, the doctor may save the mother by performing an abortion not when facing the quandary of mother *or* child dying, but only in the quandary of mother *and* child dying. But this is only a concession allowing doctors to deviate from actual Catholic teaching.

The Jesuit journal *Orientierung* for May 31, 1978, writes: "Respecting is still not the same as approving, and no one should take this serious statement, which reflects regard for a personal conscientious decision in a situation of hopeless conflict, as implying disregard for the courage, the readiness to sacrifice, the heroism of those women who prefer to die rather than betray their conscience." In other words, the only good mother is a dead mother, for the only mother who does not "betray her conscience" is the one who is ready to go under with the fetus.

In 1985 Bernhard Häring wrote: "I will not deal further with the interruption of pregnancy that has as its only final purpose (objectively) and its only intended goal (subjectively) the saving of the mother's life, when there is no further possibility of saving the life of the fetus. We must beware in such cases (extremely rare, by the way) of breeding guilt complexes that, as everyone knows, often lead to extremely disturbed interpersonal relations and to a distressed image of God" (*Theologie der Gegenwart*, 1985, 4, 219). Thus women are allowed to go on living without guilt complexes and disturbed interpersonal relationships, if the fetus, who couldn't be saved anyway, was aborted to save their lives.

But the mother has nothing at all to decide here. The mother isn't even asked about it by the German bishops. Their letter is directed to the physicians, whose conscientious decision it respects. The mothers are simply shifted from one alien jurisdiction to another. The decision about their life or death is transferred from the almighty gentlemen in black to the almighty gentlemen in white.

Nowadays many people think that in cases of mortal danger to the mother the Church allows abortion, but this is false. Rather the Church has merely agreed to respect medical decisions when otherwise both mother and child will die. This was confirmed by a letter I received from Cardinal Höffner on August 5, 1986: "With regard to your inquiry I would have you know that the statement you cite from the 'Recommendations for Physicians and Medical Personnel in Hospitals After the Change in Article §218 of the Penal Code' of May 7, 1976, is still in effect, and I firmly adhere to it. If on the program you mention another impression was given, owing to the conditions of a television interview, I can only regret this." (In a program aired over Second German Television on June 29, 1986, it was implied that in cases where the mother's life was in danger the Church affirmed abortion on medical grounds.) The cardinal then repeats the crucial lines of the letter from the German bishops, that what is at stake is the alternative "between the loss of two lives, if one lets nature take its course, or the loss of only one life." At the conclusion of the letter he stresses: "However, I should like to call attention here to the fact that the statement you recall in the corresponding section speaks about respecting the 'conscientious decision of the doctors,' in other words it refrains from any moral judgment in this boundary situation." Plainly put, in 1976 the German bishops did not approve, they only respected, the decision of the doctors that one dead body was better than two.

The official teaching of the Church, which has yet to be revoked and is still valid today, sees the situation differently. And many other countries have not yet gone so far as to evade Rome's decisions. It should be kept in mind, by the way, that the German bishops are by no means so favorable to mothers as they have been interpreted. Their declaration can just as well be turned against the mother. The bishops leave completely open the question of which of the two otherwise irrecoverably lost lives the doctor may save. The doctor may be sure of the same episcopal respect if in hopelessly conflicting situations he should decide for the life of the child and kill the mother. Fortunately, thanks to the progress of medicine and the conscience of physicians, mothers have been saved from the consequences of the sort of grisly morality advanced by the bishops.

Many theologians observe that nowadays such extreme cases, of the sort Rome passed judgment on, could no longer happen because of all the progress made in medicine. But this does not mean that theological science has made the same strides forward. Medical progress has simply made theology less dangerous for women's health, although that will not bring back to life the many women who over many centuries have fallen victim to the theologians. According to a decree from Rome dated August 1, 1886, "the most resolute will of the holiest Lord (Jesus)" sees things differently from conscientious doctors who decide to save lives. This was in confirmation of a previous decree, dated May 28, 1884: At that time Cardinal Caverot of Lyon had sent an inquiry to Rome about the surgical operation known as a craniotomy (the dismembering of the fetus's skull), when without it both mother and child will die, but with it the mother may be saved. Rome said it could not be done. On August 14, 1889, the negative response was extended to "all surgical operations that directly kill the fetus or the pregnant mother." On July 24, 1895, a doctor in Rome asked whether after the above decisions he had the right, in order to save the mother from immediate and certain death, to remove a fetus that was not yet viable. In so doing he would make use of methods and operations that would not lead to the killing of the fetus, but afterward, of course, the fetus would die since it was so premature. The response was negative. And this decision was repeated in 1898. In 1930 *Casti connubii* writes in connection with rejecting medical indications: "What could ever be a sufficient reason to justify the direct killing of an innocent being? . . . On the contrary he who aims at encompassing the death of the one or the other, under the pretence of taking therapeutic measures, or out of a falsely understood compassion, would prove himself unworthy of the noble name and reputation of a physician."

Pius XII stressed the same point in his address to the midwives on October 29, 1951 (AAS 43 [1951], 784–94). Remember that the alternative here is not mother or child, but the death of both or the mother's survival by aborting the fetus. The intrinsically correct principle, "Thou shalt not kill," which the Church thrust aside or riddled with exceptions in dealing with war and capital punishment, is here carried to absurd lengths with the death of both mother and child. It is a classical case of following the letter and not the spirit of a commandment. All the way into the second half of this century the moral theologians have been indefatigable in applauding this Roman death sentence for many women. For example, Mausbach and Tischleder's *Katholische Moraltheologie* says: "The argument that in sparing the child *two lives* are generally lost, whereas by sacrificing the child only *one* is, impresses most people . . . The violent destruction of an innocent life is simply never permitted; it cannot be allowed at all, without leading people astray into further disastrous and life-destroying steps" (1938, III, 125).

In *Das Gesetz Christi* (1967), Bernhard Häring refers to the papal decisions on this issue from 1884 to 1951 and observes "Medical people sometimes criticize the Church for rejecting the vital indications [defined by Häring as a procedure to be undertaken 'when otherwise the mother's life would be in great and immediate danger']. In reality, this was a salutary admonition to the medical community to develop its practice better, so that today even in the most difficult cases *almost* always both the mother's and the child's life may be taken care of" (ibid., 221). Many mothers owe their death to the salutary papal pronouncements from 1884 to 1951; the doctors, on the other hand, owe to these pronouncements the progress they have made, which they would not have striven for without the Vatican's brutal, inexorable stance. Had it not been for that, medicine might still find itself where it was in the Middle Ages. But now, thanks to the popes, things have "almost" reached the point where the doctors no longer need the death of mothers as a stimulus to "develop their practice." But whether or not the doctors now learn to appreciate the popes' admonitions, Häring concludes with one last clear summary: "Whatever the judgment of medical science may be, the Church sticks inexorably to the basic principle that under no circumstances can it be permitted directly to assault the life of an innocent child in the mother's womb. Cf. the address of Pope Pius XII given on October 29, 1951" (ibid.).

In that same year of 1951 Henry Morton Robinson published his best-selling novel *The Cardinal*. The book recounts how an American priest of Irish extraction rises to become a cardinal. At one point in the story the cardinal's brother-in-law, a surgeon, refuses to do a craniotomy during the birth of a child with "too large a head." It is too late for a Caesarian section, the mother dies and so does the child. The surgeon gets into difficulties because the widower takes him to court. But the cardinal supports his brother-in-law's effort to uphold the Catholic faith. The surgeon—a true martyr—loses his post at the hospital, because after the casualty the hospital demands that all doctors sign an agreement to observe the medical indications, and the surgeon refuses to sign. Catholic hospitals naturally see things the cardinal's way.

Another passage of the book describes how a mother loses her life because she gets caught in the mother-or-child alternative. Faced with his brother-in-law's decision against the craniotomy, the cardinal had prayed to God: "If this trial comes to me, Lord, grant that I may not murmur against the great severity of your love." His prayer is later answered when Mona, his favorite sister, becomes pregnant and goes into labor. Another surgeon, Dr. Parks, tells the cardinal: "If you don't give me permission to kill the embryo, there is nothing that can save your sister." During this male dialogue abut the life and death of a woman, the cardinal "clutches his chair: 'Jesus, Mary, Joseph, stand by me,' " and with the assistance of Jesus, Mary, and Joseph decides on the death of his sister. She herself is not asked at all. In this case the child is saved (Ullstein—TB, 1986, pp. 93ff. and 312ff.). Even today in such a case the cardinal would have to decide against his sister.

From 1884 onward the Catholic ban on abortion was at its absolute zenith, although in their statement of May 7, 1976, the German bishops distanced themselves from it. But let's not rejoice too soon over so much accommodation, for the debate over abortion often takes peculiar backward and forward flips. Before the harsh decisions by the Church in 1884, 1886, 1889, 1895, 1930, and 1951, which are still officially valid today, there had been progress that was later abandoned: In 1872, for example, when questioned about the permissibleness of craniotomy in cases where both the mother and child would otherwise die, Rome had evasively replied that the issue might be examined in both the older and more recent authors (*Acta sanctae sedis* 7, 1872, 516ff.).

One such "more recent" author was Magnus Jocham, a moral theologian from Freising, who wrote in 1854: "Usually saving the mother through the death of the child is probable, while saving the child through the death of the mother is doubtful. In this case one would have to advise the mother to save her own life by sacrificing the life of her child. But where there is an equal measure of hope and danger on both sides, the mother has to decide. Those who give advice always have to opt for saving the life of the mother wherever this is possible" (*Moraltheologie,* vol. III, 478). And as late as 1878, an ethician from Tübingen named Linsenmann declared: "In the cases of this sort or in which there can be a doubt, namely where without forceful surgical intervention the birth of a living child cannot take place, nature herself destines two human lives to un-avoidable death, unless medical intervention is possible. When-ever, then, the physician can through his art save one of the two lives by sacrificing the other, he cannot be assessed any respon-sibility for the death of this other. Not employing his technical operation would bring about the death of the other life as well" (*Lehrbuch der Moraltheologie,* p. 492). But such notions were quashed in 1884 by the determination that even the death of both mother and child could not justify abortion to save the mother.

This tightening of the rules on abortion took place in connec-tion with a transformation of the thinking about the exact time when the embryo acquired a soul. From the end of the nineteenth century onward belief that animation occurred at the very mo-ment of conception (simultaneous animation) won the day, and this brought with it an even stronger rejection of abortion in the earliest stages of pregnancy, not to mention the later stages. Up till the end of the nineteenth century the doctrine of successive animation had prevailed in theology. This, we recall, maintained

3 0 4

that the male embryo received a soul on or about the fortieth day, the female embryo on or about the eightieth. Hence canon law distinguished between the *fetus animatus* and the *fetus inanimatus* (anima = soul). Only the abortion of an animate fetus was punished with excommunication. And since there was no way of determining the sex of the fetus, the penalty was not incurred until the eightieth day. Only the fanatical Sixtus V had threatened abortion from the moment of conception, indeed had threatened contraception, with excommunication or even the death penalty. But in 1591 a year after his death this decision was revoked by Gregory XIV.

Since the end of the nineteenth century canon law has gotten closer to the idea of Sixtus V: Excommunication now applies to abortion from the first moment of pregnancy. The distinction between the *fetus inanimatus* and the *fetus animatus* was dropped by Pius IX in 1869. The code of canon law, as revised in 1917 and 1983, speaks only of "the fetus."

The question of when the embryo became "ensouled" was always a controversial one. In the fourth century the Church Fathers Basil the Great and Gregory of Nyssa declared—drawing upon Stoic sources—that the animation of the human embryo occurred at the moment of conception, because the soul was infused into the uterus along with the semen. Albert the Great (d. 1280) also was an opponent of successive animation, while his disciple Thomas Aquinas argued for it. Beginning in the seventeenth century there was a stronger trend toward simultaneous animation, after a physician from Louvain, Thomas Fienus, claimed that the human soul was infused not on the fortieth day, but on the third. In 1658 the Franciscan Hieronymus Florentinius demanded that every embryo, no matter how little time had passed since conception, had to be baptized when there was danger of death since it had a soul. In 1661 Innocent X's personal physician, Paul Zacchias, defended the view that the soul was infused at the moment of conception. By the beginning of the eighteenth century this was the prevailing opinion among doctors. In 1736 a theologian named Roncaglia spoke out for simultaneous animation. On the other hand, Alphonsus Liguori echoed St. Thomas, while noting that such views were "very uncertain" (*Moral Theology* III, n. 394).

Now after all this, the most important Catholic theologian in the twentieth century, Karl Rahner, was inclined once again to the successive animation theory, without specifying the instant that it occurred: "It cannot be inferred from the Church's dogmatic definitions that it would be contrary to faith to assume that the leap to spirit-person happens only during the course of the embryo's development. No theologian would claim the ability to prove that interrupting pregnancy is in every case the murder of a human being" (*Dokumente der Paulusgesellschaft,* 1962, vol. 2, 391–92). In his article "Zum Problem der genetischen Manipulation" (*Schriften zur Theologie,* 1967, vol. 8, 286ff.) Rahner points to the consequences of this for experiments with human embryonic material: "But it would be intrinsically thinkable that, if we presuppose a serious positive doubt that the experimental material was really a person, there would be reasons *for* an experiment that from a rational perspective are stronger than the uncertain right of a person whose existence is subject to doubt" (ibid., p. 301).

The question of simultaneous or successive animation, in other words of when a person is a person, has had consequences for the assessment of abortion. Thomas Sanchez (d. 1610), for centuries the standard authority on marital issues, held that when the mother is in mortal danger the abortion of an inanimate fetus is permissible (*On the Holy Sacrament of Marriage,* lib. 9, disp. 20, n. 9). But it is not true, as has been claimed, that Sanchez recognized situations where abortion was ethically and socially indicated. If a girl had been raped and upon discovering her pregnancy had to fear for her life, Sanchez would merely allow her to hasten to find a husband. Insofar as she herself was still unsure that she had conceived, she might conceal her condition from her husband, so that he would erroneously think the child who turned out to have been conceived in the rape was his own. The damage done to the husband should be rated of less importance than the mortal danger to the girl (ibid., n. 11).

But if the mother incurs mortal danger after the eightieth day, for example during birth, the fetus may under no circumstances be directly killed to save her, not even if that is her only chance of survival (ibid., n. 7). In the event of mortal danger the mother is allowed to take drugs and medications that are directly intended to cure her and only as a side effect, that is, indirectly, lead to the abortion of an animated fetus (ibid., n. 14). But then Sanchez lays down a rule that would prove fatal for many mothers, and that almost two hundred years later was made considerably worse by Alphonsus Liguori. Its dreadful implications, in fact, are still being felt to this day. Sanchez says that a mother commits a mortal sin if in mortal danger she takes a medication whose side effect can be the abortion of the fetus when it is certain or highly probable that after the mother's death the child would have lived *and could have been baptized.* In this case she is obliged to prefer the spiritual life of her child to her own bodily life. Sanchez points out that a priest who is in the process of administering emergency baptism to a dying child may not take cover from an enemy if there is a risk of the child's dying unbaptized. Just as the priest has to sacrifice his life for the baptism of a dying child, so the mother too must under certain circumstances lay down her life for the baptism of her child (ibid., n. 17).

This kind of thinking is based on the Augustinian belief that unbaptized children are eternally damned, a belief that Alphonsus Liguori carried to extremes. Alphonsus contradicts Sanchez and asserts that even if only the faintest hope exists that the child will outlive the mother long enough to be baptized, then even if medication were her only chance to recover, she may not take any, since otherwise the child would be "in danger of eternal death." She may take the medication necessary to survive only if without taking it the unborn child would die anyway before it could be baptized. Thus she may take the medication only if otherwise both child and mother will die (ibid., III, n. 194). And in 1938 the authoritative manual on moral theology by Mausbach and Tischleder pronounced: "On the other hand it is permitted . . . to employ drugs and operations that are directed, not against the pregnancy, but against a simultaneously present fatal disease of the mother, but that *per accidens* also cause an abortion. This is permitted with the presupposition that by this step the possibility of baptizing the child is not impaired" (ibid., II, p. 123).

In this context of the child's baptism taking precedence over the life of the mother, Alphonsus then exhaustively sets forth the question "whether the mother is obliged to endure the cutting open of her body so that the child can be baptized." To begin with, citing Thomas Aquinas, he determines, fortunately, that one may not kill the mother so as to be able to baptize the child. Alphonsus is so accommodating to women that he says one may not cut open the body of a woman already near death in order to pluck the child out for baptism. Nor is the mother obliged to cooperate with positive consent during the incision, if because of the operation her death is probable. She is obliged to suffer through the surgeon's cutting her up without her consent only if there is a probable hope that the child can still be baptized, and if her own death due to the surgery is not certain. For with an equal probability on both sides she has to prefer the spiritual life of the child to her own temporal life. This means that the mother must endure her possible death under the knife, if this will bring about the probable possibility of baptism, and hence of eternal life, for the child. But if her death from being cut open is certain and the prospects of getting the child baptized are questionable, then she is not obliged to accept certain death (ibid., III, n. 194).

After some theological reflections in this Jack the Ripper mode, Alphonsus turns to another Christian question, namely, whether a pregnant woman who has been condemned to death, but whose execution, for the child's sake, has been put off till after the birth, may be cut open—thus anticipating her execution—if there is a risk of the child's dying in the womb before death. Yes, says Alphonsus, citing a whole series of theologians who share his opinion. For a waiting period, which was ordered for the child's advantage anyway, would otherwise prove to his disadvantage. Since the woman would have been cut open after the execution to save the child, one might also do this before it, thereby moving ahead the time of the execution, which after all had been put off only for the child's sake (ibid., VI, n. 106).

The cruel God of Augustine, the persecutor and condemner of the newborn, of those who before their death did not manage to get baptized, is also a persecutor and torturer of mothers. And he has been this too in our century, although the discovery of anesthesia has checked his cruelty somewhat. A Catholic ethician named Franz Göpfert writes in his *Moraltheologie*

(1906) about Caesarian sections, which of course are no longer as dangerous as they were in the days of Alphonsus Liguori: "And therefore the hope . . . of being certain of baptizing the child validly excuses the danger that the operation nevertheless brings for the mother . . . Under certain circumstances, considering the eternal salvation of the child, one could claim that there is an obligation for the mother [to be operated on]" (II, p. 217).

As late as 1967 Bernhard Häring was arguing that the mother must make some sacrifices for the baptism of her child: "If there is no hope of securing the child's life *and above all its baptism* in any other way, then the mother is obliged to submit to one such operation" (*Das Gesetz Christi*, p. 225). Concerning these operations, which Häring lists (Caesarian section, severing the pelvic bone or the interpubic disk) he writes that they "primarily aim at saving the child, and no doubt pose *certain risks for the mother.*" This saving of the child, Häring says, consists "above all" in baptism. Thus there is no excluding the death of the child after baptism. Reassuringly, Häring points out to mothers that "nowadays Caesarian sections can be performed two to three times." In other words not until the fourth baptism will the mother, in certain cases, pay with her life. Häring argues that "the spiritual health of the mother, her authentically maternal thinking and feeling" must not be valued less "than the mere saving of the mother's corporeal life" (ibid., 222). In other words, a physically dead but maternally right-thinking mother is worth at least as much as one that may be alive but who lacks spiritual health.

The death of the mother can be the necessary price for the baptism of the child. Without baptism the child would be lost as far as eternal salvation is concerned. For while Catholics may not, even at the cost of their own lives, assault an "innocent child in its mother's womb," in the eyes of God the Father such a child is not as innocent as people think. God himself has pronounced the child guilty, evidently because of an offense so bad that to punish it he wishes not to associate with this child for all eternity, which means, for the child, eternal death. In order to snatch the child from God's hangman's hands and to lay it instead in God's loving hands, one must simply baptize the child. But sometimes, in exchange for not consigning the child to eternal death, God demands the earthly life of the mother.

St. Alphonsus Liguori, founder of the Redemptorists, the father of nineteenth- and, to a great extent, of twentieth-century Catholic moral theology, named a Doctor of the Church in 1871 and the patron of all confessors in 1950, is the decisive, constantly cited authority on this issue, and has stood godfather to many children of dead mothers. Alphonsus was the one who, in contrast to Thomas Sanchez, decided that an "inanimate" fetus might *not* be aborted in the event of mortal danger to the mother. Instead Alphonsus demanded that from the moment of conception abortion had to be liable to punishment. Sanchez had maintained that up until the eightieth day the fetus was "part of [the mother's] entrails." Alphonsus characterized this eighty-day grace period as a "possible" opinion, but rejected it for himself (*Theologia moralis* III, n. 394). He inspired the ideology of sacrificing the mother that has prevailed, especially from 1884 till the present. Granted, as of 1976 there has been some mitigation of this from the German bishops, but not from Rome, and even the German bishops offered only "to respect the doctor's decision." Decisions are still being made about women, but not with them, and certainly not by them. Besides, the concession to the doctors applies only to the case that otherwise both mother and child will die.

Only ignorance about what the Catholic Church has decided and not yet repealed all over the world on the subject of baptism and mothers has kept, and continues to keep, many pregnant women from panicking. Moral theologians used to discuss constantly just how far the confessor had to inform mothers about their duty to sacrifice their earthly life for the eternal life of their child, and whether they should be enlightened about their obligation to let themselves be cut open for the sake of baptizing their dying child. For the most part they advised that, since their own lives were in danger, the mothers need not be informed, in case they should not consent to their duty and thus die in mortal sin. It was a humane feature of an inhuman morality of human sacrifice to conceal, on occasion, its unmerciful principles.

But these principles are not always so agreeably concealed. Georges Simenon, the great Belgian detective novelist, reports in his *Intimate Memoirs* (Paris, 1981) the following story: Before the birth of their son Jean, he and his wife, Denise, then very far gone in her pregnancy, visited a gynecological clinic in Arizona, which had been recommended to them as the best. But they left it immediately because in the entrance hung a notice, edged in black, that "in accordance with the decision of the chief physician and the mother superior, in grave situations the fate of the child would take precedence over that of the mother." Simenon writes: "A cold shudder ran down our backs, and we tiptoed back out." Their son was born in a hospital that was less authentically Catholic (ibid., p. 247).

XXVII

ONANISM

Every age has its own delusion. In the era we call the Enlightenment the delusion of onanism broke out. Onan, as we have seen, gave his name to coitus interruptus, but after 1710 his name was also applied—falsely—to masturbation. Christian morality outlawed onanism and ranked it among the unnatural, i.e., the gravest, sins in the sexual realm. Every ejaculation that cannot lead to procreation is considered unnatural, thus onanism is a vice that according to Thomas Aquinas is worse than intercourse with one's own mother (II/II q.154 a. 11 and 12).

The history of the medical delusion over onanism proved to be a positive windfall for Catholic moral theology. For the prospect of sickness in this world has a still stronger effect on many people than fear of hellfire. This gives the theologians, as the heralds of God's will, both proofs and additional legitimization of their case. And thus the Catholic Church made good use of the medical errors about masturbation by churning out all sorts of pamphlets and treatises, especially for endangered young people. And anyone old enough to have gotten his moral theology from traditional

Catholic sources might still be persuaded today that onanism preys upon the spinal cord, softens or dries up the brain, but in any case can make you sick.

Bernhard Häring, in 1967, writes: Masturbation "also has damaging consequences for one's health." He does concede, however, that such damage "also may not occur in cases where [masturbation] is not practiced to excess (*Das Gesetz Christi*, 308). Thus of late there is a glimmer of hope for intimidated masturbators everywhere.

As far back as classical Antiquity onanism was looked upon as harmful to health (on what follows see A. and W. Leibbrand, *Formen des Eros. Kultur- und Geistesgeschichte der Liebe*, 1972). The grand progenitor of masturbation anxiety, especially the fear of tabes dorsalis (a syphilitic disease of the nervous system), was the Greek physician Hippocrates (d. ca. 375 B.C.). He was not particularly concerned with damning onanism, but with the bodily weakness brought on both by sexual intercourse and onanism. Galen (d. ca. 199 A.D.), Emperor Marcus Aurelius' personal physician, took the opposite tack, arguing that sexual intercourse and masturbation were good for maintaining one's health and for protecting the body against poisons that break it down. Abstinence, he thought, led to tremors, convulsions, and madness. Borrowing from Galen, the Muslim philosopher Avicenna (d. 1037) later spoke of medical methods for advising onanism where sexual intercourse was not possible.

It remained for Christianity to banish masturbation from the sphere of medical discussion of the pros and cons, simply damning it as immoral. Then, starting in the seventeenth century this condemnation was amplified with the worst sort of Hippocratic prognoses, so that onanism was viewed as causing disease in this life and eternal torment in the next.

In 1479, when the pastor of the Cathedral of Mainz, Johann von Wesel, faced charges of heresy before the court of the Inquisition in Mainz, the court's only concern was with morality. Medical counterarguments in the case were irrelevant. Von Wesel had familiarized himself with the theories of Galen and Avicenna and had accepted them. In his writings he dealt with the question of whether monks might not get sick as a result of continence. He wondered whether it was permissible to extract, in some artificial fashion, the semen that had gone bad and was poisoning the human body. He wanted to do this without provoking any pleasurable feelings, but he also wondered whether such pleasure might not be without sin, if the purification were taking place simply for health reasons. In the end Von Wesel had to retract his writings and was condemned to imprisonment in a monastery.

"Self-pollution" was the greatest sin against nature, and led to bodily weakness, impotence, and shortening of the lifespan through suicide. This was the claim made in London in 1640 by the Reverend Richard Capel, the preacher of Magdalen College, in his book *Temptations, Their Nature, Their Danger, Their Cure.* Oxford's Magdalen College was a center of Puritan teaching.

Calling this sickness of self-pollution "onanism" was the work of a Puritan physician in London named Bekkers, who in 1710 wrote a book called *Onania or the Loathsome Sin of Self-Pollution.* Bekkers told the world that in his day the vice was widespread among both sexes, and that hence as a doctor he felt obliged to call attention to its consequences. These were: "Disturbance of the stomach and digestion, loss of appetite or ravenous hunger, vomiting, nausea, weakening of the organs of breathing, coughing, hoarseness, paralyses, weakening of the organ of generation to the point of impotence, lack of libido, daily and nightly ejaculations, back pain, disorders of the eye and ear, total diminution of bodily powers, paleness, thinness, pimples on the face, decline in intellectual powers, loss of memory, attacks of rage, madness, idiocy, epilepsy, stiffness, fever, and finally suicide." Bekkers' book unleashed an avalanche. Hordes of young people asked him for advice about their health. He added it onto his book, which swelled to twice its original size and was translated into practically every language. The German edition appeared in Leipzig in 1736. In England the book had gone into its nineteenth edition by 1759.

In 1758 a Calvinist doctor from Lausanne named Simon-André Tissot published *Onania,* a book that managed to turn masturbation anxiety into mass hysteria. Tissot described how in one onanist the brain was so massively dried out that one could hear it rattle in the cranium. "This book worked up the subject in epoch-making style, and rigged it out to endure for centuries" (V. E. Pilgrim, *Der selbstbefriedigte Mensch,* 1975, p. 43). The last edition appeared in 1905. Tissot's book made everyone in Europe familiar with this disease. In the Foreword Tissot turned down any questions or requests for treatment, since he preferred to dedicate his time to patients with "honorable" diseases.

In *The Birth of the Modern Family* (1977) Edward Shorter reports: "Self-defilement was indeed cutting down the very flower of the nation [France] itself: the cadets in the military academies. Dr. Guillaume Daignan in 1786 related this tale of a young man's road to ruin (*Tableau des variétés de la vie humaine,* Paris, 1786): 'Joining his uncle, captain in a regiment of four battalions, he was supposed to take up the first available post. He was very well received by his numerous comrades, and soon imitated all their follies, which in this profession are not always in the direction of prudence and sagacity. He had been very well raised, polite and agreeable. These qualities, which should have guaranteed him female conquests, served only to draw him in all the more, because of his intimacy with his mates. Remorse was not delayed. First, he experienced violent cramps whenever he excited himself to such acts . . . which his whole mode of thinking should have made him detest, if he had not been swayed by the example of the multitude . . . I encouraged him to break completely with this detestable habit, and he assured me that he wished to do so all the more because he felt not at all tempted by it. But he didn't know how to avoid the occasions. Having as yet no functions to fulfill, he could scarcely sequester himself from his comrades without appearing unusual. Upon learning that this variety of orgy took place only in the evening, I counseled him to absent himself on the pretext of a migraine headache. The excuse worked for a time, but the damage was already done. The cramps returned frequently . . . And sure enough, the lad's health turned out to be permanently ruined, a nervous degenerate, deprived of the sweetness of life and the charms of sociability' " (ibid., p. 101).

Not everyone in the "Age of Reason" shared the spreading medical delusions about onanism. This can be seen in the case of one of the protagonists of the French Revolution, Count Mirabeau (d. 1791), who rejected the terroristic propaganda against onanism, and preferring Galen's theory of the toxic effects of congested semen, declared masturbation reasonable. On the other hand, Queen Marie-Antoinette got a taste of the mass hysteria at its most repulsive. Before she was guillotined, an attempt was made to justify the execution, an infamous maneuver that we read about in the documents of the trial (cf. André Castelot, *Marie Antoinette*, Paris, 1962, pp. 499ff.). In the public indictment the charge (inspired by Robespierre) is made that, aside from betraying the country, the Queen was guilty of the following: "The widow Capet (= Marie Antoinette), immoral from every point of view, is so perverse and so familiar with all vices that, forgetting her quality as a mother and with it the bounds prescribed by nature, she dares to abandon herself to filthy doings with Louis-Charles Capet, her son, as he himself testifies. The very thought and name of these obscenities make one tremble with horror." The Queen's accusers had her eight-year-old son, Louis-Charles Capet (= Louis XVII [1785–1795]), brought forward. The boy had been entrusted to a certain Antoine Simon for his "education" (which was presumably the cause of his early death). He said that Simon and his wife had surprised him several times in bed while he was engaged in "indecencies harmful to my health," which his mother had taught him.

The witness Jacques René Hébert made the following statement during the trial: "Young Capet, whose physical condition got worse from day to day, was surprised by Simon in the course of self-pollutions that were harmful to his health. When Simon asked him who had taught him this criminal behavior, he answered that his mother and aunt had done so . . . These two women often had him sleep between them in the same bed, a fact that also emerged from the statements of young Capet before the mayor of Paris and the public prosecutor of the Commune. It may be assumed that this criminal enjoyment was not taught to the youth for the sake of his pleasure but rather in the political hope of physically weakening the boy, since it was still assumed at this time that he would later ascend the throne, and in this way one could exercise influence on him. Owing to the strain and exhaustion of the activities he had been taught, the boy had gotten a hernia, so that he had to have a bandage applied to his person. As soon as the boy was no longer with his mother, he recovered his strength." Thus far witness Hébert.

To the question of what she had to say to counter this statement by the witness, Marie-Antoinette replied that she did not know what the witness was talking about. Nature forbade listening to that sort of accusation against a mother. Many of those present said she was right.

The findings of medicine supported those of theology. In 1842 the well-known ethician J. C. Debreyne, who was both a Trappist priest and a doctor, described the consequences of onanism: "Palpitations, weakened vision, headaches, dizziness, tremors, painful cramps, convulsive epileptic movements, often genuine epilepsy, general pains in the limbs or in the back of the head, in the spine, in the chest, in the stomach, great weakness of the kidneys, general paralytical phenomena" (*Essai sur la théologie morale considérée dans ses rapports avec la physiologie et la médicine*). The monk's advice for those who had contracted onanism was: sleep on your side, never on your back; drink and eat cold things, suck ice cubes, wash with salted snow water. In the case of girls, Father Debreyne proposes clitoridectomy, since the clitoris is not needed for procreation and only serves lust.

In his book *Der selbstbefriedigte Mensch*, in a chapter entitled "The 19th Century Assaults the Children," V. E. Pilgrim writes: "Nineteenth-century physicians adopted the same approach to their case histories as their predecessor Tissot. It was often reported in the 19th century that masturbation dries out the brain, so that it rattles in the skull of the onanist. Deslandes mentions the case of an eight year old boy, the back portion of whose cranium displayed extremely strange alterations. The boy had been masturbating for several years and had almost non-stop erections. 'This habit lengthened the diameter of his head in such a way that his mother found it difficult to find the lad a hat that would fit him.' " Pilgrim then describes the methods used to control onanism. "With boys wires or metal clasps were inserted through the foreskin, to prevent the withdrawal of the glans (so-called infibulation). At night metal rings with points were placed around the penis . . .

"The century's best prescription for women was clitoridectomy. The Viennese physician Gustav Braun recommended it in his *Compendium der Frauenkrankheiten* (1863). In 1858 Isaac Baker-Brown, a prominent London surgeon and later the highly esteemed president of the London Medical Society, introduced it to England. He considered the operation advisable because in his view masturbation led to hysteria, epilepsy, and varicose veins. He sought to cure masturbation by removing the organ it was done with. He performed this operation many times on both children and adults, and set up a special home for women, the London Surgical Home. In 1866 he published accounts of forty-eight of these operations" (Pilgrim, pp. 477ff.).

In 1849 a Dr. Demeaux issued an urgent call to the French Ministry of Culture. He demanded, among other things, that the dormitories in the boarding schools, colleges, and schools be set up in such a way that the beds were divided up into a foot section comprising two thirds of the bed and a head section in the other part. Both parts were to be separated from each other by a special wall. Then at night the foot section of as many has a hundred beds could be watched for suspicious movements, while the upper section was in darkness. He further demanded that trousers should not have pockets. Finally, he wanted unannounced body searches of the boys several times each year, since the onanists would catch the doctor's attention by the development of their member, by their fear of showing themselves naked, and above all by the poor state of their health; and then they could be watched with special care. Two suggestions were rejected, namely the wall over the beds, since it was pointed out that the lack of movement might harm the children, and the body searches. This, it was thought, would destroy the modesty that was precisely the most important weapon against onanism. As for removing the pockets, that was already customary all over (February 27, 1849, *Le conseil de l'Université de France,* see Jean Paul Aaron/Roger Kempf, *Le pénis et la démoralisation de l'Occident.* Paris, 1978, pp. 205ff. and 239).

The disease of onanism was also known in Russia. A Ruthenian doctor named H. Kaan wrote a *psychopathia sexualis* (1834) that appeared in a German translation in Leipzig. The work was dedicated to the Tsar's personal physician. Kaan describes onanism, the great sexual disease, in the style of Tissot, with a long list of all the mental and physical illnesses it spawned. At the end was suicide. In about 1925 Maxim Gorki wrote in his novel, *The Life of Klim Samgin*, about the protagonist: "Klim thought of the terrifying book by Professor Tarnowski about the pernicious influence of onanism, a book that his mother had pushed his way, as a precaution, some time ago."

In 1882 *L'Encéphale,* a technical French journal on nervous and mental diseases, published a long, detailed article by a doctor from Istanbul named Demetrius Zambaco on "Onanism and Mental Disturbance in Two Little Girls." The older masturbated continually, and a clitoridectomy had to be performed. Dr. Zambaco notes: "It is reasonable to concede that cauterization with a white hot iron gets rid of the sensitiveness of the clitoris, indeed that with repeated cauterization one is able to remove it completely . . . It can be readily seen that children, after they have lost feeling through cauterization, are less liable to sexual excitement and less inclined to touch themselves." Zambaco reports that he met a series of internationally known colleagues, men such as Dr. Jules Guérin in London, who had achieved excellent therapeutic results by cauterizing the clitoris.

These operations did not stop until 1905, when Freud put a halt to such mutilation of children in his *Three Contributions to the Theory of Sex.* But that in no way checked the discrediting of masturbation. In 1910 Dr. E. Sterian warned that he could recognize the "unfortunate manual-sexual types by their permanent odor of sperm" (*L'éducation sexuelle*). Ingmar Bergman, the Swedish film director who was born the son of a pastor in Uppsala in 1918, writes in *My Life* (1987, pp. 132ff.) that as a boy, taking a clue from his older brother, he looked for advice in the encyclopedia under "masturbation": "There it said in black and white that masturbation was also called self-pollution, that it was a vice of youth which had to be fought with every means available, that it led to pallor, profuse sweating, shivers, black rings beneath the eyes, difficulty in concentrating and loss of equilibrium. In severe cases the disease led to softening of the brain. It attacked the spinal cord. It could also cause epileptic fits, loss of consciousness and a premature death. With these prospects for the future before my eyes, I went on with my handiwork with terror and delight. There was no one I could speak to. I couldn't ask anyone, I had to be continually on guard, continually hiding my horrible secret . . . In the night before I first took the Eucharist I tried with all my might to overcome my demon. I struggled with him till the early morning, but lost the battle. Jesus punished me with a huge pimple in the middle of my pale forehead."

In 1956 the book *In All Candor,* by an English minister named Leslie D. Weatherhead, was published in Zurich. The book relates how for thousands of English men and women onanism is the greatest problem in life, how they have nervous breakdowns over it. Weatherhead warns against approving masturbation, since it is a sin. In 1967 Abbé M. Petit-mangin argued that onanism had to be combated by every expedient, that it was a vice, as contraception was for married people. In 1975 Pope Paul VI, in his "Declaration on Some Questions in Sexual Ethics," attacked the grave sin of onanism. Now that the doctors and educators, at long last, have dismissed the problem of masturbation, it is once again in good hands with the theologians. The Pope writes that the masturbator forfeits the love of God. Beyond that, masturbation is a mortal sin, "even though it is not possible to prove unequivocally that Holy Scripture expressly repudiates this sin as such." At any rate, on doubtful questions the Pope's word is always more important than Scripture, and so one need not be disturbed by the Bible's silence on masturbation.

In addition to all this, the Church is now getting some unexpected help in this matter from the East, and, of all countries, from the one where contraception is imposed by the state, namely China. Hubert Dobiosch reports from a student trip to China in 1985 that came about through an invitation to the chair of moral theology in Augsburg, by agreement with the German Bishops Conference, in order to "build a bridge to the Church in China, cut off from the rest of the world." Dobiosch writes: "To realize the program of family planning, the Chinese are carrying out intensive educational efforts. Young people are emphatically urged to practice continence. Young men and women are told the following: 1. Early marriage is harmful, leading to exaggerated sexuality. 2. Intensive sexual life leads to impotence. 3. Masturbation results in impotence, brain damage, and nearsightedness. 4. The following countermeasures are recommended: a) absorption in the works of Marx, Lenin, and Mao, b) gymnastics, c) early rising, etc., d) not sleeping on one's belly, e) not using warm covers, f) not wearing tight-fitting underwear, g) shadowboxing is warmly recommended and widely practiced" (*Theologie der Gegenwart,* 1982, 2, 106–7).

So in one-child China a great missionary field is opening up for the Catholic Church's gospel of continence. The fact that the Chinese are becoming nearsighted because of onanism—as it is claimed—is fortunate and promises that more and more of them will flock to hear the good news of Christianity. The farsightedness of the German Bishops Conference is justified in seeking fruitful soil for the future in China. This can be seen, with regard to onanism, from an article in *Der Spiegel* (No. 13, 1986, 189) on education in China: "The pamphlet, for example, on 'General Information on the Hygiene and Biology of Young Persons,' warns that 'masturbation impairs health' . . . 'underwear that is too tight' or 'heavy blankets' are to be avoided."

XXVIII

HOMOSEXUALITY

G*reek and Judeo-Christian* myths about the origin of humanity are agreed that every person is an incomplete half. But they disagree about whether for the man another man or a woman completes his half and makes a whole. In the biblical account of Creation the becoming-one-flesh of a man and a woman is expressed through the image of Eve being fashioned from Adam's rib.

Obviously this is not meant to be understood scientifically: Genesis does not contradict evolution since Eve, like Adam, developed from an animal body. The biblical version of the original relationship between man and woman is a metaphorical expression of their profound interconnectedness. When God brings Eve to him, Adam says: "This at last is bone of my bones/ and flesh of my flesh." And the passage closes with the reflection: "Therefore a man leaves his father and his mother and cleaves to his wife, and they become one flesh" (Gen. 2:23–24). Thus they will return, in a certain sense, to the closest physical association in which they once found themselves when woman was still an integral part of man. *Because* of this primal unity woman will once again become one in body with him, and this in the state of marriage. From the standpoint of this original unity revived in marriage, Judaism, Christianity, and Islam see homosexuality as unnatural. By nature man seeks only to be joined with woman, and woman with man.

The Greek myth, as Plato (d. 348/347) presents it in the *Symposium,* looks different: Our natural makeup now is different from what it once was. Originally there were three kinds of complete human being, spherical creatures, some consisting of a man and a man, others of a woman and a woman, and finally the heterosexual ones made up of a man and a woman. As a punishment from the gods these spherical humans were sliced in half, and now each half runs around in search of his other half. The Greek myth speaks of the heterosexual halves with scorn: "Then all men who are a cutting of the old common sex which was called manwoman are fond of women, and adulterers generally come of that sex, and all women who are mad for men, and adulteresses." Then after a brief mention of lesbians, the myth continues: "But those which are a cutting of the male pursue the male . . . and these are the best of boys and lads because they are naturally bravest . . . Here is a great proof: when they grow up, such as these alone are men in public affairs . . . [They] do not trouble about marriage and getting a family, but that law and custom compels them" (191E–192A, translated by W. H. D. Rouse).

Thus what the Christian world, which had many homosexuals burned at the stake down through its history, labels as "unnatural," the Greek myth calls "natural." The Church's celibates, whose minds were not set on "marriage and getting a family" either, would have been seen in ancient Greece as classical representatives of the homosexual species of human. Evidently, people's ideas of what is "natural" and "unnatural" are not always and everywhere the same.

In the Letter to the Romans, Paul the Jew reckons homosexual and lesbian love among typical Greek vices—and they fill him with disgust. But even among the Greeks homosexuality was sometimes challenged, as shown by the following scene: Plutarch (d. ca. 120 A.D.) reports about an elite homosexual corps, the "Lovers Battalion" from Thebes. It functioned in accordance with the principle that "it is good to put a lover side by side with his beloved," because when danger arrives one is most concerned about one's beloved. Furthermore lovers especially want to distinguish themselves in the eyes of their beloved. This unit from Thebes, also called the "holy troop," remained undefeated until the battle of Chaironeia. There they were defeated by Philip II, the father of Alexander the Great, in ca. 338 B.C. "After the battle, when Philip went to look at the fallen, and came to the place where the three hundred lay, as they had all marched straight into the enemy's spears and sunk down together, he is said to have been astonished, and when he heard that this was the troop of the lovers and the beloved, he wept and cried out: 'Let them die who suspect such people of having done something dishonorable' " (*Parallel Lives, Pelopidas* 18). The fact of Philip's assaulting the detractors of homosexuals shows that they existed.

Such contempt for homosexuals can also be found, for example, in the words of Seneca the Elder (father of the famous Seneca the Younger, whom Nero forced to commit suicide in 65). He describes the decadence of these individuals: "Unhealthy passion for singing and dancing fills the souls of these effeminates. They curl their hair, they make their voices thin, to make them resemble the voices of women. They vie with women in the softness of their movements, and abandon themselves to obscene explorations. This is the ideal of our young men. Effete and nervous by birth, they remain that way of their own free will, always ready to violate the chastity of others and to pay no heed to their own" (*Controversiae* I, prologue 8). The Stoic Epictetus (d. ca. 135 A.D.) describes the orators as so perfumed and curly-haired that one wondered if they were men or women (*Dissertationes* III, 1). And the same Aristophanes (d. ca. 380 B.C.), whom Plato makes the author of the myth of the three sexes, mocks the effeminate poet Agathon in the *Thesmophoriazusae:* "One little rosy nail/ Prattles over the lyre, One little tepid hand/ Coyly arched with silks and your hair not rank merely but netted./ A woman's girdle, a skin smarmed up with oil like a wrestler,/ Dangling a sword in one hand, a looking glass in the other./ Are you horned or slatted, you twilight of the genders?" (Translated by Ian Fletcher, *Anion* [University of Texas], vol. II, no. 3, 1963.) Thus the positive estimate of homosexuality in ancient Greece was never univocal.

Christianity adopted Judaism's revulsion for homosexuality; and as soon as they came to power, Christians tried to eradicate homosexuals in 390 by a law that threatened them with burning at the stake. Article 116 of Emperor Charles V's "Penal Rules" (1532) laid down: "They are to be condemned to pass from life to death by fire, in accordance with the common custom." The only thing Catholicism has in common with homosexuality is the contempt for women that in the warlike masculine society of Antiquity was associated with homosexuals. In particular Catholicism borrowed the Aristotelian idea that woman were not capable of friendship, that friendship, i.e., the highest form of relationship between adults, was possible only among men. As we have seen, the two great pillars of Catholic Christianity, Augustine and Thomas Aquinas, made it clear that woman had been joined to man as a "helpmeet," but only for childbearing, while for comfort in isolation "man is a better help to a man." In keeping with its sexual pessimism, within its own ranks Catholicism desexualized homosexuality and then went on cultivating it as a misogynistic male society.

In the case of sympathetic churchmen one cannot speak of their despising, but rather of their ignoring, women. Thus John XXIII wrote in his spiritual diary in 1948: "After more than forty years I still warmly recall the edifying conversations that I had in the episcopal palace in Bergamo with my revered bishop, Msgr. Radini

Tedeschi. About the persons in the Vatican, from the Holy Father downwards, there was never an expression that was not respectful, no, never. But as for women or their shape or what concerned them, no word was ever spoken. It was as if there were no women in the world. This absolute silence, this lack of any familiarity with regard to the other sex, was one of the most powerful and profound lessons of my young life as a priest, and even today I thankfully keep the excellent and beneficial memory of that man who raised me in this discipline."

For this exclusively male world, this womanless terrarium in which popes and their educators move and which, by placing them in a totally separate society, is supposed to preserve them from what they would see as the beginning of their gravest error, namely the perception of the other half of the human race, for this ghetto of the male church, women are still only objects to be ignored in the process whereby the celibates take protective measures for maintaining their chaste little world apart. They strive to behave "as if there were no women," and in this surrealistic effort to dive back again into that paradisiacal time before God created Eve, in their infantile flight into a sort of male uterus of a womanless world, they can have no vision for the real world, that is, for a world full of men *and* women, which means for a world of human beings.

XXIX

THE MORAL THEOLOGY OF THE TWENTIETH CENTURY

S*exuality is a realm* of human life that more than most has fallen victim to a highly specialized form of the discipline of theology, one might say of a peculiar excrescence of the field, namely, moral theology. The biblical foundations of this ethical system are extremely feeble, since there is nothing like it in the New Testament. What moral theology wants to be, among other things, namely, "Christian service instructions for all foreseeable cases in life" (*Lexikon für Theologie und Kirche,* vol. 7, 1962, 613) is something it has had basically to work out on its own. Those involved in this effort must have felt more or less abandoned by Christ, since Jesus' preaching "was a presentation, neither complete nor systematic, of the ethics of qualifying for the Kingdom of God" (ibid., 618).

The Church remedied this gap in Jesus' preaching by completing, systematizing, and concretizing his moral theology, bringing out the essential characteristics of coherent structure and detailed casuistry. In the course of time casuistry became the most striking feature of the system. A Christianity that once moved about in daylight turned into a discreetly darkened whisper in the confessional, which increasingly and ever more indiscreetly concentrated on the sins of the flesh. Churchmen believed that no sexual lapse could ever be trivial, as Rome officially decided on February 4, 1611. In contrast to Luther's canceling of the carefully measured distinctions between sin and sin, the Councils of Trent (1545–63) demanded that sins had to be reported with information about their kind, number of times committed, and the circumstances in question. This enhanced the moral theological interest in the most detailed possible behavioral norms and rules, while gearing the inquisition in the confessional toward the particulars of the sins. Beginning in the sixteenth century practically all orders published collections of case law, and most of what the army of casuists brooded over and hatched is still valid even today.

The one great name that has to be stressed here is our old friend Alphonsus Maria Liguori (d. 1787). His comprehensive work *Theologiae moralis* had a decisive impact on the further development of Catholic ethics. Alphonsus Liguori was loaded down with all the honors the Church had to give: He was beatified in 1816, canonized in 1839. In 1871 he was raised to a Doctor of the Church by Pius IX, who attested that there was nothing in his works that did not agree with the truth taught by the Church. In 1950 Pius XII made Alphonsus Liguori the patron of all confessors and moralists.

The official Redemptorist biography of Alphonsus, whose "sense of reality" has been celebrated in this century by Bernhard Häring, tells us that: "As a bishop he gave audiences to women only in the presence of a servant. Once he received a very old woman by having her sit on the end of a long bench, while he sat at the other end with his back turned. In confirming women he never touched their bare cheeks, when he had to give the slap on the cheek prescribed by the Church, but only the head covering of the confirmands" (quoted in Karlheinz Deschner, *Das Kreuz mit der Kirche: Eine Sexualgeschichte des Christentums*, pp. 325–26).

His work has gone into more than seventy editions. Hundreds of moral theologians have copied him, and all together they have set down in characters of bronze a wretched moral theology that not only presupposes the individual's status as a minor, but systematically works to train people for it. This theology has made consciences not broader and deeper but full of scrupulous fears. Sexual morality has become as specialized science for celibate experts. The ethicist Franz Göpfert wrote in 1906 that "the ordinary, uneducated people cannot distinguish between unchastity, sensuality, and dishonorableness" (*Moraltheologie*, 346). Such distinctions can be grasped only by unmarried judges in the confessional. The ordinary person, whether educated or not, with only his normal knowledge to rely on, simply can't handle it. We find the same incomprehensible moral-theological jargon in Häring: "Sexual pleasure, culpable, caused by shameless acts, but not directly and voluntarily affirmed, is by its nature gravely sinful" (*Das Gesetz Christi*, 1967, III, p. 301). It is clear to the confessors that the penitents can't cope with this sort of thing: "The confessor must beware of demanding a material completeness in the confession that would correspond to the technical distinctions" (ibid., 317). If the confessor did not shrink from insisting on complete technical accuracy, or what he took to be such, then he would have to stockpile provisions in the confessional, because it would be a long time before he got home.

Children present a special problem. As Göpfert writes, "With children it cannot be denied that they see many things as playing and naughtiness, without recognizing any serious sin in it, for example, when they touch one another, look at others *uncleanly* or let themselves be seen in this way" (ibid., p. 346).

Alphonsus also continued the process of demonizing sexuality. Thanks to him, the *incubus*, the male devil who lies on top, and the *succubus*, the female devil who lies on the bottom, enter the confessional booth, even in the twentieth century. People keep accusing themselves of sexual intercourse with the devil. Admittedly, Göpfert warns confessors against "readily believing" (*Moraltheologie*, II, p. 365) such confessions, and he speaks in this context of "madmen or fantasies of hysterical people." But it's too easy to slander the victims of an abstruse theology, rather than looking for madness or hysteria first of all among the originators of this whole idea. Göpfert thinks of sex with the devil not as something to be "readily believed," but still believable. Only at the end of our century has the theological to-do over this specter disappeared, and hence any belief in it. So under the pressure of an enlightened age theology has had to surrender a once extensive subject and realm of knowledge.

On the foundation of the sexual casuistry worked out by Alphonsus a broad field of activity was built up and made available for sexual pessimists, even in the twentieth century. There was an especially rich material outside of marriage (within marriage theology concentrated on the "misuse of marriage" = contraception). The pleasure-hating ethicians found many a stone that they managed to turn, under which they discovered all sorts of unchaste or shameless vermin. For "by unchastity we understand every kind of enjoyment of sexual pleasure that is counter to the divinely willed purpose of the sexual drive. Unchastity seeks pleasure outside the bounds of duty, which according to God's will is bound to the exercise of sexual intercourse in marriage" (Fritz Tillmann, *Die katholische Sittenlehre*, IV 2, p. 117). Pleasure was the red flag of the pleasure they took in hating pleasure. When one hears such words as "pleasure" "lust," or "desire," one must not immediately imagine the worst. "On the way to the consummated external act lie impure glances, touches, embrace, and kisses, in which there is a strong inbuilt tendency to proceed to the extreme" (ibid., p. 122).

For dealing with this broad area between glancing and kissing that theologians termed "immodesty," as early as the sixteenth century they developed a practicable method for ethical labeling. Thus, just as beef is classified into different grades, human beings were broken down into higher, lower, and objectionable body parts. A person's relation to or attitude toward his own parts or his relation to or attitude toward another person's parts corresponded to the relation of man to God and vice versa. "Because of their different influence on the excitement of sexual pleasure the parts of the body were divided into honorable [face, hands, feet], less honorable [chest, back, arms, thighs], and dishonorable [sexual parts and parts very close to them]" (H. Jone, *Katholische Moraltheologie,* 1930, p. 189). As had the tradition before him, Göpfert also calls the "dishonorable" body parts "shameful" and "obscene" (*Moraltheologie,* II, p. 366).

The consequences of immorality as defined by the Church can sometimes be grim: "Thus the light touch of a woman's hand can be a mortal sin, if it occurs with impure intent." It "can" be a mortal sin, but kisses on the arm are "regularly mortal sins; for no just reason to do this is thinkable. But if there is no just reason, then they take place either from lust or at the least they are highly provoking." By the way, one should not make light of a touch of the hand, either, because it is always a venial sin: "Touches on the honorable . . . parts, if they take place in passing out of thoughtless, joking, or curiosity, are venial sins. Thus it is a venial sin to touch lightly and in passing the fingers, hands or face of a person of the opposite sex without a perverse intention and sexual desire and danger of acquiescing in sensual pleasure, provided that if sexual pleasure arises, it is repulsed and one abstains from these acts" (ibid., p. 368). And Göpfert points to a series of moral theologians who have taught the same doctrine, for example, Alphonsus Liguori. On the other hand Göpfert declared in an earlier edition that, "In dancing, lightly holding the hand of a woman is either no sin or only a venial sin"

(*Moraltheologie*, 1900, II, p. 336). Göpfert seemed not to be quite sure of this point himself, and so in 1906 he dropped the whole sentence just to be safe.

Along with the sinful touches there are also sinful looks. Here one distinguishes dishonorable glances from extremely dishonorable glances. Dishonorable glances can be dishonorable even if the object of their attention is itself honorable, but so much for that subject. In any case one has to keep in mind—to give one example of systematic moral theology—that the danger of such glances must be judged in accordance with 1. the object, 2. the intention of the person glancing, 3. the disposition of the person glancing, and 4. the manner of glancing. According to the predominant opinion of ethicians, the disposition of the person being glanced at does not justify any specific distinction. But one has to distinguish the dishonorable glances from the extremely dishonorable glances. We can already guess what is meant here, namely the sight of "dishonorable" bodily parts, and not only naked ones: "It is likewise a grave sin to see such things through a net or a very thin, transparent veil; for this stimulates lust rather than extinguishing it" (ibid., 1906, II, p. 376).

The same moralistic spirit can be found in Häring in 1967. He divides the "sins of immodesty" into a) looks, b) touches ("The public conveyances, which are often crowded to overflowing nowadays, offer a host of dangerous opportunities for anonymous flirtation"), c) conversations, d) reading ("How seriously attentive we must be in this area is shown by the maternal care of the Church in banning bad books," [ibid., p. 315]). The introductory sentence is: "Everything immodest that is done with the express intention for provoking lust is unchaste because of this very intention and a grave sin" (ibid., 312). In connection with b) touches, Häring does, however, find words of comfort for the normal Christians: "But where real Christian love and helpfulness (care of the sick, etc.) call for and motivate touching, experience shows that with normal individuals there is nothing to fear."

As far as touching, kisses, and embraces go, engaged couples are allowed no more than unengaged ones, and that means, in principle: nothing of the sort, "because engagement gives the couple no rights at all to each other's body," as Göpfert writes (ibid., p. 372). Acquaintanceships between girls and young men may only be made "for a good purpose, in other words, to enter upon marriage directly. . . . Intercourse (not sexual, but social) should take place only in a limited way, which means not too often and not for too long. Greater frequency can be tolerated when the marriage will occur within a short time, say one or two months; visits should be less frequent the further the marriage is put off. Greater frequence can be tolerated if the girl is never alone, but always under a watchful eye; visits should be less frequent when the engaged couple are always by themselves" (ibid., pp. 373–74). In 1967 Häring maintained that: "Although in today's dynamic open society parental supervision in the old style, which corresponded to a closed society, is hardly possible any more, still even today sensible rules of behavior have to be worked out. On this point Christians have to realize clearly that the conventional ways of behaving in today's society are derived from ideologies incompatible with Christianity" (ibid., pp. 377–78).

But the moral theologians noticed no such incompatibility under the Nazis. On the contrary, for many of the important points of Catholic ethics national socialism seemed to promise help, and the Church was zealously engaged in seizing this opportunity. The first personal meeting between Hitler and a Catholic bishop, namely Bishop Berning of Osnabrück and Vicar General Steinmann, the representative of Bishop Schreiber of Berlin, who was ill, took place on April 26, 1933. In Berning's minutes we read: "The conversation (1 and ¼ hrs.) was amiable and businesslike. The bishops joyfully acknowledged that because of the new state Christianity was being promoted, the level of morality raised, and the struggle against bolshevism and atheism carried on with energy and success" (Hans Müller, *Katholische Kirche und Nationalsozialismus, Dokumente 1930–1935,* 1963, p. 117). At the Bishops Conference in Fulda, May 30–June 1, 1933, the great pastoral letter was promulgated with its "thanks to Hitler," because from now on "immorality . . . would [no longer] threaten and ravage the soul of the German people." For the German bishops the battle against immorality meant fighting "for chaste education of young people" and against "excesses in group bathing" (ibid., pp. 146 and 156). In August 1933 at the exhibition of the Holy Coat in Trier Monsignor Steinmann greeted the crowd with "Heil Hitler!" When he was criticized for this in New York, he said that the German bishops saw in Hitler a bulwark against "the plague of dirty literature" (Friedrich Heer, *Gottes erste Liebe*, p. 409).

During the Nazi period Marian devotion, the Catholic ideal of chastity, and celibacy were all colored brown. In a book entitled *On Being a Virgin*, by Father E. Breit, which was published in Kevelaer in 1936 (with an imprimatur from the diocese of Münster under Bishop von Galen), Mary is supported with racist Nazi thinking: "Thus there blossomed about the image of Mary a healthy, pure, kindly womanhood. We need not explain in any further detail what that brought us as far as *racial health and racial ennoblement* were concerned" (pp. 34–35). What "Mary wishes to cultivate, protect, and complete" is the "primeval German kind of woman" (ibid., p. 35). As for chastity or unchastity, "From the standpoint of the bond between the individual person and his people and with humanity as a whole all unchastity means a squandering of the holy life-source. Hence it is an offence against the community of the people" (Tillmann, pp. 119–20).

The Catholic phobia about squandering the sacred semen and the Nazi mania of racial purity were thus united. Bishop Wilhelm Berning of Osnabrück, who in an article on "The Catholic Church and German National Characteristics" argued for the "return to the bonds of blood, which means the hereditary biological connections" (*Das Neue Reich*, no. 7, 1934, 9), saw the Nazi fantasies as also being the best soil for nurturing the Church's brand of celibacy: "Again and again, as a result of cooperation between a good biological legacy and a suitable environment, which also embraces the supernatural, we see children from these families growing up to be priests and religious. They constitute a radiant antithesis to those criminal families whose young members fill the insane asylums and prisons" (ibid., pp. 14–15).

And so such clergymen agreed with the Nazis that the state had to do something against the danger to the nation's biological legacy. Tillmann, a moral theologian, wrote in 1940: "The results of research on heredity, given the sharp increase of people with inherited handicaps, has led to reflections about how to prevent a new generation afflicted with hereditary diseases from coming into existence. Education or a ban on marriage are clearly inadequate owing to the intellectual inferiority of most handicapped individuals as well as to their unrestrained instincts. But the goal could probably be achieved by institutionalization, which would, however, have to last as long as their reproductive careers" (Tillmann, 415). Thus the author rejects sterilization, but the reasons he cites are hair-raising: "In fact, the gravest moral objection to sterilization lies in the way it separates sensual satisfaction from responsibility, which can have disastrous effects on inferior individuals, who often display an uncontrolled sexual drive" (ibid., p. 419).

Pleasure-hating clerical celibates preferred concentration camps to sterilization. Cardinal Faulhaber reports a conversation he had with Hitler in 1936, where the Führer argued in favor of sterilizing the so-called "hereditarily diseased" to prevent the birth of a sickly new generation. Said Hitler: "The operation is simple and doesn't incapacitate them for a trade or for marriage, and now the Church is holding us back." To which Faulhaber replied: "From the Church's standpoint, Herr Chancellor, the State is not forbidden to isolate these vermin from the community, out of self-defence, and within the framework of the moral law. But instead of physical mutilation other defensive measures must be tried, and there is such a measure: interning the people with hereditary diseases" (*Literary Remains of Cardinal Faulhaber*, no. 8203).

Internment camps meant concentration camps, which were evidently within the "framework of the moral law," but sterilization, whether voluntary or involuntary, never was because it means a capacity for pleasure without a capacity for procreation. Pope Sixtus V's "lecherous eunuchs" of 1587 were not granted the right to marry until 1977.

Genetic considerations and the Church's hatred of pleasure make common cause in alarming fashion in Bernhard Häring's chapter on "Choosing a Spouse Responsibly" (1967): "Genuine willingness to be of service to the Creator and Redeemer will lead the Christian to look for the spouse from whom one may expect . . . given the available possibilities, the best children and their best education as children of God. Eugenics is increasingly developing into an important science that aims to provide information as to which choice of spouse can best naturally serve the marriage's legacy to the offspring. Responsibility to marriage, to service to life absolutely forbids choosing a partner one has every prospect of expecting only severely handicapped . . . children from. A certain hereditary handicap . . . which gives rise to fears that the children will be burdened with sickness and disabilities (for example, hemophilia, nearsightedness, perhaps even blindness and deafness), but will nevertheless be intellectually normal, does not in principle exclude anyone from marrying, even though *in serious cases it may be grounds for urgently discouraging marriage*. An experienced Catholic eugenicist maintains with good reason that marrying people with severe hereditary disabilities is absolutely irresponsible from a moral point of view . . . It is desirable that before getting engaged a couple exchange certificates of their personal and hereditary health, drawn up by a physician who is an expert in psychology and eugenics . . . The Church's ban on marriage between relatives (which according to current canon law applies only up to and including the third degree of the collateral line) fulfills a beneficial eugenic function" (*Das Gesetz Christi*, pp. 342–43).

Nobody has anything against healthy children, everybody aspires to have them. Back in Antiquity people saw *euteknia* (= handsome, healthy offspring) as an important topic. But forbidding blind and deaf people and hemophiliacs from marrying, or "urgently discouraging" it, instead of leaving it up to them, whether they want children despite their problems or, if they don't want them, however they may want to practice contraception in their marriage, is a misanthropic attitude. The human eugenics approach, with certificates of personal and hereditary health, à la Häring, puts the Church on the side of totalitarian systems. As for Häring's notion that the Church issued its ban on marriage between relatives because of its "beneficial eugenic function," that did not occur to theologians till the nineteenth century. As we have seen in the chapter on "Incest," the prohibition was nothing more than a variation on the eternal clerical theme of hostility to pleasure and marriage.

Recently Catholic moral theology has lost much of its prestige. With its contrived elaborations it stands today, practically speaking, facing the ash-heap. It is a folly that poses as religion and invokes the name of God, but has distorted the consciences of countless people. It has burdened them with hairsplitting nonsense and has tried to train them to be moral acrobats, instead of making them more human and kinder to their fellow men and women. In the name of a supernatural world that is alien and hostile to humanity it has oppressed the nature and naturalness of people, which like an overstretched bow, inevitably had to break. Its theology is no theology, and its morality is no morality. It has come to grief on its own stupidity. It thought it could deprive people of their personal experience of God's will, and replace the discovering of this will by a proliferating system of casuistry. It broke down because of its own hard-heartedness, when it tried to subject men and women to the shackles of its own laws, instead of letting them obey the commandments of God, which call them to freedom.

Karl Rahner was right when he said about moral theology: "But it is part of the tragic and irreducibly obscure historicity of the Church that in both theory and practice it used bad arguments to defend moral maxims based on problematic, historically conditioned pre-convictions, 'prejudices' . . . This dark tragedy of the Church's intellectual history is so burdensome because we are dealing here, in all or very many cases, with questions that penetrated deeply into the concrete lives of human beings, because such false maxims, which were never objectively valid . . . placed burdens on people . . . that from the standpoint of the freedom of the Gospel were not legitimate" (*Schriften zur Theologie* [1978], vol. 13, 99–100).

The best advice for the Church's ethical experts on sex would have been to keep silence. But instead we hear moral theologians such as H. J. Müller, speaking out in 1983, in an article, "Marriage Without a License": "There were times when in a way we cannot imagine today objective norms were violated without the persons involved feeling guilty about it. Think of the witch trials . . . Something like this may be said about the attitude of many young people nowadays toward sexual behavior. Even those committed to the Church cannot understand, as they say, why their serious, thoughtful decision to live together without, at first, getting married, should be a sin." Müller thinks "everything must be done" to "enlighten" the benighted values of these people (*Theologie der Gegenwart,* 1983, 4, 259). For moral theologians the witch trials of past centuries are the equivalent of marriage without a license in our time. But just to make this comparison represents a greater obscuring of values than all the darkness which all the couples married without a license are able to occupy.

Many people today regard themselves as married, although others (e.g., Church and state) deny it. Others again don't want to marry, because for them living together is a private matter and not subject to political or ecclesiastical formalities. They reject licenses. Evidently we find ourselves today in a shift of the older forms and norms for contracting marriage. But the lamentation one hears about marriage being in danger is unjustified. What danger there is threatens, at most, the marriage licenses, and they don't go very far back anyway.

How did marriages take place in the old days? Many people did get married in church with the priest to bless them and a wreath and veil for the bride. But for many others things happened something like this: They went for a walk, and he said to her: I love you, you're my wife, and she said: Yes. As far as Roman law was concerned (on which the Church based her own law), they were married ("the will to be married constitutes marriage"). The only witness was the moon, if that. Such marriages were called clandestine, but nobody questioned that they were proper marriages. Starting in 1215 the Church called for publications of the banns, but many did not comply with this.

Secret marriages caused legal uncertainty. Many a woman swore that another woman's fiancé, who intended to get married in church, was in reality her husband. Many a husband married in church, once he got tired of his wife, swore that he had been secretly married before, so that the present marriage was invalid. In the year 1349 in Augsburg, for example, there were 111 lawsuits where abandoned spouses petitioned that their runaway mates be adjudicated to them. In 101 of these the plaintiffs were women; 80 of them had to be turned down, however, because the marriage could not be documented.

There were continual efforts to master this legal confusion. Luther, for instance, argued that if a marriage were contracted without the parents' (concretely, the father's) permission, the father had the power to declare it invalid, even if children had been born from the union (*Sermon for Epiphany* WA, vol. 10, I, 1; cf G. H. Joyce, *Christian Marriage,* pp. 103ff.). Luther's friend and fellow reformer Melanchthon, on the other hand, believed that a clandestine marriage, once consummated, could not be declared invalid by the father (ibid., p. 119). The Reformed Protestants were strict in their insistence on parental rights. The Anglican bishop Thomas Barlow (d. 1691) said: "Surely a father, by the right of God and nature, has the legitimate power . . . to use even flogging and lashes to bring his children to do their duty and to obey his just commands (concerning marriage)" (ibid., p. 82).

In the sixteenth century the Catholic Church took a different approach from that of the Protestants, as it tried to defuse the problem of clandestine marriages. In 1563 through the decree *Tametsi* ("Although") it introduced the so-called formal obligation: Although there was no doubt that secret marriages were valid, from now on a specific form for contracting marriage had to be observed, namely a wedding in the presence of one's own pastor and at least two witnesses—otherwise the marriage was invalid.

This priestly solution did not suit the Protestants. They pleaded for the wishes of the parents: As early as 1526 the Reutlinger Church Regulations, inspired by Luther, stated: "According to papal custom many people get married behind their parents' backs." A church marriage that took place behind the parents' backs was invalid, "because God's commandment to obey one's father and mother cancels such a promise of marriage."

In the course of the next centuries (e.g., in the "Declaratio Benedictina," 1741), the Catholic Church made it clear that it did not demand the Catholic form of marriage for non-Catholic, e.g., Protestant, couples. Protestant marriages were valid without the observance of forms, as were all marriages before 1563.

In 1975 Pope Paul VI complained: "Meanwhile a moral decline is becoming increasingly widespread, and among its most serious symptoms is the boundless glorification of the sexual." For the Church's celibates sex is always the most serious thing. The Pope continues: "Nowadays some demand the right to premarital intercourse, at least in cases where a serious intention of getting married and a certain sort of marital inclination in the hearts of both partners demand the fulfillment that they deem natural. This is especially the case when the wedding celebration is delayed by external circumstances." The Pope labels such a relationship "fornication." He maintains that such unions "in no way guarantee the honesty and fidelity of the interpersonal relations of husband and wife" (*Declaration on Certain Questions of Sexual Ethics*, 1975).

This Vatican pronouncement is for the most part loveless, unjust, and theologically slipshod. It condemns out of hand, without distinction, the premarital relations of both Catholic and non-Catholic couples as "fornication." As far as non-Catholic couples are concerned, the Pope is violating his own canon law, which says that non-Catholic couples are not subject to any formal obligation in contracting marriage. That is, they don't need either a civil or religious ceremony, the only thing necessary for them to be validly married is that they wish to remain together forever as man and wife. The wish to be married, "the marital inclination," which the Pope acknowledges, is enough.

But even in the case of Catholic couples the Pope should avoid the word "fornication." Since 1563 Catholics are obliged to observe the forms, but canon law also has an extraordinary form (=

statement of the wish to be married in the presence of two witnesses), the so-called emergency marriage (can. 1116), specifically for situations where "grave disadvantages" are involved with
the normal, prescribed marriage ceremony. Such difficulties can
be altogether material in nature. Hence Canon 1116 could also be
applied, for example, to student couples, pensioners, etc., who
because of external circumstances don't get married in the usual
form.

But even if the Church cannot see its way clear to recognizing
the Catholic couples as "emergency marriages" in the sense of
Canon 1116, it should still be possible to show them respect
instead of labeling them as fornicators and discriminating against
them. It is unrealistic to believe that a marriage contracted with
all the proper forms "guarantees honesty and fidelity." Calling
such relationships fornication is emotional and irrelevant. It fails
to take into account the fact that marriage is based on the will of
two people and that all external forms are historically conditioned
and of secondary importance.

For a long time now the state has gotten involved in marriage.
In 1580 in the Netherlands the first civil marriage was contracted. Since 1875 in Germany the civil marriage has taken
place before the church wedding. But a marriage license from the
state is of no consequence for the Catholic Church where Catholic couples are concerned, and vice versa: What the Church
views as a marriage (e.g., in accordance with Canon 1116) is no
marriage for the state. By their reciprocal nonrecognition of civil
and religious marriage the Church and the State together rela-
tivize the value of a marriage license.

Thus the form by which a marriage comes into existence has
continually changed in the course of time. Since many people
nowadays reject the old forms, new forms and norms should be
sought so as to do better justice to the will of the couple.

The fact that the Church disregards its own canon law has
meant suffering not just for couples living together without benefit of clergy (labeled without distinction as "fornicators" by Pope
Paul VI) but for many divorced people who have remarried. We
have already seen in Chapter III that the Catholic Church can-

not invoke Jesus to justify its unbending harshness toward those who have remarried after divorce. But in many cases it cannot even invoke its own canon law. Catholic canon lawyers estimate that about 30 percent of all divorced Catholics were not married validly according to canonical law, and so their marriages could be annulled by the Church. After their divorce they would then not *remarry*, but get married for the first time.

The German episcopacy, to be sure, has operated in obscurantist fashion here. It has done nothing to help this 30 percent, where appropriate, to get their rights. Rather it leaves the individuals concerned in error, believing that whoever is divorced was also married validly. And the bishops punish whether or not there is anything to punish. In recent days one continually read about Catholic kindergarten teachers being fired for marrying a divorced man. And government courts back the Church up in such cases. But this is altogether unfair at least until there has been a test to see whether the state of affairs that the Church persecutes so harshly even exists.

All this is different, for example, in Spain. Every reader of popular Spanish magazines knows Isabel Preysler, the most elegant woman in Spain. After her church marriage to singer Julio Iglesias (with whom she has three children) was annulled, she married the Marquis de Grinón, whom she later divorced in order to marry the banker Miguel Boyer—this time only in a civil ceremony. Then there is Franco's eldest granddaughter, Carmen, whose marriage to Alfonso de Borbón, Duke of Cadiz (with whom she had two children), was annulled by the Church, enabling her to have a valid church wedding with Jean-Marie Rossi, to whom she is now married. Or the singer Isabel Pantoja, who was married to the divorced star matador Paquirri (since killed in a bullfighting accident), after Paquirri's first marriage was annulled.

The term "nulidad del matrimonio" (annulment of marriage), which often appears in banner headlines in Spain, is not a familiar one in German to magazine readers but only to a small group of canon lawyers, and is kept secret, as much as possible, from the people it applies to.

To enlighten divorced individuals who have remarried here is a crash course in Catholic marriage law. There is a whole series of grounds for annulment. The most important reason why a marriage does not take place to begin with is a defective will to marry. For example, if someone enters matrimony with the reservation (or with the express or hidden condition) that, "If things go badly, I'll get a divorce," if he or she, that is to say, enters into a so-called trial marriage, then that person has excluded the factor of indissolubility from his will to marriage. The marriage is invalid. Or if someone says: "I wish to marry you, but only if we agree not to have children, in other words to have a marriage based on the pill or the condom or the calendar," then the marriage is invalid. In all these cases it can be annulled.

The Catholic Church, which under the current Pope is taking special plans to prevent people from becoming aware of Church law on marriage, does this by canceling annulments for lack of proof of defective will to marry. But whether proved or unproved, with a defective will to marry no marriage takes place, for *consensus facit matrimonium*—the will to marry makes a marriage. Being right and getting one's rights, however, are two different things, especially in Germany.

XXX

Notes on Mariology

In *the history of* Christian theology and piety, Mary, the Mother of Jesus, has always played a special, an outstanding role. This is understandable, for as the mother of the man whom Christians acknowledge to be their Redeemer, she has fascinated the minds of believers from the very beginning. It was a good thing that a woman played such a prominent role in the mental life of the Church and prevented the Church and the world from becoming even more totally masculine than they did. Women in particular have always seen in Mary a place of refuge, a woman to whom they could flee as to their mother and sister, sometimes even to her and away from a God who seemed only too much like an angry man.

But Mariology, the Church's teaching about Mary, was developed not by women, but by men, unmarried men at that. These clerical celibates affirmed that their unmarried state, which they called and still call "virginity," was superior to marriage. Marriage and the sexuality bound up with it have never had a lobby in the Church, and there was always something morally dubious about them.

But Mary was a married woman and bore a child. If we read the New Testament accounts with an open mind, we see that she had quite a number of sons and daughters. But if we were to take the text as it stands, that would mean that Mary's way of life was quite alien to celibacy, and so it was necessary to reform the image of Mary as it is presented in the New Testament, i.e., as a mother of children.

And so she was disallowed her children, with the exception of her one son, Jesus. They were taken away from her and, at first, declared to be the children of a fictitious first marriage of her husband, Joseph. But then her environment was even more stringently cleansed of everything marital. Even her husband had to have been unmarried. He too had to be virginal, and thus Mary's sons and daughters couldn't be Joseph's sons and daughters either. This would have damaged Mary's virginal status, hence the brothers and sisters of Jesus were finally transformed into his cousins.

Then even the birth of her one remaining son was taken away from her. She was not allowed to give birth as women in this world do, for that would have impaired her "virginity in childbirth" and hence done away with her "perpetual virginity." Even today the Pope keeps stressing that Mary was "intact." This means that during delivery her hymen was not permitted to tear, otherwise she would have been damaged and injured the way all other mothers are by the birth of a child and so cease to be "as good as new." And so Mary could not give birth in the ordinary female way.

This doctrine of "virginity in childbirth," which cannot be abandoned without having the whole artificial structure of Mary's "perpetual virginity" collapsing on itself, is an especially crass example of what fantastic lengths people will go to in order to make Mary over into a virgin. The traditional teaching of virginity in childbirth states that 1. Mary's hymen remained intact, that 2. the birth was painless, and that 3. there was no afterbirth (Lat. *sordes* = filth). Mary is supposed to have borne Jesus as if he were a ray of light or transfigured, as he was after his resurrection, or like the burning bush, which was not consumed, or "the way spirits pass through bodies without resistance" (M. J. Scheeben, *Handbuch der katholischen Dogmatik,* 1878, II. 939). Putting aside the question of whether Christ, if he was born like a sort of ray, nevertheless became man, the dignity of a woman cannot be manifested by making her into the mother of a beam of light. By separating Mary so radically from other women who have borne children, one may have given her, from the Mariological standpoint, something crucially important. But from the human standpoint one has taken something just as crucial away. Anyone who claims that Mary maintained her biological virginity in childbirth—like the birth of an idea of a pure spirit—has to realize that he is robbing her of her motherhood.

And in fact with the doctrine of the Virgin Birth theologians have stolen Mary's motherhood. The intention was to make her an exception to the curse that, as the Church's celibates saw it, weighed down on the normal motherhood of normal mothers. But this curse is merely a monstrous product of neurotic sexual fantasy. For the Mariologist Alois Müller the damage done to the mother in childbirth is a special "sign of the curse of original sin" (*Mysterium salutis,* 1969, III, 2, pp. 464–65), which hangs over mothers and motherhood. Only Mary's childbirth was painless, while all others get to feel God's curse (Genesis 3): "In pain you shall bring forth children." "After original sin this painful cursing of her motherhood struck Eve herself" (ibid., p. 463), and since then all mothers have been cursed except for one. They are cursed in their pains. Seven times in one page (464) Müller uses the word "curse" with reference to motherhood. But the more some Mariologists insist on having mothers cursed, the stronger grow one's suspicions that this is not God's curse but a curse in the eyes of celibate theologians.

Mary's childbirth, by the way, was painless for yet another reason, which was contributed by Augustine (d. 430), the father of our pleasure-hating sexual morality: "She conceived without carnal pleasure and therefore gave birth without pain." Theologians never tire of asserting this, even in our century. By comparison with Mary, therefore, all other mothers are damaged, punished and cursed by pain, and finally besmirched. Only of Mary can it be said: "She has borne a child, *but still* remained pure maid," to quote the famous German Christmas carol *"Es ist ein Ros' entsprungen."*

The notion of Mary's intactness in childbirth essentially goes back to an account in the so-called Proto-Gospel of James, an apocryphal text that was presumably composed in the second half of the second century. Its author tried to pass himself off as James, the brother of the Lord. This forgery had a substantial— one can say an enormous—influence on the whole further development of Mariology. Admittedly, in the West, unlike the East, the Proto-Gospel was basically rejected, because in it Jesus' brothers and sisters still appear as Joseph's children from a first marriage. And the theologians, especially Jerome, were ready at hand to make Jesus' siblings into cousins; but despite the document's being denied by Western theologians, its contents (for example, the legendary names of Mary's parents, Joachim and Anne) were accepted. And the Proto-Gospel launched the intact hymen on its career through Mariology. The report on this topic is not distinguished by its discretion. It seems rather to display features of a theological pornography, with sexual fantasies disguised as piety.

The passage in question reads: "And the midwife came forth from the cavern, and met Salome, and she said: 'Salome, Salome, I have to tell you of a spectacle that has never occurred before: A virgin has given birth, which nature never permits.' And Salome said: 'As sure as the Lord, my God, lives, until I place my finger inside and examine her condition, I shall not believe that a virgin has given birth.' And Salome went in and prepared Mary for the examination. And she gave a scream of pain, and cried out: 'I have tempted the living God. See, my hand is consumed by fire and is falling off.' And she prayed to the Lord. And behold, an angel of the Lord stood before Salome and told her: 'The Lord God has heard your prayer. Come here and take hold of the child, and you will be healed.' And Salome did so, and she was healed, as she had prayed, and went out of the cavern."

We can see how crudely the author has gone about cutting and trimming the image of a woman, not shying away from degrading Mary by this theological meat inspection, so as to come up with a virgin that meets ideal celibate specifications. For all that, the Wetzer/Welte *Kirchenlexikon* says of the Proto-Gospel of James that "it is designed to glorify the mother of the Lord" (1, 1071), and in the same passage emphasizes the "dignity" of the representation.

After Mary has had to submit to this inspection, she turns out to be demonstrably what the male theologians expected and demanded of her: a perpetual virgin. The *one* intact mother while the others are all more or less violated, the *one* pure mother, while the others are all impure. The theologians have dumped their theological rubbish on mothers, believing in their pious zeal that this would paint the mother of Jesus as all the more spotless. But in unloading a perpetual curse on all others, in contrast to the perpetual virgin, they lost sight of women as a group, their notion of women as a whole was narrowed, that is, if they ever had such a notion to begin with.

The Church's celibates wanted to paint a picture of Mary that had nothing in common with the image of other women. And they succeeded. But in so doing they distorted a human face past all recognition. The veneration for the one Pure Woman, in comparison and contrast to all other other Impure ones, may be helpful for celibate existence in a womanless world, which because of this vacuum often equals a state of forlorn human exile. But for many other people the celibates have done great harm.

It may be that some individuals long for the image of a queen of heaven, but many more long for a human person. And all those who might have met the image of a real person in a less miraculous and therefore more truthful image of Mary have been cheated and deprived of that encounter by the doctrine of an incomprehensible and therefore existentially meaningless natural wonder. Because of this human deficit in Mariology, living the faith is made impossible for Christians, insofar as Mary is supposed to be their concrete religious model. How is a woman to recognize herself in Mary when the Litany of Loreto hymns Mary as *mater inviolata?* That makes all other mothers *matres violatae,* women who have had been violated, mistreated, besmirched, defiled, injured, shamed, and desecrated—by maternity.

In Catholic theology Mariology has stood on its head long enough. It is time to set it on its feet again. What turned it topsy-turvy is the fact that very early on it became a masculine— and celibate, to boot—Mariology. In this way the usual male reversals of the world and its values took over the lion's share of Mariology. Traditional Mariology does not deserve its name. It has become a sort of anti-Mariology, since although it purports to exalt the greatness and dignity of a woman and to paint them in scholarly theological fashion against a gold background, in reality its clumsy fingers crush what constitutes feminine dignity in particular (Mary) and in general (all women).

It is a grim fate for a woman to have to live in a dogmatic corset made by men. Mary encountered this in an unparalleled way. She was not allowed a share in anything having to do with female sexuality, in anything connected with the natural process of conceiving and bearing a child. She was not allowed to get her only son through the love of a man, it had to be the Holy Spirit, and there could be no pleasure. She was not allowed to bear her son in the natural way, because she had to remain intact in childbirth. Finally she was not allowed to have other children later on, for that would have meant violation and shame. Thus she was turned into a sort of sexless creature, to a shadow of a wife and mother, reduced to her function in salvation history. She was granted real life by the lords of creation only insofar as was necessary to function properly. Beyond that it was denied her.

On the subject of her wisdom Thomas Aquinas wrote: "There is no doubt that the blessed Virgin received the gift of wisdom to an exceptional degree" (*Summa Theologiae* III q. 27 a. 5 ad 3). But on closer inspection this gift of wisdom proves to be very limited, since "she had the use of wisdom in contemplation, but

she did not have the use of wisdom with regard to teaching"
(ibid.). The gentlemen of the Church wish to teach about her,
not to be taught by her. But one need not wonder very long why
St. Thomas concedes the mother of Jesus such a strictly limited
amount of wisdom, making her unfit to be a teacher. Teaching,
he says, "is not suitable to the female sex" (ibid.). Celibate arrogance doesn't even stop in the face of Mary.

At bottom the Church's male celibates despite—but perhaps
still more precisely because of—all their dogmatic elaborations
about Mary have always passed her over as a person and as a real
woman. They have seen her role in salvation history in their
celibate fashion, and in this role they have bestowed on her
miraculous and abstruse attributes. They have hung this image,
so alien to humanity, on the walls of their sterile masculine
mental world. Bishop Hermann Volk, for example, notes down
this sort of thin masculine cogitation: "Mary is honored and mentioned in the Gospel not for her own sake, but rather for the sake
of her function and service in God's plan of salvation" (Gesam-
melte Schriften, 1966, vol. 2, 78). A celibate would obviously find
it sinful to honor a woman for her own sake. Mary is important
and worthy of honor merely as one who carries out a plan. The
theologians have given her the title of Mother of God, and have
thereby done their utmost in dogmatic appreciation of her, but
they have ignored the fact that a woman is also something more
than the bearer of a child according to a plan. This holds for
Mary and for all women with her, and the Church's celibates
have missed the point in her case as much as in all the others.

Beyond this, it should be noted that over time the traditional
teaching of Mary's perpetual virginity—the claim that she was a
virgin before, during, and after childbirth—has been shaken in
the minds of many Catholics. Theologians are increasingly recognizing that "virginity" is an intellectual model, appropriate to
New Testament times, for the new beginning of history with
Christ. Hence we are obscuring the actual, salvation-history sense
of the Gospel and distorting it into unbelievable and unimportant
miracles, if we take literally the Gospel accounts in question.

Given the slowly dawning realization of the exclusively theological nature of the New Testament narratives about the Virgin Birth, the Pope, with his tireless emphasis on biological miracles in Mary's case, finds himself in a growing shambles of outdated ideas. There's nothing new about a pope sticking to old assertions; the last thing one expects from a pope is progress in theology. But we have to be surprised that lately he has been backed up by some bishops who, as scholars, have themselves contributed to the findings that the Pope refuses to accept.

An example: In his Marian encyclical *Redemptoris Mater* (1987) John Paul II stresses that Mary "preserved her virginity intact," meaning, quite concretely, that her hymen was intact. But the current president of the German Bishops Conference, Bishop Karl Lehmann, does not think in the same drastically biological terms as the Pope, as we see in the book he edited, *Vor dem Geheimnis Gottes den Menschen verstehen, Karl Rahner zum 80. Geburtstag* (1984). In the introduction to this Festschrift Lehmann praises Professor Rudolf Pesch for "trying, in dialogue with Karl Rahner, to think further about the difficult question of the 'Virgin birth' " (p. 8). And in the conclusion of the book Bishop Lehmann once again voices his thanks to Pesch: "Let me once again strongly underscore the gratitude that I feel toward all the participants, and that I already expressed in the Introduction" (ibid., p. 138).

Framed in this way by praise and thanks from Lehmann, we find statements by theologian Pesch such as the following: "Rudolf Schnackenburg, for example, has established that: 'If we weigh the arguments for and against Jesus' having full brothers and sisters [born after him], we have to admit that there is stronger evidence for assuming that these siblings existed . . . The evident meaning of the oldest testimony, Mk. 6:3, supports this position.' " And Pesch states that this is a finding "that I also reached in the excursus 'On the Question of Jesus' Brothers and Sisters' " (ibid., p. 25).

Thus, Schnackenburg and Pesch are inclined to assume that Jesus had brothers and sisters. And the man who became president of the German Bishops Conference, Karl Lehmann, praised Pesch for thinking further about these issues than some other Catholics.

In the Lehmann book Pesch goes even further. He cites with

approval the Catholic theologian Gerhard Lohfink: "The New Testament confesses and proclaims that Jesus is the Son of God, but not that Jesus was conceived without an earthly father" (ibid., p. 26). That means that the biological Virgin Birth is not a biblical truth of faith.

On the one hand then, in 1984 Lehmann joined with Pesch, Schnackenburg, and Lohfink in not viewing the Virgin Birth as a biological fact; instead he praised and thanked theologians who pressed their thinking beyond that. On the other hand, Lehmann joined with John Paul II in understanding the Virgin Birth in a completely biological sense; and in 1987 he canceled the authorization to teach of a theologian (the present writer) who understands the Virgin Birth not biologically, but theologically (as he himself did in 1984).

Pesch's article in the Lehmann book bears the significant heading: "Against a Double Truth." But despite this warning, Bishop Lehmann understands the Virgin Birth in a double sense, depending upon whether he is editing papers by German scholars for a Festschrift to honor Karl Rahner, or concurring with the Pope in the year he was elected to the German Bishops Conference. Thus we hear from him two different truths about Mary's virginity, one for professors of theology, another for the Pope— with the second one also intended for the mass of believers.

During the trial of Galileo, Cardinal Bellarmine (who played a decisive part in it) wrote on April 12, 1615, to the Carmelite monk Paolo Antonio Foscarini: To assert that the earth revolves around the sun "is as erroneous as to claim that Jesus was not born of a virgin." This equating by the Church of the ideas, first, that the earth is the immovable center of the universe and, second, that Mary gave birth as a virgin, means that Bellarmine's proposition can also be reversed, so that Mary no more gave birth as a virgin than the sun revolves around the earth. Now that the error about the sun can no longer be maintained, and the earth has been given permission to be a planet, the error about the Virgin is still to be corrected. For too long human understanding and Christian faith were violated by the false doctrine that the sun revolves around the earth. To this day they are being violated by the false doctrine of the Virgin Birth.

BIBLIOGRAPHY
(FREQUENTLY CITED WORKS)

Brandl, Leopold. *Die Sexualethik des hl. Albertus Magnus.* 1954.

Browe, Peter. *Beiträge zur Sexualethik des Mittelalters,* 1932.

Deschner, Karlheinz. *Das Kreuz mit der Kirche: Eine Sexualgeschichte des Christentums.* 1974; 2d ed. 1987.

Franzen, August. *Zölibat und Priesterehe.* 1969.

Fuchs, Josef. *Die Sexualethik des heiligen Thomas von Aquin.* 1949.

Goldmann-Posch, Ursula. *Unheilige Ehen: Gespräche mit Priesterfrauen.* 1985.

Göpfert, Franz Adam. *Moraltheologie.* Vol. 2. 1906.

Häring, Bernhard. *Das Gesetz Christi* (E.T. *Law of Christ*). 8th ed. Vol. 3. 1967.

Heer, Friedrich. *Gottes erste Liebe: Die Juden im Spannungsfeld der Geschichte.* 1981.

Hefele, Carl Joseph. *Konziliengeschichte.* Vol. 1. 1855. Vol. 5, 1863. Vol. 6, 1867.

Joyce, G. H. *Christian Marriage,* London, 1948.

Klomps, Heinrich. *Ehemoral und Jansenismus.* 1964.

Lindner, Dominikus. *Der Usus matrimonii.* 1929.

Mausbach, Josef and Tischleder, Peter. *Katholische Moraltheologie* (many volumes). 1938.

Müller, Michael. *Die Lehre des hl. Augustinus von der Paradiesesehe und ihre Auswirkung in der Sexualethik des 12. und 13. Jahrhunderts bis Thomas von Aquin,* 1954.

———. *Grundlagen der katholischen Sexualethik.* 1968.

Noonan, John T. *Contraception.* 1965, 1986[2].

Pastor, Ludwig von. *Geschichte der Päpste* (E.T. *History of the Popes*). Vol. 10. 1926.

Schmaus, Michael. *Katholische Dogmatik.* Vol. 5, *Mariologie.* 1955.

Strack, H. L. and Billerbeck, P. *Kommentar zum Neuen Testament aus Talmud und Midrasch.* 1924–61.

Tillmann, Fritz. *Handbuch der katholischen Sittenlehre.* Vol. 4. 2d ed. 1940.

Wetzer, Heinrich Joseph and Welte, Benedict. *Kirchenlexikon* (many volumes). 1886–1903.

ABOUT THE AUTHOR

UTA RANKE-HEINEMANN holds a Ph.D. in Catholic Theology. She qualified as a university lecturer in 1969, the first woman ever to do so in the field of Catholic theology. In 1970, she became a Professor of Catholic Theology. She lost her academic chair (New Testament and Ancient Church History) at the University of Essen, West Germany, for interpreting Mary's Virgin Birth theologically and not biologically. Since late 1987, she has held the chair for the History of Religion at the University of Essen.

INDEX OF NAMES

INDEX OF SUBJECTS